D1612471

A History of the French Anarchist Movement, 1917 to 1945

AK
PRESS

David Berry
A History of the French Anarchist Movement, 1917 to 1945

© 2009 David Berry
Introduction © 2008 Barry Pateman
This edition © 2009 AK Press (Oakland, Edinburgh, West Virginia)

ISBN-13 9781904859826

Library of Congress Control Number: 2008927322

AK Press
674-A 23rd Street
Oakland, CA 94612
USA
www.akpress.org
akpress@akpress.org

AK Press
PO Box 12766
Edinburgh, EH8 9YE
Scotland
www.akuk.com
ak@akedin.demon.co.uk

The above addresses would be delighted to provide you with the latest AK Press distribution catalog, which features the several thousand books, pamphlets, zines, audio and video
products, and stylish apparel published and/or distributed by AK Press. Alternatively,
visit our web site for the complete catalog, latest news, and secure ordering.

Printed in Canada on acid free, recycled paper with union labor.

Cover design by Clifford Harper and Jayne Clementson
Interior design and layout by JR

This book is dedicated to the memory of all those anarchists, some of whom are named here, who lost their lives in the struggle against fascism.

Roger Badard/Baudard (Perdiguera, 17 October 1936)

Juliette Baudard/Baudart (Perdiguera, 17 October 1936)

Jean Bégué/Béguez (Belchite, September 1936)

Mario Berard (Perdiguera, 17 October 1936)

Raymond Berge/Bergé (Perdiguera, 17 October 1936)

Charles Berthelot (Germany, 1945)

Louis Berthomieu/Berthonnieux (Perdiguera, 17 October 1936)

Emile Boff (Casa del Campo, 12 November 1936)

Marcel Bonvalet (Ravensbruck)

Boudoux (Perdiguera, 17 October 1936)

Eugénie Casteu (Spain, 1937)

Georges Charrang[eau?] (Perdiguera, 17 October 1936)

Lucien Chatelain (Aragon, March 1937)

Philippe Colombet (Codo, August 1937)

Commeurec (Germany, 1943/44)

Emile Cottin (Farlete, 8 September 1936)

Henri Cottin (France, shot by Gestapo, 11 June 1944)

Pierre Darrot (Mauthausen, February 1945)

Jean Delalain (Perdiguera, 17 October 1936)

Henri Delaruelle (Perdiguera, 17 October 1936)

Max Détang (Albacete, December 1936)

Gérard Duvergé (Agen, tortured by Gestapo, 2 February 1944)

Jean Ferrand (Barna, 5 May 1937)

Fons (Santa Quiteria, April 1937)

René Frémont (Sedan, June 1940)

René Galissot (Perdiguera, 17 October 1936)

Marcel Gérard (Teruel, December 1936)

Georges Gessaume (Tortosa, 26 July 1938)

Jean Giral/Giralt (Perdiguera, 17 October 1936)

Georges Gourdin (Elbrück, 23 January 1945)

Marcel Greffier (Cuesta de la Reina, 1937/38)

Suzanne Hans (Farlete, November 1936)

Georgette Kokoczinski (Perdiguera, 17 October 1936)

Jules Le Gall (Buchenwald, 14 June 1944)
François Le Levé (Neuengamme, 20 January 1945)
Lemère (Farlete, 8 September 1936)
Raoul Lion (Mauthausen, 1943/44/45)
Henri Lion (Mauthausen, 1943/44/45)
Bernard Meller (Huesca, November 1936)
Georges Monnard (Quinto, December 1936)
Pelcot/Pellecot (France, shot by German troops)
Yves [?] R????s[?] (Perdiguera, 17 October 1936)
Maurice Rajaud (Spain, 1936/37/38)
Louis Recoulis/Recoules (Farlete, November 1936)
Pierre Ruff (Neuengamme, 1945)
Bixio Sorbi (Dachau, 20 October 1944)
Jean Trontin (Perdiguera, 17 October 1936)
Yves Vitrac (Perdiguera, 17 October 1936)

Contents

Acknowledgements

There are many people who over the years have helped me in different ways with the preparation of this book and to whom I would like to offer my thanks.

Firstly, the staff of the various libraries and archive centres in which I have worked, who have been unfailingly helpful: the Bibliothèque Nationale, the Archives Nationales, the Centre de Recherches sur l'Histoire des Mouvements Sociaux et du Syndicalisme, the Institut Français d'Histoire Sociale, the Musée Social and the Archives de la Préfecture de Police in Paris; the Bibliothèque de Documentation Internationale Contemporaine in Nanterre; the Internationaal Instituut voor Sociale Geschiedenis in Amsterdam; the British Library in London. I would also like to thank the comrades of the Secrétariat d'histoire et d'édition of the Fédération Anarchiste in Paris and of the Kate Sharpley Library in Peterborough.

Many others have helped me in various ways, by sharing the results of their unpublished work with me; sending me photocopies of otherwise inaccessible documents; pointing me in the direction of previously unknown sources; translating Spanish documents for me; reading drafts and suggesting improvements: Jean-Louis Blanchon, Sylvain Boulouque, Phil Casoar, Colette Chambelland, Rolf Dupuy, Georges Fontenis, Sharif Gemie, John Horne, Jeremy Jennings, Paul Kennedy, Jean-Michel Lebas, the late Jean Maitron, Gaetano Manfredonia, Janet Mayes, the late Peter Morris, Dieter Nelles, Barry Pateman, Marc Prévôtel, Siân Reynolds, Paul Sharkey, Alexandre Skirda and Reiner Toßtorff.

A special mention must be made of Rod Kedward, who first suggested this research topic and who guided my first steps as a historian and researcher; the late René Bianco and Marianne Enckell of the CIRA (Centre international de recherches sur l'anarchisme) in Marseille and Lausanne respectively, who could not have been more helpful and whose knowledge of the anarchist movement seems to be encyclopædic; and Gill Allwood for her constant support and encouragement and for being my first reader.

I am especially grateful to those veteran militants who agreed to share with me their memories of the 20s and 30s: Louis Anderson, Pierre-Valentin Berthier, Henri Bouyé, Charles-François Carpentier,

Nicolas Faucier, Daniel Guérin, Maurice Joyeux, Paul Lapeyre, René Lochu, Roger Pantais, André Senez, Georges Sossenko.

Finally, I would like to acknowledge financial assistance from the Wolfson Foundation (administered by the British Academy) and the Nuffield Foundation which made research in Paris possible.

I am also grateful to Cambridge University Press, Oxford University Press, and the Lukas Verlag for permission to re-use previously published material (chapters 8, 12 and 13 respectively).

List of Initials

AEAR	Association des écrivains et artistes révolutionnaires
AFA	Association des fédéralistes anarchistes
AIT	Association internationale des travailleurs
ARAC	Association républicaine des anciens combattants
ARME	Association révolutionnaire des miliciens d'Espagne
CAI	Comité d'action internationale contre la guerre
CAS	Comité anarcho-syndicaliste
CASDLPE	Comité anarcho-syndicaliste pour la défense et la libération du prolétariat espagnol
CDS	Comité de défense syndicaliste
CEL	Comité pour l'Espagne libre
CGT	Confédération générale du travail
CGTR	Confédération générale du travail révolutionnaire
CGTSR	Confédération générale du travail syndicaliste révolutionnaire
CGTU	Confédération générale du travail unitaire
CNT	Confederación nacional del trabajo
CRRI	Comité pour la reprise des relations internationales
CSR	Comité syndicaliste révolutionnaire
CVIA	Comité de vigilance des intellectuels antifascistes
FA	Fédération anarchiste
FACR	Fédération anarchiste communiste révolutionnaire
FAF	Fédération anarchiste de langue française
FAI	Federación anarquista iberica
FCEEAF	Federación de comités españoles de accion antifascista en Francia
FCL	Fédération communiste libertaire
FCRA	Fédération communiste révolutionnaire anarchiste
FCS	Fédération communiste des soviets
FIJL	Federación iberica de juventudes libertarias
FSI	Fédération syndicale internationale
GR	Gauche révolutionnaire
ISR	Internationale syndicale rouge
JA	Jeunesses anarchistes
JAC	Jeunesses anarchistes communistes
JC	Jeunesses communistes

JEUNES	Jeunes équipes réunies pour une nouvelle économie sociale
NKVD	People's Commissariat for International Affairs
PC	Parti communiste
PCF	Parti communiste français
PS	Parti socialiste — Section française de l'Internationale ouvrière
PSOP	Parti socialiste ouvrier et paysan
SFIC	Section française de l'Internationale communiste
SFIO	Section française de l'Internationale ouvrière
SIA	Solidarité internationale antifasciste
UA	Union anarchiste
UAC	Union anarchiste communiste
UACR	Union anarchiste communiste révolutionnaire
UFSA	Union fédérative des syndicats autonomes
UD	Union départementale
UL	Union locale
USC	Union socialiste communiste
USI	Unione syndicale italiana

List of Tables

Introduction, by Barry Pateman

For those of us who have been working, in some way, on the history of anarchism, anarchists, and anarchy this is an interesting yet, truth be told, somewhat worrying time. There can be no doubt that considerable work has been done in clearing the ground and engaging in examinations of the lives, ideas and practices of some of those who have identified themselves as anarchists. As a result our knowledge base has increased considerably over the last twenty-five years and some of the work produced has been astonishingly good. Yet, probably because we are engaged in the research of complex ideas and practices, this impressive research (as all good research does) has led to unexpected challenges and concerns.

I'd like to begin with two that we can see in both the academy, for want of a better word, and also that critical grey area between independent anarchist scholarship and the academy. These concerns are to do with what we are doing when we research the history of anarchism and anarchists. Some recent scholarship appears to suggest that the lives of anarchists—their hopes, fears, contradictions and yes, moments of inspiration—are no more than objects for intellectual experimentation. Currently in-vogue terms and intellectual strategies are marshaled to "prove" an impressive point. Sometimes though, one fears that all the facts, ideas and experiences have been incisively filleted to fit the idea at hand. The very worst of this scholarship has been presented in a discourse that reminds one of the philosophical and intellectual onanism so resonant in the Marxism of the last thirty years. I'd like to think we could do better than that.

Secondly, there is an ongoing concern as to what we should be researching and where we should be working. Perhaps we have been too narrow, too cut off from the world at large and not paying enough attention to the social contexts within which anarchists act and live. As Sharif Gemie argued, "in reality when we see anarchist organizations in action, we find that they interact with a great variety of different groups, traditions, and individuals—vegetarians, free schools, contraception rights activists, avant-garde artists and poets, anti-clericals and also, more worryingly, anti-Semites, nationalists, misogynists, demagogues, and so on. These points suggest that the forms for anarchist histories should be a milieu or a political culture whose centre is in informal lived relationships!"[1]

It is a seductive suggestion, and well made, suggesting the richness of some anarchist lives sorely absent in some research. Yet something in its approach is disturbingly missing. After all, thousands upon thousands of people have taken an intellectual, emotional and intuitive journey to become anarchists. Granted that these journeys need to be explored more and may, indeed, consist of interacting with numerous milieus, yet we can still assert that to call oneself an anarchist suggests at least two things: First, an identification with others who used the same word to describe their feelings and practices and, second, a separation, however slight, nuanced or sympathetic, from those who didn't! We ignore the experiences that made this journey possible or the self-identification gained by journey's end at our own peril. Of course Gemie's suggestions raise other points. Is radical opposition, then, simply a collection of individual milieus criss-crossed by various people? Is it impossible for anarchist organizations or affinity groups to embrace these milieus? However we answer these critical questions I remain unconvinced that we know enough about the anarchism and anarchy that anarchists brought to, say, freethought or rent strikes, to simply take that very anarchism for granted.

A separate challenge that we, as historians in this field, face is the practice of some contemporary anarchists who, prompted by the urgency of the reality around them, find the past, in so many ways, irrelevant. Capitalism is so corrupt, so emotionally crippling, so destructive of our very planet that we need a new anarchy and we have little to learn from our past. Indeed, like Shelley, some of us are beginning to believe that, "The world is weary of the past. O' might it die or rest at last." (*Hellas*) What anarchists did in Spain, France, China, Bulgaria etc. is interesting and even impressive. Circumstances today, though, mean they have little of importance to say to us except, possibly, their failures and bravery. Does our work, then, address anything of relevance to inspire us today? Does our work furnish any tools to challenge capitalism, or are we lonely readers engaged in the search for the irrelevant?

David Berry's monumental *A History of the French Anarchist Movement* directly or indirectly touches on all of these worries. It is a work that obviously reflects years of careful, critical and respectful research in the field, and a work that clearly reminds English-language readers how much essential material is available in other languages — material

---

1   Sharif Gemie, "Historians, Anarchism and Political Culture," *Anarchist Studies* 6.2 (October 1998):

we urgently need to have generally available before we can make too many confident assertions about anarchist ideas and behavior.

Above all, though, I think Berry's book deals with two constant and re-occurring questions in the history of anarchist practice: Are anarchists ever able to create organizations that are supple and nuanced enough to be faithful to the complexities of anarchist practices and relationships, and who should, or can, anarchists work with in order to dismantle capitalism and replace it with a society predicated on voluntary agreement, equality, and mutual aid?

The working out of these questions can make for challenging reading. Acronyms abound in the book, groups change shape, perspective and name. Sometimes, yes, due to personality clashes, but equally from the need to find the right direction, the most comfortable and suitable organizational structure. An organizational structure that can both bring people to anarchy and anarchism, preventing it from being a perpetually peripheral activity and, still somehow remain true to the principals of anarchists' practices and beliefs.

Relationships between communists, trotskyists, left communists, and anarchists are carefully described by Berry. Attempts to reconcile anarchism and Marxism are balanced with the perspicacity and concerns of Luigi Fabbri and others, and the seduction of anarchists by the apparent possibilities of the events in Russia—a new world of hope, a world that could be ours—is sensitively examined. We see groups of anarchists negotiating, clarifying—sometimes in a clear-headed manner, sometimes almost in a dream. Sometimes being proactive, other times just reacting. And his impressive organizational narrative continues; Popular Fronts and Anti-Fascism, working for Spain and the revolution, dealing with the German occupation. Anarchists found allies where they could, some dubious, some surprising. These are no easy narratives and David Berry is to be commended for his clarity and sure footedness as he guides us on these journeys among anarchists that are never treated as topics for any intellectual thesis.

There is, also, another narrative: that of individuals who sometimes move from organization to organization, reminding us that anarchism is more than a newspaper or a policy statement. This is an anarchism of anarchists placing all of their energy and hope into small groups of like-minded comrades. It is an anarchism of those volunteers in Spain—a narrative that allows us to begin the necessary reclamation of those for whom anarchism was not just an organization or support group, but also something worth dying and physically suffering for—Georgette Kokoczinski, shot and killed, fighting with the Durruti Column in October 1936, René Prince imprisoned in Spain by the communists, alongside, probably, forty other French anarchist volunteers. We learn of those who took part in the Resistance to the German occupation—and those who did not. These are narratives both of clandestinity and, yes, collaboration.

Of course we may have disagreements with some of Berry's emphasis. Surely Emile Cottin and Germaine Berton deserve a little more sympathy. André Prudhommeaux's remarkable clear-sightedness on events in Spain might be a little more kindly treated by the author. Perhaps the prescience of those "on the margins," in Berry's words, with their early critique of Bolshevism might be a little more rewarded. These disagreements, though, are because the book has challenged and often inspired us to reflect on our own ideas and challenge our own preconceptions. It will be a constant reference point for years to come, in the same way we use Avrich's *The Modern School Movement* or *The Haymarket Tragedy*, and it will, like those books, present us with other stories and narratives to be researched and told whenever we re-read it. Who were the forty or so French anarchist volunteers imprisoned in Spain? What can we learn about those Russian and Spanish exile communities in France? What difference in narratives might be applied to key events? What can we find about the inter-relationships of those individuals who comprised each organization? How far can we rely on newspapers as central research tools? The book is dedicated to those who lost their lives in the struggle against fascism and each name on that list is a story waiting to be told. Who knows what each story might inform us about anarchy and anarchism and how people embraced these most beautiful of ideals?

Above all, though, research of this high quality reminds us that we have much more to do before we start throwing around too many generalizations about where we are now as anarchists and what needs to be done to allow anarchy to flourish and grow. There is still much for us all to learn. Time to get on with it.

Barry Pateman
2008

Preface to the AK Press edition

I have made no significant changes to the text of this book as published originally by Greenwood Press in 2002, but there are three small things I want to do for this AK Press edition.

Firstly, it seems appropriate to update my comments on the literature. As far as I am aware, little has been published on the interwar French anarchist movement in the last few years, but there are a few very useful studies which should be mentioned—and I am grateful to Marianne Enckell and the comrades of the collective "Les Giménologues" for their help with this. The latter, in fact, have published the autobiography of an unknown Italian anarchist, originally named Bruno Salvadori, who became a member of the International Group in the Durruti Column: Antoine Gimenez and les Giménologues, *Les Fils de la nuit: Souvenirs de la guerre d'Espagne (juillet 1936 – février 1939)* (Montreuil & Marseille: L'Insomniaque & Les Giménologues, 2006). This includes a very thoroughly researched study of the context which contains an enormous amount of useful detail on the anarchist militias and the foreign volunteers in them. The Fédération Anarchiste has just published Michel Sahuc, *Un regard noir: la mouvance anarchiste française au seuil de la seconde guerre mondiale et sous l'occupation nazie (1936–1945)* (Paris: Editions du Monde libertaire, 2008). And finally, Michel Léger has just written (and published himself) a biography of his father Robert, entitled *De brigades en brigades*.

Secondly, I have added to a footnote in ch.13 in order to remove a possible ambiguity regarding a particular activist's war-time activities.

Finally, I would like to thank a few people: Zach and others at AK for taking it on; Clifford Harper for such a beautiful cover; and Barry Pateman for his encouraging comments.

Introduction

Surely no political idea has been subjected to a more withering barrage of condemnation than anarchism ever since Proudhon first attached the anarchist label to himself.

William O. Reichert[1]

It is impossible to understand the evolution of the labour movement without studying the history of its minorities, since they propose other methods and other perspectives than those of the bigger organizations. It is therefore impossible to analyze the dead ends in which we find ourselves today without evaluating as accurately as possible both the positive contribution and the more problematic aspects of the anarchist movement.

Denis Berger[2]

It hardly seems necessary to explain the interest that anarchism holds for historians and others interested in French working-class movements, or the interest that France holds for anarchists and others interested in the history of anarchism. If France gave the world the concept of "Jacobinism," it was also a Frenchman, Pierre-Joseph Proudhon, who coined the term "anarchist" and was the acknowledged "father" of the anarchist movement. France was for some years the adopted home of Michael Bakunin and of Peter Kropotkin, associated respectively with anarchism's development as a "collectivist" then as a "communist" doctrine. It was in France that anarchism first became a significant social force: with the Proudhonists and Bakuninists in the First International, then with the anarchists' *rôle* in the development of "revolutionary syndicalism." It was also in France that, through its rather tenuous connection with the terrorist and illegalist actions of a few individuals, anarchism gained most notoriety. At the same time and partly because of this, anarchism also found favour with many prominent "*fin de siècle*" writers, artists and intellectuals in France.

Yet despite the important position that anarchism has occupied in French history, despite the general acknowledgement of the breadth and depth of its influence in many areas of French social, political and cultural life, from the co-operative movement to symbolist poetry, from anti-clericalism to free love, histories of the anarchist *movement* have not, on the whole, been either numerous or impressive. It is worth quoting at length some comments originally made in 1965 by Daniel Guérin, since it is one aim of this study to address precisely the points he makes regarding some widespread criticisms (and misrepresentations) of anarchism:

> Anarchism has for many years suffered from an undeserved disrepute, from an injustice which has manifested itself in three ways.
> Firstly, its detractors claim that it is simply a thing of the past. It did not survive the great revolutionary tests of our time: the Russian revolution and the Spanish revolution. It has no place in the modern world, a world characterized by centralization, by large political and economic entities, by the idea of totalitarianism. There is nothing left for the anarchists to do but, "by force of circumstance" as Victor Serge put it, to "join the revolutionary marxists".
> Secondly, the better to devalue it, those who would slander anarchism serve up a tendentious interpretation of its doctrine. Anarchism is essentially individualistic, particularistic, hostile to any form of organization. It leads to fragmentation, to the egocentric withdrawal of small local units of administration and production. It is incapable of centralizing or of planning. It is nostalgic for the 'golden age'. It tends to resurrect archaic social forms. It suffers from a childish optimism; its 'idealism' takes no account of the solid realities of the material infrastructure. It is incurably petit-bourgeois; it places itself outside of the class movement of the modern proletariat. In a word, it is 'reactionary'.
> And finally, certain of its commentators take care to rescue from oblivion and to draw attention to only its most controversial deviations, such as terrorism, individual assassinations, propaganda by explosives.[3]

Communists have often been among the worst offenders in this respect. Firstly because anarchism, like syndicalism (many of whose distinctive features had their origins in the influence of anarchism), has been seen as the doctrine of a particular stage of development of capitalist societies and of particular social strata, doomed to be superseded by communism, the "scientific" doctrine of modern industrial capitalism and of the industrial, urban working class. Anarchism and other non-marxist forms of socialism have thus tended to be seen as immature, *pre-* or *proto*-marxist socialisms. Such a linear view of the evolution of socialist thought and action has been increasingly challenged of late.[4]

Secondly, of course, the international communist movement's willingness to use slander (not to mention physical violence) against its rivals and enemies on the left—and not just under Stalin—has been well documented. This has ranged from attempts to discredit French syndicalists who insisted on publicizing some of the "excesses" of bolshevik rule in the early days of the Comintern and Profintern (which will be discussed in this study), through Yaroslavsky's highly spurious 1937 booklet on anarchism in Russia, to more or less dishonest attempts after 1968 to dismiss newly popular anarchism as an irrelevance in the modern world.[5]

Indeed, looking at some of the histories of French anarchism produced (not just by communists) since 1945, one might be inclined to agree with the anarchist Le Négus in Malraux's *L'Espoir*, speaking of a communist play he had seen and in which there had been some anarchist characters: "And what were they like? Like communists as seen by the bourgeois."[6] Most of these histories have done little better than Boisson, whose 1931 history of *Les attentats sous la troisième république* (Terrorism under the Third Republic) at least had the virtue of an honest litle.[7] Indeed, the persistence of the cluster of stereotypes attached to the words "anarchism" and "anarchist" has proved to be such that one writer felt compelled to entitle an article "Les Anarchistes Doux" ("The Gentle Anarchists"), simply because it did not concern itself with violent marginals.[8] Chronicles such as those by Salmon, Sergent and Ulrich, although not without interest, tended to adopt a sensationalist, journalistic approach, concentrating on the individualists, the terrorists, the illegalists and the moralists.[9] Guilleminault and Mahé's study represented only a slight exception in so far as it devoted a little attention to the 1914–18 war and the founding of the French Communist Party at the end of 1920.[10] More recently, Parry and Caruchet have chosen to devote yet more space to the illegalists of the Bonnot gang, and a chapter in Pierre Miquel's study of the Parisian police lumps together anarchists, thugs, "apaches," child beaters, prostitutes and petty criminals under the title "Le Paris des anarchistes et l'anarchie de Paris" ("The anarchists' Paris and the anarchy of Paris").[11]

For a long time the only real attempt to produce a properly researched historical study of the French anarchist movement was Jean Maitron's doctoral thesis, published in 1951.[12] As for the inter-war years, however, research on the French anarchist movement has tended to be neglected by historians of working-class movements between the wars in favour, notably, of work on the nascent communist movement.

Only after the 1960s, and particularly after the events of May 1968, did anarchism internationally become the subject of a revival of interest.[13] In France, a number of master's dissertations and doctoral theses were undertaken in the early 1970s, mostly of a bibliographical nature or concentrating on only one newspaper. This unpublished research, together with Maitron's more or less regular updates on research of anarchism and related areas published in the labour history journal *Mouvement social*, culminated in the publication by Maitron of *Le mouvement anarchiste en France*, the second volume of which took the story up to 1975.[14] But the main reason for the publication of the second volume was the inclusion of an extensive bibliography, and as the period covered is so broad, only around 50 pages are devoted to the inter-war years. This brevity made impossible any detailed treatment of the anarchist movement in this period, led to misrepresentation of the anarchists' positions and activities at certain points and meant that significant developments within anarchism were neglected. Biard's study, published a year after Maitron's, does not remedy the situation, being concerned primarily with the period 1945–75 and devoting only an introductory chapter to the inter-war years.[15] The last 20 years or so have seen many more unpublished postgraduate dissertations and theses on aspects of French anarchism,[16] as well as a series of autobiographies by veteran militants[17] (including Georges Fontenis' partially autobiographical study of the libertarian communist tradition, which also focuses on the post-war years[18]) and the publication of "academic" studies by Amdur, Auzias, Brémand, Colson, Jennings, Maricourt, Pessin, Sonn, Thorpe, Vincent and others.[19] On the 1920s and 30s, much research nevertheless remains to be done.[20]

Despite periodic resurgences of interest in anarchism, despite occasional assertions of the reappearance of anarchist or syndicalist ideas and practices (as, arguably, in France over the last decade), the most sympathetic historian cannot deny that as a movement anarchism is nowadays marginal in comparison with the first decades of the 20th century, and it was never a mass movement. Nevertheless it would be a mistake to fall prey to what James Joll has called "the historians' cult of success," an ahistorical approach that, in Edward Thompson's words, "reads history in the light of subsequent preoccupations, and not as in fact it occurred."[21] To understand the appearance of new strategies within the labour and socialist movements, those which are being discarded must be properly understood: "The orthodox options themselves only have meaning and can only be explained and evaluated in their context and through their contrast with the totality of options habitually hidden."[22] To understand the causes and modalities of the decline of the anarchist movement we must study the 1920s and 30s, the period following what is generally regarded as its heyday. In examining the anarchists' responses to the Russian and Spanish revolutions, it becomes easier to assess the nature of anarchism as a doctrine, faced as it was, for the first time, with actual revolutions — and in particular with revolutions where anarchist movements played a rôle. As Guérin argued:

> 19th century anarchism can be clearly distinguished from·20th century anarchism. 19th century anarchism was essentially doctrinal. It is true that Proudhon was more or less involved in the revolution of 1848 and that Bakunin's followers played some rôle in the Paris Commune. But these 19th century revolutions were not, essentially, libertarian revolutions; they were to a certain extent 'jacobin' revolutions. The 20th century, on the other hand, was for the anarchists the century of revolutionary practice. They played an active rôle in the two Russian revolutions and had an even more important place in the Spanish revolution.[23]

So this study proposes to analyze the anarchist response to these revolutions, thus making it possible to comprehend the dilemmas facing anarchism at historically crucial moments and to illuminate its critique both of capitalism and of the dominant forces in the working-class movement. But although this is a study primarily at the level of ideology and organization, I have endeavoured to avoid producing a history dealing solely with leaders or faceless organizations. I have tried — as far as the sources permit — to emphasize the feelings, the beliefs and the commitments of ordinary "grass roots" militants, to show them struggling with new and difficult situations, to rescue the memory of these otherwise unknown militants from the "enormous condescension of posterity."[24] As Geneviève Fraisse has put it, "Naming the 'obscure' activist gives substance to reality and counteracts the anonymity in which the hegemonic forces wish to abandon them. ... To concern ourselves with the lives of unknown individuals is to bring into question the representativity of an analysis founded on the study of the leaders and organizational structures of a movement. In order to understand this movement, the lives, the statements, the actions of the leaders are not enough."[25] This study nevertheless makes no claim to provide a social or cultural history of anarchism. Others, such as Auzias and Sonn, have focussed more on the cultural aspect of anarchist milieux (in interwar Lyon and turn-of-the-century Paris respectively) and more work of this kind would shed light on the meaning of anarchism in terms of activists' everyday lives. On the other hand, serious sociological or prosopographical research on anarchism is still, as far as I am aware, comparatively unknown territory.[26]

My choice of level of analysis has led to another lacuna, but it is one for which I make no apologies: by their self-isolation from "the social question" the individualist anarchists eliminate themselves from any lengthy consideration here. Indeed, it will be one of the main conclusions of this study that the nature and parameters of the anarchist movement changed in this period: that it came to be dominated by anarchist communism to a greater extent than ever before; that there was an increased distance both in terms of ideology and practice between anarchist communism and anarchist individualism; and that the period as a whole can be characterized as one of revision of what had by 1914 already come to be seen as "traditional" anarchism.

Notes

1.   William O. Reichert, "The anarchist as elitist: a critique," p.63, in *Our Generation* vol.18, no.1 (Fall/Winter 1986), pp.63–86.

2.   Denis Berger, "Communisme, pouvoir, liberté," p.48, review of Georges Fontenis, *L'autre communisme. Histoire subversive du mouvement libertaire* (Mauléon: Acratie, 1990) in *Critique communiste* no.113–114 (January 1992), pp.47–50. All translations are mine unless otherwise stated.

3.   Preface of 1970 to Daniel Guérin (ed.), *Ni Dieu ni Maître. Anthologie de l'anarchisme* (Paris: La Découverte, 1999), vol. I, pp.6–7.

4.   See, for example, Kathryn E. Amdur, *Syndicalist Legacy: Trade Unions and Politics in Two French Cities in the Era of World War I* (Urbana & Chicago: University of Illinois Press, 1986); Daniel Colson, *Anarcho-syndicalisme et communisme. Saint-Etienne 1920–1925* (Saint-Etienne: Université de Saint-Etienne/Centre d'Etudes Foréziennes/Atelier de Création Libertaire, 1986); Jeremy Jennings, *Syndicalism in France. A Study of Ideas* (Basingstoke & London: Macmillan in association with St. Antony's College, Oxford: 1990); Wayne Thorpe, *"The Workers Themselves." Revolutionary Syndicalism and International Labour, 1913–1923* (Amsterdam: International Institute of Social History & Dordrecht/Boston/London: Kluwer Academic Publishers, 1989); K. Steven Vincent, *Between Marxism and Anarchism: Benoît Malon and French Reformist Socialism* (Berkeley, CA: University of California Press, 1992). For a recent discussion of the historiography of revolutionary syndicalism, see Marcel van der Linden, "Second thoughts on revolutionary syndicalism" in *Labour History Review*, vol.63, no.2 (Summer 1998), pp.182–96. I know of no comparable review of the historiography of anarchism, though many of the central issues are similar.

5.   E. Yaroslavsky, *Anarchism in Russia* (London: Lawrence Wishart, n.d.), published in France as Em. Iaroslavski, *L'Anarchisme en Russie: Comment l'Histoire a tranché au cours de la Révolution russe la controverse entre anarchistes et communistes* (Paris: Bureau d'Editions, 1937). Examples of post-68 publications are Maurice Moissonnier, "Anarchismes d'hier et d'aujourd'hui," in *La Nouvelle Critique* no.24 (May 1969), pp.6–9; and Eric Hobsbawm,

"Reflections on Anarchism" in *The Debate on Anarchism* (Nottingham: The Bertrand Russell Peace Foundation for *The Spokesman*, 1973).

6.   André Malraux, *L'Espoir* (Paris: Gallimard, 1937), p.239.

7.   Marius Boisson, *Les attentats sous la troisième république* (Paris: Editions de France, 1931).

8.   Abel Clarté's "Les Anarchistes Doux" in *Les dossiers de l'histoire* no.13 (May–June 1978), pp.88–89, did not however contribute a great deal to the restoration of anarchist history, since it merely conformed to alternative and equally misleading stereotypes: it was a brief comment on the intellectual Pioch and the individualist Lacaze-Duthiers. The ways in which the stereotypical associations of anarchism came into being would make an interesting object of study and have not yet, to my knowledge, been studied with regard to France. Cf. Nhat Hong, *The Anarchist Beast: The Anti-Anarchist Crusade in Periodical Literature (1884–1906)* (Minneapolis: Soil of Liberty, n.d.).

9.   André Salmon, *La Terreur Noire: chronique du mouvement libertaire* (Paris: Jean-Jacques Pauvert, 1959); Alain Sergent, *Les Anarchistes: Scènes et Portraits* (Paris: Frédéric Chambriand, 1951); Paul Ulrich (ed.), *Histoire de l'Anarchie* (Geneva: Famot, 1974), 2 vols.

10.   Gilbert Guilleminault and André Mahé, *L'épopée de la Révolte: Le roman vrai d'un siècle d'anarchie (1862–1962)* (Paris: Denoël, 1963).

11.   Richard Parry, *The Bonnot Gang* (London: Rebel Press, 1987); William Caruchet, *Ils ont tué Bonnot. Les révélations des archives policières* (Paris: Calmann-Lévy, 1990); Pierre Miquel, *La Main courante. Les archives indiscrètes de la Police parisienne, 1900–1945* (Paris: Albin Michel, 1997), pp.109–46.

12.   Jean Maitron, *Histoire du mouvement anarchiste en France (1880–1914)* (Paris: SUDEL, 1951).

13.   On the bibliographical aspect of this revival, see Nicolas Walter's comparison of the situation in 1945–60 and 1970: "Anarchism in Print: Yesterday and Today," in "Anarchism Today," special number of *Government and Opposition*, vol.5 no.4 (Autumn 1970), pp.523–40.

14.   Jean Maitron, *Le mouvement anarchiste en France* (Paris: Maspero, 1975), vol.I: "Des origines à 1914"; vol.II: "De 1914 à nos jours." This will be referred to throughout this study simply as Maitron.

15.   Roland Biard, *Histoire du mouvement anarchiste 1945–1975* (Paris: Galilée, 1976).

16.   From the point of view of research, the most important is undoubtedly René Bianco, *Un siècle de presse anarchiste d'expression française dans le monde, 1880–1983* (Doctorat d'Etat, Université de Provence, 1988).

17.   Nicolas Faucier, *Pacifisme et Antimilitarisme dans l'entre-deux-guerres (1919–1939)* (Paris: Spartacus, 1983) and *Dans la mêlée sociale. Itinéraire d'un anarcho-syndicaliste* (Quimperlé: La Digitale, 1988); Lucien Feuillade, *Une vie comme ça* (Paris: Quai Voltaire, 1988); Maurice Joyeux, *Souvenirs d'un anarchiste* and *Sous les plis du drapeau noir* (Paris: Le Monde libertaire, 1986 & 1988); René Lochu, *Libertaires, mes compagnons de Brest et d'ailleurs* (Quimperlé: La Digitale, 1983); Pierre Martin, *L'Armée? Non merci! (Candide face au Moloch)* (Arudy: Utovie, 1983); Louis Mercier-Vega, *La Chevauchée anonyme* (Geneva: Editions Noir, 1978); René Michaud, *J'avais vingt ans. Un jeune ouvrier au début du siècle* (Paris: Syros, 1983); Georges Navel, *Passages* (Paris: Gallimard, 1991); May Picqueray, *May la réfractaire. Pour mes 81 ans d'anarchie* (Atelier Marcel Jullian, 1979).

18.   Georges Fontenis, *L'autre communisme. Histoire subversive du mouvement libertaire* (Mauléon: Acratie, 1990). A revised and enlarged edition was published as *Changer le*

monde. Histoire du mouvement communiste libertaire, 1945–1997 (Paris: Le Coquelicot/Alternative libertaire, 2000).

19.   Amdur, *Syndicalist Legacy*; Claire Auzias, *Mémoires libertaires: Lyon, 1919–1939* (Paris: L'Harmattan, 1993); Nathalie Brémand, *Cempuis: Une expérience d'éducation libertaire à l'époque de Jules Ferry* (Paris: Editions du *Monde libertaire*, 1992); Colson, *Anarcho-syndicalisme et communisme*; Jennings, *Syndicalism in France*; Thierry Maricourt, *Histoire de la littérature libertaire en France* (Paris: Albin Michel, 1990); Richard D. Sonn, *Anarchism and Cultural Politics in Fin de Siècle France* (Lincoln & London: University of Nebraska Press, 1989); Thorpe, *The Workers Themselves*; Vincent, *Benoît Malon*. See also David Berry, Amedeo Bertolo, Sylvain Boulouque, Phil Casoar, Marianne Enckell & Charles Jacquier, *Présence de Louis Mercier* (Lyon: Atelier de création libertaire, 1999); "Anarchism," ch.6 of Robert Gildea, *The Past in French History* (New Haven & London: Yale University Press, 1994), pp.260–97. This list is not intended to be comprehensive.

20.   Limitations of space prevent a comprehensive review of the literature here. See René Bianco, "Où en est l'histoire de l'anarchisme?" in *Mouvement social* no.144 (October–November 1988), pp.45–54; René Bianco with Philippe Equy, "Où en est l'histoire de l'anarchisme?," *Bulletin du CIRA* (Centre international de recherches sur l'anarchisme, Marseille) no.34 (1993). Both CIRA produce regular updates on research and publications in their bulletins: CIRA, BP 40, 13382 Marseille Cedex 13, France; CIRA, Beaumont 24, 1012 Lausanne, Switzerland. See also the multi-lingual *Research on Anarchism* web site (http://melior.univ-montp3.fr/ra_forum/), which includes amongst other things the full text of a growing number of published and unpublished studies; the site is also connected to an e-mail discussion list which is a useful source of information on current research and new publications.

21.   James Joll, *The Anarchists* (London: Eyre & Spottiswoode, 1964), p.12; E.P. Thompson, *The Making of the English Working Class* (Harmondsworth: Penguin, 1980), p.12.

22.   Robert Pagès, "André Prudhommeaux et le choix de l'autonomie (1902–1968)," p.9, introduction to André Prudhommeaux, *L'effort libertaire* (Paris: Spartacus, 1978).

23.   Daniel Guérin, "Un procès de réhabilitation," p.22, in *A la recherche d'un communisme libertaire* (Paris: Spartacus, 1984), pp.22–3.

24.   Thompson, *The Making of the English Working Class*, p.12.

25.   Geneviève Fraisse, "Du bon usage de l'individu féministe," p.48, in *Vingtième siècle* no.14 (April 1987), pp.45–54.

26.   Nicolas Faucier, "Rapport sur le mouvement anarchiste en France, sa composition, son comportement durant la période 1930–1940" in "Communauté de travail du CIRA," *Société et contre-société* (Genève: Librairie Adversaire, 1974); Jean Maitron, "Un 'anar', qu'est-ce que c'est?," in *Mouvement social* no.83 (April–June 1973), pp.23–45. With regard to the recent trend towards prosopography (collective biography), see Michel Dreyfus, Claude Pennetier & Nathalie Viet-Depaule (eds.), *La Part des militants. Biographie et mouvement ouvrier: Autour du Maitron, Dictionnaire biographique du mouvement ouvrier français* (Paris: Edns. de l'Atelier/Edns. ouvrières, 1996), especially René Bianco, "Les anarchistes dans le Dictionnaire biographique du mouvement ouvrier français," pp.185–92. See also my "Contribution to a Collective Biography of the French Anarchist Movement: French Anarchist Volunteers in Spain, 1936–39" (paper given to a conference on the International Brigades, University of Lausanne, 1997; proceedings in French translation edited by Jean Batou forthcoming; original version on the *Research on Anarchism* web site). Mimmo Pucciarelli has attempted a study of the present-day anarchist movement: "Qui sont les anar-

chistes?" in *Alternative libertaire* no.219 (summer 1999) (available at http://www.citeweb. net/albelgik/archive/99/219-ete/som-219.htm).

1

The Context: Anarchism in France from the 1840s to 1917

> Do not imagine that Anarchy is a dogma, an unchallen-
> geable doctrine, venerated by its supporters. ... No: the
> absolute freedom which we demand means that our ideas
> are constantly developing; it lifts them towards new ho-
> rizons ... and pushes them beyond the narrow confines
> of all forms of regulation and codification. We are not
> 'believers'.
>
> *Émile Henry*[1]

There may well be some value for intellectual historians in tracing the politico-philosophical roots of modern anarchism through its major "thinkers" right back to antiquity. Eugène Armand, leading light of individualist anarchism between the wars, was to do just that in his 1933 study of the movement's "precursors," looking at everything and everybody from the Satan and Prometheus myths, through Zeno and Plato, medieval Christianity, the writers and thinkers of the Renaissance, to Diderot, Schiller and Godwin.[2] But to do this, as Georges Fontenis has quite rightly insisted, is to confuse "the history of the revolutionary anarchist movement with the universal history of anti-authoritarian thought" and tends to produce a distorted image of the origins of anarchism as a historically situated movement.[3] The present study aims to restore anarchism within the history of inter-war French society and to situate the movement in that period in terms of its own "internal" history. Hence the need to begin with a brief overview of the development of French anarchism as an articulate and identifiable trend over the seventy or so years preceding the First World War. The intention is to show how, over that period, anarchism in France evolved as an ideology and as a practice through several phases in response to both political and socio-economic developments. Such periodization can be over-schematic and misleading, if it is not borne in mind that such historical breaks are rarely, if ever, clean. Nevertheless, if the limitations of the exercise are not forgotten, it can be a useful way of making clearer certain developments in later periods. It should also put into perspective recurring debates after 1914 about the "true" meaning of anarchism and the need to revise or reaffirm anarchist "principles."

1840–71: THE DEVELOPMENT OF ANARCHISM AS A DISTINCT IDEOLOGY

Anarchism first appeared in France as a distinct ideology in a period characterized by the development of industrial capitalism. From 1815 on, and especially after the July revolution of 1830, the new industrial technology and the free market economy began to establish themselves. The results were rapid urbanization and immigration into the towns from the countryside, social dislocation, the birth of a factory proletariat, the gradual decline of the artisanat. It was amongst the latter, during the years after 1830, that the origins of a working-class consciousness can be located: "The French working class was born in the workshops, not the factory, among artisans whose immediate experience in the July Monarchy were reflected through values lodged deep in their culture-norms, profoundly antagonistic to the ethos of the capitalist emphasis on profit maximization. ... Relative, if threatened affluence and a sense of community and professional pride made them the vanguard of worker resistance movements."[4] It was from the standpoint of this class that Proudhon, "the father of anarchy," engaged with other early socialist theorists such as Louis Blanc, Pierre Leroux and Louis Auguste Blanqui and developed a doctrine, "mutualism," which represented a break not only with contemporary non-anarchist socialists but also with a "pre-anarchist" tradition going back to the "*enragés*" of 1793–95.

Firstly, rejecting both capitalism and communism, Proudhon "transposes the social position of the master artisans who rejected equally vigorously both absorption into the capitalist factory and the threat of dispossession. For the Lyon mutualist as for the French craft worker, possession of the tools of their trade (as opposed to property as a source of profit) was the guarantor of economic activity and, as Proudhon would argue later, of the freedom of the producer."[5] Secondly, repeated evidence of the willingness of a supposedly progressive republican bourgeoisie to resort to violent repression of the working classes had led Proudhon, like many of his class and generation, to lose faith in politics and the state and to put the emphasis on working-class autonomy and on the question of socio-economic organization.[6] For Proudhon and the mutualists, the lessons of the workers' uprisings of 1830 and 1848 were that the powers of the state were merely another aspect of the powers of capital, and both were to be resisted equally strongly.[7] As he wrote shortly after 1848, "All revolutions are accomplished through the spontaneity of the people. To the extent that governments have sometimes followed the people's lead, it was because they had little choice. Almost always, governments have restrained, repressed and hit out with violence."[8] Finally, the critique of the present always went hand in hand with the development of the future organization of society, modelled economically on the artisanal workshop and socially on the workers' associations, and characterized by a simultaneous insistence on decentralized autonomy and federalist organization.

In the 1850s and 1860s Proudhonist mutualism was the dominant influence among the most active sections of the nascent French labour movement. At the first two congresses of the First International or IWMA (the International Workingmen's Association, or Association internationale des travailleurs) in 1866 and 1867, the French, Belgian and Swiss delegations adopted very Proudhonian positions, both in their acceptance of private property, and in their rejection of parliamentary politics. But by 1868, due to the increase in membership of the French section of the IWMA, the growth of aggressive trade unionism, government attacks on the mutualist-led Paris section and growing doubts about the capacity of mutualist co-operatives to organize virtual monopolies such as national transport, a transition from mutualism to "antistatist" or "antiauthoritarian collectivism" had begun. Indeed, the 1867 congress had already voted in favour of public (though not state) ownership of the means of transport and exchange.[9] This collectivist tendency was the dominant one by the time of the 1869 congress, which voted unanimously for the creation of trade unions. The French delegates agreed with this so long as the unions were to have revolution as their aim, but they still saw strikes as useless. Further development of the anarchist tendency within the IWMA was interrupted by Bakunin's failed attempt at insurrection in Lyon in September 1870, and by the Paris Commune of 1871. The consequent repression—by a bourgeois democratic republic based on universal male suffrage—left 20–25,000 dead, and although it reinforced the anarchists' rejection of "democratic" politics, it effectively meant the end of the IWMA in France. Internationally, the IWMA was a mere rump after the 1872 La Haye congress, when marxists and anarchists split over the question of involvement in parliamentary politics.

1871–1880: THE JURA FEDERATION

After the Commune, the French labour movement was decimated. The French Federation of the IWMA was represented from 1877 by Paul Brousse's newspaper, *l'Avant-Garde* (whose international section was

written by Kropotkin). The paper's attitude as far as labour organization was concerned consisted of a rejection of reformist syndicalism in
favour of revolutionary action. At the time, this tended to compound anarchism's isolation in what was already a very unfavourable situation.

In fact, for the decade following the Commune, anarchism developed not in France, but within the Jura Federation on the Franco-Swiss
border. The Jura Federation refused to accept the decisions of the La
Haye congress, and held its own congress later the same year at Saint-
Imier, effectively founding a rival "antiauthoritarian" International. Expelled from the IWMA in 1873 because of its attitude to political parties
and political action, Jura's ideology was "revolutionary collectivism," a
kind of synthesis of Proudhonian mutualism and collectivism. The Federation embraced the strike as a revolutionary tool, whilst still denying it any value as a means of achieving wage rises or improvements in
conditions.

It was during the late 1870s that the notion of "propaganda by the
deed" developed within the Federation. In the words of Paul Brousse,
"The idea advances on the basis of two complementary forces: the influence of the act and the strength of the theory, and if one of these forces
is more effective than the other, it is the act."[10] Given the state of the
movement, the insurrectionalism of some French and Italian comrades,
and the influence of contemporary Russian terrorism, it seems almost
inevitable that such "propaganda by the deed" should have developed
in the direction of illegal and violent action, rather than through other
more peaceful and less dramatic means.

The late 1870s also saw a new development in the definition of the
society aimed for. French anarchism had initially been mutualist, then
had adopted a limited collectivism, that is to say collective ownership of
the means of production, but individual ownership of the fruits of his/
her own labour. By 1880, after an intervention by Kropotkin the previous year, communism had been adopted as the aim ("anarchist communism" or "libertarian communism" in order to distinguish it from "authoritarian" or "State communism").[11] The new society would be based
on the commune and on the free federation of producers and consumers.
Tactics, a previously neglected question, were now also defined: the destruction of the State by force, the use of illegal methods, the propa-
gation of "the revolutionary idea" and of "the spirit of revolt" and the
autonomy of groups (though with some co-ordination of activity).

This then was the state of French anarchism when, with the return of the amnestied communards in 1880, France again became the
centre of gravity of revolutionary activity.

1881–1892: THE BIRTH OF AN INDEPENDENT ANARCHIST MOVEMENT

The split on an international level between marxists and anarchists over the question of whether to take part in political institutions was mirrored on a national level at the French Socialist Workers' Congresses organized in 1879 and 1880. These two congresses produced profound disagreements and organizational division followed in 1881, when the anarchists withdrew from the socialist congress in order to hold a separate "Independent Revolutionary Socialist Congress." For Maitron, the date of that congress, 22 May 1881, marks the birth of an autonomous anarchist "party" whose programme and tactics differed clearly from those of other socialist currents.[12] In the following months, various regional congresses saw similar splits. In some cases the anarchists were the minority, in others they represented the majority. Anarchist federations were subsequently established in some regions.

Such attempts at co-ordination and organization were to have little future, though, and through to the early 1890s there was no national organization in France; there were only local groups with limited links between them. This was due partly to circumstances, partly to principle. Circumstances, because when a congress was organized in London in 1881 in an attempt to reconstitute the IWMA, memories of the first international bureau were such that the new bureau was given very little power. Principle, because of the insistence on "autonomy" and "free initiative." This applied both internationally and nationally. For instance the Barcelona anarchist paper, *El Productor*, commented after an international anarchist conference held in Paris in 1889 that "the mania for non-organization has rendered impossible any discussion of an international organization, which could give such excellent service to the cause of revolution."[13] But a majority of French anarchists were certainly very reticent about any co-ordination beyond the most short term activities. As an article in *le Révolté* argued: "We do not believe in long term associations, federations, etc. For us, a group should come together only for a clearly defined objective or short term action; once the action is accomplished, the group should reform on a new basis, either with the same elements, or with new ones."[14] Similarly, the stress was placed on "antiauthoritarianism" to such an extent that some anarchists could complain about the national distribution of an anarchist manifesto on the grounds that it constituted a kind of "moral dictatorship."[15]

At that time, the social revolution was believed by many activists to be imminent. When Kropotkin declared in 1883 that "the social revolution is near! It will break out within ten years," some thought his "ten years" was pessimistic.[16] "*La sociale*" was to be revolution through strikes, but not through strikes with reformist aims. Strikes were seen as a process through which workers asserted and became conscious of their dignity as the producers of social wealth, and through which they learned the meaning of class struggle. Anarchists encouraged the development of violent, expropriatory strikes and, ultimately, the insurrectionary general strike synonymous with social revolution. They emphasized the rôle of individual revolutionaries in triggering strikes, rather than the action of trade union organizations. The Great Depression (1873–96) saw industrial recession of varying degrees of severity according to sector and region, and the period was typified by violent strikes and riots such as at Montceau-les-Mines in 1882 and Decazeville in 1886. Such events and the use of violence against both people and property were glorified by the anarchist press, even though most of those involved were not of course conscious anarchists. The consequences, in any case, were a period of severe repression and the Lyon trial of 1883 at which the authorities handed down harsh sentences on many leading anarchist activists.

The depression also produced much unemployment, and the years 1883–85 saw a profusion of protest meetings and demonstrations. Whereas the guesdists advised the sending of legal delegations to elected representatives and the authorities, the anarchists encouraged illegal action and "expropriation," warning the unemployed to expect nothing of their elected representatives. Although this was no longer fertile ground for proselytism after about 1885, the anarchists continued to concentrate their propaganda work on "marginals," appealing in their own words "to the vagabonds, to the beggars, to the outlaws; …to those who are attacked as 'pimps' and 'prostitutes'; …to all the wretched, to all who suffer."[17]

From the mid- to late 1880s, however, in response to the decline of strike movements and of protests by the unemployed, *"la reprise individuelle"* (individual appropriation) made its appearance and became very common. It was never unanimously accepted by anarchists. Some, like Sébastien Faure, a prominent anarchist orator and propagandist, and Elisée Reclus, the famous geographer, Bakuninist and Communard, saw such theft as a revolutionary act.[18] Others, like Jean Grave, the Parisian shoemaker and editor of the leading anarchist newspapers of the time, condemned it as uncomradely, immoral and a deviation which ordinary people would not understand.[19] It represented, in fact, the beginning of anarchist "illegalism" as a particular minority tendency within the movement.

A not dissimilar ambivalence manifested itself in respect of the first May Day demonstrations in France in 1890 and 1891. On the one

hand, the anarchists were spontaneist and anti-organizationalist, opposing the aims of the demonstrations ("the three eights": eight hours of
work, eight hours of free time, eight hours of sleep) as reformist and
anti-revolutionary: "History, especially modern history, has recorded no
revolution nor even any movement of profit to the revolution which was
not the product of a spontaneous explosion of the masses' discontent
and anger."[20] Yet anarchism was a working-class movement, and such
an attitude would have meant isolating anarchism from an important
manifestation and symbol of working-class solidarity. The response
was therefore uncertain: "It is not enough to argue against May Day on
the grounds that it cannot achieve anything, that it would play into the
hands of the present government. In order to combat the proposal effectively, we have to put forward an alternative. What? We do not know. It
is up to the anarchists to find something."[21]

1892–94: TERRORISM

The very brief period during which political assassination hit the headlines in France is really a postscript to the 1880s. The policy of propaganda by the deed had been sanctioned by the IWMA at its London
congress of 1881, and for several years the use of poison, guns, knives
and explosives had been preached continually in the French anarchist
press. It corresponded to the revolutionary strategy of the 1880s: it was
based on the belief that the revolution was near; that it would erupt
spontaneously, provoked by the violent actions of individuals or small
groups; and that both legal procedures and mass organization were useless or even harmful.

In response to the actions of the "anarchist terrorists" (Ravachol,
Auguste Vaillant, Émile Henry and the Italian Santo Caserio) the government introduced the so-called "lois scélérates" (literally: villainous
laws, 1893–94), which were used against all revolutionaries, and initiated a massive wave of repression specifically against anarchist circles.[22]
Most anarchist newspapers disappeared. Leading activists were either
arrested or on the run. It prohibited all revolutionary propaganda, anarchist or not, at a time when Third Republic politicians were particularly
vulnerable, notably because of the Panama affair. After the "Trial of the
Thirty" in August 1894, terrorist attacks diminished and had ceased by
the end of the year.

On the whole, the terrorist era had very little positive effect. The
strategy gained no wide popular support and seems to have become
endemic for a while only through the circular logic of martyrdom and
revenge. The attacks stopped because of the "Trial of the Thirty," when

the jury acquitted the anarchist propagandists accused of being the accomplices of criminals; because of the very tight police surveillance of anarchist activists; but mostly because of the increasing strength of the labour movement.

The Fédération nationale des syndicats (National Federation of Trade Unions) had been founded in 1886, but in the words of Fernand Pelloutier, anarchist and early apologist for revolutionary syndicalism, this had been the "war-machine at the service of the French Workers' Party."[23] Anarchists had thus seen the Federation as a deviation from the revolution. Yet its 1888 congress saw the adoption of the general strike policy and by 1894 the syndicalist tendency within the Federation won out over the guesdists. What was called "economic action" (in other words, extra-parliamentary direct action) was thus given priority over "political action" (parliamentary party politics). The early 1890s also saw the development of the Fédération des Bourses du Travail (Federation of Trades Councils[24]) under the dominance of the anarchists and other anti-guesdist socialists. Thus from 1894, the labour movement was predominantly libertarian in orientation.

For the syndicalist Louzon, the terrorist phase was "the alarm bell which raised the French proletariat from the state of prostration and despair in which it had been plunged by the massacres of the Commune."[25] The evidence actually seems to suggest the opposite: namely, that the terrorist/illegalist era achieved nothing other than the isolation of the anarchists, the increased hostility of other socialist tendencies, increased repression and a negative, violent image which it has been difficult for anarchists to dispel ever since. The move towards labour organization seems to have been a reaction against the sterility of terrorism, "this infantile disorder of anarchism" as Maitron calls it.[26] For not all anarchists were terrorists by any means. Many leading activists, whilst not disowning dynamiters—in whom they saw "free spirits" and revolutionaries, however misguided tactically—did not praise their actions either. Evolution in the minds of activists was already under way in this period. The first warning in the press against too one-sided an interpretation of the expression "propaganda by the deed" appeared in 1886: "How many opportunities for action present themselves every day for less glorious action than we dream of perhaps, but action which is just as effective."[27] The anarchists' papers continual encouragement of terrorism came to an end by 1888. Significantly, it was Kropotkin, one of the leading anarchists to have contributed to the violent interpretation of propaganda by the deed, who wrote in 1891 that "an edifice which is built on centuries of history will not be destroyed by a few kilos of explosives." The revolution would not be brought about by the heroic acts of individuals: anarchist communism must win over the masses.[28]

1894–1914: REVOLUTIONARY SYNDICALISM

Repression following the terrorist period more or less destroyed the anarchist movement. Militants were exiled, imprisoned or under surveillance. From the spring of 1894, no important anarchist weekly appeared for over a year. Some contemporaries thought it was the death of the movement. But, in 1895, three important new anarchist newspapers appeared: Grave's *les Temps nouveaux*, Emile Pouget's *la Sociale* and Sébastien Faure's *le Libertaire*. As the first issue of the appropriately-named *les Temps nouveaux* (The New Times) put it: "We are now entering a new phase of the struggle."[29]

The new tactic for anarchist-communists—spreading the word more widely amongst the working class by entering labour organizations—was first suggested around 1890 and Kropotkin was one of the first. There was still much initial resistance, however, and the new tactic did not mean the total abandonment of certain "traditional" anarchist attitudes. The trade unions were still seen as worse than useless if their only aims were wage rises or reductions in working hours. The new policy was not really one of spontaneous mass action, but one of "active minorities." It was, in that respect, "avant-gardist": "The revolution will be made by the pressure of the masses. But these masses themselves are looking for people to take the initiative, they are looking for men and women who can better formulate their thoughts, who will be able to win over the hesitant and carry with them the timid."[30] It was a question of "individual initiative, put at the service of the collectivity."[31]

The attitudes of the different tendencies nevertheless varied. With *la Sociale*, support for syndicalism was clear. Pouget had been an active syndicalist from the late 1870s. In 1894 he criticized the anarchists' "affinity groups" because of their tendency to isolate anarchists from anyone who did not already agree with them. In 1900, he became editor of the CGT (Confédération générale du travail, General Confederation of Labour, created in 1895) weekly, *la Voix du peuple*.

Jean Grave was less convinced, but from 1895 *les Temps nouveaux* nevertheless had among its contributors leading syndicalists like Paul Delesalle, Amédée Dunois, Pierre Monatte, Georges Dumoulin and especially Fernand Pelloutier. It also carried a regular column with labour movement news. Pelloutier accepted that anarchists had in the past been right to be wary of trade unions, "veritable breeding ground of aspiring deputies."[32] But with the trade union movement's increasing militancy from the early 1890s and their growing scepticism towards political institutions, Pelloutier had become representative of those activists for whom, after 1895, anarchism was more or less synonymous with syndicalism.

The activists around *le Libertaire* did not think at all in the same way and were until 1899 violently anti-syndicalist. This was because of the "iron law of wages," whereby it was supposedly impossible to increase the totality of wages paid to the working class or to decrease the totality of hours worked by the working class. Hence syndicalists were considered bourgeois, objectively reactionary, and so on. Such anarchists supported only spontaneous strikes, seen as a rebellion against the whole system rather than as directed at a wage rise or some other piecemeal reform. The "respectable," organized working class was not to their taste: "The last hope, for those of us who are angry, impatient, revolutionary, is the dark mass of unemployed and starving proletarians—these are the ones who must be the starting-point of anarchist demands."[33] This began to change in 1899, when Grandidier could write: "Let us cease posing as the ferocious guardians of an inviolable dogma. Let us for once be rather more practical. Let us leave this ivory tower in which we are suffocating. Let us enter the trade unions."[34] From 1900, regular columns appeared on labour affairs and on strikes, and in 1901 Georges Yvetot, secretary of the Fédération des Bourses, became a contributor.

Around *le Libertaire* there was much clearer support for syndicalism with the departure of the individualists in 1905, when the weekly *l'Anarchie* appeared and became the focus of individualist anarchism until 1914. This latter paper was consistently anti-syndicalist on the grounds that the unions were too powerful, that *"les abrutis,"* as the working class were often referred to (the word means literally "numbed by toil"), would thus be able to win improvements, and that this would then reduce their will to revolt, thereby prolonging the reign of capital. The paper's main editors were André Lorulot, Mauricius and Albert Libertad.[35]

The individualist positon might be summed up as follows:

1. Only individuals exist, not classes. Among individuals, some co-operate with the system, others not. The latter are anarchists. The others vote, accept laws, work in factories, exploit people, agree to be exploited; all these limit the freedom of the free spirit, and are therefore enemies.
2. Society consists of exploiters and exploited; the ideal is to be neither. This implies working in co-operatives or communes or similar with other anarchists, but the position also led to "individual appropriation."

3. Trade unions are an adaptation to capitalism and are therefore to be disdained. Membership of them means accepting the rule of the majority, which is a form of oppression of the individual. They also encourage sectional competition.

For the socialist/collectivist anarchists, on the other hand, there was a clear lineage from the "labour movement anarchism" of the IWMA to the "anarchist syndicalism" of the CGT. The two periods were separated only by 20 years, and anarchist syndicalists were keen to establish a lineage with Bakunin and Jura. It was Bakunin who had written in 1869: "There is only one method of emancipation. It is the workers' struggle in solidarity against the bosses. It is the organization and the federation of strike funds."[36] This notion that it was the "only method" led to the idea of the self-sufficiency of syndicalism. Direct action and the general strike were also inherited from the IWMA. In other words, the anarchist syndicalism of the turn of the century was a revival of a tactic that had disappeared with the Bakuninist International and the Jurassians.

Whatever the differing views within anarchism, French labour organization was dominated by libertarianism from 1894 when, at the Nantes congress, the anarchist-influenced syndicalists beat the marxist-influenced socialists into a minority and "economic action" was given priority over "political action." The split at Nantes was confirmed and accentuated by the decision of the 1896 socialist conference in London to exclude anarchists because of their refusal to endorse parliamentarism. The Fédération des Bourses du Travail, founded at Saint-Etienne in 1892, rapidly became an anarchist stronghold. It was animated by all the tendencies hostile to the marxist Workers' Party (possibilists, blanquists, allemanists, anarchists and independents). The anarchist Pelloutier, who disliked the glorification of Ravachol and condemned revolutionary verbiage, irresponsible gesturing and propaganda by the deed, was the soul of the Federation from 1894 until his death in 1901.

Thus between 1894 and 1906, anarchists conquered many of the leading posts in the movement and the CGT came to be impregnated with anarchist ideology.[37] The famous resolution insisting on the CGT's revolutionism and apoliticism, adopted at the Amiens Congress of 1906, was seen as the "charter" of revolutionary syndicalism. But syndicalism, born of anarchism to a large extent, took on a life of its own and, arguably, came to threaten anarchism. The celebrated international anarchist conference at Amsterdam in 1907 saw the clash of the new revolutionary syndicalists and those who shall be referred to in this study as anarchist syndicalists (in other words, militants who saw themselves primarily as anarchists but who were also active in their trade union). For the latter, represented at Amsterdam by the prominent Italian Errico Malatesta, syndicalism was an important aspect of the revolutionary struggle, but only one amongst many; it was a part of anarchism, but by its nature only partial. Malatesta also questioned a basic premiss of syndicalism, namely that the exclusion of party politics from the trade union sphere would allow class consciousness to unite the working class in revolutionary opposition to capital. Malatesta denied the efficacy of common economic interests as compared to the solidarity born of a shared ideal.

For activists such as the young Pierre Monatte, on the other hand, revolutionary syndicalism had developed in struggle because of the failure of the existing tendencies, including anarchism, and was now the revolutionary movement *par excellence*. As Amédée Dunois — like Monatte, an anarchist won over to syndicalism — put it, syndicalism was a synthesis of Bakunin and Marx, born of a double reaction against "the deviation of socialism into parliamentary politics, the deviation of anarchism into intellectualism."[38] Dunois justified his abandonment of the "straight" anarchist movement and his commitment to syndicalism thus: "Revolutionary syndicalism *is* anarchism, but an anarchism which has been refreshed and given new life by proletarian ways of thinking; it is a realistic and concrete anarchism which unlike the old anarchism is no longer satisfied with negation or with abstract assertions; it is a proletarian anarchism to be realized not by initiates, but by the working class strengthened by years of struggle."[39] The veteran James Guillaume would similarly attack the anarchists' insistence on the rôle of "idealism" rather than on the concrete realities of class conflict: "You think that the starting point is the revolutionary ideal and that the workers' struggle against the bosses only comes afterwards, as a consequence of the adoption of the 'ideal'; I think on the contrary … that the starting point is the struggle and that the ideal comes after, that it takes form in the workers' minds as the incidents of the class war give birth to it and cause it to develop."[40]

1894–1914: THE "FORCES OF REVOLUTION"

Over those same 20 years preceding the Great War, there was a scattering of anarchists active in many different fields. Like syndicalism, these sometimes became effectively synonymous with anarchism for such activists, not just a part of it. Thus, anarchists involved in the co-operatist and pacifist movements were sometimes lost to anarchism. Illegalism had a similar effect though in a different way. For others, "Anarchism can be considered their crowning synthesis," and "neo-malthusianism"

(family planning), education and anti-militarism were valid and necessary fields of activity for anarchists working for a total social revolution.[41] Thus, anarchists were to be found involved in anti-clericalism,
naturism, vegetarianism, communalism and even on the fringes of the
SFIO (Section française de l'Internationale ouvrière, the French Section of the Second International, the United Socialist Party created in
1905), as well as in those areas already mentioned. There were various
reasons for this. Firstly, anarchists had believed the revolution to be imminent, and yet it seemed always to recede into the future. Communalist
and co-operatist experiments were a way of making the revolution instantly in one's everyday life. Secondly, because of the lack of doctrinal
cohesion. Since activists refused to lay down any dogma as to which
was the one true path, then anarchists could do what they as individuals
thought best, or simply what they felt like doing. The impatience felt by
many anarchists, especially on the individualist wing, is illustrated by
this quotation from a letter written to Jean Grave:

> It is stupid that those who have understood are forced to wait
> until the mass of fools blocking the way forward have evolved.
> The herd will always be the herd. Let us leave them to shuffle
> along, and let us work for our own emancipation. ... The Fa-
> therland, Society and Morality have collapsed. ... That is good,
> but do not help resurrect new entities: the Idea, the Revolution,
> Propaganda, Solidarity, we could not care less about them.
> What we want is to live, to be able to take our ease and en-
> joy the pleasures to which we have a right. What we want to
> achieve is the integral development of our individuality in all
> senses of the word.[42]

1894–1914: MOVEMENT AND ORGANIZATION

What might be called the "traditionalist" position was typified by Grave
and the *Temps nouveaux* group: organization is alright for those making
a political revolution, but not for anarchists, since it reproduces the authoritarian structures intended to be destroyed; individuals must be free
to organize as they wish, according to their affinities, and for clearly-
defined actions only, the organization disappearing when the purpose
is fulfilled; organization stifles individual initiative; unity of view leads
to stagnation. To a large extent, this was a reflection of the nature of
the broader labour movement around the turn of the century. Organizations of the left (parties or unions) tended not to have very clearly
defined ideological positions; organizational structures were loose; activists came and went, passing from one grouping to another according

to how active particular groups were and with scant regard for doctrinal niceties; a non-theoretical, instinctive class consciousness seems to have been an adequate basis for co-operation.[43] Lequin has written of the influence of anarchist militants in the labour movement that it was "not the influence of an organization; it was the influence of ephemeral leaders during the high points of worker agitation. ... The smallest strike was the opportunity for direct action."[44]

Such dispersion and discontinuity was not to the liking of everybody. It has already been noted that individualist anarchism became a separate minority tendency around 1905. By the time of the 1907 Amsterdam conference, French anarchist-communism was split between the traditionalists (who did not attend the conference because they disapproved) and those who put their hopes to a greater or lesser degree in syndicalism. Over the next few years, there were various attempts at establishing permanent anarchist organizations, but the difficulties were enormous. Commenting on the possibility of such organization, Dunois summed up the different tendencies within the movement:

1. Anarchists who create groups, but who lack influence, culture and — very often also — seriousness;
2. Influential, educated, honourable anarchists who do not want to hear speak of organization;
3. Syndicalist anarchists for whom the ideological grouping has become vain and superfluous (need I add that I am close to sharing this opinion?);
4. Anarchists affiliated to the Socialist Party who have nevertheless remained faithful to the spirit, if not to the formulae, of anarchism.
With elements like these, one can not make an anarchist organization.[45]

The dissatisfaction of many was such that a real danger was presented to anarchism when Gustave Hervé and others on the revolutionary wing of the SFIO proposed to create a new party on a libertarian basis. Nothing came of the idea, however, different projects from 1910 on finally culminated in the creation in 1913 of a Fédération communiste révolutionnaire anarchiste (FCRA, Anarchist Revolutionary Communist Federation). At its founding conference, the individualists were expelled because of the strength of feeling provoked by the actions of the Bonnot gang. By October 1913, 25 groups and 9 individuals were members of the FCRA, and regional federations were being created or strengthened all over France. Maitron estimates that in 1893 there were 50 groups, and 60–70 groups (with about 2,500 members) by 1913.[46]

1914: THE "GREAT WAR"

Although, in some respects, post-war developments on the left and in the labour movement were a continuation of trends already clearly visible before 1914 (the CGT's drift towards greater reformism, for instance, or the anarchist movement's attempts to organize itself), it is nevertheless true that the "Great War," as it quickly became known, quite apart from the deaths and the destruction it caused, also represented a traumatic episode for the French revolutionary movement:

> Wars have always been perceived as moments of rapid accel-
> eration of history, … a shaking up of references such that ev-
> erything seems to start again from square one, consigning old,
> 'pre-war' references and arrangements to the museum. Like the
> fault in a geological fold, the war years constitute a spectacu-
> lar break: for those who lived through them, first of all, in the
> suddenly outdated image they imposed on certain people and
> certain ideas, and this inevitably played a rôle in the transfor-
> mation of forms of activism in a movement where reference to
> the past had an important function.[47]

The outbreak of war, the "betrayal" of the CGT and SFIO leaderships in supporting the "*Union sacrée*" (Holy Union, the national war effort), the absence of mass opposition to mobilization, all of this represented the failure of many years of hard work in the labour movement and of revolutionary antimilitarist and antipatriotic propaganda. The war provoked the collapse of experiments in libertarian education and in communal living; it came at a time when, after decades of trying, the communist wing of the anarchist movement had at last managed to set up a national organization, however imperfect; and it saw what was in the eyes of most, the "defection" or "betrayal" of leading anarchists such as Jean Grave, Charles Malato and even Peter Kropotkin, who supported the war effort against "Prussian militarism."

The shock, the disillusion and the anger were profound. Louis Lecoin, a labourer already well-known in the anarchist and syndicalist movements in Paris, was traumatized by, what was for him, the scandalous and inexcusable betrayal by his former heroes of all his hopes and ideals:

> It was as if, in August 1914, a shadow had fallen on the faith
> I had in human beings. The leaders of the CGT who had been
> my teachers now caused me only revulsion. And the antipatriot
> Hervé—for whom I would willingly have been torn to pieces
> before 1912—was even more repugnant to me. These ex-pac-
> ifists now showed themselves to be the most ferocious in their

pursuit of the destruction of lives. How I hated them! I could not forgive them for having undermined my hitherto unspoiled confidence in others. So whether I would die was of no importance to me now. So long as I gave a meaning to my death.[48]

Lecoin, the pacifist, was later arrested looking for the turncoat Hervé with a loaded revolver in his pocket, and he ended up spending the duration of the war in gaol for refusing to join his unit.

Anarchism had been critical of authoritarian leaders, of hierarchies and of initiative-destroying centralization, and had advocated instead spontaneous popular revolution. Thus Jean Grave, whilst also berating the leaders of the labour and socialist movements, including the anarchists, for not being equal to the task, was profoundly affected by the failure of the "masses" to move:

> With the ideas of initiative we thought we had sown, we had hoped that the masses would not wait for the word from their leaders to act, that they would be able to do what was necessary themselves, that they would spontaneously find the correct solution for each situation. Yet a revolutionary situation arose without the masses, without the revolutionary leaders realizing. … The masses in action, that is how I had envisaged the successful revolution, with the anarchists working amongst them. But on this occasion, the masses remained inactive, passive. They showed no more understanding than the leaders.[49]

The anarchist movement was in total disarray. Organizations collapsed, papers disappeared, supporters were arrested or called up. The French as a whole were dismayed when the war proved to be not a short episode as they had at first believed, but dragged on and on.[50] But the weight of their shame and despair was to be lightened a little by the first news that the universally loathed Tsarist régime had at last collapsed.

Notes

1. Quoted in Daniel Guérin, *L'anarchisme* (Paris: Gallimard, 1981), p.12.

2. Eugène Armand, *Les Précurseurs de l'anarchisme* (Orléans: Éditions de *l'en dehors*, 1933). As a young man, Armand (1872–1962) had been an ardent propagandist first for the Salvation Army (for which he worked in various capacities) and then for Tolstoyan (Christian) anarchism. From 1911 he was supported by his wife, a schoolteacher, and was able to devote himself entirely to propaganda. See Jean Maitron & Claude Pennetier (eds.), *Dictionnaire biographique du mouvement ouvrier français* (Paris: Editions Ouvrières, 1964–1993), vols.10 and 17 (henceforth *DBMOF*).

3.   Georges Fontenis, *Changer le monde. Histoire du mouvement communiste libertaire, 1945–1997* (Editions Le Coquelicot/Alternative libertaire, 2000), p.16.

4.   Roger Magraw, *France 1815–1914: The Bourgeois Century* (London: Fontana, 1983), pp.96–7.

5.   Pierre Ansart, *Naissance de l'anarchisme. Esquisse d'une explication sociologique du proudhonisme* (Paris: Presses Universitaires de France, 1970), p.201.

6.   See Robert Gildea, *The Past in French History* (New Haven & London: Yale University Press, 1994), ch.6.

7.   It is worth noting, though, that Proudhonian antiauthoritarianism was very different from that of the later individualists: "The revolt against authority is not in the name of subjectivity or in the name of individual freedom, but in the name of social freedom and of the autonomy of the freely associated producers." Ansart, *Naissance*, p.202.

8.   Quoted in Guérin, *L'anarchisme*, p.49.

9.   For a brief explanation of these early discussions about the administration of large scale public services and about whether to use the word "state" to describe such structures, see Guérin, *L'anarchisme*, pp.86–90.

10.   Paul Brousse, *L'Avant-Garde*, 17 June 1878, quoted by Alexandre Croix in "Le Terrorisme anarchiste," *Le Crapouillot* (January 1938).

11.   As Bakunin had put it, distinguishing between his "collectivism" and Marxian "communism": "I am no communist because communism concentrates and absorbs all the powers of society in the State, because it leads necessarily to the concentration of property in the hands of the State, while I want the abolition of the State—the radical extirpation of this principle of authority and of the tutelage of the State, which, under the pretext of making men moral and civil, has up to now enslaved, oppressed, exploited and depraved them. I want the organization of society and of collective or social property to proceed from the bottom up, by way of free association, and not from the top down by means of any authority whatsoever." In James Guillaume, *L'Internationale: documents et souvenirs (1864–1878)* (Paris: Société Nouvelle de Librairie et d'Edition & P.V. Stock, 1905–10), vol.I, p.75.

12.   Maitron, vol.I, p.112. The word "party" had of course a much less precise meaning in those days, meaning something like "movement" or "organization."

13.   Quoted in *la Révolte*, 19–25 October 1889.

14.   *Le Révolté*, 13–26 September 1885.

15.   Maitron, vol.I, p.150.

16.   Quoted in Maitron, vol.I, p.152.

17.   Appeal made at a soup kitchen in Paris in 1891. Maitron, vol.I, p.182.

18.   Sébastien Faure (1858–1942) was a leading propagandist for anarchism from the late 1880s until his death. By the 1920s he was already the venerable old man of the movement and was widely liked and respected. Faure came from a wealthy family, had initially been destined for the priesthood, and had worked for a time in insurance before becoming increasingly politically active. See *DBMOF*, vols.2 and 27. Elisée Reclus (1830–1905) was, with his brother, a member of Bakunin's Social Democratic Alliance; he fought in the Commune of 1871. See *DBMOF*, vol.15.

19.   Jean Grave (1854–1939), a Parisian shoemaker, was a leading anarchist militant before 1914, being responsible for the production of *le Révolté*, *la Révolte* and *les Temps nouveaux*. He was increasingly isolated after 1914 because of his support, however qualified and justified, for the allied war effort. See *DBMOF*, vols. 12 and 30, and his autobiography, *Quarante ans de propagande anarchiste* (Paris: Flammarion, 1973).

20.   *La Révolte*, 18–24 October 1890.

21.   *La Révolte*, 30 January–5 February 1892.

22.   The first of these three laws was directed not just against direct incitement to crime, but even against vindication; the second made conspiracy with intent a crime, even when no actual criminal act was committed; the third attacked anyone guilty of an "anarchistic act of propaganda." See Maitron, vol.I, p.252, note 2. See also Albert Vilar, *Les lois de 1893–1894 dites "lois scélérates"—Etude Historique* (Paris: Editions de l'Unité Ouvrière, 1930).

23.   Quoted in Maitron, vol.I, p.284. The *Parti ouvrier français* was led by the marxist socialist Jules Guesde, renowned for being dogmatic and authoritarian, and for his opinion that the trade unions should limit themselves to issues directly concerned with the workplace, whilst it was the task of the party to consider the bigger political questions such as revolution.

24.   *"Bourse du travail"* literally means labour exchange, which was one of their original purposes, but they came to fulfil many more rôles and functioned as a kind of local trades council.

25.   *Révolution prolétarienne*, 10 November 1937.

26.   Maitron, vol.I, p.259.

27.   *Le Révolté*, 4–10 September 1886.

28.   *La Révolte*, 18–24 March 1891.

29.   *Les Temps nouveaux*, 4–10 May 1895.

30.   *La Révolte*, 28 May–2 June 1892.

31.   *La Révolte*, 28 May–2 June 1892.

32.   *Les Temps nouveaux*, 2–8 November 1895.

33.   Ernest Girault in *le Libertaire*, 3–9 June 1897. Ironically, Girault would eventually fetch up in the Communist Party.

34.   *Le Libertaire*, 5–12 November 1899.

35.   Lorulot (1885–1963), real name André Roulot, was from a working-class Parisian background and had various jobs as a youth. He met Libertad in 1905, when they co-founded *l'Anarchie*. See *DBMOF*, vol.13. The Parisian Mauricius (1886–1974), real name Maurice Vandamme, was involved with the individualist anarchists until 1917. An architect's assistant, he was a member of the Draughtsmen's, Clerks' and Associated Workers' Union within the Building-workers' Federation. See *DBMOF*, vol.14. Libertad (1875–1908) was a mysterious character, somewhat larger than life. He was a central figure on the individualist scene from 1892 until his death. See *DBMOF*, vol.13.

36.   Quoted in Maitron, vol.I, p.279.

37.   Indeed, as Maitron pointed out, the extent of the influence of anarchism among the organized working class can be gauged from the enormous number of elected union officers who were known anarchists. It has been calculated that even in 1914, when anarchist influence in the CGT had already declined somewhat, in the region of 100,000 syndicalists—supported anarchist positions at CGT congresses—through their elected delegates. Groupe Louis Bertho-Lepetit de la Fédération Anarchiste, *L'influence anarcho-syndicaliste dans la CGT 1902–1923* (n.d.).

38.   Quoted in Maitron, vol.I, p.324.

39.   Quoted in Maitron, vol.I, p.323, note 175.

40.   *La Vie ouvrière*, 20 June 1914, quoted in Daniel Colson, *Anarcho-syndicalisme et communisme, Saint-Etienne 1920–1925* (Saint-Etienne: Université de Saint-Etienne/Centre d'Etudes Foréziennes/Atelier de Création Libertaire, 1986), p.43.

41.   Sébastien Faure, "Les Forces de Révolution," p.263, in *Propos Subversifs* (Paris: Les Amis de Sébastien Faure, n.d.[1950/51?]), pp.263–294. The "Forces of Revolution" actually listed by Faure are the rationalist and humanist movement, the Socialist Party, syndicalism, the co-operative movement and anarchism (p.264).

42.   Maitron, vol.I, p.414.

43.   See Colson's discussion of the work of historians such as M. Perrot and Y. Lequin and its relevance for our understanding of revolutionary syndicalism, in *Anarcho-syndicalisme*, pp.53–9.

44.   Yves Lequin, *Les ouvriers de là région lyonnaise, 1848–1914* (Lyon: Presses universitaires de Lyon, 1977) vol.II, p.283.

45.   Quoted in Maitron, vol.I, p.446.

46.   Maitron, vol.II, pp.123–35.

47.   Colson, *Anarcho-syndicalisme*, p.51. For an account of the anarchist movement at that time, see Maitron, vol.II, pp.9–23; Nicolas Faucier, *Pacifisme et Antimilitarisme dans l'entre-deux-guerres (1919–1939)* (Paris: Spartacus, 1983), pp.38–44; and Grave, *Quarante ans*, chs.23–26.

48.   Louis Lecoin, *Le Cours d'une Vie* (Paris: Louis Lecoin, 1965), p.70. Lecoin (1888–1971) was from a poor rural background: his father was an agricultural labourer. Working at various jobs, Lecoin moved to Paris in 1905 and became active as a syndicalist and anarchist. See *DBMOF*, vol.13.

49.   Grave, *Quarante ans*, pp.474–5.

50.   See Jean-Jacques Becker, *Les Français dans la guerre* (Paris: Éditions Robert Laffont, 1980).

Part I

The Aftermath of War and the Challenge of Bolshevism, 1917–1924

2

The New Dawn in the East

It is above all the Russian Revolution which deserves our
gratitude. For it was the Russian Revolution which threw
off the yoke of autocracy and, in the face of a world gone
berserk with murder, and to the great dismay of the gen-
erals and of the privileged, sent out its appeal for peace,
for reason, for universal fraternity and for the struggle
against capitalism.

Claude Content[1]

As was the case for all of my generation, the Russian
Revolution ... was for me an object of total fascination.

René Michaud[2]

Commenting on his initial enthusiasm for Lenin and the bolsheviks,
Louis Lecoin wrote in his autobiography: "I seem to remember that the
initiative for the first political manifesto to appear in France in favour of
the maximalists—as the Russian bolsheviks were known at the time—
came from the anarchists in the *Santé* prison in the summer of 1917."[3]
It is unclear what this manifesto was, but it is certainly true that the
anarchists were among the first to welcome the February revolution. As
early as 31 March 1917, anarchists of the CRRI (Comité pour la reprise
des relations internationales, Committee for the Resumption of International Relations) and of a certain *Groupe scientifique* jointly decided that
either Jules Lepetit (a prominent anarchist and leading member of the
Seine Building Labourers' Union) or Sébastien Faure would intervene,
by force if necessary, at a meeting of the Human Rights League the following day in order to speak "in honour of the Russian Revolution."[4]
A fortnight later, at a "matinée concert" of L'Entr'aide (Mutual Aid, a
prisoners' support group), the anarchist miners' leader Broutchoux addressed a "fraternal greeting" to the Russian revolutionaries, holding up
their achievement as an example to French and other revolutionaries,
before closing his speech with a warmly received "Down with war!"[5]
F. Elosu, writing in Faure's non-partisan anti-war weekly *Ce qu'il faut*

dire, founded in April 1916, waxed lyrical on the subject of "Revolution and History": "The annals of the nascent 20th century will after all not be filled by death alone. Revolution will infuse them with its noble spirit and give them new life with its pure and fruitful action. After a long night of anguish and oppression which has weighed heavily on our hearts and minds, at last, far in the East, glows a dawn of liberty. The Russian Revolution is good, true, magnificent History."[6] A special number of *le Libertaire*, brought out illegally by Lepetit in June 1917, adopted a similarly enthusiastic tone, though in less poetic language: "As for us, we must not allow the Russian revolution to be crushed. It is perhaps the beginning of a new era in world history. Despite the crisis in which it is now struggling, the Russian revolution has opened up a way forward for the proletariat enslaved by capitalism and bourgeois governments."[7]

AGAINST KERENSKY

The February revolution thus provided a glimmer of hope amidst the despair of the Great War, and already the Russian experience is offered up as a model. However, unlike the majority of the European left, the anarchists were not satisfied with the overthrow of the Tsar and the installation of a bourgeois democratic government. The anarchists wanted to see a further revolution in Russia, supported by a general uprising in the West and, as in pre-war anarchist and syndicalist propaganda amongst young French soldiers, conscripts were urged to use their weapons accordingly: "So, French workers, do not lay down your arms. ... The Russian, Bulgarian, Austrian and German workers are calling on you to join in the great class struggle which they have begun."[8] This, they believed, would have the effect of ending the war instantly.[9] It would also guarantee a revolutionary socialist outcome to the complex situation in Russia: "It is only by rising up immediately and overthrowing our own tyrants, our own exploiters, that we will help our Russian comrades in stopping the intrigues which threaten them."[10]

These "intrigues" threatening the Russian revolution were twofold. First: the efforts of the Provisional Government to restore "order" and establish a bourgeois democratic government. June's special number of *le Libertaire* had been clearly pro-bolshevik—reckoning that "Lenin's Central Committee" had the support of four-fifths of the Russian working class. In *Ce qu'il faut dire*, Mauricius could refer to "our comrade Lenin,"[11] and Genold to "our loyal friend Trotsky."[12] The February revolution had only seen an expansion of "political" freedoms, and as the émigré Russian anarchist Fouchs put it: "The people want above

all to make the economic revolution, all the more so as they are suffering from famine and from a lack of clothes and fuel."[13] Several articles
in *Ce qu'il faut dire* are very clear about the danger represented by the
Kerensky government. Siegfried, emphasizing the popular nature of the
February uprising and the revolutionary fervour of the Russian working class, warns of the danger if "governmental opportunism born, like
a mushroom, of the new state of affairs, succeeds in its efforts to break,
channel or in some way block the revolutionary tide."[14]

The second of the two threats to the revolution was the efforts
both of Kerensky's Provisional Government and of its allies to make
sure that Russia would carry on fighting. Mauricius, explicitly making
the link between rejection of the war and support for a further revolution, wrote: "I call out to our Russian friends: 'Beware the capitalist
oligarchy which will attempt to steer the Revolution towards nationalist
ends. Do not stop at the political Revolution, make the Social Revolution.'"[15]

But in the West, even members of the SFIO seemed to the anarchists to be working in the interests of capital, rather than in the interests of a starving and war-weary proletariat. Sent by the French government, three Socialist *députés* —Marius Moutet, Marcel Cachin and
Ernest Lafont—arrived in Moscow on 1 May 1917, to encourage the
Kerensky government in its pursuance of the war against Germany.[16]
The CRRI branded them the "official ambassadors of the French imperialist bourgeoisie."[17] For *le Libertaire*, they had been sent "to defend the
interests of French big business, threatened by the practical socialism
of the Russian social-democrats. Whereas the allied governments and
their socialist and syndicalist retainers sing the praises of the revolution
and organize meetings to salute the liberation of the slav peoples, they do
everything they can behind the scenes to crush the revolution."[18] To the
"résistant" anarchists (those who opposed the national war effort), revolutionary defeatism—the turning of the war into a civil war—was the
only acceptable policy, and Mauricius admiringly quoted Lenin: "A true
socialist cannot not wish for the defeat of their own government."[19]

Approval of the downfall of the most despotic régime in Europe
was common to the whole of the political left, but certain aspects of
the anarchist response were nevertheless distinctive. Because of their
extreme antimilitarism and their belief in the imminence of revolution,
the anarchist movement was perhaps more affected than other sectors
of the labour movement by the failure to prevent the outbreak of war, or
at least hinder mobilization in 1914. The downfall of the Tsar opened up
the prospect of a rapid end to the slaughter. Thus the anarchists' immediate reaction was gratitude and hope. Their impenitent revolutionism

led them to imagine a conflagration on a European scale provoked by the proletarian internationalism they had vainly hoped would manifest itself in 1914. So as early as the spring of 1917, the anarchists in France were already calling for a socialist revolution in Russia to complete the bourgeois revolution of February; for the internationalization, or at least Europeanization, of the revolution; and for an immediate end to the war.

Their position was shared by only small minorities in the SFIO and the CGT, and they were constantly appealing for more support. As André Girard wrote: "Socialists, syndicalists, when will you be ashamed of yourselves?"[20] It is interesting and, with hindsight, ironic to note that in this respect, they were in a minority not only in western Europe: when Lenin returned to Russia in April 1917, he was himself isolated in his own party on all these questions.[21]

FOR THE OCTOBER REVOLUTION

The October revolution—"the true Russian revolution"[22]—was greeted in *Ce qu'il faut dire* with a long and prophetic article by Boris Souvarine, a socialist and a member of the CRRI.[23] Imbued with a feeling for the historic significance of the event, the article labels the bolsheviks "those descendants of the Commune"; the struggle is seen as "a battle whose outcome will have a profound influence on the fate of the international working class." The article is also undoubtedly enthusiastic: "Is there at present a single rebel against the bourgeois order whose heart does not beat faster at news of events in Petrograd, who does not see the Russian revolutionaries as their comrades in thought and in revolt, who does not embrace their cause, who is not moved and fearful as they follow the ups and downs of the struggle, who does not suffer at the thought of an eventual defeat?"

But Souvarine also formulated certain reservations and fears. Expressing his wish that socialists of all tendencies in Russia should cooperate to produce a stable system, "which would truly be the power of the people and not that of an individual, however intelligent and honest they might be," he was nevertheless concerned at possible clashes between socialists: "It is to be feared that for Lenin and his friends, the 'dictatorship of the proletariat' must be the dictatorship of the bolsheviks and of their leader." Souvarine also seems to have shared, to some extent at least, the anarchist conviction that decentralization is the most practical and effective approach for coping with large and complex social structures, for he insisted on the enormity of the task and on the consequent impracticability of excessive centralization: the man or the party in power "would always be preoccupied above all with maintaining their authority, which would be forever being threatened." These prophetic comments only expressed concern for possible future developments, however, and did not prevent Souvarine going on to become a member of the SFIC (Section française de l'Internationale communiste, the Communist Party) and a delegate to the Executive Committee of the Comintern in 1921. Looking back on this period, anarchists have manifested little sympathy for activists such as Souvarine or Monatte who, realizing their mistake too late, worked with the bolsheviks before either leaving the SFIC or being expelled from it.[24] Lecoin, for example, wrote: "There is no doubt that the supporters of dictatorship would not have caused so much damage in our labour movement if honest and respected revolutionaries like Monatte had not acted as their apologists and intermediaries and helped them gain positions of power."[25] And Maurice Joyeux, prominent in the anarchist movement after the Second World War, referred to the "naïvety, not to say the gullibility" of such activists.[26]

REVISIONISM AND RECOMPOSITION

In 1917, the main organ for anarchist-communism was the weekly *Ce qu'il faut dire*. This was not, however, an anarchist paper in the usual sense. Founded by Mauricius and Sébastien Faure in April 1916, it was the only revolutionary antimilitarist paper in existence at the time,[27] and given the redefinition of boundaries within the labour movement produced by the question of support for, or opposition to, the war effort, it thus attracted the collaboration of minority syndicalists and socialists. It was to cease publication in December 1917, but followed by the short-lived weekly *Franchise* (again founded by Mauricius) and especially the more theoretical monthly *l'Avenir international* (founded by ex-members of the *Temps nouveaux* group), it was to develop a very sympathetic and above all a very libertarian reading of events in Russia, in general, and of bolshevism, in particular. Some contributors also adopted a very critical stance with regard to traditional, pre-war anarchism. In these respects, it foreshadowed the development of "sovietism," a kind of libertarian communism or "council anarchism" which was to manifest itself in the creation of Péricat's Parti communiste, and later a Fédération communiste des soviets (Communist Soviet Federation). These developments need to be followed in some detail in order to make clear their significance for anarchist ideology and practice as the movement endeavoured to come to terms with the defeat of 1914 and with the Russian revolution. To begin with, there was an understanding that the axis of the international revolutionary movement had shifted. It was no longer centred on France, "the predestined land of revolutions, the holy land of communism and of syndicalism."[28] The French anarchists were disillusioned and ashamed at their failure to prevent war, and there was much admiration for the bolsheviks: it was the latter who were now seen to be carrying forward the European revolutionary tradition. For Souvarine they were the heirs of the Communards. Writing many years later, Mauricius put Marx, Engels and the leading anarchist theorists together in the same revolutionary tradition, the culmination of which was bolshevism: "The news of the triumph of the Bolshevik Revolution was greeted with enthusiasm the world over. It was no longer a question of a simple political revolution, a mere change of government: it was the Social Revolution which all the great thinkers of the 19th century—Proudhon, Marx, Engels, Bakunin, Kropotkin, Malatesta *et al*—had so ardently desired."[29]

It was in fact Mauricius who articulated many of the criticisms of pre-war anarchism and many of the suggestions for a reorientation of the movement, but his new position seems to have been welcomed by a large number of activists. Mauricius appears to have followed a political trajectory not unlike that of Victor Serge.[30] An individualist anarchist before the war—he was obliged to leave the founding congress of the FCRA in 1913 for that very reason[31]—by March 1917 he was writing pieces on Russia that read like attempts at historical materialist analysis.[32] By May, he was not only trying to link up all the anarchists, syndicalists and socialists who were united in the *Ce qu'il faut dire* support groups, he had also launched a proposal for a Third International.[33] To this end, Mauricius was corresponding with anarchist activists in other countries, especially with Armando Borghi and others in the Unione syndicale italiana (USI, Italian Syndicalist Union), and with comrades of a certain Comitato d'azione internazionale anarchico. As a first step towards a Third International, he proposed that the anarchists should attend the projected international socialist conference in Stockholm.[34] His aim was to launch the idea of a new International whose members would be "exclusively and unreservedly internationalist."[35] He therefore demanded that the ruling of the 1896 London conference excluding antiparliamentarians be dropped;[36] for, as he put it: "With regard to the concepts of patriotism, war and militarism, only the anarchists had precise, clear, definitive and irrefutable ideas."[37] The corollary of this was that he wanted to see banned from the conference all those socialists and trade unionists who had supported their respective countries' war effort: "The International must be composed of internationalists and not of politicians and weathercocks."[38] Mauricius was keen to hear the opinions of other comrades on his proposals. We know that as early as September 1917 the syndicalist Raymond Péricat supported the idea of an International uniting anarchists, syndicalists and socialists.[39] It also seems reasonable to suppose that Faure was not averse to the idea. It was he who jointly created *Ce qu'il faut dire* with its clear policy of inviting the collaboration of activists on the left wing of the CGT and of the SFIO; he was the editor-in-chief of the paper; and it was he who was criticized by Lecoin for co-operating too much with non-anarchists.[40] In an article in *Ce qu'il faut dire* Mauricius also gave the impression he was supported and indeed encouraged by a bolshevik called Goldenberg, a representative of the Petrograd soviet, whom he claimed to have met at least twice: once in Paris and once in Rome.[41] He also had the agreement of various groups of Italian anarchists: the USI, the Comitato d'azione internazionale anarchico and the activists around *Avenire anarchico* and *Guerra di Classe*.[42]

Of the Italians with whom Mauricius was in contact, only the comrades around *Cronaca libertaria* opposed the idea.[43] But the most detailed critique came from the French individualist anarchist Pierre Chardon. Chardon raised the usual individualist objections to any kind of *rapprochement* with even the revolutionary wing of the socialist parties or with revolutionary syndicalists: "I persist in considering harmful a tactic which consists in according too much importance to developments in the socialist and syndicalist movements."[44] He clearly had a profoundly different view of the rôle and aims of the anarchist movement, and referring to Mauricius' desire to use Stockholm as a propaganda platform, he wrote: "Anarchist action—patient, hidden, tenacious, involving individuals, eating away at institutions like a worm eats away at fruit, as termites undermine majestic trees—such action does not lend itself to the theatrical effects of those who wish to draw attention to themselves."[45] Chardon thus summed up the more individualist interpretation of anarchist strategy, believing anarchism to be totally irreconcilable with socialism and syndicalism: "We only accomplish anything useful when we work with those like ourselves. ... Nothing will come out of this congress but chaos, confusion, ambiguity, compromise, a temporary and artificial balance ... between the different tendencies, the whole translated into ambiguous resolutions that will satisfy everybody and nobody."[46]

The problem for Mauricius was not anarchism's critical theory ("In every area of social criticism, the anarchists have been beyond compare"[47]), but its revolutionary practice, and he had come to question the effectiveness of the traditional anarchist attitude: "I admire the anarchist draped in the splendours of the pure idea who refuses to condescend to relativities, but does this attitude contribute to actually diminishing the power and harmfulness of authority? That is the question."[48] For Mauricius, Chardon and others paid lip-service to the notion of learning from experience, but were in fact unwilling to change one iota of their theory or practice. Referring to Chardon's understanding of anarchist tactics, Mauricius wrote: "Thus reasons the flea biting the lion … Only no sooner has the flea managed to suck a few drops of blood from the ferocious beast that the latter, with one bite, feeds itself another pint—unless with one swipe of its paw it does not suppress the flea and its logic."[49] What was absolutely essential, according to Mauricius, was unity. The movement needed to group "around a few precise, concrete principles the greatest number of people possible";[50] it needed cadres—"that is to say aware, enlightened, educated and energetic militants"—and it needed organization: "There is no shortage of 'men and women of principle acting according to their convictions'; but if they act without co-ordination or planning, inconsistently and each as he or she wishes, then as far as the progress of the human race is concerned, they may as well not have bothered."[51]

Armand Beaure was to emphasize in the pages of *Ce qu'il faut dire* the number of activists who had left the anarchist movement to join the SFIO.[52] Mauricius, continuing his reply to Chardon, and becoming more and more bitter in his criticisms of pre-war anarchism, also laments the movement's inability to hold within it many a sympathetic activist, who, having tried to work with the anarchists, eventually gives up and leaves because "they see rising up before them, in the name of liberty, the crowd of sectarian morons declaring that anarchy consists in contemplating your navel, doing a moonlight flit and practising free love."[53] Finally, in an equally biting outburst, Mauricius makes clear the influence on his thinking of revolutionary marxism in general and of the achievements of the bolshevik party in particular: "I declare that Trotsky, that Lenin, that Liebknecht, that Friedrich Adler, that Rühle, and many other famous and intransigent socialists appeal more to me, that I feel closer to their actions,—despite differences of view—and that I would be happier co-operating with them than with the horde of boorish, incoherent nonentities who claim to represent anarchism."[54]

Despite a running battle with government censorship and despite police harassment in the form, for instance, of raids on their premises, *Ce qu'il faut dire* managed to keep going from April 1916 to December 1917.[55] Its last number—22 December 1917—carried a front page article on the French bourgeoisie by Trotsky, "who was our comrade during his stay in Paris and of whom all our comrades have the best of memories."[56] It was succeeded, the following March, by another paper founded by Mauricius: *Franchise*.[57] The editorial in the first issue placed it clearly in the same lineage, making even more clear the extent to which some anarchists believed redefinition and realignment to be the order of the day: "What use are labels? A storm has overturned our table of values, the old frameworks within which we once enclosed our sectarian spirits have shattered. Anarchists! Syndicalists! Socialists! Old outdated formulas. Romain Rolland is closer to us than Kropotkin, and Liebknecht is not the same as Albert Thomas."[58]

FOR A RECONCILIATION OF ANARCHISM AND MARXISM

For most anarchists, the October revolution was a libertarian revolution. A certain Lisitchine had written in *Ce qu'il faut dire*: "It is not Lenin and his friends who are imposing their doctrines on the Russian people, it is Lenin who is obeying the Russian people, identifying with the peasants, the workers and the soldiers of revolutionary Russia."[59] This theme, as well as the critique of pre-war anarchism and the campaign for a recomposition of the left, were continued by another group of anarchists in another new review. Founded in reaction against the war and preoccupied with events in Russia, *l'Avenir International* (The International Future) was created in January 1918 by activists such as A. Mignon and André Girard who had abandoned Jean Grave over the latter's support for the war effort.[60] The anarchist-communist Siegfried, writing in March 1918, bemoaned the hesitancy and the lack of support for the Russian revolutionaries shown by many socialists, syndicalists and even anarchists:

> How all our talk must seem obsolete and futile to the Russians, our perpetual evocations of the French Revolution, of its methods and of its glories, the intellectuals' chatter about the League of Nations and their obsession with law and nothing else, our watery and rhetorical conceptions of a socialism with no muscle, in a word our Franco-centric, entirely ideological and hollow incomprehension of the present fratricide. ... In the meantime, the Workers' and Soldiers' Councils are in the process of doing the job for us and putting into practice the old ideas that so many generations, that so many martyrs here as in Russia made fertile with their blood.[61]

This criticism of the impotence of French anarchism in contrast with Russian bolshevism is also explicit with André Girard, for whom the Russian revolution was, as late as September 1918, an "antiparliamentary, decentralizing and federative revolution leading to an organisation based on the self-government of the people."[62] The dissatisfactions to which Girard gives voice are very similar to those expressed by Mauricius, though couched in less colourful language: "We have had occasion to note, since the outbreak of war, that to many comrades' minds, our ideas, whilst resting on very sincere convictions, sometimes lacked a critical basis, a realistic foundation."[63]

The criticisms are the ones usually made of anarchism, then as now: that anarchist aspirations are sincere and noble, but based more on enthusiasm and wishful thinking than on observation of the facts and on rigorous thinking. Hence the many spurious "deviations," "due to the lack of a clear sense of direction."[64] Anarchism, Girard suggests, lacks a solid theoretical grounding, and is unable to provide a positive, constructive strategy to match its essentially negative critique. What does Girard suggest to remedy the situation? Within the anarchist movement, says Girard, the class struggle and working-class internationalism have for many years been, "if not a credo — we accept none — at least two stable principles."[65] Hence his interest in Marx. This article was in fact written in response to harsh criticisms he had received from certain anarchist readers after an earlier article written to commemorate the hundredth anniversary of Marx's birth.[66] Girard was clearly aware that many of his readers would not appreciate his endeavours: "Anarchists commemorating Karl Marx?!... I can already hear the stones being piled up ready for pelting us with."[67] He tries to play down the significance of what he is doing, suggesting that the only reason he produced an article on Marx rather than on Proudhon or Kropotkin was the anniversary of the former's birth. Besides, he goes on, his attitude to all the theorists is the same: they must not become masters, none of them is perfect. "The failing common to all disciples is that they stick rigorously to the letter of the master's doctrine, considered to be immutable and unconditioned by time or space."[68] This protects Girard against charges of slavishly taking on board marxist dogma. Equally, though, the implication is that the anarchist "masters" may also be re-examined in the light of events and may be found lacking: "It is not in Bakunin's Panslavism or his Germanophobia, it is not in Proudhon's plan for a State Bank or in his mutualism that we would have looked for support."[69]

L'Avenir international as a whole — and notably through Girard, Mignon and Dunois — was concerned to effect not only a *rapprochement* on a practical level between anarchists, syndicalists and socialists, but also on a theoretical and permanent organizational level, continuing the drift towards some kind of as yet ill-defined libertarian or left-wing or council communism. All three take care not to shock or alienate their anarchist readers, presenting as revolutionary and anti-authoritarian a picture as possible of marxism.

Girard warns that it is a mistake for anarchists to be sectarian "to the point of imprisoning ourselves in our narrow sect."[70] Mignon brings together the names of Bakunin and Marx, but not for the reason anarchists usually do so: "Not in order to stress that each one represents, in a sense, a different way of liberating the world, authoritarian collectivism with Marx, libertarian federalism with Bakunin, but in order to effect a *rapprochement*: both were revolutionaries, both fought against the ruling classes and showed the ways to liberation."[71] It has already been noted that Girard emphasized the importance to anarchism of class struggle and its corollary, international working-class solidarity. For him these represent "the fundamental essential principle" of marxism, and are "the keystone of modern socialism."[72] Thus the anarchists are situated clearly within a wider revolutionary socialist labour movement. The journalist Amédee Dunois—once an anarchist, but by this time already committed to revolutionary syndicalism—continued this rehabilitation of marxism in three long and very closely argued articles, in which the traditional conflict between anarchists and marxists was re-examined.[73] These articles did two things. First, they gave a more conciliatory view than the usual anarchist one of the conflicts between Marx and Proudhon and between Marx and Bakunin, pointing out the similarities—especially between the latter two as compared to the non-communist Proudhon— and presenting the conflict as a misunderstanding and a difference of temperament, rather than as a substantive political disagreement. Second, they presented a libertarian, anti-dogmatic and revolutionary interpretation of marxism, thus separating marxism in the minds of anarchist readers, both from the stereotypically authoritarian communism that anarchists have traditionally seen in the figure of Marx, "the stereotype of the rebarbative authoritarian socialist," and from parliamentary socialism, especially French parliamentary socialism: "Amongst those who claim to be socialist, there are some bitter critics of the Soviet régime who reproach it with having broken with the parliamentary tradition of bourgeois democracy by dissolving the Constituent Assembly. Further proof of the lack of marxist spirit which has always characterized French socialism."[74]

For Dunois, communism was based on class struggle, working-class autonomy and internationalism: "Statism, reformism, revisionism—all that is opposed to marxism, because it is opposed to the autonomous movement of the revolutionary proletariat."[75] Thus, for him, revolutionary syndicalism was a marxist movement *par excellence*. Bakuninist anarchism also had much in common with what he calls Marx's "critical communism," because of the centrality of such notions as class struggle and working-class internationalism, and also because of what Dunois saw as a basic historical materialism. All these aspects of anarchism had been subverted, according to Dunois, by the likes of Kropotkin and Grave.[76] The only real difference of opinion was over "political action"—not to be confused with "parliamentary action."[77] As for the question of political power, this too is discussed by Dunois in a way calculated to alienate revolutionary anarchist-communists as little as possible: "Power is nothing more than the ability to put into effect our ideas, the strength to destroy the institutions of the past, the strength to create the institutions of the future. There is no revolutionary who does not ultimately depend on the exercise of force, in other words political power."[78]

The whole point of this discussion of the traditional anarchist-marxist conflict was, of course, the question of potential anarchist support, first, for the Russian bolsheviks, and, second, for the building of some kind of communist party in France, which would be more or less modelled on the former. Thus, having expounded his interpretation of both marxism and anarchism, Dunois tells the reader: "It is my profound conviction that were Marx alive today, he would join us in hailing this decentralized soviet régime which has been installed in Russia by the revolutionary proletariat and which has not left intact a single part of the old bourgeois machinery of state. He would see in it a perfected form of the free government a first version of which he saluted in the Commune in June 1871."[79]

The dilemmas brought to the surface by the events of 1914–16 and also by the Russian revolutions clearly represented a historical break, and they were perceived as such. Criticisms of "traditional" anarchism were being made, there was talk of new developments in the international revolutionary movement, the need to take account of events was often evoked. And yet there was also a continuity of sorts. This whole debate about the nature of anarchism, its relation to other socialisms, its relation to labour, organization and so on, all this was a continuing debate within the movement. Dunois reminded the anarchists, "my brothers in arms in former times, my comrades still,"[80] that they had once stood at a similar crossroads: the dilemma of what attitude to adopt *vis-à-vis* syndicalism. Dunois found it interesting, in the context of the Russian revolution and attempts to build a communist party in France, to quote what the renowned socialist leader Jean Jaurès had said of the anarchist movement in 1896:

> Anarchism is at present going through a profound crisis; it is in the midst of a transformation. It is clear that it repudiates more and more not only propaganda by the deed, but also individual action. It is rejecting the individualist elements and it is not far from changing its name: it is known more and more as anarchist

communism or libertarian communism or even simply antipar-
liamentarian communism. It is entering the trade unions; it is
accepting delegation, representation in congresses; one more
step and it will accept representation in parliaments, and under
the inspiration of men like Hamon and Bernard Lazare, *it will
become no more than a form of protest within socialism itself against
that which many see in marxist socialism as too authoritarian and narrow.* That is, in my opinion, an incorrect and superficial view
of marxism. But when we are separated from anarchism only
by this difference of interpretation, when the certain evolution
of anarchism towards socialism is complete, then there will no
longer be anything preventing all the anticapitalist forces from
working together.[81]

This *rapprochement*, according to Dunois, had now become even
easier because the "political question" had assumed different forms: recent revolutionary events had shown that it was possible thoroughly to
destroy the bourgeois state apparatus and replace it with a system based
on the Russian soviets and on the German workers' councils. Would the
anarchist-communists join forces with other revolutionary communists,
or would they stay on the outside?

THE STATE AND THE DICTATORSHIP OF THE PROLETARIAT

One contributor to *l'Avenir international* who adopted a markedly different stance, notably in a series of articles on *"L'Infatuation Marxiste,"*
was the well-known Italian anarchist, Luigi Fabbri.[82] In particular, Fabbri emphasized the specificity of the anarchist analysis of the state, an
analysis that should prevent anarchists from fully approving the policies
of the Russian bolsheviks, however much the latter might have been
deserving of support when under attack from bourgeois democracy and
tsarist reaction.[83] For Fabbri, the state is not just "the guardian of capital," as the marxist analysis would have it:

> The State has a vitality of its own and constitutes … a veri-
> table social class apart from other classes …; and this class has
> its own particular parasitical and usurious interests, in conflict
> with those of the rest of the collectivity which the State itself
> claims to represent. … The State, being the depositary of soci-
> ety's greatest physical and material force, has too much power
> in its hands to resign itself to being no more than the capitalists'
> guard-dog.[84]

Fabbri's attitude is, then, much more guarded. Anarchists, for him, were right to admire and help those involved in the international anti-war conferences at Zimmerwald and Kienthal, they were right to defend the bolsheviks against bourgeois lies and to support them in their struggle against tsarists, bourgeois democrats and "social patriots." But they were wrong to "idolize" Marx, and wrong to accept the "dictatorship of the proletariat."

Despite Fabbri's interventions, however, the group of French anarchists around *l'Avenir international* seem ultimately to have found Dunois' type of argument more attractive and/or their disillusion with anarchism greater. Girard, whilst agreeing that "dictatorship" was to be avoided, lent his support to something which he preferred to call "social control by the Proletariat," and stressed that anarchists must be clear on what exactly they meant when they spoke about social revolution. How could an anticapitalist revolution possibly be defended against a bourgeois counter-revolution, especially in its early days? "How ... will we be able to defend the revolution other than by using coercion against those who would try to prevent the revolution from being successful? On the pretext of safeguarding freedom ... will we allow them to destroy the new society ...? Will it not be necessary, in the interests of our task, in order to ensure its safety, to keep them, for a certain time, from attacking the revolution?"[85]

This sounds very much like the first step towards accepting some kind of transitional period, some kind of "dictatorship of the proletariat"—both anathema to anarchism—though Girard did not discuss in any detail the socio-political structures involved in such a situation. Also, Dunois' appeal to the anarchist-communists to join the socialists received a favourable response. Mauricius had, as early as May 1917, called for the creation of a Third International uniting the revolutionary antimilitarist elements of anarchism, syndicalism and socialism. Dwelshauver—the journalist and art historian better known as Jacques Mesnil—echoed this appeal in the pages of *l'Avenir international* in October 1918.[86] Mesnil directed his proposal at anarchist-communists, revolutionary syndicalists and other "federalists" and declared himself ready to accept "political action"—though unfortunately without defining the phrase.[87] In December 1918, Dunois appealed to the anarchists to join the SFIO and turn it into a revolutionary party. The following month, André Mignon claimed that the Dunois article had the approval of Mignon's local anarchist group, and also of the Parisian anarchists around the review. The only thing preventing them all from joining the SFIO was, he claimed, the latter's insistence on parliamentary politics, and if the party would declare its support for open class struggle and for the building of workers' councils, he predicted that "all French communists would join *en masse*."[88] The extent of the group's political development and their new commitment can finally be seen in the fact that when *l'Avenir international* had to fold, for financial reasons, in the autumn of 1920, they decided to accept an offer from the pro-bolshevik Committee of the Third International to combine their efforts and contribute to the *Bulletin communiste*, directed by Souvarine.[89]

We must now consider how this re-shuffling of the different tendencies on the left led to the creation of new organizations, and, arguably, of a new ideological current within the revolutionary movement.

Notes

1. From the leaflet "Au Peuple Français" (To the French People), a summary of which is given in a police report of 15 December 1918 (BA1545). The leaflet was printed, in modified form, as an article in *le Libertaire*, 2 February 1919. See also *le Journal du Peuple*, 1 March 1919. According to the police report, 15,000 copies of the leaflet were printed. Content (1892–1927) was at that time administrator of *le Libertaire*. See *DBMOF*, vol.23.

2. René Michaud, *J'avais vingt ans. Un jeune ouvrier au début du siècle* (Paris: Syros, 1983), p.85. Michaud was the pseudonym of Adrien Provost, adopted initially when Provost deserted from the army in 1921. He was heavily involved with the anarchists in the 1920s, but later moved towards oppositional communism and then joined the SFIO whilst remaining a syndicalist activist.

3. Louis Lecoin, *Le cours d'une vie* (Paris: Louis Lecoin, 1965), p.92.

4. Police report "Notes russes," 1 April 1917, F7/15055. Judging by a further report of 13 May 1917, the *Groupe scientifique* seems to have been one of those educational discussion groups so common in the anarchist movement at that time. It met in Montmartre, and included among its members the prominent militants Loréal, Mauricius and Genold. The anarchists would intervene at meetings of the Human Rights League on other occasions, heckling its president V. Basch for having supported the Union sacrée. See "Les incidents des 'droits de l'homme'. Une réponse des 'perturbateurs'. Une nouvelle lettre de M. Basch" in *le Journal du Peuple*, 11 January 1919; see also the issue of 29 December 1918.

5. *L'Entr'aide* was a not unsuccessful organisation of support for political prisoners and their families. The concert in question was attended by about 600 people. Police report, 16 April 1917, F7/15054. On Benoît Broutchoux see *DBMOF*, vols.11 and 20.

6. *Ce qu'il faut dire*, 21 April 1917. On Elosu see *DBMOF*, vol.12.

7. *Le Libertaire (Organe Anarchiste)*, "Numéro spécial de propagande," June 1917. BA1494. On Louis Bertho (1889–1920), known as Lepetit, see *DBMOF*, vol.10.

8. From the leaflet "Au Peuple Français." A similar message was contained in a leaflet produced by the CDS (Comité de défense syndicaliste, Committee for the Defence of Syndicalism), "Aux Travailleurs de France." Report of 24 November 1918, BA1545. The rôle of the CDS and its connection with the anarchist movement will be discussed in the next chapter.

9. See the leaflet "Au Peuple de Paris. La Paix! Sans annexions, sans conquêtes et sans indemnités," published by the CDS. 10,000 copies were printed, paid for by the Building-workers' and Garment Industry Workers' Unions. BA1494.

10. *Le Libertaire*, June 1917.

11. *Ce qu'il faut dire*, 9 June 1917.

12. *Ce qu'il faut dire*, 5 May 1917. Genold was the pseudonym of Delong (1882–1954), who wrote of himself in *Ce qu'il faut dire*, 10 March 1917: "I am a man of the people, a real one, the son of peasants, I lived in a cottage with a floor of beaten earth then, still a small child, the slums of Paris and the street: the street where since the age of 15 …, I had to find a pittance for myself, as a clerk, a porter, a labourer, a vagabond."

13. According to police reports, Fouchs was living in Paris during the war, and had opposed the national war effort. A friend of Vsevelod Eichenbaum (better known under his pseudonym Voline), Fouchs was a member of the *Temps nouveaux* group and of a "Russian Anarchist-Communist Group" in Paris. Reports of 13 May 1917 and 20 April 1918, F7/13055.

14. *Ce qu'il faut dire*, 24 March 1917.

15. *Ce qu'il faut dire*, 28 April 1917.

16. Jacques Fauvet, *Histoire du Parti communiste français 1920–1976* (Paris: Fayard, 1977), pp.21–22.

17. CRRI leaflet, "Les bons Apôtres." BA1545. The CRRI was created in February 1916 by the coming together of anarchists and revolutionary syndicalists from the Comité d'Action Internationale contre la Guerre (International Action Committee against the War) and Socialist Party militants involved with the Zimmerwald conference.

18. *Le Libertaire*, June 1917. Cachin, for one, would have the unpleasant experience at the 1922 congress of the Comintern of having to sit through a long and biting indictment of his record in this period by Trotsky: "Cachin tried to defend himself in an abject and servile speech, stammering with embarrassment, promising to become a good communist and begging the confidence of those who had punished him. It was revolting." Clara & Pavel Thalmann, *Combats pour la liberté: Moscou, Madrid, Paris* (Paris: Spartacus/La Digitale, 1983), pp.43–44.

19. *Ce qu'il faut dire*, 21 April 1917.

20. *Ce qu'il faut dire*, 8 December 1917.

21. Marcel Liebman, *Leninism under Lenin* (London: Merlin Press, 1980), pp.116–147.

22. In April, Mauricius had written: "The true Russian revolution is about to begin." *Ce qu'il faut dire*, 21 April 1917. .

23. By the western calendar, of course, the "October Revolution" occurred on 7 November 1917. The article by Souvarine—the first one to appear on the subject in *Ce qu'il faut dire*—appeared on 17 November 1917. Although, as shall be explained in more detail later, Souvarine was far from being the only non-anarchist to contribute to *Ce qu'il faut dire*, he must have felt it necessary to justify such collaboration, and opened his article with the following remarks: "Like my friend Rappoport, I feel no contempt for the anarchists; but I do feel revulsion for politicians, of whatever sort, and especially for those who wear the socialist mask."

24. Souvarine and Monatte were both expelled from the Communist Party in 1924.

25. Lecoin, *Le cours d'une vie*, p.93.

26. Maurice Joyeux, *L'anarchie dans la société contemporaine* (Paris: Casterman, 1977), p.15.

27.   *Ce qu'il faut dire* also had a bookshop at 69 Boulevard de Belleville, Paris 11. *La Plèbe*, which would bring together anarchists, syndicalists, socialists and feminists, and which saw itself as the organ of the Zimmerwald movement, did not appear until April 1918. *Le Libertaire* did not reappear until January 1919. Pierre Monatte's *la Vie ouvrière* disappeared with the outbreak of war and did not reappear until April 1919.

28.   J. Sadoul in *L'Internationale Communiste*, the official organ of the Executive Committee of the Comintern, November–December 1919. Quoted by Annie Kriegel, *Aux origines du communisme français, 1914–1920* (Paris & La Haye: Mouton, 1964), vol.I, p.269.

29.   Mauricius, "En Souvenir d'Armando Borghi" (5pp. TS), p.2. "Fonds Mauricius," IFHS 14AS292B/II.

30.   See Serge, *Mémoires d'un révolutionnaire 1901–1941* (Paris: Seuil, 1951).

31.   See Maitron, vol.II, pp.449–50.

32.   See for example *Ce qu'il faut dire*, 24 and 31 March 1917. In 1936 Mauricius actually joined the SFIO and he was a conference delegate for the party on at least two occasions in the 1940s and 50s. See the "Fonds Berthier-Vandamme," IFHS 14/AS/451.

33.   *Ce qu'il faut dire*, 19 and 26 May and 9 June 1917.

34.   Planned for August of that year, the conference never materialized.

35.   *Ce qu'il faut dire*, 19 May 1917.

36.   *Ce qu'il faut dire*, 15 September 1917.

37.   *Ce qu'il faut dire*, 19 May 1917.

38.   *Ce qu'il faut dire*, 15 September 1917.

39.   *Ce qu'il faut dire*, 29 September 1917. There is a photograph of Péricat in *le Journal du Peuple*, 9 November 1918.

40.   Although, as we shall see below, there were some criticisms of Mauricius, notably and not surprisingly, from the young individualist Pierre Chardon. According to a police report (F7/13054), Lecoin took Faure and *Ce qu'il faut dire* to task for having too many links with non-anarchists. Can we assume that since Faure was the editor-in-chief, he was at least partially in agreement with Mauricius?

41.   *Ce qu'il faut dire*, 15 September 1917. I have been unable to identify Goldenberg with any certainty. Serge (*Mémoires*, p.185) refers to a "Dr. Goldenberg, an old bolshevik who lived in Berlin and whom Lenin sent for urgently at the onset of his illness." A more likely candidate perhaps is Boris Goldenberg, a Russian *émigré* who would be a leader of the German Communist Party's student movement before moving closer to Trotsky and becoming a prominent member of the oppositional SAP (Sozialistische Arbeiter Partei). He eventually emigrated to France and joined the SFIO, becoming a member of Pivert's "Revolutionary Left" faction, whose manifesto he wrote. Pierre Broué, *Histoire de l'Internationale communiste, 1919–1943* (Paris: Fayard, 1997), pp.534 and 1006, and *Trotsky* (Paris: Fayard, 1988), p.1057; Daniel Guérin, *Front populaire, révolution manquée* (Arles: Actes Sud, 1997), p.162.

42.   *Ce qu'il faut dire*, 29 September 1917.

43.   *Ce qu'il faut dire*, 29 September 1917.

44.   *Ce qu'il faut dire*, 20 October 1917. Maurice Charron, known as Chardon, still only in his mid-20s, was an accountant in Châteauroux. *DBMOF*, vol.11.

45.   Ibid.

46.   *Ce qu'il faut dire*, 27 October 1917.

47.   *Ce qu'il faut dire*, 17 November 1917.

48   *Ce qu'il faut dire*, 29 September 1917.

49.   *Ce qu'il faut dire*, 17 November 1917.

50.   *Ce qu'il faut dire*, 29 September 1917.

51.   *Ce qu'il faut dire*, 17 November 1917.

52.   *Ce qu'il faut dire*, 3 November 1917.

53.   *Ce qu'il faut dire*, 17 November 1917.

54.   *Ce qu'il faut dire*, 17 November 1917.

55.   See for example, *Ce qu'il faut dire*, 10 November 1917. On repressive measures taken by the Clemenceau government against the labour and antimilitarist movements, see Kriegel, *Aux origines du communisme français* vol.I, section 2, ch.2.

56.   *Ce qu'il faut dire*, 22 December 1917.

57.   Only three numbers of *Franchise* appeared: 31 March, 7 April and 14 April 1918.

58.   *Franchise*, 31 March 1918. The writer Romain Rolland had opposed the war, whereas Kropotkin justified it; Karl Liebknecht, the German marxist socialist, was a founder of the German Communist Party and an international symbol of opposition to the war, whereas the French socialist Thomas was Armaments Minister in 1916–17.

59.   Lisitchine, "Les événements en Russie," *Ce qu'il faut dire*, December 1917.

60.   The core group behind the review was, according to Mignon, "the old *Temps nouveaux* propaganda group (which we formed but the ownership (sic) of whose name is claimed by Jean Grave)." *L'Avenir international*, June 1918. For a brief account of the split in the *Temps nouveaux* group, see Maitron, vol.II, p.14. For a more detailed, but obviously more partisan account, see Grave, *Quarante ans de propagande anarchiste* (Paris: Flammarion, 1973), chs.26–27. Having noted the continuity, it is also worth bearing in mind the comments of one activist for whom *Ce qu'il faut dire* was "entirely in the hands of the individualists," and the forthcoming *l'Avenir international* "will be a voice for anarchist-communism, which is hardly heard of at all at the moment." Letter from a G. Thomas (Baubres, Indre) to the syndicalist Charles Benoît (Paris) dated 12 November 1917. PP BA1562: "Correspondence des Pacifistes de Juillet 1917 à Avril 1918." Benoît (1878–1950) was another of the Mignon-Girard group—see *DBMOF*, vol.10.

61.   Siegfried, "La Révolution Russe, L' 'Expérience Socialiste,'" *l'Avenir international*, March 1918.

62.   André Girard, "Pourquoi Marx?," *l'Avenir international*, September 1918.

63.   Ibid.

64.   Ibid.

65.   Ibid.

66.   André Girard, "Karl Marx et l'Internationalisme," *l'Avenir international*, June 1918.

67.   Ibid.

68.   Ibid.

69.   André Girard, "Pourquoi Marx?," *l'Avenir international*, September 1918.

70.   *L'Avenir international*, June 1918.

71.   A. Mignon, "Bakounine et Marx," *l'Avenir international*, June 1918.

72   *L'Avenir international*, June 1918.

73.   A. Dunois, "Marxisme et Liberté," *l'Avenir international*, June, August & December 1918.

74.   *L'Avenir international*, August 1918.

75.   Ibid.

76.   Ibid. This is an interpretation common to the libertarian communist wing of the anarchist movement. See for example Daniel Guérin's *L'Anarchisme* (Paris: Gallimard, 1981),

Part 3, Ch. 1. Cf. Maximilien Rubel, *Marx théoricien de l'anarchisme* (Saint-Denis: Cahiers du Vent du Chemin, 1983).

77.   *L'Avenir international*, August 1918.

78.   Ibid.. Cf. Engels' comments on anti-authoritarianism in "On Authority," in Marx, Engels, Lenin, *Anarchism and Anarcho-Syndicalism* (Moscow: Progress Publishers, 1972), pp.102–5.

79.   *L'Avenir international*, August 1918.

80.   *L'Avenir international*, December l918.

81.   Jean Jaurès, *la Petite République*, 9 August 1896; quoted by Dunois in "Marxisme et Liberté," *l'Avenir international*, December 1918. It should be noted that Jaurès was one of the very few socialist politicians who had the respect and admiration of many anarchists. See, for example, René Michaud, *J'avais vingt ans* (Paris: Syros, 1983), p.110; and Grave, *Quarante ans de propagande anarchiste*, p.471.

82.   *L'Avenir international*, July and August–October 1920.

83.   Fabbri, "Le problème de l'État et la Guerre (Réflexions d'un anarchiste)," *l'Avenir international*, June and July 1919.

84.   *L'Avenir international*, June 1918.

85.   André Girard, "Le Communisme organisé: le contrôle social du Prolétariat," *l'Avenir international*, January 1920.

86.   Dwelshauver was to work with the SFIC and its paper *l'Humanité* for a few years, before deciding, after Kronstadt, that bolshevism was "far too oppressive"—see *DBMOF*, vol.12.

87.   Jacques Mesnil, "Vers la troisième Internationale," *l'Avenir international*, October 1918.

88.   Mignon, "Les Anarchistes et le P.S.U.," *l'Avenir international*, October 1919. The article was written in January, but appeared in the review much later because the MS was among papers seized by police.

89.   *L'Avenir international*, August–October 1920.

3

Sovietism as Council Anarchism

The old organizations are in turmoil. The classifications of yesteryear no longer correspond to those of today. New currents have taken form, unforeseen affinities have brought together tendencies which were ignorant of each other or which were in conflict, new antagonisms have broken up hitherto compact forces. ... In France, the complexity of these divorces and attractions is greater than anywhere else.

Boris Souvarine[1]

The best way to help Russia is to follow their revolutionary example in every country. Let us create everywhere our own soviets. ... Long live Communism! Long live World Revolution! Long live the Emancipatory General Strike!

Lacoste[2]

We are entering a major new period of organization.

M.S.[3]

It is generally accepted, both by historians and by contemporaries, that developments within the labour and socialist movements during and immediately after the Great War were of a quite exceptional complexity in France. Lenin himself underlined the fact that whilst the creation of "a new type of party, truly revolutionary and truly communist" would inevitably always be difficult, it was particularly so in France.[4] The bolsheviks believed European revolution to be imminent: in May 1919 Zinoviev declared that the whole continent would be communist within a year. And they also believed that of the European countries, France and Italy were the nearest to revolution. They were thus concerned that, going on from the campaign against the war and against the allied intervention in Russia, French revolutionaries should now urgently campaign to build a new communist party.[5] They were well aware of the main problem in France that this strategy, with its immediate revolutionary perspective, would come up against: the factious nature of the French revolutionary movement.

TOWARDS THE "REVOLUTIONARY BLOC"

The proposed solution was the formation of a "revolutionary bloc," defined by Henri Guilbeaux as follows:

> Applied to France, this formula means that the regrouping of the revolutionary forces must include the left Zimmerwaldians who, within the Socialist Party, formed a bloc around comrades Loriot and Saumoneau; the anti-parliamentarian syndicalists who throughout the war remained resolutely attached to the class struggle and declared against reformism and the League of Nations; all the left-wing elements who defended the Russian revolution whose general directives they accepted and which were grouped around *La Vie Ouvrière*, *La Plèbe*, *Ce qu'il faut dire*, *L'Avenir International*, *L'Internationale*, etc. These elements fought, moreover, in groups such as the CRRI, the CDS, and the Anarchist Communist Federation.[6]

For socialists and syndicalists answering the bolshevik's call, the main stumbling block had to do with the modalities of splitting their present organization—basically: when and along which lines. This was complicated by the advent of the general election in November 1919. Those developments will not be commented on here, except insofar as they directly involved anarchists or are necessary to an understanding of developments within anarchism. For the anarchists, the main problem was ideological, having to do with the nature of anarchism and the nature of bolshevism. In a sense, anarchism was in a doctrinal void. Ideologically it had developed over the previous 70–80 years through different phases, the latest being its very close relation with syndicalism: the CGT had to a large extent been seen as anarchism's creature. For five years or so before the war, this had no longer been the case, but despite a certain dispersion of efforts in various directions, anarchist communism had been struggling to build a more cohesive organization. This process had been rudely interrupted by the war, whose effects on morale have already been stressed. In that context, certain elements of anarchism were to continue to move toward both a greater concern with cohesiveness and an increased identification with organized labour. We have already seen the favourable reaction of many French anarchist-communists towards bolshevism; their revolutionism; their belief in the possibility of immediate revolution in western Europe, specifically in France; and their willingness to criticize pre-war anarchism and to organize with non-anarchist revolutionaries in a Third International. The next step was to be an even greater commitment to bolshevism, although clearly to a very particular interpretation of bolshevism. The nature of that commitment and that interpretation are what must now be considered in more detail.

THE COMMITTEE FOR THE DEFENCE OF SYNDICALISM, 1916–19

The CRRI (created in February 1916) represented the coming together of the anarchists and syndicalists of the International Action Committee against the War (founded late in 1915 and including such activists as Albert Bourderon, Marcel Hasfeld, Jules Lepetit, Alphonse Merrheim, Marcel Vergeat and Raymond Péricat) with the socialists and syndicalists involved in the Zimmerwald and Kienthal conferences (1915 and 1916). However, cohabitation proved difficult, even during a joint campaign against the war, and the two tendencies formed two "commissions"— one uniting the socialists and some syndicalists, the other the anarchists and libertarian syndicalists. By August 1916 the latter had become the independent Comité de Défense Syndicaliste (CDS, Committee for the Defence of Syndicalism).[7] The CDS was clearly libertarian in orientation, including among its leading members anarchist syndicalists such as Veber and Boudoux, and in March 1917 Péricat became its secretary. This—what Kriegel called the "ultra-left" current—is the one which primarily interests us here. It is nevertheless important to note the overlaps between this current and the "extreme left" CRRI, which in May 1919 became the Comité de la Troisième Internationale (Committee of the Third International), and that brought together SFIO members such as Souvarine, Saumoneau and Loriot with syndicalists such as Monatte and Monmousseau, Péricat and Sirolle. These overlaps, the co-operation between socialists, syndicalists and anarchists in a common effort to overcome the apparent failure of all three ideologies in 1914, have already been noted. What gradually became clear, however, was the basic difference of approach between these two currents. On the one hand, were the anarchists and those close to them who would have no compromise with the "reformists" and the "social patriots." The CDS and its heirs—the Parti communiste (PC) and the Fédération communiste des soviets (FCS)—wanted to rely only on the revolutionary elements within anarchism, socialism and syndicalism in its efforts to build a new organization. And they wanted to act immediately to take advantage of the revolutionary tide that swept much of Europe at the end of the war. In 1919, this was also what the bolsheviks wanted.[8] On the other hand, were members of the SFIO and of the CGT wanted to win over as many as possible within their organizations. Thus, whilst we must note the presence within the Committee of the Third International of anarchists or syndicalists like Péricat and Sirolle, and others connected with the first PC, it must also be stressed that the Committee's tactic was clearly to work within the SFIO. As Loriot and Saumoneau made clear in May 1919, "The aim of the members of the Committee of the Third International is to conduct propaganda in all the revolutionary parties in favour of this new International. They must therefore remain members of the groups to which they belong."[9] So although Article 2 of the Committee's statutes stated that membership was open to members of libertarian, socialist or communist groups, in practice the principle aim of the Committee was to campaign within the SFIO for membership of the Third International.

From its creation in the summer of 1916, the CDS included anarchists as well as revolutionary syndicalists. A manifesto of the CDS was published in August of that year defending "the Russian maximalist socialists and anarchists" against their French detractors—ex-Zimmerwaldians, the majorities in the CGT and the SFIO, *l'Humanité* and *le Populaire*. The manifesto, published in *la Tranchée Républicaine*, was signed by Péricat, Faure, Einfalt and Mauricius (of *Ce qu'il faut dire*), Boudoux and Baril (of *le Libertaire*) by Decouzon (of the Pharmaceuticals Industry Workers' Union) and his wife, and by the anarchist syndicalist Broutchoux.[10]

Until December 1917 this current had been able to carry on its pro-bolshevik propaganda through the pages of *Ce qu'il faut dire*. After that time its only outlets were, for a few weeks in the spring of 1918, the very shortlived *Franchise* and *la Plèbe* or, from January 1918, *l'Avenir international*.[11] The latter, however, was a review rather than a campaigning newspaper, and appeared only monthly. Thus in February 1919—the same month as the first post-war conference of the Second International in Bern and a month before the creation of the Third International or Comintern in Moscow—Péricat and others launched *l'Internationale*. Collaborators included anarchists like Despres and Vergeat (the latter, a leading member of the Seine Metal-workers' Union); anarchist sympathizers like the intellectuals Méric and Pioch; revolutionary syndicalists like Martinet, Monatte and Monmousseau; and socialists like Loriot and Saumoneau. Its pages were also open to *l'Entraide*, administered by the anarchists Jahane and Le Meillour; and to the Bureau de propagande antiparlementaire (Bureau for Antiparliamentary Propaganda),

Table 1

The Evolution of Revolutionary Left Groupings, 1915–1921

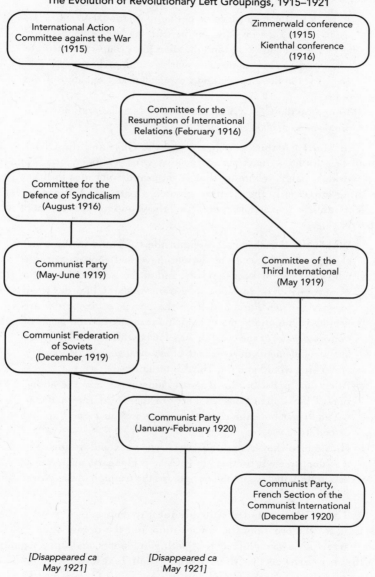

initiated by what was at that time referred to as the Fédération anarchiste.[12] The aims of the paper were laid out in the first number:

> To work for the reconstitution of the International on a new basis; to act as a liaison between the extreme-left elements of the CGT, the Socialist Party and the anarchist groups; to constitute a link between internationalist workers and intellectuals; ...
>
> To work for the emancipation of women and equality of the sexes.
>
> To oppose the CGT's programme of class collaboration with a programme of class struggle.[13]

In March, Arthur Bouchez urged the CDS and the CRRI to go ahead and found a "maximalist-socialist workers' party" or "communist workers' party," claiming that "a thousand comrades in France are awaiting impatiently the creation of such a party."[14] A fortnight later, Péricat published an article committing the group to the creation of such a party:

> Within the Socialist Party, within the CGT and in the anarchist groups, there are many who have had enough of those who want us to take a step back and of the organizations who want to march on the spot, they want to march in order to go forwards. From Paris and from the provinces, comrades are writing to me urging me to launch a campaign in the pages of *l'Internationale* for the creation of a Party which would rally the left-wing elements of socialism, of syndicalism and of anarchy, and which would join the Third International.
>
> After the appeal by the Russian communists and the affiliation of the Italian Socialist Party to the Third International, we no longer have the right to hesitate, we must stand up and be counted.
>
> [It is the bolsheviks and the spartacists we intend to side with, it is alongside our brothers in Russia, in Hungary, in Germany and in Italy that we intend to fight for the triumph of the World Revolution.][15]

The article concluded with a request to comrades to send in their ideas as to "the creation, the constitution and the organization" of the new party. In May a manifesto originating in Nantes, and signed notably by the secretaries of the Metal-workers' and Textile-workers' Unions, asked that the CDS, the CRRI and the Anarchist Communist Federation join together to produce a communist party belonging to the Third International.[16] The same number of the paper reproduced a list of organizations willing to affiliate to the Third International. The list included sections and federations of the SFIO, various syndicalist organizations and the newspaper *la Vie Ouvrière*.[17]

The first brief and somewhat vague outlines of how such a party would look were also put forward at this time, and the bolshevik influence was evident, if only in the nomenclature: the local group would be called a "soviet" or "communist council" and it would elect two sets of delegates; one to a "regional soviet," one to a "confederal council," and members of the latter would be called "people's delegate" or "commissioner" (*commissaire*). Despite such terminology, the proposal was clearly anarchist-inspired. Defining workers' councils, it continued: "These Workers' Councils are composed of three autonomous groups, socialist, syndicalist and anarchist, with delegates from economic, political, social, trade union, co-operative, humanist, libertarian, affinity group, tenants' and other groupings."[18] The means to be adopted were class struggle, internationalism, the programmes of Zimmerwald and Kienthal, of bolshevism, of the Spartakus League and of the Moscow International. "Communes" were to have full autonomy under the new revolutionary régime, but there was also to be a "temporary dictatorship." These "proposals" were anonymous and they clearly had little to do with ideological clarification or organizational cohesiveness, demonstrating a remarkable degree of eclecticism and muddled thinking. Such an approach was not common to all collaborators of *l'Internationale*, however, and the Tours "Communist Group" adopted an attitude more like that of *l'Avenir International*: "Whatever their other failings, the bolsheviks had one merit, a clear programme; it was one of the major causes of their success. Let us have clear programmes, a sure sign of clear thinking and of a lucidity which fears nothing."[19]

THE FIRST COMMUNIST PARTY, 1919

How, then, did this "Communist Party" eventually come to be founded? On the same day, 8 May 1919, both the CDS and the CRRI (the latter simultaneously re-naming itself the Committee of the Third International) decided on their affiliation to the Moscow International.[20] On 30 May, at an extraordinary meeting of the CDS, the manifesto and statutes of France's first *"Parti communiste"* were finally produced.[21] At that meeting a commission was also delegated to contact the Committee of the Third International with a view to inviting their participation in the creation of the new party. However, a meeting on 8 June failed to produce agreement between the two groups, foundering on the question of whether activists should remain within the SFIO and CGT. This was clearly unacceptable to the CDS, which therefore decided to create the PC alone, and, at a meeting on 20 June, a provisional executive committee was elected.[22] Sigrand was general secretary, Mondange treasurer and Péricat director of *l'Internationale*.[23]

The party seems, however, to have been riddled with disunity and rivalry from the start, rivalry notably between Péricat, Sigrand and Lacoste. Violent quarrels became the norm as members divided into conflicting factions, and Paule Mondange, for one, was soon to give up and leave the party. In September the newspaper changed its name to *l'Internationale Communiste*, and was printed in a much smaller format.[24] Since the paper already had large debts, the PC decided not to take on that burden by buying it from Péricat, whose property it was, but to start a fresh newspaper. Although *l'Internationale Communiste* continued to appear until December, it was therefore rivalled for a while by *le Communiste*, official organ of the PC "and of the Soviets belonging to the French Section of the Third, Moscow International and of the Workers', Peasants' and Soldiers' Councils," which appeared in October. Sigrand, a railway worker and ex-member of the SFIO, adopted increasingly authoritarian methods, accumulating all the functions of the executive committee and, despite the legend "Written and Controlled by the People itself" appended to the paper's masthead, taking control of *le Communiste*.[25]

Before long, an "Autonomous Regional Soviet" had appeared on the scene in Paris. This was to form a centre of resistance to Sigrand within the PC, and forced a congress to be held in Paris, 25–28 December 1919. Sixty-five delegates representing 35 "soviets" were present at the congress, which opened with Thomas (secretary of the Commission d'organisation) reading a report highly critical of Sigrand. After discussion of the different points of view, the only point on which all were agreed was the Party's lack of a clear programme and statutes, and it was with this question that the rest of the congress was taken up. As early as August, the socialist and PC supporter François Mayoux had warned that the Party would have to change, that it could not survive in its present form—founded, he claimed, on a basic contradiction: "the reconciliation of two irreconcilable theses, freedom on the one hand, authority on the other."[26] The congress of December in fact represented the clash between these two tendencies within the PC. This clash was embodied in the final confrontation between two proposals for organizational structure. The first was moved by Ernest Girault (the delegate for Argenteuil) and the proposal caused a stir at the conference, being perceived as hierarchical and centralist.[27] An article by Girault on relations between the soviets and the trade unions had appeared in *le*

Communiste two months before. This had also betrayed a conception of the revolutionary and post-revolutionary organization that owed little to anarchist-communist workerism and spontaneism. It had more in common with the SFIO's attitude to syndicalism or with the leninist analysis of "trade union consciousness," and betrayed the influence of the individualist anarchists' disdain for the "herd." The soviet, for Girault, was the brain, the trade union the brawn: "The toiling masses are incapable of creating the communist society themselves, they do not possess the mental capacity necessary for such a task of radical transformation. Trade unionists cannot, because of their inherited defects, their distorted education, the prejudices of their milieu and their physiological weaknesses become by themselves a revolutionary force."[28] What was necessary, according to Girault, was a "directing authority."

At Lacoste's suggestion those delegates who had alternative, more libertarian proposals — Lebourg, Chauvelon, Emile Giraud, Robelot (or Roblot?) and Lacoste himself — put together a joint project that was presented to the conference in opposition to Girault's.[29] Ernest Girault's proposal was rejected by a vote of about 2 to 1; the libertarian alternative was then accepted by all but 4 delegates, who abstained. Based principally on Lebourg's proposal, the libertarian organizational structure was as follows:

1. At the lowest level, Workers' Councils based on the work place; these would be concerned only with the economic sphere;
2. Soviets would bring together delegates of the Workers' Councils and of other sections of the community, and would concern themselves with propaganda and administrative work within the locality; Soviets and Workers' Councils would work in collaboration with each other;
3. Regional Soviets would be composed of delegates from the Workers' Councils and the Soviets, and would concern themselves with the general organization and administration of the region;
4. A Central Soviet or Administrative Commission would be composed of one delegate from each region, and would co-ordinate activity in the regions; the Central Soviet would be responsible to the Congress;
5. The Congress of Soviets would be composed of delegates from each Workers' Council and local Soviet; it would meet every three months, and would be the only body able to take decisions regarding policy.

THE COMMUNIST FEDERATION OF SOVIETS

When the conference voted to adopt this organizational structure, it also voted to transform the Communist Party into the Communist Federation of Soviets. The new federal structure was justified, notably, on the grounds that it was more difficult than a centralized one for the authorities to suppress. It was also argued that the PC had concentrated too much on the "political domain," thus laying itself open to domination by intellectuals. A new Administrative Commission was elected, and although it included both Sigrand and Girault, neither of them became members of the bureau.[30] At a later meeting of the Commission, Marius Hanot was elected general secretary, Alex Lebourg assistant secretary, and Emile Giraud treasurer. Significantly, both Lebourg and Giraud were members of the Anarchist Federation. Hanot was a member of the committee of Henri Barbusse's ARAC (Association Républicaine des Anciens Combattants, Republican Association of Veterans) and editor of its newspaper *le Combattant*.

Not surprisingly, conflict soon arose between Sigrand and the new bureau. According to the police account, Sigrand and others resigned after a meeting of the Administrative Commission on 23 January 1920, because of Emile Giraud's proposal that local Soviet members should be allowed to attend meetings of the Commission. According to Sigrand's account, he resigned on 7 February "because of tactical differences."[31] He was followed by Lacoste and Fabre, and a little later by Ernest Girault and Henri Bott. Early in April this group decided to resurrect the moribund PC, and a Central Committee was named shortly after.[32] At least one member of this Committee—Beauchet, better known as Pierre Mualdès—was a well-known anarchist. Although we know little or nothing about most of the names involved here, it would therefore seem reasonable to assume, unless Mualdès was a complete exception, that the PC-FCS split was not simply one between anarchists and non-anarchists.

The FCS soon started a new paper, the fortnightly *Soviet*, whose very name indicated the concern with direct democracy. It ran from March 1920 to May 1921.[33] The last number of *le Communiste* as organ of the first PC had been no.5 (14 December 1918). It was resurrected as weekly organ of the new, secessionist PC in July 1920, but lasted only five numbers.[34] Unity acts as a multiplier of support, and as we shall see below in more detail, both the FCS and the PC suffered from their splitting. The Federation's last major action was the organization on 8 December 1920 of a meeting in honour of Raymond Lefebvre, Vergeat and Lepetit, French delegates to the second congress of the Comintern who had died at sea during the return journey. After the creation of the SFIC at the Tours congress of December 1920, the PC considered entering this new party, which would in effect have meant becoming its left wing. A majority decided against this, however, and after some fruitless attempts to re-merge with the FCS,[35] the PC dissolved itself on

25 March 1921, forming a Groupe d'études de propagande (Study and Propaganda Group).

"SOVIETISM" AS NEW REVOLUTIONARY TRADITION

In March 1920 Alex Lebourg, a member of the Anarchist Federation and assistant secretary of the FCS, gave a talk entitled "Anarchism and Sovietism." Five months later, criticizing anarchism, he wrote: "Faced with the facts, we need to make one thing clear: a new revolutionary tradition is taking shape."[36] What exactly was meant by "sovietism" and what was its relation to anarchism and bolshevism?

We have already seen the gelling of the "ultra-left" tendency in France, and how the anarchist elements within that tendency developed from opposition to the war, through a critique of certain aspects of anarchism and an admiration of the Russian revolutions, to an anarchism that saw itself as part of the revolutionary socialist movement. The first organizational manifestation of this pro-bolshevik tendency, the CDS with its paper *l'Internationale*, was still relatively eclectic. On the one hand it played host to what we might call "straight" anarchism, with its emphasis on the spontaneity of revolution and its condemnation of the "tyranny of the majority." On the other, it could publish the manifesto of the PC with its declaration that the French revolutionary labour movement "envisages the temporary dictatorship of the proletariat replacing the dictatorship of the bourgeoisie until the complete realization of communism."[37]

And whilst *l'Internationale* condemned "state socialism" as "the most oppressive machine for the people which is subjected to it,"[38] activists such as Maurice Heine carried on as members of both the SFIO and the PC.[39] For the first six months of its existence, the PC had no clear statutes, no common understanding of how it should function as a revolutionary organization in France. The only unanimous position was approval of Russian bolshevism and support for the Third International. Activists such as the ex-anarchist Girault were to embrace positions that represented a total abandonment of their earlier libertarian principles. It is nevertheless not entirely clear to what extent the second PC (from the spring of 1920) was substantively more "authoritarian" than the more "libertarian" FCS. It was still vehemently opposed to legalism and parliamentary politics, for example, and was workerist.[40] And it managed to retain someone like Mualdès, who stayed loyal enough to his anarchist principles to return to the movement after the demise of the PC and FCS.

But was this mere eclecticism? Was it simply confusion, disagreement? Partly, no doubt. But gradually, especially with the creation of the FCS, there did emerge a doctrine that was clearly seen by many activists as a synthesis of marxism and anarchism, as a new ideological current: sovietism.[41] Its inspiration was not only Russian bolshevism, but also German councilism.[42] For one activist it could be called "sovietism/communism/direct democracy/government by the people for the people."[43] For Girault, it was a new idealism: "Only communist morality, born of marxist Socialism and of anarchism, can build a new social order. It is the morality of the Soviet."[44] How did this translate into a party programme? The PC, founded in May 1919, accepted the unavoidability of the dictatorship of the proletariat.[45] It was still influenced by its own libertarian background in that it emphasized the temporary nature of the dictatorship; and by its syndicalist background in that revolution was conceived of in the form of a general strike. The PC was also rigorously anti-parliamentarian. A leaflet by the anarchist André Lorulot and a pamphlet by Marius Hanot both set parliamentarianism and sovietism in total opposition the one to the other.[46] The PC was egalitarian: the collectivity would benefit equally from production, since it would control production, but "the worker will manage the factory."[47] Technology would be developed in ways that would improve the quality of life. Marriage would be abolished as an oppressive institution, and schools would be created with the motto: "Neither god nor master."[48] Supporters of the first PC had also been concerned with the forms of post-revolutionary social organization. Lipin wrote on the need for workers' councils, stressing that these must not be the expression of any one party or grouping.[49] Prouvost, claiming there was general dissatisfaction in France with the ideas of the parliamentary and "authoritarian" socialists, wrote: "People no longer want anything but temporary and conditional delegates acting on binding mandates, as mere instruments in the hands of the citizens. … This is the general feeling at the moment, let us take advantage of it now."[50]

But it was the FCS which developed the idea of sovietism, its own internal structure reflecting the emphasis on grass roots control which was central to it. The Federation's declaration in the first number of its paper, *le Soviet*, echoes the Russian call: "All power to the soviets!," and stresses the need for "People's Economic Councils" and "Factory and Workshop Committees." Familiar themes such as the revocability of delegates and the autonomy of soviets occur again and again. "Sovietism is the direct self-government of the world proletariat," we are told.[51] But the most enlightening explanation of what the Federation was about was provided by two anarchists, Genold and Lebourg. Lebourg, in an

article entitled "Federation or Party, Communism and Sovietism," anal-
ysed the different tendencies within the European pro-bolshevik camp.
Interestingly, he saw the situation as a re-play of the struggles within the
First International:

> Quite naturally, the European crisis brought on by the war,
> in making each of us aware of the imminence of the collapse
> of capitalism and of the inevitable social transformation, has
> reawakened the antagonisms which have always divided the
> revolutionary proletariat into two groups: the centralists and
> the federalists, those who favour political action and those who
> favour direct class action, the authoritarian communists and
> the libertarian communists. We are at present witnessing a re-
> grouping, within the Communist International, of the partisans
> of these two tendencies.[52]

MARX V BAKUNIN REVISITED

Thus, whilst granting that some pro-bolshevik French revolutionaries
remained true to their principles during the 1914–18 war, Lebourg in-
sists that they were nevertheless still "statist, centralist, authoritarian
communists; yesterday they were active members of the of the Socialist
Party, a party engaged in parliamentary politics." This was why—and
here the target was presumably Sigrand *et al*, as well as the Committee
of the Third International—they preferred the label "communist" and
why they still maintained the idea of a "party." The danger, for Lebourg,
was "national solidarity inevitably produced by political action": "A party is inevitably a political organism and as everyday political action can
only take place within the limits, within the framework of the nation, we
can say that all political parties are fated to adapt to the governmental
organization of the nation in which it was formed."[53] The other tendency
insisted on the word "soviet," preferred to call themselves "sovietists,"
and had as their main concern "the constitution of a new class struggle
organization."[54] Clearly the central point here was the quest for an organizational form that was compatible with revolutionary aims, and the
question of post-revolutionary social structure. Having dismissed the
political party, Lebourg declared: "The communism of tomorrow will be
sovietist or it will not be communist."[55]

By reviving the old Marx-Bakunin dichotomy of the First International, Lebourg reversed the tendency towards revolutionary socialist
unification apparent in the groups around *Ce qu'il faut dire* (April 1916
to December 1917) and *l'Avenir international* (January 1918 to October
1920), and in the CDS and early PC (spring 1917 to December 1919).

But the appraisal of the Russian revolution and its contribution to the European revolutionary movement was still thoroughly positive as late as June 1920:

> The diffusion throughout the world of the principles of the Soviet has aroused the enthusiasm of all Federalists and libertarian communists; the Russian revolution, in making everyone aware of what the Soviet represents, has helped the Proletariat take a great step forward. The Soviet, an organization of the working class, interprofessional, based on the commune, federalist, non-hierarchical, enabling the system of short-term mandates, instituting the permanent control of delegates held individually responsible, appeared to many as the solution which has been sought after for so long (and which Fernand Pelloutier came close to formulating); the Soviet was revealed as the form of organization truly able to realize the transformation of society towards Federalist Communism.[56]

SOVIETISM V BOLSHEVISM

Lebourg did not refer to bolshevism in his analysis: he referred to the Russian revolution and to its creation, the soviet. And it was this that was most important: "Through a telegramme sent by Zinoviev, the Executive Committee of the Third International welcomed the French anarchist syndicalists who, grouped around Péricat, had just affiliated to the Communist International; we must not hide the fact that Federalists were attracted above all by Sovietism."[57] This represents a subtle shift within the ultra-left tendency. It was with the FCS that this kind of distinction was first made. As Lebourg pointed out later in the same article, the bolsheviks were only able to succeed because of "a mass movement whose slogan was 'All power to the Soviets!'" And again, in September 1920, Jean Hermitte emphasized that bolshevism was the doctrine of a political party, sovietism a system of direct democracy. Hermitte's interpretation of the Russian revolution was again an essentially libertarian one: the bolsheviks had only been successful in gaining mass popular support because they had been seen to favour the soviets, which were the spontaneous creation of the people in revolution, not a bolshevik innovation. Indeed, the FCS was almost becoming critical towards the bolsheviks: "The Bolsheviks acted therefore above all as the interpreters of the will of the Russian people. They were excellent 'messengers'. They will continue to be so to the extent that they observe the system of Direct Democracy and act less as a Party, to the extent that they are Sovietists more than they are bolsheviks."[58] Thus it becomes clearer how

Lebourg could explicitly claim for sovietism the heritage of bakuninism and Pelloutier's conception of direct action syndicalism.[59] In the 1890s the anarchist syndicalists had seen themselves as taking up the torch of bakuninist anarchism, the latter having embraced collectivism and the need for a revolutionary organization based on labour. Lebourg and the FCS saw councilism or sovietism as the latest development in the same tradition.

By this time—the spring and summer of 1920—the FCS was being rivalled by the second PC. Within the SFIO the centrists were gradually being won over to the bolshevik cause, and the campaign for the party's membership of the Moscow International was well advanced. Already in May, Chauvelon had warned against what the revolutionists perceived to be the coming dangers: "We are antiparliamentarians because we are sovietists. That is the essential and decisive point. The intermediate position (sovietist-parliamentarian) is not only absurd, but dangerous. It represents the thin edge of the wedge leading to the worst weaknesses, the worst compromises, the worst betrayals."[60]

SOVIETISM V ANARCHISM

But although the sovietists were distancing themselves both from Russian bolshevism and from French "parliamentarian communism," at the same time as claiming ideological descent from the anti-authoritarians of the First International and from direct action syndicalism, they were nevertheless to distance themselves also from certain aspects of anarchism. This critique took the form notably of an attack on the absolute anti-authoritarianism of the anarchist movement, and on what was held to be anarchism's unrealistic, outmoded understanding of revolution in the 20th century. Both Genold and Lebourg thought anarchist talk of "freedom" abstract and idealist. Genold lumped together liberals and anarchists, accusing them of being moralistic in their attitude towards the bolsheviks:

> Certain liberals—and certain anarchists—combat maximalism because of an attachment to the old principles of freedom; which freedom are they talking about? The freedom of the poor or of the wealthy, that of the capitalists or that of the proletariat? Careful study of our societies shows that there is no such thing as Freedom, there are freedoms, which become more contradictory as social chaos increases. And Monsieur Clemenceau, the lawyer of the business class, was right when, addressing the revolutionaries, he said: "Between you and us, it is a question of force." ... Wanting to give people freedom before equality

really is putting the cart before the horse. Quoting the Declaration of the Rights of Man and of the Citizen to the impoverished worker looking through restaurant windows at bourgeois couples dining is an insult to human reason.[61]

Genold's criticisms were linked also to an attack on the individualist, or what he calls the "Rynerian," approach to revolution: namely, the belief that social revolution was pointless unless the individuals making up society had all evolved sufficiently within themselves first.[62] Emile Giraud was also to take up this argument. Revolutions do not wait, he pointed out, and this implies limitations on one's behaviour in a revolutionary situation: "If we were masters of the crowd, if we could decide on the hour of the revolution and wait for the masses' education to be completed, the anarchists would be right; but we cannot decree the Revolution, on the contrary it is the Revolution which carries us along like corks on the water, and which forces us into taking certain necessary actions."[63] Other anarchists writing in *le Soviet* made similar criticisms.[64] But again it was Lebourg who conducted a thoroughgoing critique of these aspects of pre-war anarchism: "We were educated in a school of revolution which we could without exaggeration qualify as idyllic."[65] The revolution, he argued, would not be over after three days of street-fighting: "How many times have we heard comrades talk about 'the day after the revolution'; Jean Grave wrote a tome with the primitive title: 'The Workers on the Day after the Revolution"; it was so simple, people were practically embracing by the barricades."[66]

SOVIETISM, REVOLUTION AND "DICTATORSHIP"

Lebourg wanted to emphasize one of the major lessons of the Great War and of the Russian revolution: namely, that just as the nature of wars had changed considerably, so had the nature of revolutions:

> We know that the coming Revolution, in France as elsewhere, will not be child's play. When our French comrades know of the suffering endured by the Russian proletariat; when they know how the atrocities committed by the bandits of the allied forces and by the tsarist generals surpassed even those of the counter-revolutionary Vendée, of the infernal columns of Versaillais and of Satory; when our comrades in the occupied lands and those who were prisoners in Germany realize that the blockade of Soviet Russia is more terrible than anything they themselves suffered, then all will understand better the scale and the severity of the struggle; it will be evident to us all, even the anarchists, that the proletarian dictatorship is a necessity.[67]

This was the crux of the matter. Despite the sovietists' rejection of bolshevism and of authoritarian socialism, they had come to be convinced that the exercise of authority in a violent revolution was both unavoidable and morally justifiable. They therefore found themselves justifying the "dictatorship of the proletariat" in Russia against the criticisms of the anarchists around *le Libertaire*, which had by that time reappeared.[68] In attempting to persuade anarchists of the correctness of his argument, and trying to bring the argument onto more familiar and more concrete territory, Lebourg used the example of the syndicalist's treatment of a strike-breaker:

> There was a time … when the leaders of the CGT would explain that the duty of class solidarity was more important than anything else; that when the unionized workers decided on a strike in a factory, an industry or even nationally, all workers, unionized or not, should follow the strike call; that strikers had the right to use force if necessary to prevent non-strikers from working; that whoever, in the name of freedom, effectively became a defender of the bourgeoisie, whether consciously or not, would be a renegade and a traitor.
> Well, that is the dictatorship of the proletariat.[69]

That was the argument from the duty of proletarian solidarity. There were two other arguments. The first was simply that if the revolution was to take power away from the bourgeoisie and give it to the working class, then: "the political expropriation of the bourgeoisie is the indispensable corollary of their economic expropriation." Proletarian dictatorship was made necessary by the violent resistance of the bourgeoisie and, Lebourg added vaguely but significantly, "of the reactionary parts of the population." Finally, he argued, the whole set of economic problems brought about by a revolution require "discipline on the part of the working class": disruption of the economy caused by workers' being away in the army, sabotage by counter-revolutionaries, the problems of economic conversion and reorganization, and so on.

SOVIETISM: AN ASSESSMENT

The FCS had therefore covered quite a lot of ground since the unquestioning and undifferentiated support accorded bolshevism and the Russian revolution by the CDS and the PC in the heady days of 1917–19. The sovietism developed by the anarchists and others in the FCS did indeed represent, as Lebourg claimed, a new revolutionary current. It involved an emphasis on the need for tighter organization, structured in a libertarian and federal way, but with a much greater degree of ideological and practical cohesiveness. It was workerist, anti-parliamentarian, revolutionist. It developed out of the anarchist movement, claiming descent from Bakunin and Pelloutier. At the same time, it was very critical of the idealism and individualism of some forms of anarchism. It also drew on German councilism and especially on Russian sovietism. Its analysis of what happened in Russia led it to the conclusion not only that the revolutionary organization must be much better prepared for the decisive moment, but also that during and after the revolution there would inevitably be a transitional period (though that phrase was not used), during which the exercise of authority and violence against the counter-revolutionary forces would be inevitable, justifiable and quite compatible with the anti-authoritarian democratic structures of the post-revolutionary society.

For the anarchist historian Alexandre Skirda, sovietism was nothing but a mirage; the anarchists were ignorant, fascinated by the success of the bolsheviks and blinded to reality; those who justified the dictatorship were despicable hypocrites.[70] This seems rather harsh. The sovietism of the French "ultra-left" seems to have been less a "mirage," than a perfectly valid attempt to develop out of anarchist-communism, and anarchist syndicalism a realistic revolutionary doctrine which would take account of the lessons of 1914 and 1917 and of the new situation in the French labour movement; and which would enable revolutionaries to take advantage of the situation at the end of the war. It is certainly true that the first PC was generally enthusiastic about the Russian revolution, bolshevism and western councilism, and often was quite happy to confuse them. But everybody belonging to the European far left reacted that way.[71] And by mid-1920 the FCS had become critical of the bolsheviks, whilst still maintaining its enthusiasm for the achievements of the Russian revolution, and defending both against western critics. Besides, a libertarian reading of the early period of the Russian revolution was certainly not limited to the anarchists, nor was it unjustified. The Russian revolution was indeed a libertarian one, the soviets had much to recommend themselves to anarchists, and the bolsheviks were indeed only able to come to power by identifying themselves with the radical, spontaneous popular movement.[72]

Skirda, continuing his attack on the sovietists, also delights in pointing out that "the existence of these communist organizations was at no time recognized by Moscow, since it was the party born of the split in the Socialist Party at its Tours Congress which won its favours."[73] It is of course true that it was eventually the SFIO majority which became the French section of the Comintern. It is also true, as Kriegel points out, that it was the socialist Loriot who was felt by the bolsheviks to be their best representative in France.[74] But this does not mean to say that the PC, the FCS and the anarchists in general were disregarded by the bolsheviks. Far from it. In August 1919, in a letter to Sylvia Pankhurst, Lenin wrote: "Very many anarchist workers are now becoming sincere supporters of Soviet power, and that being so, it proves them to be our best comrades and friends, the best of revolutionaries, who have been enemies of Marxism only through misunderstanding, or, more correctly, not through misunderstanding but because the official socialism prevailing in the epoch of the Second International (1889–1914) betrayed Marxism."[75] If we are to believe Raymond Péricat's autobiographical notes, he was also thought highly of by Lenin. For according to Péricat, Lenin made a speech in Moscow in March 1919, about the founding of the Comintern, in which he said: "Citizen Péricat is one of the rare representatives of the French labour movement who is in general in agreement with us."[76] Liebman recounts how Radek was removed from his post as secretary of the Comintern, just before the second congress in July 1920, for opposing the decision to invite anarchists and anarchist syndicalists.[77] Alfred Rosmer, himself from an anarchist and then revolutionary syndicalist background, and a member of the CRRI, tells us how much non-marxist revolutionaries were impressed and attracted by Lenin's writings, such as *The State and Revolution*, written in 1917: "Besides these texts, in which they could find a language akin to their own, a conception of socialism which resembled their own, what particularly pleased revolutionaries from the anarchist and syndicalist traditions, and attracted them towards Bolshevism, was the merciless condemnation of opportunism."[78] Mauricius was to confirm this. Writing of his travels in Russia, he recounts how Lenin had the first French-language edition of *The State and Revolution* sent to a group of French-speaking delegates: "On reading it we were surprised and reassured, since it revealed to us an aspect of Karl Marx and of Friedrich Engels which we had not studied adequately. The marxist conception of the state was not what we had been led to believe by the passionate and biased debates between Proudhon, Bakunin and Marx."[79] And as late as 1921, *le Soviet* printed an open letter from Victor Serge, in which he tried to win over anarchists to the bolshevik cause.[80] His letter contained the usual criticisms of a traditional anarchism which refused to revise its ideology, but basically it flattered anarchists, trying to convince them of their indispensability to the Comintern: "If you do not intervene, the enthusiasm which the Russian revolution has aroused among the best of the working class movement could well be channelled, used, diverted by 'socialist' and 'syndicalist' politicians. The habits of inaction which they maintain with such eloquence could delay the successful outcome of the struggle in Russia by years."

So when Kriegel and others point out the lack of understanding demonstrated by the anarchists and syndicalists, it must be seen in this light. To which one must, of course, add that the revolution and thus bolshevik theory were in flux, and the attitude of the bolsheviks towards the anarchists was therefore also evolving. The principles of bolshevism and the new International were not really settled until the second international congress of July 1920. To begin with, the campaign conducted within the SFIO in favour of membership of the Comintern, first by the Committee of the Third International and later by centrists such as Cachin and Ludovic-Oscar Frossard, was beginning to bear fruit. After the SFIO's Strasbourg congress in February 1920, at which the pro-Comintern camp made substantial gains, Lenin changed tactic: he now agreed with Rosmer and others connected with the Committee of the Third International that it was possible and desirable to win over as many members of the SFIO as possible. In April 1920, Lenin also wrote *"Left-Wing" Communism, an Infantile Disorder*. This represented a significant shift away from the libertarianism of *The State and Revolution*. The leftists' refusal to compromise by co-operating with reformists or by involving themselves in parliamentary politics had previously been praised to some extent as a guarantee of their revolutionary integrity and reliability. Now it was attacked as childish and unrealistic, incompatible with the new emphasis on a uniform international strategy and on the rôle of the party as a centralized leadership. Such an evolution in the bolsheviks' stance was bound to have a negative effect on libertarian support for the French PC and FCS; not just because of the increasingly authoritarian organizational principles, but also because the bolsheviks were now seen to be welcoming socialists such as Marcel Cachin, universally loathed by anarchists because of the extreme tardiness of his conversion to communism and antimilitarism. Indeed, the Parti Communiste—Section Française de l'Internationale Communiste (Communist Party—French Section of the Communist International) created by the SFIO's Tours congress of December 1920 contained many elements that could never be accepted by the anarchists.

But this is to anticipate, for by 1920 there was, in any case, no longer any real possibility that the leftists' original project might succeed: the project having been first to unify the revolutionary movement under the auspices of a Third International, and second to organize a social revolution in France. Those celebrated characteristics of French politics right across the spectrum—ideological plurality, factionalism, weakness of organization—were from the start to plague this attempt to achieve revolutionary unity, despite the rhetoric on both sides and despite the fluid nature of the movement at that time. The CRRI was the first attempt to unite, and that lasted about a year, from the spring of 1916 to the spring of 1917. A subsequent attempt to re-unite in May–June 1919 also failed because of the tactical differences between the so-called "ultra-left" and "extreme left" over how to form the communist party. The "two irreconcilable traditions of freedom and authority" clashed within the PC—"an almost ludicrous example of the divisive tendencies of the French working-class movement," according to Wohl—almost as soon as it was created, and led to the split of December 1919.[81] This seems to have been due to the political origins of those concerned: the SFIO on the one hand, anarchism and syndicalism on the other hand. Also, looking back on the period, Péricat was to blame Sigrand's abuse of his position for the collapse of the party, as well as hostility caused at least partly by its working-class constitution.[82] A police report of August 1920 on bolshevik propaganda referred to the existence of a multitude of small groups "whose mutual relations are less than cordial and which devote most of their time and energy to barbed polemics over questions of detail in the application of principles and over personality clashes."[83]

Space forbids any real analysis here of whether there was in fact a revolutionary situation in France between 1917 and 1920, and the question has already been considered at length by Annie Kriegel.[84] But as Kriegel says: "Whether they were plausible or not, the revolutionary objectives of the ultra-left were not achieved. The failure of the strikes of the spring of 1919 to develop to the stage of a social revolution definitively undermined the idea that the proletariat could, through general strike and under the leadership of the PC, overthrow the regime."[85]

THE INFLUENCE OF SOVIETISM

So the ultra-left failed in both respects. But had this tendency been entirely without influence? Clearly not, though support is difficult to estimate with any precision. *Ce qu'il faut dire*, appearing in very difficult times and constantly under attack from the censors, nevertheless had a print-run of 20,000 at the end of 1916, with 3,000 subscribers. The following year there were about 50 support groups (of which 20 or so were in Paris), and the paper was also very popular with the troops at the front.[86] The monthly, rather more theoretical *l'Avenir International* had a print-run of only 3,000.[87] Péricat claimed an attendance of between 5,000 and 6,000 for the "Fête de l'Internationale" in Marseille on 25 May 1919.[88] The weekly *l'Internationale* claimed to have sold only 2,400 copies of its first number (out of a print run of 6,000), but that this figure had risen to 7,500 (out of a print-run of 11,000) by July 1919.[89]

What of the organizations whose creation these publications had helped to prepare? Sigrand was to claim that the first PC had 40,000 copies of its manifesto printed, although according to Kriegel, the figure was 20,000.[90] A police report of 22 July 1920 tells us that 5,000 copies of *le Communiste* no.2 (18 July) were printed; and that of these, 3,000 were distributed to the kiosks in Paris, 600 to the provinces, and that 1,400 were distributed through the party's sections to be sold at meetings.[91] A report produced a month later gave a figure of 6,000 for the print-run of *le Communiste*, 15,000 for *le Soviet*.[92]

In considering the number of groups belonging to the two PCs and the FCS, one has to bear in mind the unreliability of police reports when it came to distinguishing between different tendencies in the movement; the fact that, when it came to debating ideological or tactical differences between the leaders in Paris, activists in the provinces were often less than interested; and that it is often difficult to assess to what extent some groups had any real existence.[93] With these caveats in mind, what do we know about the strength of the "sovietist" organizations? We know that at the congress of December 1919, there were delegates from about 33 member soviets present: 10 from Paris, 15 from the Paris region, and 8 from the provinces.[94] The size of groups seems to have varied considerably, ranging from 10 or less to more than 100. The previous September, Bott had received a membership card numbered 1484.[95]

The split between the FCS and the second PC was, not surprisingly, very damaging. There was a period of uncertainty during which member soviets had to decide which organization they belonged to. Most remained with the majority, the FCS.[96] An undated police report covering Paris and region lists 11 PC groups (of which 6 had become inactive), and 12 FCS groups (of which 4 had become inactive).[97] The report of January 1920 gave the following figures for the FCS: 11 soviets in Paris, 24 in the Paris region; 20 in the provinces.[98] And it also pointed out that the pre-congress PC membership of 3,500 had fallen to 700 for the FCS. The report of April 1920 claimed that membership of both organisations together had fallen from 700 to 400.[99] Whatever the uncertainty about all these figures, one thing is clear: after 1919, both the FCS and PC gradually faded away. By August 1920, the police could describe the organization of the FCS as "a bare skeleton," with only about 300 members in Paris and the north, the PC as having no real existence in numerical terms.[100] A long, detailed and abnormally accurate police report, produced in the spring or early summer of 1921, ended with the following assessment: "As for the 'Communist Federation of Soviets' and the 'Communist Party', their level of activity is zero and their membership insignificant. Both organizations, whose programmes are incidentally more anarchist than communist, are fated to disappear very shortly."[101]

Amdur nevertheless questions the kind of interpretation of the multiplicity of postwar leftist groups offered by Kriegel (and subsequently by other historians, notably communists), whereby they are seen as representing a linear development from "the 'ultra-left' (anarcho-communism) to the 'extreme left' (revolutionary syndicalism) and finally, after the failure of each, to Bolshevism."[102] This underestimates the continuity of support in certain localities for the "earlier" ultra-leftism, where it had significant influence on later movements "even though it lost its formal, institutional bases of support."[103] What Ansart has called this "largely mythic" idea of successive ideological phases was in fact a polemical invention of the communists in the early 1920s that enabled them to attack as "infantile" or "outdated" those who questioned bolshevization.[104]

RECONCILING SOCIALISM AND FREEDOM

The "sovietists" merit study if only because, as Kriegel points out, they might potentially have played a much more significant rôle. They have a particular interest for us also because, of all the European leftist currents in this period, the French sovietists were the only ones to be rooted to such an extent in anarchism, rather than in marxism. And because Péricat's PC "represents a testing ground—in some respects a pretty poor one but nevertheless representative—for a doctrinal quest which cannot leave historians in the second half of the 20th century indifferent, since its aim was to reconcile socialism and freedom."[105]

Notes

1.   "Brûlons les vieilles etiquettes!," *l'Avenir international* no.25 (January 1920).

2.   *Le Communiste*, 25 October 1919.

3.   Ibid.

4.   Quoted by Annie Kriegel, *Aux origines du communisme français 1914–1920* (Paris & La Haye: Mouton, 1964), vol.I, p 275–6.

5.   Kriegel has emphasized the links between these campaigns: how the campaign against the war became a campaign against the allied intervention, and how this facilitated the shift to a defence of the Russian revolution, this in turn becoming "the struggle for the defence of the bolshevik revolution." *Origines* (1964), vol.I, p 277.

6.   Quoted in Kriegel, *Aux origines du communisme français* (Paris: Flammarion, 1969), p.53. Henri Guilbeaux, an anarchist and syndicalist, had been involved with the Zimmerwald conference in Switzerland during the war, and went to Russia in 1917. He was to become a member of the first French PC and later became the Moscow correspondent of *l'Humanité*, by that time the paper of the SFIC.

7.   According to Péricat, one of the reasons for the split was that the socialists were interested only in writing pamphlets, whereas the CDS was to be actively involved in, for example, the May Day disturbances of 1919 and the metalworkers' strike of June 1919. Péricat also counted bourgeois intellectual arrogance as a contributing factor in the failure of the PC: it was never taken seriously, he was later to claim, because it was "the work of manual workers." Péricat (1873–1957) was himself a building-worker and was secretary of the Building-workers' Federation 1908–1913. "Raconte nous tes Souvenirs," 7pp. TS (n.d.[1945]) and "Un Parti Communiste en France: Un peu d'histoire," 25pp. MS (June 1956), "Archives Péricat," IFHS 14AS205(a)1. *DBMOF*, vol.14.

8.   Kriegel, *Origines* (1969), p.56. The bolsheviks wanted the immediate creation of a communist organization, led by the socialist Loriot, and including anarchists and syndicalists like Péricat.

9.   Quoted in Kriegel, *Origines* (1969), p.121.

10.   Péricat, "La Révolution Russe." 3pp. MS (n.d.), in the "Archives Péricat," IHFS, 14AS205(a)1.

11.   *La Plèbe* survived four numbers in the spring of 1918. It was produced by Fernand Despres (1879–1949), a shoemaker turned journalist who was to join the SFIC at its founding, only to leave again in October 1922. *DBMOF*, vol.12.

12.   See "L'Antiparlementarisme," *l'Internationale*, 17 May 1919. The Bureau consisted of about a dozen fairly well-known anarchist militants—the *"responsables"* were Rimbault and Bidault—plus "the best elements of the different syndicalist, revolutionary, communist and anarchist currents." Notice that "communism" is assumed to be anti-parliamentarian.

13.   *L'Internationale*, 15 February 1919. It is interesting to note the quite unusual emphasis on feminism, and not just in the statement of aims. The paper was to carry many articles by Louise Saumoneau and others on the particular problems of women. Also, judging by listings in the paper, about a third of the contacts for local PC groups were women.

14.   *L'Internationale*, 22 March 1919.

15.   *L'Internationale*, 5 April 1919. The final paragraph (in square brackets) did not appear in the newspaper, having been cut by the censor. The text can be found in "Un Parti Communiste en France: Un peu d'histoire," "Archives Péricat," IFHS, 14 AS 205(a)1. Notice the prominence accorded the Spartacists as well as the bolsheviks. The repression of the Spartakus uprising in Berlin by a socialist-led government contributed significantly to the parliamentary socialists' being considered outright enemies.

16.   *L'Internationale*, 10 May 1919.

17.   *La Vie Ouvrière* reappeared in April 1919. On the ideology of the group around this paper, see Colette Chambelland, *Pierre Monatte, une autre voix syndicaliste* (Paris: Les Editions de l'atelier/Editions ouvrières, 1999); Daniel Colson, *Anarcho-syndicalisme et communisme. Saint-Etienne 1920–1925* (Saint-Etienne: Université de Saint-Etienne/Centre d'Etudes Foréziennes/Atelier de Création Libertaire, 1986), pp.33–49; Jeremy Jennings, *Syndicalism in France: A Study of Ideas* (Basingstoke & London: Macmillan in association with St. Antony's College, Oxford: 1990).

18.   *L'Internationale*, 10 May 1919.

19.   *L'Internationale*, 5 July 1919.

20.   See 14pp. TS police report (n.d.[between March and July 1921]), F7/13090.

21.   See *l'Internationale*, 7 June 1919 and *le Communiste*, 25 October 1919.

22.   See police report cited above, F7/13090. At the CDS meeting, according to this report, "it had been formally agreed that the Committee of the Third International would be invited to join the Committee for the Defence of Syndicalism, which would be at the head of the movement." The names of the members of the provisional committee were published in *l'Internationale*, 28 June 1919: Fabre, Péricat, Sigrand, Jouteau, Juste, Capus, Baudey, Lacoste, May, Paule Mondange, Louisette Rossi, Marguerite Gaillard, Jeanne Couvreur.

23.   The information reproduced here derives, unless otherwise referenced, from the various reports—to be found in the Archives Nationales—produced on the CDS, the PC, the FCS, and related developments: "Le Parti Communiste. Le Congres de Décembre 1919," 12pp. TS (January 1920), BB18/6465; "Le Parti Communiste et la Fédération Communiste des Soviets," 6pp. TS (4 April 1920), BB18/6465; Note from Minister of Justice[?], 7pp. TS (n.d.), BB18/6465; "Parti Communiste/Comité de la 3ème Internationale/ Fédération Communiste des Soviets," 4pp. TS (n.d.), F7/13091; 14pp. TS (n.d.[between March and July 1921]), F7/13090.

24.   The paper was called *l'Internationale Communiste* from no.30 (15 September 1919). The last edition was no.36 (16 December 1919).

25.   According to a police report, "not a single article appeared in this paper ... that was not censored by the general secretary." "Le Parti Communiste," January 1920, BB18/6465.

26.   See Constant Bougon (pseudonym of F. Mayoux), "Pour un parti révolutionnaire," *l'Internationale*, 9 August 1919. Mayoux pointed out that he believed the exercise of authority unavoidable in a revolution.

27.   Ernest Girault (1871–1933) was in fact a veteran of the anarchist movement. In the late 1880s he had been a member of the *le Libertaire* group which had been violently hostile to syndicalism. He was an active member of the anarchist-dominated Antimilitarist League and was a founding member of an individualist-anarchist "colony" established at Saint-Germain-en-Laye in 1906. Clearly his attitude changed considerably over the following two decades, since by 1926 he was a member of the SFIC and would write the booklet *Pourquoi les Anarchistes-Communistes français ont rallié la IIIe Internationale* (Paris: Librairie de *l'Humanité*, 1926).

28.   *Le Communiste*, 25 October 1919.

29.   These were the delegates for Rouen/Sotteville, Paris 20, Courbevoie, Charenton and Paris 3 respectively. Péricat's "Un Parti Communiste en France," already cited, gives the impression that Emile Chauvelon, who taught French and Latin at the Lycée Voltaire, was the only "*bourgeois*" in the PC. Interestingly, police reports (of 3 May and 29 May 1920, BB18/64655) claim he had been elected to the Executive Committee of the Committee of the Third International early in May 1919, and that he did not leave the Committee until February 1920; he joined the PC, but after the conference of December 1919, joined the FCS which was born of it. Either the police report is wrong, or this is yet further evidence of the complexity (or confusion) of the situation.

30.   The Commission members were Lebourg, Chauvelon, Sigrand, Carl, Hanot, Girault (Ernest), Bott, Giraud (Emile), Lacoste, Fabre, Le Dréant.

31.   See Sigrand's open letter to the Minister of Justice in *le Communiste*, 8 August 1920.

32.   Sigrand, Lacoste, Fabre, Bott, Hutin, Mayre, Brossault, Arnault, Lucas, Beauchet (alias Pierre Mualdès), Marguerite Gaillard.

33.   Emile Giraud was the administrator. The anarchist Genold was to be a contributor to the paper.

34.   *Le Communiste. Organe officiel du Parti Communiste. Section Française de l'Internationale Communiste.* Notice the dropping of the earlier reference to soviets in the sub-title. Also, the party's local groups were no longer called "soviets," but "sections." According to Maitron (vol.II, p.286) the paper reappeared on 4 July 1920. I have found only nos. 3, 4 and 5, dated 25 July, 1 August and 5 August 1920.

35.   According to a police report cited by Kriegel, the two groups did form together a Revolutionary Action Committee, which nevertheless left both groups complete autonomy of action. Kriegel, *Origines* (1964), vol.I, p.305.

36.   Alex, "La Dictature du Prolétariat," *le Soviet*, 29 August 1920.

37.   *L'Internationale*, 7 June 1919. The PC manifesto was also published in *le Communiste* no.1 (25 October 1919).

38.   *L'Internationale*, 7 June 1919.

39.   Heine was a delegate of the Paris 14 soviet to the PC conference of December 1919, and being one of the more outspoken critics of Sigrand's alleged authoritarianism, he then joined the FCS. "Le Parti Communiste et la Fedération Communiste des Soviets" (4 April 1920), BB18/6465. According to Kriegel (*Origines* 1964, p.285–6), he was a delegate to the SFIO's Tours congress in December 1920.

40.   See, for example, Louis Laérol, "Vers le 'Front unique'?," *le Communiste*, 1 August 1920.

41.   Symbolic of this was the fact that the PC (even after the split with the FCS) used a black and red banner—see *le Communiste*, 8 August 1920. In France at that time, the red flag was the symbol not only of socialism and communism, but of the labour movement generally, as numerous accounts of demonstrations testify, and anarchists could happily march behind it. The anarchist Georges Yvetot's booklet *A.B.C. syndicaliste* (1908, 1911, 1931) also refers to CGT members as "les syndiqués rouges," "red union members." The black flag was specifically anarchist. Was this the first time a black and red flag was used?

42.   Chauvelon, "Base Marxiste, Forme Soviétique," *le Soviet*, 30 April 1920. On councilism, see: Denis Authier and Jean Barrot, *La Gauche Communiste en Allemagne 1918–1921* (Paris: Payot, 1976); Richard Gombin, *The Origins of Modern Leftism* (Harmondsworth: Penguin, 1975); Kriegel, *Origines* (1964), vol.I, pp.282–6.

43.   Léon Prouvost, "Vers le Communisme," *l'Internationale*, 28 August 1919.

44.   *L'Internationale Communiste*, 1 October 1919.

45.   See the manifesto of the PC in *le Communiste* no.1 (25 October 1919).

46.   The Lorulot leaflet, "Qu'est-ce que le Soviet?," was distributed in Bordeaux, at a meeting of the mechanics' union, just before the May Day demonstration of 1919. BB18/6465. Hanot's pamphlet, "Soviet ou Parlement?", was also published in 1919 (Paris: Imprimerie "La Productrice"). For an example taken from the press, see also Lacoste's violent attack on the SFIO in "Elections ou Grève générale," *le Communiste*, 8 November 1919.

47.   Manifesto of the PC, *le Communiste*, 25 October 1919.

48.   Ibid.

49.   Lipin, "L'Essence du Régime Soviétique," *l'Internationale*, 1 December 1919.

50.   Léon Prouvost, "Vers le Communisme," *l'Internationale*, 28 August 1919.

51.   See "Déclaration" and "Pourquoi ce journal? Pourquoi ce titre?" in *le Soviet* no.1 (21 March 1920). The latter article was written by Chauvelon, and was responsible for the prosecution of Emile Giraud (the paper's administrator and therefore legally responsible)

for "provocation to theft and pillage, provocation to murder, provocation of members of the armed forces to disobey orders." See report of 1 April 1920, BB18/6465. The authorities also considered banning the FCS almost as soon as it was created. See report of 21 July 1920, BB18/6465.

52. *Le Soviet*, 20 June 1920.

53. Ibid. See also an article by Lebourg in *le Soviet*, 25 July 1920.

54. *Le Soviet*, 20 June 1920.

55. Ibid.

56. Ibid.

57. Ibid.

58. "Régime Direct. Soviétisme et Bolchevisme," *le Soviet*, 26 September 1920. According to this article, Hermitte had written a book in 1901 entitled: *Horizons, études sur les idées qui préparent l'avènement d'un régime nouveau*; and had stood in the general election of 1910 in the 13th arrondissement, on a "sovietist" ticket.

59. See Jacques Julliard, *Fernand Pelloutier et les origines du syndicalisme d'action directe* (Paris: Editions du Seuil, 1971). The organization of the early CGT involved a "horizontal" structure and a "vertical" one, both organized federally. The vertical was represented by the unions of a particular industry, federated nationally. The horizontal was represented by the different unions of a particular locality, coming together in the Bourse du Travail and their local and regional "unions," and being concerned at a local level with the co-ordination of production and distribution to match needs and capacities. The vertical and horizontal would be confederated, with overall national co-ordination. These structures were envisaged as both revolutionist organizations under capitalism, and as the basic structures of the post-revolutionary society.

60. "Soviétisme ou Parlementarisme—Il faut choisir," *le Soviet*, 9 May 1920.

61. *Le Soviet*, 9 May 1920. The article was reproduced from Genold's own paper *Notre Voix* (5 March 1920), copies of which have proved impossible to unearth.

62. Henri Ner—or Han Ryner as he liked to call himself—was a writer of rather moral, philosophical stories. He was looked up to by many on the individualist/pacifist wing of the movement.

63. Emile Giraud, "A Propos d'un livre de Lénine," *le Soviet*, 15 January 1921. Giraud was here reviewing Lenin's *La Maladie Infantile du Communisme*, which had just been published in France by the Committee of the Third International.

64. See for example Albert Pilot's "Appel aux anarchistes," *le Soviet*, 1 November 1919; or Arthur Bouchez, "Aux Libertaires Communistes," *le Soviet*, 7 December 1919. These were not attacks on the anarchists, but on traditional anarchist ideology, and were usually accompanied by appeals to the anarchist-communists and anarchist-syndicalists to join with the FCS.

65. Alex, "La Dictature du Prolétariat," *le Soviet*, 29 August 1920.

66. *Le Soviet*, 20 September 1920. Grave was to recognize this himself when writing his autobiography, published in 1930. Describing the helplessness of the anarchists in 1914—a moment full of revolutionary potential, he thought— Grave admitted: "It is true that, although we had talked a great deal about revolution, we had never realized what a revolution actually is, nor what forms a revolution can take." Grave, *Quarante ans*, p.475.

67. Alex, "La Dictature du Prolétariat," *le Soviet*, 29 August 1920.

68. According to Giraud, a recent public meeting by Faure and Pioch at which they had attacked the bolshevik dictatorship "created a rift between the communists and the

libertarians which I fear is insurmountable, and that is extremely regrettable." *Le Soviet*, 15 January 1921.

69.   *Le Soviet*, 26 September 1920.

70.   Alexandre Skirda, *Autonomie Individuelle et Force Collective. Les anarchistes et l'organisation de Proudhon à nos jours* (Paris: Alexandre Skirda, 1987), ch.14: "Le 'mirage du soviétisme' et la crise de l'anarchisme."

71.   The British syndicalist Tom Mann, for instance, wrote in the first post-war number of *la Vie ouvrière* that "bolshevism, spartakism, syndicalism had the same revolutionary meaning." Quoted by Pierre Monatte, *Trois Scissions Syndicales* (Paris: Les Editions Ouvrières, 1958), p.243.

72.   On sovietism as essentially anarchistic, see, for example, G. P. Maksimov, "The Soviet of Workers', Soldiers' and Peasants' Deputies," in Paul Avrich (ed.), *The Anarchists in the Russian Revolution* (London: Thames & Hudson, 1973), pp.102–6 [first published in 1918 in Russian]; & Pano Vassilev, *L'Idée des Soviets* (Fresnes-Antony: Editions du Groupe Fresnes-Antony de la Fédération Anarchiste, 1983) [first published in 1933 in Bulgarian]. See also Régis Gayraud, *La Grande mêlée des utopies. La Russie libertaire (1905–1921)* (Paris: Nautilus, 2001).

73.   Skirda, *Autonomie Individuelle et Force Collective*, p.155.

74.   Kriegel, *Origines* (1964), vol.I, pp.279–80.

75.   Quoted by Marcel Liebman, *Leninism under Lenin* (London: Merlin Press, 1975), p.261.

76.   Péricat, "Raconte nous tes Souvenirs," 7pp. TS (n.d.[1945]). Péricat's gloss: "I am — I confess — very proud of this declaration."

77.   Liebman, *Leninism*, p.396.

78.   Quoted in Liebman, *Leninism*, p.396. Rosmer played an important role in the nascent communist movement. He was a member of the Executive Committee of the International from 1920, and a leading member of the SFIC from 1922. Like Souvarine and Monatte, he would be expelled from the Party in 1924. He wrote about his experiences in Russia in *Moscou sons Lénine* (Paris: Maspéro, 1970), 2 vols. I am grateful to Ian Birchall for giving me a copy of a paper presented to the London Socialist Historians Group in 2000, "Alfred Rosmer and the RILU. The Sublation of Syndicalism."

79.   Mauricius, "En Souvenir d'Armando Borghi," "Fonds Mauricius," IFHS 14 AS 292B/II. Another file in the Mauricius archives (14 AS 291/27) contains a copy of *L'Etat et la révolution* published in Moscow in 1919 by the Executive Committee of the Comintern. It was republished many times in French: there were at least four other editions between the wars.

80.   *Le Soviet*, 15 January 1921. The letter was dated August 1920.

81.   Robert Wohl, *French Communism in the Making, 1914–1924* (Stanford: Stanford University Press, 1966), p.142.

82.   Péricat, "Un Parti Communiste en France: Un peu d'histoire," 25pp MS (June 1956), pp.1–2. "Archives Péricat," IFHS 14 AS 205(a)1. The first number of *le Communiste* (25 October 1919) pointed out that the party had no famous names, no influential personalities: "It is humble workers who are expressing their ways of thinking; and if it is not perfect, if syntax is not always respected, we at least feel that these comrades are saying what they think …!"

83.   Report dated August 1920, F7/13090.

84.   Kriegel, *Origines* (1964), vol.I. Hopes were certainly high among activists. The police intercepted a letter to Péricat from Mathieu Peyron, treasurer of the Syndicat des

Métallurgistes de Firminy et Unieux (Loire) expressing pleasure at the success of the May Day demonstration and adding: "the moment is close for we know what we want, the masses are with us, we only need to give the signal." See AN F7/13061. And Kriegel cites the case of a railway worker who, during the strikes of June 1919, "believing that the revolution was imminent, took the place of the foreman in the workshop and declared to his workmates that there would be no more bosses." Kriegel, *Origines* (1964), vol.I, p.278, note 1.

85.   Kriegel, *Origines* (1964), vol.I, p.303.

86.   See "Correspondence des Pacifistes de Juillet 1917 à Avril 1918," especially reports dated 16 July, 31 August and 3 December 1917, PP BA1562. See also Maitron vol.II, p.16.

87.   See two police reports, one entitled "Sur la propagande bolcheviste en France" (24 Angust 1920), another untitled and undated, produced by the Sûreté. F7/13090.

88.   *L'Internationale*, 31 May 1919. No figures were given for a similar *fête* held on 18 May in Paris.

89.   *L'Internationale*, 12 July 1919.

90.   *Le Communiste*, 8 August 1920. Kriegel, *Origines* (1964), vol.I, p.287. Kriegel gives no source reference.

91.   BL/56/114, BB18/6465.

92.   "Sur la propagande bolcheviste en France" (24 August 1920), F7/13090. For comparison's sake, the same report also gave the following figures: *l'Humanité* (SFIO), 100,000; *Bulletin communiste* (Committee of the Third International), 5,000; *la Vie Ouvrière* (revolutionary syndicalist minority in the CGT), 20,000.

93.   "Soviets existant en France au 13 Juillet 1920," 15pp. TS, p.11. F7/13091.

94.   "Le Parti Communiste" (January 1920), BB18/6465.

95.   Kriegel, *Origines* (1964), vol.I, p.293.

96.   "Le Parti Communiste et la Fédération Communiste des Soviets" (4 April 1920), 6pp. TS, p.5. BB18/6465.

97.   F7/13091.

98.   BB18/6465. The report also tells us that, according to Sigrand, some soviets existed in the army and navy.

99.   "Le Parti Communiste et la Fédération Communiste des Soviets" (4 April 1920), 6pp. TS. BB18/6465.

100.   "Sur la propagande bolcheviste en France" (24 August 1920), F7/13090.

101.   Undated report [Between March and July 1921], 14pp. TS. F7/13090.

102.   Kriegel, *Aux origines* (1964), vol.I, pp.275–353.

103.   See Kathryn E. Amdur, *Syndicalist Legacy: Trade Unions and Politics in Two French Cities in the Era of World War I* (Urbana & Chicago: University of Illinois Press, 1986), pp.154–6, where she analyses the itinerary of some of the locally influential "anarcho-bolshevist" groups in the Loire and Haute-Vienne. See also Colson, *Anarcho-syndicalisme*, pp.86–7, on the rôle played by Saint-Etienne anarchists alongside left Socialists in the "Amis de *la Vague*" groups and with councilists in La Ruche communiste.

104.   Pierre Ansart, preface to Colson, *Anarcho-syndicalisme*, p.6. See also Colson's ch.2: "Le mythe de l'anarcho-syndicalisme."

105.   Kriegel, *Origines* (1964), vol.I, p.306.

4

The Mainstream: From Revision to Reaffirmation of Anarchism

The anarchists no longer know where they are and can be found far from each other in various hybrid clans.

Boris Souvarine[1]

On the one hand, those who believe there is nothing in need of revision in our doctrine or our philosophy. On the other, those who believe the opposite, that is to say, the anarchist neo-communists(?) who have become apologists for dictatorship.

Pierre Le Meillour[2]

THE RE-ESTABLISHMENT OF ANARCHIST COMMUNISM

If the PC and FCS both, in the stance they adopted with regard to the Russian revolution, attracted much anarchist support, they by no means attracted all the anarchists, and anarchist opinion also evolved. Despite widespread early enthusiasm and support for the Russian revolution, by July 1920 the Anarchist Federation (i.e. the mainstream anarchist communists grouped primarily around *le Libertaire*) seemed to a leading member of the PC to be "fiercely intransigent" on the question of "dictatorship."[3] This had quickly become one of the major questions coming between the Russian bolsheviks and wholehearted anarchist support in France. Indeed, one of the factors that contributed to the demise of the sovietist groups was the reestablishment of the straight anarchist press and organizations, which offered yet another centre around which to organize. *Le Libertaire*, especially, became a rival, and Péricat was not pleased by its reappearance. Although it happily carried notices for *l'Internationale* and its events, it also organized an outing to the countryside for the same day in May 1919 that *l'Internationale* had chosen for its fête.[4] According to the anarchist syndicalist Henri Sirolle, who was to be a part of the French delegation to the founding congress of the Profintern in Moscow in July 1921: "Rivalries have sprung up between the different tendencies and ... jealousy reigns between groupings which ought to be working together. Thus *le Libertaire* is jealous of *L'Internationale*. If this situation carries on ... I shall end up becoming an individualist."[5]

ANARCHIST COMMUNISM AND SYNDICALISM IN THE NORTH: *GERMINAL*

But *le Libertaire* was not the only rival. The mainstream of post-war anarchist communism was represented primarily, it is true, by *le Libertaire*, weekly organ of the FA (or, from 1920, the UA or Anarchist Union) and based in Paris; but also by *Germinal*, a regional weekly based in Amiens, around which was to be created a Fédération communiste libertaire du Nord (FCL, Libertarian Communist Federation). *Le Libertaire* reappeared in January 1919 and the FA was "definitively constituted" in August of that year, though it would not hold its first post-war congress until November 1920.[6] *Germinal* reappeared in August 1919, and the founding congress of the FCL was held in September 1920.

Like *le Libertaire*, *Germinal* was much stronger after the war than before. *Le Libertaire* was in a stronger position within the movement partly because it was no longer rivalled on a national level by *les Temps nouveaux*. The individualist André Lorulot, in an assessment in 1922 of the state of the movement nationally, was even to describe *le Libertaire* simply as "the only French anarchist periodical," and he estimated its print-run at that time to be 20,000.[7] Two years before, the Sûreté had put it at 8,000.[8] *Germinal* had, before the war, appeared only very infrequently. From its reappearance in 1919 until 1933 it appeared regularly every week. From October 1920 two editions were produced, one for the Somme, one for the Oise; from July 1925 a further edition was produced for the Nord-Pas-de-Calais. It therefore had very strong local links and syndicalist connections, especially in Amiens, where it also ran a bookshop. *Germinal*'s director was Georges Bastien, secretary of the Textiles Union in Amiens.[9] Another important contributor was François Rose of the local Building-workers' Union. Of the funds raised to launch the paper, nearly half were supplied by local syndicalist organizations.[10] In the first year or so, its total readership initially hovered between 3,500 and 5,500, reaching a peak of 8,500 during the strikes of the spring of 1920.[11] But if the paper's own accounts are to be believed, these figures rocketed after the paper spread to cover the neighbouring *département*, and readership in 1921–22 was around 15,000–17,000 (including 1,500–2,500 subscribers).

Suffice it to say that *Germinal* was a paper with very strong roots in the local and regional organized working class, and this no doubt had to do with the fact, that for at least a year or two, *Germinal* was at the heart of the strong, unifying groundswell of support for the Russian revolution. Unity was the watchword of the period, and the co-operation between anarchists, socialists and syndicalists already familiar to us in Paris (around *Ce qu'il faut dire* and *l'Avenir international, l'Internationale* and *le Communiste*) was characteristic also of the north. This included propaganda through public meetings and the press, and also the setting up of unitary groups. In October 1919, with another local syndicalist and with Pierre Monatte, François Rose of the *Germinal* group took part in a public meeting in favour of the Russian revolution.[12] The following year, the paper encouraged all its local readers to attend a "Grand Reunion in support of the Russian Revolution and of the Rights of Peoples."[13] The paper published the Clarté group's manifesto, "For the Russian Revolution," which insisted not only that Russia was "boldly and completely socialist," but also that "if you remain indifferent, you are a party to counter-revolution."[14] On the same page as the Clarté manifesto, *Germinal* also printed the manifesto of the FA, which was also pro-Russian.[15] On 15 October 1919 an article appeared announcing the existence in Amiens of a "Revolutionary Communist Group."[16] In February 1920 there was a call in the pages of *Germinal* for a "Revolutionary Congress" to re-launch a revolutionary front which had existed in the Somme before the war, the appeal being directed at "all revolutionary comrades, libertarians, communists, syndicalists, socialists, all who are disgusted with the antics of careerist politicians."[17] We know there was a "soviet" belonging to the FCS in the Oise, but *Germinal* carried only one notice for the group.[18] Similarly, a notice appeared advertising the existence of the "Propaganda Bureau of the Workers' Trade Union Councils."[19]

THE FCL AND OPPOSITION TO BOLSHEVISM

It is difficult to know exactly what the activities of such groups were, and to what extent they overlapped with each other and with existing socialist, syndicalist and anarchist organizations. Perhaps the culmination of all these efforts was the "Revolutionary Congress" held in Amiens on 15 August 1920, which decided on the formation of a "Revolutionary Communist Federation" "bringing together all the elements of the avant-garde."[20] That preliminary meeting led to the Amiens congress of 19 September 1920, which paradoxically was to mark a turning-point in terms of the *Germinal* group's attitude to the bolsheviks, and hence in terms of revolutionary unity in the north of France. It was at that congress that "we parted company with the authoritarian elements and founded the Libertarian Communist Federation of the Nord region."[21] As the new Federation's constitution put it: "All organizations are in a state of complete confusion. Because of this confusion, many militants no longer know which path to follow and the hour of action may be lost."[22] The Federation reaffirmed the principles of anarchist communism, and made it clear that it had no truck with the importation of bolshevism into France: "Tomorrow, the constitution of a State, of a government—whether it is called dictatorship of the proletariat or given some other label—would simply be the pretext for the installation of a new aristocracy, a new authority, a new form of exploitation and a new class of parasites."[23]

The Federation can nevertheless be situated in the same lineage as the sovietists in the sense that it was unequivocal on the need for tactical as well as strategic unity, and was concerned that all members should accept the organization's "line of conduct." Even the fact that there was a fixed subscription rate (of 1 franc per member per month) was significant in an anarchist organization: the level of subscriptions in the UA were decided by each member group.[24] Also like the sovietists, *Germinal* had identified strongly with the Russian revolution. For Rose, the Third International was "the Great International we have so often praised," "the only hope we had after the war."[25] Bastien, in January 1920, went so far as to write: "anyone who rejects robbery and invasion is a bolshevik."[26] Bastien's interpretation of the revolution was the libertarian one common to many on the left: the revolution and the soviet system were spontaneous and popular; the bolsheviks gained power and initiated a more centralized system only because it was necessitated by foreign intervention and the civil war; despite all the difficulties, bolshevism had been able to build in Russia "a regime which, although not the ideal of which we used to dream, nevertheless represents a formidable transformation of the foundations of society, entirely to the advantage of the class of producers. Bolshevism, class struggle, the dictatorship of the proletariat, these are all just pure collectivism, socialism in direct action."[27] Even as late as August 1920, in an article entitled "Vive la Russie!," Bastien had nothing but praise for the victorious Red Army: "The Red Army defends the gains of the revolution. The Red Army defends the happiness of a whole people, the elderly, women and children. The Red Army is a popular army, inspired by the conviction of the justness of its cause and by faith in the human ideal."[28] This is significant because of the anarchists' antimilitarism, and it was a question that would receive much more attention during the Spanish civil war. In April 1919 the Ukrainian anarchists were already declaring their opposition to the structure of the Red Army: that is, a centralized, hierarchically structured army, as opposed to a revolutionary workers' militia, voluntary, elected and, to some extent, decentralized.[29] According to Péricat, the creation of the Red Army was the first step in the alienation of the French anarchists from support of the bolsheviks.[30]

It has been claimed that it was thanks to a common front of anarchists and communists, originating in the campaign in favour of the Black Sea Mutineers, that Bastien was, in April 1921, elected assistant secretary of the Departmental Union.[31] This seems quite plausible, but it is further claimed that Bastien was moving towards the SFIC and that this evolution was "brutally interrupted by the news of the events at Cronstadt."[32] On the evidence of what Bastien wrote in *Germinal*, this would seem something of an exaggeration. Bastien insisted in November 1919: "We are not Bolsheviks. But we will fight for them because for us they represent sincere, honest, courageous action."[33] And the founding congress of the FCL, with its reaffirmation of anarchist-communist principles and its explicit rejection of the dictatorship of the proletariat, took place six months before the Kronstadt uprising. A month after that congress, Bastien wrote for *Germinal* the first of many articles to appear in the paper making clear the group's rejection not just of bolshevism in Russia, but of the pro-bolshevik camp within French socialism. Bastien expressed his surprise that so many comrades had been taken in by the idea that a dictatorship was necessary; he repeated his belief that the revolution had initially been "a spontaneous uprising of the masses," and had not survived simply because of the dictatorship of a minority. Bolshevism, for Bastien, had now become an anti-working-class ideology, since it denied the capacity of the working class to organize itself.[34] François Rose seems to have undergone an equally rapid evolution away from bolshevism, both French and Russian. Just a month before the Tours congress, he wrote:

> It is just when the ideas and the organizations of the avantgarde need to reaffirm themselves forcefully and clearly and win the confidence of the masses, that the principal militants of the Socialist Party are getting bogged down in the swamp of affiliation to the Third International, that the entire party has its eyes turned to Moscow, like believers facing their god. They do not seem to realize what is going on in our country and are allowing the reactionary forces to organize and gain ground.[35]

So the break would seem to have taken place in the autumn of 1920, not in the spring of 1921. This is interesting to the extent that it suggests the alienation of the anarchists around *Germinal* from the nascent international communist movement was not caused initially by developments in Russia. Criticisms of the bolsheviks' excessive authoritarianism had not stopped the anarchists from maintaining their support for the Russian regime.[36] There is nothing in the pages of *Germinal* to suggest that its militants knew much at all about the repression of anarchists and socialist-revolutionaries in Russia. The Cheka's attacks on the Russian anarchists had, after all, begun in April 1918, and it was in September 1919 that some anarchists had joined with socialist-revolutionaries to bomb the bolsheviks' Moscow headquarters. By the end of 1920, the Cheka had swept the entire country in its efforts to destroy anarchist opposition to the regime. *Germinal* seems to have paid little attention to these developments—partly no doubt because of the shortage of reliable information at that time.

On the other hand, *Germinal's* comment on the French socialists became increasingly hostile from about the middle of 1920. This coincides with the gradual winning over to the Third International of increasing numbers of centrists within the party. The feeling emerges from a reading of *Germinal* that the anarchists had felt the Russian revolution to be their revolution: they had been the first to offer their wholehearted support to Lenin and the bolsheviks, and now the French socialists—"these revolutionaries who discovered the Russian revolution a year after the anarchists"[37]—were taking it over and perverting it. So perhaps the anarchist syndicalists around *Germinal*—apparently so favourable towards the bolsheviks and to attempts to form a unitary communist organization—were in fact repelled more by the immediate prospect of belonging to the same camp as a parliamentary socialist like Cachin, than by the more distant and abstract problem of having to square support of a dictatorship with anarchist principles.

THE ANARCHIST UNION AND *LE LIBERTAIRE*

The same can be said to some extent of *le Libertaire*, and a similar, though not identical, chronology can be observed in the FA/UA. Before the Paris congress of November 1920 the organizing committee circulated a list of questions for consideration. The first item on the list was the organization of the FA. The second was anarchist theory: "Against confusionism; reaffirmation and not revision of our doctrine; against the State, against Authority, for Federalism."[38] The third was the question of what attitude to adopt with regard to other groups and parties: "The need for an intransigent and consistently anarchist attitude in accordance with our philosophy." The preamble to the resolutions of the congress defined it as only the first step in the reorganization of the anarchist movement, and referred darkly to "certain individual deviations from anarchist action."[39] The FA congress played the same rôle as the founding congress of the FCL in the north. Whilst granting that the Russian revolution had instituted new social forms and had, at least in its origins, been permeated by the principles of anarchist communism, on the whole it nevertheless perpetuated "the faults inherent in all States":[40] "The development of authority in the form of the dictatorship of the proletariat and the hold which words have had on the inadequately prepared minds of the people, oblige the anarchists, with the sole aim of putting an end to any confusion, to reiterate their doctrine."[41]

The Russian revolution, it was claimed, had conformed to none of the "conditions of marxist dogma," and therefore "marxist doctrine ... has been absolutely proved wrong by the facts." The congress also reaffirmed that political parties were by their nature authoritarian, and therefore to be opposed by anarchists. The congress specified how the Federation would be organized, and strongly recommended working in the labour movement: "Without wishing to oblige anyone to join a union, the anarchists envisage fully supporting the task of proletarian emancipation, which can be accomplished on condition that it is inspired by an idea of social transformation clearly opposed to authoritarian and centralist systems. In the unions, the anarchists will have no greater priority than arousing the spirit of revolt."[42] So the main site of struggle, according to the newly created UA, was to be the syndicalist movement; and the two main aims within the syndicalist movement were to be to combat authoritarianism and to foster the revolutionary spirit.

Thus, the same turning-point can be seen in the FA/UA as in the *Germinal* group: after a period of "revision" or of "confusion," the FCL and the UA founding congresses, in September and November 1920, put an end to uncritical support for bolshevism and put a damper on comradely feelings towards non-anarchist revolutionaries. The *Germinal* group's change of heart seems to have been relatively sudden: they seem to have maintained their favourable attitude towards both bolshevism and bolshevism's supporters in France until quite late into 1920. *Le Libertaire*'s honeymoon with bolshevism only really lasted four months or so. The creation of the PC in May 1919 produced both favourable and unfavourable reactions in the ranks of the FA, with some militants like Bontemps and Mualdès being members of both simultaneously. But, in the summer of 1919, the FA as a whole began to distance itself from bolshevism, from the PC and from the SFIO, and by September 1920 the great majority were hostile, even though maintaining their defence of the Russian revolution against those on the right. The difference between the *le Libertaire* and *Germinal* groups perhaps had to do with *Germinal*'s very deep roots in the local and regional CGT. The daily activities of many *Germinal* activists and supporters necessitated working together with people of different political opinions. It is perhaps significant that *Germinal* was initially sub-titled "*Journal du Peuple*," and only felt a need to nail its anarchist colours to the mast, changing that sub-title to "*Organe communiste libertaire*," in October 1920. For the *Libertaire* group, which put to the fore the action of the FA as a specifically anarchist organization, with specifically anarchist methods and solutions, the emphasis was different—even if the labour movement was seen as a prime site for its activities. With this in mind, let us look at developments within the FA in more detail.

Some of the articles that appeared in *le Libertaire* early in 1919 were comparable in their enthusiasm and lyricism to those printed by *Ce qu'il faut dire* in late 1917—clearly opinions had not changed that much in over a year. The Russian revolution was "this revivifying wind … sweeping away at one go the privileges acquired over centuries of plundering."[43] It was the Russian revolution—not Wilson, not Clemenceau, not the allied victories—which had made the armistice possible.[44] And *le Libertaire* welcomed the spread of "sovietism" to Hungary, Bavaria and. … France:

> Péricat knows very well that he is satisfying the greatest desire of those who are tired of a unity which has become more and more problematic. He also knows that it is impossible, for such a radical task as the Social Revolution, to have anything to do with militants whose record has consisted entirely of loitering in the waiting rooms of ministerial antechambers. And he understands that international working-class solidarity demands, for the triumph of the common cause, the grouping into a single bloc of the honest and resolute forces of the Universal Revolution. Bravo, Péricat! Take courage! Bolshevism is on the march.[45]

But apart from the public meetings being held by Sébastien Faure as late as December 1919—which remained very favourable, if not entirely uncritical towards the Russian revolutionaries[46]—and the occasional optimistic article by Dr. Madeleine Pelletier on the situation of women and children in revolutionary Russia,[47] the debate was soon transformed into a fairly abstract one of doctrine (revolving around the dictatorship of the proletariat), and into a more immediate tactical one (regarding the desirability or otherwise of co-operating with non-anarchists).

THE UA'S CRITIQUE OF BOLSHEVISM

Reimeringer was one of those contributors to the UA's weekly organ, *le Libertaire* who believed that bolshevism was "a socially viable régime."[48] Dolcino argued that anarchism was not "an immutable dogma"; that it was, on the contrary, "a doctrine of life"; and that "there has been the Russian revolution and the lessons that are to be drawn from it mean more than theories."[49] His basic argument was that, given the lack of consciousness of the masses, given the opposition of the middle classes (*classes moyennes*) as well as of the bourgeoisie, and given the likelihood of foreign intervention, the leadership of a politically conscious revolutionary minority and the installation of some kind of dictatorship would in the early stages of a revolution be inevitable: "To allow the different counter-revolutionary currents to act with impunity at such a time would without doubt mean the collapse of the revolution and the destruction of its conquests."[50] To adopt such a stance was not, according to Dolcino, to abandon anarchism. It was merely to accept the unavoidability of a period of transition from capitalism to pure, anarchistic communism: "the unavoidable stage of authoritarian socialism"[51]: "Where significant minorities urge the masses on in an irresistible, egalitarian movement, the dictatorship will not take the form of a bloody terrorism. We see it rather as a strict control exercized by the workers over production and distribution until such time as scarcity is a thing of the past and mentalities have evolved sufficiently for the full application of the libertarian formula: To each according to their needs."[52]

Others made more effort to emphasize the popular and mass nature of the "dictatorship" — "that of the great majority."[53] R. Caillaux, a member of the PC, emphasized in the pages of *le Libertaire* that the PC aimed for a federal economic system, and for a dictatorship of the proletariat "from below": "For we believe that the ruling classes will never allow themselves to be expropriated without resistance, and that the fact of being a revolutionary inevitably, logically implies the idea that we want to impose on or dictate to our masters, the dictators of today, that we no longer want to be slaves and pariahs, but free men."[54] Barday was even convinced there was no significant ideological difference between the FA and the PC, "other than the title."[55]

The arguments, in short, were the well-rehearsed ones we have already examined: that anarchism's pure anti-authoritarianism with its outright refusal to countenance any kind of post-revolutionary transitional period had been proved idyllic by the experience of the Russian revolution. Several factors were adduced to show that the exercize of authority would be necessary in a revolution: the backwardness of the masses; the reactionary nature of the petty bourgeoisie as well as of the ruling classes; the probability of foreign military and economic intervention. Thus bolshevism was not in fact to be criticized, but lauded. Attempts to establish a communist party in France under the auspices of the bolshevik regime were to be actively encouraged; especially so since the major difference separating anarchist and non-anarchist revolutionaries—the question of authority—had been blurred to such an extent that organizational unity with socialists and syndicalists no longer presented any real problem. In effect, the specificity of anarchism as a revolutionary doctrine distinct from others was being denied.

This point of view was held by a very significant minority of contributors to *le Libertaire*, but the majority very quickly began to reassert themselves. Rhillon was quick to point out the rôle in the Russian revolution of anarchists and revolutionary socialists other than the bolsheviks: "Indeed we would be justified in arguing that it was thanks to their contribution, thanks to the libertarian economic programme that the Revolution was able to function."[56] Rhillon once again put forward the view that Lenin had only been able to gain power by appropriating anarchist methods and anarchist slogans, and that once in a sufficiently powerful position, both the slogans and the allies were unscrupulously dropped: "It was the authoritarian hijack of a libertarian Revolution. The masses rose up with the cry of 'Socialization!' The bolsheviks applied nationalization. The workers and peasants were favourable to federalist ideas, to organization from the bottom up, the bolsheviks immediately instituted a heavy and extremely centralized bureaucracy. The original Sovietism was purely and simply the application of the federalist idea. The bolsheviks perverted its meaning and its spirit." Rhillon's was an unforgiving picture of a libertarian revolution being knowingly and deliberately perverted by megalomaniac authoritarians. Unfortunately, he went on, many in the west had been taken in because of the civil war with the Whites: "The counter-revolutionary threat of Denikin and the Kolchaks did Lenin a great service. It was this which enabled him to pose as the incarnation of the revolutionary resistance of the Russian people."

The reassertion of the specificity of anarchism and of the dangers of centralization and authoritarianism also brought to the fore a profound mistrust of "state socialists," a fear of being used and absorbed. The Third International and the PC were therefore given short shrift. In June 1919, when the PC and the Committee of the Third International had just announced their membership of the Moscow International, Content called for the creation of an Anarchist International.[57] The onslaught against the PC was led by E. Haussard, Pierre Le Meillour and François. In a long article outlining the experience of the war and the post-war crisis—"a situation which many militants judge to be revolutionary"—François explained why many anarchists saw unification with non-anarchists as necessary: because "the anarchists are still too few and above all too disorganized to take the place they merit."[58] Whilst not denying the good intentions of others associated with the Third International, François thought that what they and the anarchists had in common was enough for unity "in certain limited conditions and for a short-term purpose," but not enough for a common programme: "For let us not forget that in order to act effectively, it is necessary to be united by identical conceptions and principles, and such is not the case here." The CRRI was, he insisted, proof of this truth, that to try to unify would only make matters worse, and would make the disagreements more visible to outsiders.[59] Besides, he claimed, it was always the most "advanced" elements within any such alliance (i.e. the anarchists) who had to compromise on their principles and programme. E. Haussard made the same point. For him, there was a clear difference between authoritarian and anti-authoritarian communists, and no amount of re-defining the word "dictatorship" would alter that fact: "Dictatorship implies command, authority; authority implies laws; laws imply gendarmes, prisons, etc, in other words quite the opposite of anarchism. And please let us hear no more about the rights of the majority, an anti-anarchist notion if ever there was one."[60] Thus for Le Meillour the communists ought to start their own party by themselves.[61]

It is interesting to note that even in July 1919, Le Meillour was already convinced that the Third International would eventually welcome those who had voted the war credits.[62] There was a general suspicion of the relations between the new International and the SFIO; a fear that the SFIO minority was playing the role of Trojan horse and that it would enable the rehabilitation—in the revolutionaries' eyes—of many socialists generally regarded on the far left as at best reformist and at worst reactionary and nationalistic. It was suggested that bolshevism was now a fashion, a useful political bandwagon: "Workers, beware of the schemers who under the pretence of *bolshevism* are preparing to return, at your expense, to their profitable electoral dealings! ... Who does not claim to be a bolshevik to hoodwink the masses? The *député* Longuet and *le Populaire* are bolshevik. The *député* Cachin and *l'Humanité* are bolshevik. The *député* Brizon and *la Vague* are bolshevik."[63]

Segond Casteu was equally cynical about "our professional politicians." According to him they were bound soon to move towards the Third International, like rats leaving a sinking ship, since "the old ship of social-democracy is making water": "Do not forget that their profession is politics. That says it all. Sooner or later, they will land on their feet, by which I mean that they will jump on the brand new ship which is communism, just as soon as it gets a little wind in its sails."[64] Casteu also pointed out that anarchists too often devoted themselves to other people's projects, and were present everywhere. … except in the FA. There was clearly a great deal of concern among anarchists about the dilemma this presented, since co-operative campaigns like that against intervention in Russia and for an amnesty for the mutineers—campaigns in which the anarchists played an important part[65]—meant that the anarchist message was lost:

> Once again the workers of France who read in the papers that a joint meeting was addressed, at the Paris Circus, by Le Meillour, Péache, Sirolle, Cachin and Longuet, will never know what was said by Le Meillour, Péache and Sirolle. They will only know one thing: that our anarchist comrades quite happily go and make speeches in the company of the worst crooks. And the masses inevitably come to the conclusion that those crooks cannot therefore be as crooked as all that! That those supposed crooks must be OK after all! And that if those who accused them of being crooks really meant what they said then they would not share a platform with them. The moral: it is the antiparliamentarians who finish up looking like liars or jokers. It is a serious dilemma.[66]

And as with the *Germinal* group, such was the anarchists' dislike of socialists like Cachin, Longuet and Frossard, that when it became clear that Cachin was going to be accepted into the Third International, it was taken to be final proof of Lenin's treacherousness: "It is an axiomatic truth that power makes you stupid": "We know Cachin. It was Cachin who was the obliging, complacent and self-interested accessory to the government's lies and crimes during the four years of the war. It was Cachin, the ignoble charlatan, who declared himself a socialist at the same time as he voted the war credits destined to be used to combat the Bolsheviks!" And now Cachin "has the nerve to catechize the masses in the name of Lenin!"[67]

From September 1920, the FA was decidedly hostile towards all elements of the SFIO. Its analysis of the Russian revolution was that the experience confirmed the anarchist doctrine: the revolution had been popular and successful because it had been libertarian, now it was being perverted by authoritarianism. Not only that, but Lenin and the bolsheviks were now seen to be in cahoots with French politicians who were regarded by the anarchists as the worst, most dishonourable enemies of the working class. Nevertheless, although the Russian revolution was regarded as being by no means perfect, it still had to be protected against reaction: "We will refrain from criticizing too harshly the achievements of the Russian maximalists and from playing into the hands of those who are fearful for their lives of luxury and whose digestion is disturbed by talk of bolshevism."[68]

It is then quite clear that to a great extent the anarchists' attitude to bolshevism was influenced not only by developments within Russia, but also by the evolution of the SFIO between the Strasbourg and Tours congresses of February and December 1920; that is, their opinion of Lenin seems to have been very much influenced by Moscow's acceptance of the SFIO centre. It is of course also clear that the anarchists would be alienated by the concentration of power in Russia, by the increasingly repressive nature of the regime, and by what they saw as the loss of revolutionary impetus—all held to be further evidence of the correctness of their analysis, that a dictatorship was by its nature incapable of introducing socialism. The announcement of the New Economic Policy in 1921 was seen as the re-installation of capitalism, as a capitulation; and the recognition of the USSR by France in 1924 was seen as proof that the bolshevik regime was no longer a danger to international capital, that the bolshevik state had now been re-admitted to the club.[69]

NEWS FROM RUSSIA

Strong reaction was also provoked by the increasing repressiveness of bolshevism. Because of the very great difficulties at first with both post and travel between Russia and the west, it was only from about 1920 that more information of a reliable nature began to get through. Getting hold of news remained difficult, though, and access to it in the west was uneven. In *le Libertaire*, for example, there was to be no reasonably full account of the Kronstadt uprising of March 1921 before the following December;[70] and yet *les Temps nouveaux* published a fairly detailed analysis of its political significance, including the text of the Kronstadt manifesto, in their April–May edition.[71] Makhno was not even mentioned in *le Libertaire* until January 1920, and was described then as an "anarchist intellectual."[72] Maitron has already shown how ill-informed western anarchists were for a long time about the true nature of the makhnovchina: when Sirolle was at the founding congress of the Profintern in Moscow in the summer of 1921, he could deny that the makhnovchina had anything to do with anarchism.[73] Nevertheless, the flow of information was gradually improving, and by the time Makhno eventually made it as far as Paris in 1924, the French anarchist movement was reasonably well-informed about the reality both of Nestor Makhno and of the insurrectionary militia he had led.[74]

THE CAMPAIGN AGAINST POLITICAL REPRESSION IN RUSSIA

The French anarchists got their information from various sources: newspapers and official documents of the international communist movement; correspondence with anarchists still in Russia; Russian revolutionaries in exile in the west; French activists on visits to Russia.[75] As early as September 1920, le *Libertaire* printed a list of political prisoners who were being held in Moscow, and demanded from the "French bolsheviks" a formal confirmation or denial of the veracity of their information.[76] At about the same time, concern began to increase in the west about Kropotkin's health, and the bolsheviks' refusal to grant him and his daughter Sacha passports so Kropotkin could benefit from a warmer climate. Consequently, western anarchists began to raise money to buy the Kropotkin family food and clothes.[77] More or less organized campaigns were subsequently launched which raised money simultaneously for victims of the dreadful famine in Russia; for Russian revolutionaries—of whatever socialist current—who were now political prisoners under the bolshevik regime; and even, it would seem, for strikers in France. *Germinal* opened a donations list for victims of the famine in August 1921, a famine for which the blockade and military intervention were held primarily responsible.[78] In October of that year, *Germinal* announced the creation of an "Action Committee for Russia," which had already, despite its name, sent 300 francs to striking textile workers in the Nord, as well as a similar amount to the Russians.[79] *Le Libertaire*'s subscription list for relief of the famine had raised over 8,000 francs by the end of 1921.[80] And by the spring of 1922, the Russian Anarchist-Communist Federation's Black Cross began appealing for funds to help victims both of famine and of political repression in Russia.[81]

In fact, the campaign around revolutionaries—especially, though not exclusively, anarchists—imprisoned, exiled or executed by the bolshevik regime had, by late 1921, become a major part of the French anarchists' activities. And Russians living in exile in France played a major part in the developing campaign against bolshevism. The "Union of Russian Anarchist and Anarcho-Syndicalist Organizations" were the authors of an appeal, "To the World Proletariat," which appeared in *Germinal* in May 1922, and which took the form of a lengthy and detailed account of the repression of non-bolshevik revolutionaries in Russia.[82] In 1923, the IWMA's "Russian Anarcho-Syndicalist Defence Committee" launched a further appeal "For the struggle against reaction in Russia":

Do you not protest against fascism, against the executions by the English in South Africa, against reaction in Spain? Are you not moved by the fate of Max Holz and of Marty? Are you not engaged in a battle to save the life and freedom of Sacco? … And what of Russia? Why have you forgotten Russia? Do you really believe that over there among the thousands of exiled prisoners there are not some Saccos, some Vanzettis, some Cottins, some Max Holzes?[83]

A similar equation between political prisoners in Russia on the one hand, and in right-wing and so-called democratic regimes on the other, was made by the "Group for the Defence of Revolutionaries Imprisoned in Russia," created in January 1924 by French anarchists and syndicalists with the aim of co-ordinating a large scale campaign in the press and through public meetings.[84] It is indicative of the breadth of support for such action within the labour movement that of the 21 signatories, 12 were currently trade union representatives. We have some evidence that such campaigns did actually help in attaining the release of certain activists. Schapiro, for example, who had been given a passport to attend the syndicalist conference of October 1921 in Berlin, and then arrested on his return by the Cheka. His case was taken up in France by the CDS, in particular by its secretary Pierre Besnard and by Henri Totti, and Schapiro was expelled from Russia in the autumn of 1922.[85] Similarly, the interview with Trotsky which May Picqueray and Lucien Chevalier were granted in 1922 seems to have been not unconnected with the subsequent release from prison and sending into external exile of the two Russian anarchists Mollie Steimer and Senya Fleshin.[86]

The UA was even prepared to use the threat of violence against leading bolsheviks to persuade the Russian regime to cease its attacks on political adversaries on the left. The UA congress of November 1921, held at Lyon, resolved that "practical action" had to be taken in favour of the Russian anarchists, and passed the following resolution: "This practical action … could take the form of an ultimatum to the bolshevik government with the threat of reprisals against the person of the highest representatives of the bolshevik regime."[87] The same threat was contained in an open letter to the Profintern congress of 1921, printed in *le Libertaire* and *Germinal*.[88] I have found no evidence that this resolve was ever acted on. Indeed, when Mauricius tried to push the Berlin conference of October 1921 to consider effective means of bringing influence to bear, he did not get very far. Long and heated discussions apparently revealed "very clearly the differences of temperament and of character between the different nationalities."[89] A vague resolution was eventually adopted urging all anarchists to undertake "the necessary agitation in favour of our Russian friends."[90]

The French anarchists, then, launched themselves into a campaign against bolshevism, using the press, of course, and leaflets and public meetings. The FA, for example, organized a meeting on "The Anarchists and Dictatorship" in the CGT's premises in the rue Grange-aux-Belles in Paris in December 1920—a meeting for which they provided five of their best known speakers: Faure, Lecoin, Le Meillour, Veber, Sirolle and Boudoux.[91] Some of these militants seem to have given similar meetings for at least a year, and, as was often the case, the anarchists publicly invited their adversaries to attend and take part in a debate. Anarchists also often intervened at meetings organized by communists, in order to make their voice heard.[92] By 1922, the campaign included the publication by the UA's Librairie Sociale of short books such as *La Persécution des Anarchistes et des Syndicalistes révolutionnaires dans la Russie soviétique* (The Persecution of Anarchists and Revolutionary Syndicalists in Soviet Russia), translated by Voline and with an introduction by André Colomer.[93]

Mauricius' *Au Pays des Soviets* was published in 1922. *Neuf Mois d'Aventures*, his account of a visit to Russia that began in July 1920, when he left Paris with credentials provided by Péricat and the PC, and which ended in March 1921 in the Santé prison.[94] The experiences of people like Mauricius, the few French militants who had actually travelled fairly extensively in Russia and met a variety of people (rather than just official representatives), must have been as important to the French anarchist movement as the knowledge of exiled Russians. Mauricius certainly undertook an extensive speaking tour on his release from prison.[95]

THE LEPETIT, VERGEAT AND LEFEBVRE AFFAIR

Indeed, were it not for the importance attached to such first-hand accounts, it seems improbable that the tragic deaths of Lepetit, Vergeat, Toubine and Lefebvre would have given rise to the suspicions and rumours which further embittered relations between anarchists and communists in the 1920s. Bertho Lepetit and Marcel Vergeat—both anarchist syndicalists—and Lefebvre—a pro-bolshevik socialist—were delegates to the second congress of the Comintern in July 1920. Toubine was a Russian comrade who accompanied them as an interpreter. For reasons which remain unclear and controversial, they were obliged, unusually, to return to France *via* Murmansk and the Baltic, and died at sea in the autumn of 1920. The importance that this affair acquired resided in the fact that the impressions brought back by the dead men—respected militants—might have been important for the future ideological evolution of the CGT. There followed an unseemly and sordid quarrel between the two factions—one more or less in favour of links between syndicalism and bolshevism, the other wishing to retain total independence—as to whether or not the delegates had been impressed by what they had seen in Russia. Despite claims by Cachin (of the SFIC) and Michel Kneller (of the Labourers' Union) that Lepetit returned transformed from an interview with Lenin,[96] the evidence in fact suggests not only that Lepetit and Vergeat set off for home still firm in their anarchist convictions and very critical of many aspects of bolshevism, but also that even the marxist Lefebvre was unhappy about some of what he learned.[97] Letters which Lepetit had written to his partner and to his union, the Seine Labourers' Union, and that contained a detailed account of his experiences in Russia, were published in *le Libertaire* in December 1920 and January 1921.[98] Unpleasant things began to be rumoured.[99] There seemed to be no reason why they should have been more or less forced by the bolsheviks to take such an unusual and obviously perilous route, "whereas the converted and bought pilgrim Cachin was able, at the same time, to make the journey with other communist delegates unhindered and to return home in time to repeat to the congress delegates at Tours the lessons they had been taught in Moscow."[100]

Interestingly enough, though, a syndicalist who had spent six months in Russia and who had met Lepetit and Vergeat whilst over there was convinced there had been no deliberate delaying of the delegates' return (or worse): "I can hardly be suspected of bias towards the bolsheviks. But the truth which emerges from all the information I have been able to gather is that the Russian comrades did nothing to hinder their return to France. And one can say that the accusations reproduced in the bourgeois press on this matter constitute yet another of their slanders."[101]

THE VILKENS AFFAIR

The visit of that syndicalist to Russia, and especially the articles he wrote for *le Libertaire* on his return, gave rise to another "affair." Vilkens (or sometimes Wilkens, though his real name was only ever given as "G...") was actually Spanish, though he had settled in the north of France.[102] He was a carpenter and a founder member of the Building-workers' Union in Chauny (Aisne). In June 1920 he was mandated by the "Trade Union Committee for the Defence of Spanish Workers" in the Nord to go to Russia and report back on his impressions. Before he left, he was apparently a fervent marxist, and all his friends were supporters of the "bolshevik dictatorship." Indeed, the secretary of Vilkens' union, Marcel Bila, commented: "Before setting off for Russia, 'G.' was pro-bolshevik to such an extent that I did not think there was much point in his going. It was the experience of the Russian Revolution which showed him the error of his ways. His evidence is all the more valuable."[103]

When Vilkens came back, he wrote a long series of articles called "Six Months in Russia" for *le Libertaire* which were quite damning for the new regime. Vilkens claimed to have got to know not only bolshevik officials whilst in Russia, but to have lived in the homes of ordinary workers and peasants; to have been with the Red Army, both in the barracks and at the front; to have spoken to oppositional revolutionaries; and to have been in prison... The range and detail of his articles were indeed exceptional—the original intention was to publish them as a book—but the project was never realized.[104]

Vilkens had indeed been arrested by the Cheka, on 13 October 1920, and had not been released until 22 November. He had been denounced as suspect by a Spanish communist, though apparently for no other reason than his criticisms of the regime. However, early in 1921, back in France, the syndicalist Victor Godonnèche and the *Vie ouvrière* group denounced Vilkens and his information as suspect, and the accusations were only dropped at a meeting with the *Vie ouvrière* group after interventions from the German anarchist Augustin Souchy, and from Bila.[105] The *Vie ouvrière* group were in the end convinced only because it was clear the Russians themselves had released Vilkens and had given him papers with which to return to France.[106]

Nevertheless, despite this apparent clarification, the hostilities were to continue. At a congress of the CGT minority in October 1921, Monatte still did not want Vilkens to be allowed to speak, and when a majority voted in favour of Vilkens, Monatte left the room.[107] From about this time—especially after the founding of the Profintern, when Rosmer, Monatte and other syndicalists were to distance themselves from the anarchists and move closer to the communists—this kind of thing became more or less the norm. Disputes between the anarchist communists on the one hand and *l'Humanité*—regularly accused of biased and selective news coverage—and *la Vie ouvrière*—"that defamatory rag *par excellence*"[108]—became more and more frequent. Salomon Lozovsky, the head of the Profintern, complained to Monatte in May 1922: "The sad thing about this business is that the Communist Party has not dared to undertake a serious campaign against the insupportable fuss those muddle-headed anarchists are making in the pages of *le Libertaire* and their other papers."[109] This was not how the anarchists saw things from their side, though. Indeed, Renato Souvarine titled two articles of October 1921: "The Campaign of the Communist International"—one article concerning itself to a great extent with the publication by Victor Serge of Bakunin's confession to Tsar Nicholas I.[110]

If it is possible to point to a watershed for relations between the anarchists and the French supporters of bolshevism, then it would be 1924 and the shooting in the Maison des Syndicats, rue Grange-aux-Belles. At a meeting of syndicalists on 11 January, an argument between anarchists and communists led to a fight, and two apparently unarmed anarchists—Adrien Poncet and Clot—were shot dead.[111] There followed months of recriminations on both sides, and an official committee of enquiry composed equally of members of the majority and of the minority in the CGTU (Confédération générale du travail unitaire) concluded that the individual responsible was a CGTU official and Communist Party member. According to two Italian eye-witnesses, this event "profoundly saddened and made a great impression on the proletariat of all countries, for this sinister and ominous event was not the result of a fight between subversives and the police, but represented something tragically new in the history of the international proletariat. Brother had killed brother."[112]

Notes

1. "Brûlons les vieilles étiquettes!," *l'Avenir international*, January 1920.

2. "Le Congres Anarchiste." *le Libertaire*, 24 October 1920.

3. Emile Arnault, "Faisons le point," *le Communiste*, 25 July 1920: "The F.A. remains fiercely intransigent. No dictatorship, they say, not even provisionally." The first national organization founded at the Paris congress of 1913 had been called the Fédération communiste révolutionnaire anarchiste (or sometimes the Fédération communiste anarchiste révolutionnaire). During the war and immediately after it was usually referred to simply as the *Fédération anarchiste* (FA). It was only at the first post-war congress, held in Paris in 1920, that the organization became known as the Union des anarchistes de langue française, or Union anarchiste (UA). See Table 2, "Evolution of principal anarchist organizations, 1913–39."

4. Kriegel, *Origines* (1964), vol.I, p.296 and note 4. The walk in the countryside was a standard event in the anarchist movement, being a mixture between a social and a political event, accompanied as it often was by a discussion or a speech. This particular one, at Garches just outside Paris, attracted about a hundred anarchists.

5. Ibid. Sirolle, an electrician on the railways, was secretary of the "Anarchist Railway-workers Group" before the war; in 1920 he was to become secretary of the Railway-workers' Union (Paris-Invalides) and a member of the Federation bureau. See *DBMOF*, vol.15.

6.   *Le Libertaire*, 17 August 1919. Le Meillour was the FA's secretary, Haussard the treasurer. The Jeunesses Anarchistes (Anarchist Youth) was also founded in June 1919, and, with Léon Oupiter (known as Outer) as secretary, was very successful. See Report of 10 May 1922, F7/13054, for a detailed report on the history of the JA 1913–1922.

7.   André Lorulot, "Où en est l'anarchisme? — II: L'avenir du mouvement anarchiste," *le Réveil de l'Esclave*, 1 January 1922.

8.   Sûreté Générale report, "Sur les moyens de diffusion des idées bolchevistes en France" (n.d. [1920]). F7/13090.

9.   On Georges Bastien, see *DBMOF*, vol.18.

10.   These were the Railway-workers, Printers, Market-Traders, Metal-workers, Building-workers, Weavers, Clerical-workers, Tram-workers, Dyers and Leather-workers; the "Union" co-operative, the Bourse du Travail, the Departemental Union, and the "*Prévoyance ouvrière*" friendly society (Ailly-sur-Somme). *Germinal*, 10 January 1920. The paper's full accounts were published regularly.

11.   In the early years, however, sales were very localized: only about one-fifth or one-sixth were outside Amiens. See *Germinal*, 10 January 1920 and 24 July 1920.

12.   *Germinal*, 1 November 1919.

13.   *Germinal*, 13 November 1920.

14.   *Germinal*, 13 September 1919. Clarté was a movement of antimilitarist revolutionary intellectuals with a review of the same name, founded in 1916 by the novelist Henri Barbusse. Barbusse was to join the SFIC in 1923. The manifesto in question was signed by, among others, the anarchists Steinlen (the impressionist painter) and Laurent Tailhade (the poet).

15.   Of ways of imposing international peace, the manifesto said: "We know of only one, but it is not one which can be decreed from above. It is the means employed by the Russian people."

16.   *Germinal*, 18 October 1919.

17.   *Germinal*, 14 February 1920.

18.   *Germinal*, 7 March 1920. The notice for the Oise Revolutionary Group was placed by André Savanier (of Nogent): the group's secretary was Marcel Rigault (of Beauvais).

19.   *Germinal*, 20 March 1920. The Conseil d'Ouvriers Syndiqués (COS) were described in a leaflet put out by the Anti-Parliamentary Bureau/Propaganda by the Pamphlet Group in 1919: "Pour ne pas voter — Déclaration," in which soviets and the COS were contrasted with parliamentarianism: "The Councils teach workers in the capitalist society, under the leadership of technicians affiliated to the CGT, to face up to their revolutionary responsibilities. Having no dealings with the bosses, the rôle of the COS is in technical revolutionary education. They are organized in their workshops, shops, farms, communist schools, etc., etc., in order to ensure the effective organization of everyday life in the communist society after the workers' revolution .... For us antiparliamentarians, our ideal is *full communism according to the programme of the Anarchist Federation*." BN, *Tracts politiques de groupements anarchistes et libertaires, 1919–1939*.

20.   *Germinal*, 21 August 1920. The conference was organized by Lemarchand (of Amiens), and there were delegates present — "libertarians, communists, extremist syndicalists" — from Crillon, Beauvais and Creil (Oise); Aumale (Seine-Maritime); Le Vimeu and Corbie (Somme).

21.   See Segond Casteu's introduction to an article by Malatesta, "Ce qu'est la Dictature du Prolétariat" (taken from the Italian anarchist paper *Umanita Nova*), *Germinal*, 9 October 1920. S. Casteu was apparently fluent in Italian, because he often acted as a translator/interpreter for the movement. The September conference was attended by delegates from

Amiens, Corbie, Montdidier and Le Vimeu (Somme), Creil and Beauvais (Oise), and a few individuals. Lemarchand (Amiens) and Rigault (Beauvais) were the only two out of 24 delegates who favoured a "Russian-style" revolutionary government. The Federation elected Foulin as secretary. See G. Bastien, "Le Congrès d'Amiens," *le Libertaire*, 26 September 1920.

22. *Germinal*, 25 September 1920.

23. Ibid.

24. Ibid.; *Germinal*, 4 December 1920. *Le Libertaire*, 26 September and 28 November 1920.

25. *Germinal*, 20 September 1919.

26. *Germinal*, 24 January 1920.

27. *Germinal*, 1 November 1919.

28. *Germinal*, 14 August 1920.

29. Paul Avrich (ed.), *The Anarchists in the Russian Revolution* (London: Thames & Hudson, 1973), pp.125–7.

30. Péricat, "La Révolution Russe," 3pp. MS (n.d.), p.3. IFHS, Péricat Archive, 14AS205(a)1. According to this account, the anarchists (presumably the *le Libertaire* group) organized a big meeting in Paris, at which Faure criticized the bolsheviks for creating the Red Army, and Péricat spoke against him, justifying the Red Army as necessary to deal with the intervention.

31. *DBMOF*, vol.18.

32. The Kronstadt uprising (March 1921), according to the libertarian analysis, was an attempt to halt the bureaucratisation of the new regime and to force a return to the truly revolutionary, democratic sovietism of the early days. See Avrich (ed.), *The Anarchists in the Russian Revolution*, pp.156–68. Interestingly, the police files contain a report on a public meeting in Lorient (Morbihan) in 1927, at which Bastien was outlining, for an audience of about 200, the principles of anarchist communism. When criticized by communists in the audience, Bastien counter-attacked by talking about the authoritarianism of communism, and apparently reduced his opponents to silence by mentioning "the 30,000 murders at Cronstadt, where the flag of the Soviets did not shy away from making itself red with the blood of the workers." According to the police he was greatly applauded. Report of Commissariat de Police, Lorient, 15 June 1927. AN F7/13060.

33. *Germinal*, 1 November 1919.

34. *Germinal*, 20 November 1920.

35. *Germinal*, 27 November 1920. For Bastien, writing during the Tours congress, the Moscow International was "purely political." *Germinal*, 1 January 1921.

36. See for example Bourdon, "La Semaine," *Germinal*, 24 April 1920.

37. *Germinal*, 24 April 1920. See also Maurice Dommanget, "Les Masses sont-elles prêtes?" *Germinal*, 11 September 1920.

38. The circular was printed in *Germinal*, 6 November 1920.

39. *Germinal*, 4 December 1920.

40. *Le Libertaire*, 28 November 1920 and *Germinal*, 4 December 1920.

41. *Le Libertaire*, 28 November 1920.

42. Ibid.

43. *Le Libertaire*, 23 March 1919.

44. *Le Libertaire*, 30 March 1919.

45. *Le Libertaire*, 13 April 1919.

46.   See the report on one such meeting in *le Libertaire*, 28 December 1919: "Russia is illuminating the darkness and showing the way. Let this beacon never be extinguished! We must be at the sides of the Russian revolutionaries in their attempts to build the communist society, whatever criticisms we may have from the anarchist point of view. It is our duty to do everything we possibly can to put an end to intervention and the blockade."

47.   See for example "La Russie révolutionnaire et la Culture intellectuelle," *le Libertaire*, 31 August 1919. The feminist Pelletier was a member of the SFIO, but had close ties with the anarchists until the end of 1921 (see "Une réponse de Madeleine Pelletier," *le Libertaire*, 30 December 1921). When she visited Russia at the end of 1920 she was in fact very disappointed as far as the situation of women was concerned. See Claude Maignien's preface to Madeleine Pelletier, *L'éducation féministe des filles* (Paris: Editions Syros, 1978), pp.7–55.

48   *Le Libertaire*, 25 May 1919.

49.   *Le Libertaire*, 8 June 1919.

50.   Ibid.

51.   *Le Libertaire*, 25 May 1919.

52.   *Le Libertaire*, 8 June 1919.

53.   Barday in *le Libertaire*, 29 June 1919.

54.   *Le Libertaire*, 3 August 1919.

55.   *Le Libertaire*, 29 June 1919.

56.   *Le Libertaire*, 13 July 1919.

57.   *Le Libertaire*, 1 June 1919.

58.   *Le Libertaire*, 29 June 1919.

59.   Content, too, stressed the danger of differences being increased by a false unity "to the greater benefit of reaction, which will enjoy watching the revolutionaries tear each other apart." *Le Libertaire*, 3 August 1919.

60.   *Le Libertaire*, 15 June and 13 July 1919. A police report of 22 April 1919 (F7/13061) represents Haussard as expressing a different opinion. In the FA's bookshop in Paris, the Librairie Sociale, on 21 April 1919, Haussard, Le Meillour, Bidault and four or five other anarchists were discussing the different tendencies within the SFIO. There was a general preference for the Zimmerwald socialists like Loriot, and Haussard argued that a working-class dictatorship was necessary in Russia "in order to combat the parties which will want to use the revolution to benefit the interests of the new bourgesoisie." Bidault disagreed, saying that that would be "anti-anarchist," but the others agreed with Haussard.

61.   *Le Libertaire*, 27 July 1919. By the time of the Paris congress, Le Meillour was demanding that it make the "necessary selection" between those who did not wish to revise anarchist philosophy, and the "anarchist neo-communists … apologists for dictatorship." *Le Libertaire*, 24 October 1920.

62.   *Le Libertaire*, 27 July 1919. Within the socialist movement, the whole debate about who was to be admitted to the Moscow International and about the "Twenty-one conditions" did not really begin until 1920. See Liebman, *Leninism*, pp.391–3.

63.   *Le Libertaire*, 1 June 1919.

64.   *Le Libertaire*, 13 July 1919.

65.   By the spring of 1920, the FA was campaigning simultaneously for conscientious objectors, deserters, mutineers of the army and navy, Emile Cottin (the anarchist who attempted to assassinate Clemenceau in February 1919) and political prisoners in Russia. See, for example, report of Procureur Général, Poitiers, 18 March 1920. A report from the Procureur Général, Bordeaux, in the same period (22 March 1920) shows that the

authorities there were somewhat worried about the strength of the anarchists' campaigns: "The numbers of posters put up, of newspapers published and of pamphlets distributed implies considerable expenditure." BB18/6465.

66. *Le Libertaire*, 4 January 1920. Péache was a prominent member of the JA.

67. *Le Libertaire*, 26 September 1920.

68. *Le Libertaire*, 4 January 1920.

69. Both the NEP and the recognition of the USSR (created in December 1922) by France were seen as "the end of the revolution." *Germinal*, 5 November 1921 and 1 November 1924.

70. *Le Libertaire*, 23 December 1921.

71. See M. Isidine, "La Vérité sur Cronstadt—Une Tentative de Révolution Soviétique Libertaire," *les Temps nouveaux*, April–May 1921. For the Kronstadt rebellion's own declarations and anarchist comment, see Avrich, *The Anarchists in the Russian Revolution*, pp.156–68; Avrich, *Kronstadt 1921* (Princeton: The University Press, 1970); Ida Mett, *The Kronstadt Uprising* (London: Solidarity, 1967; first published in Paris, 1949); Voline, *La Révolution Inconnue: Russie 1917–1921* (Paris: Belfond, 1986 edn.), pp.405–506.

72. See *le Libertaire*, 11 January 1920. Makhno was of the rural working class, and he never left his class to become the schoolteacher others often claimed he had become.

73. Maitron, vol.II, pp.52–3.

74. On Makhno's exile in Paris, see Skirda, *Nestor Makhno*, ch.27. In 1937, the bolsheviks were still trying to portray the makhnovchina as bandits and were still purveying an almost entirely fictional portrait of Makhno. See E. Yaroslavsky, *History of anarchism in Russia* (London: Lawrence and Wishart, n.d.), published in France as Em. Iaroslavski, *L'anarchisme en Russie: Comment l'Histoire a tranché, au cours de la Révolution russe, la controverse entre anarchistes et communistes* (Paris: Bureau d'Editions, 1937).

75. On the phenomenon of the first "tourists" to post-revolutionary Russia, see Fred Kupferman (ed.), *Au Pays des Soviets (Le voyage français en Union soviétique 1917–1939)* (Paris: Editions Gallimard/Julliard, 1979). On the particular question of the many communist sympathisers whose account of what they saw was, to say the least, partial, see also Jean Maitron's preface to Emilio Guarnaschelli, *Une petite pierre: L'exil, la déportation et la mort d'un ouvrier communiste italien en URSS 1933–1939* (Paris: Maspéro, 1979), pp.17–21: "Although soviet 'socialism' already had its inquisition and its witch hunts, we actually knew little about them at that stage and it seemed unthinkable to us to join our voice to those of its declared enemies." —p.20.

76. "Dans les prisons bolcheviques...," *le Libertaire*, 26 September 1920. The list of prisoners included 42 socialist-revolutionaries, 72 left socialist-revolutionaries, 27 "maximalists" [SR maximalists? bolsheviks?], 3 "social-democrats" [mensheviks?] and 80 anarchists.

77. See the appeal, for example, in *le Libertaire*, 24 October 1920. Bidault was treasurer of the appeal fund.

78. *Germinal*, 13 and 20 August 1921.

79. *Germinal*, 1 October 1921. The secretary of the committee was J. Dupois. It was not specified how the money was to be sent to Russia nor how it would be distributed.

80. *Le Libertaire*, 14 October 1921.

81. See *les Temps nouveaux*, April 1922 and 13 May 1922, and *Publications de "la Révolte" et "Temps nouveaux,"* April 1922. The Anarchist Black Cross was resurrected in 1967 by the Scottish anarchist Stuart Christie.

82. *Germinal*, 20 May 1922 and 27 May 1922.

83. *Germinal*, 28 April 1923. On the creation in the winter of 1922–23 of the *Association Internationale des Travailleurs* (AIT) or International Working-mens' Association (IWMA), as an anarchist-syndicalist alternative to the reformist and communist trade union Internationals, see chapter 6.

84   The group's declaration was signed by the following: V. Battini (Seine CGT Departmental Union); L. Bert (Rail-workers P.O.); P. Besnard; B. Broutchoux & Chevalier (CGTU Metal-workers); Cordier (CGT Building-workers); L. Digat (CGT Post Office workers); E. Dondicol; J. Gaudeaux (Travelling Sales Representatives' Union); L. Guérineau (UA); G. Guiraud (Seine CGT Union); L. Haussard (UA); A. Hodée (CGT Agricultural Workers' Federation); A. Hugnin (Rail-workers Paris Etat Rive-Gauche); Jolivet (Autonomous Building-workers): Z. Lafonta; Massot (CGTU Metal-workers); Marc Pierrot; Paul Reclus; H. Totti; Georges Yvetot. The group's contact was Jacques Reclus (in Paris). See *Germinal*, 26 January 1924. The Fedeli Archive at the IISG contains undated circulars of a Comité de Défense des Révolutionnaires emprisonnés en Russie, whose secretary was the anarchist militant Chazoff. The leaflets insisted: "Our Committee is above all political parties, its aims are purely humanitarian." The committee claimed to include socialists, syndicalists and oppositional communists as well as anarchists. One leaflet announced the appearance of a *Bulletin* the following June, but I have not been able to find any copies.

85.   See *Germinal*, 30 September 1922, 21 October 1922 and 18 November 1922. This CDS is not to be confused with the CDS of which Raymond Péricat was secretary and which became the PC in 1919. After the creation of the CGTU in 1922 — which brought together the anarchists, communists and revolutionary syndicalists who opposed the reformist leadership of the CGT — a new CDS was founded by the anarcho-syndicalist minority, with Besnard as secretary. See chapter 6.

86.   Employed as she was as administrative secretary of the Metal-workers' Federation (CGTU), Picqueray accompanied the Federation's secretary and delegate, Lucien Chevallier, to the Profintern's 1922 congress in Moscow. She had been asked by the Black Cross in Berlin not only to carry messages in, but to intervene on behalf of Steimer and Fleshin. On their journey home in January 1923, Picqueray and Chevallier were arrested by the French police for having false papers and revolvers, and Picqueray believed the Russians to have betrayed them. Chevallier was sentenced to 3 months imprisonment and a 500 franc fine, Picqueray to 40 days and a 500 franc fine. The list the police made of the documentation Picqueray and Chevalier were bringing back with them runs to nearly six pages of foolscap: Reports of Procureur Général, Douai, 10 January, 9 February, 3, 7, 8, and 23 March 1923, BB18/6468. On her visit to Russia, see May Picqueray, *May la réfractaire Pour mes 81 ans d'anarchie* (Paris: Atelier Marcel Jullian, 1979), pp 83–121. For a very brief account by Chevallier of their intervention, and the text of the letter he sent to Trotsky, see Abe Bluestein (ed), *Fighters for anarchism: Mollie Steimer and Senya Fleshin. A memorial volume* (USA Libertarian Publications Group, 1983), pp.47–8.

87.   *Germinal*, 10 December 1921.

88.   "Les Anarchistes Français au Secours des Révolutionnaires Russes. Une lettre au Congrès International Syndicaliste de Moscou," *le Libertaire*, 1 July 1921 and *Germinal*, 9 July 1921. Requesting that Russian anarchists not be persecuted, and that they be allowed to attend the Berlin conference planned for the following autumn, the letter concluded that if these demands were not met, "we would have no choice but to reciprocate, that is, to impose on the protagonists of State socialism operating in our milieux the sanctions required by the circumstances."

89.   *Le Libertaire*, 3 February 1922.

90.   Ibid.

91.   *Le Libertaire*, 5 and 12 December 1920. An account of the meeting is given in *Le Libertaire*, 19 December 1920.

92.   Thus an anarchist called Prescot intervened at a meeting of the SFIC in Onnaing in February 1923: "It was a lecture on anarchy, its aims and its methods. The speaker talked of the Russian revolution, but not to hold it up as an example, because it has replaced the mechanisms of the previous regime by others which are no better." Report of Procureur Général, Douai, 28 February 1923, BB18/6468.

93.   See *le Libertaire*, 15 and 22 December 1922.

94   Mauricius, *Au Pays des Soviets. Neuf Mois d'Aventures* (Paris: Eugène Figuière, n.d.[late 1921/early 1922]). The book carries an advertisement for a second volume, *La Vérité sur les Bolcheviki (Ce qu'ils sont réellement. Ce qu'ils ont fait. Ce qu'ils veulent)*, which was to appear in June 1922, but which was never published. The "Fonds Berthier-Vandamme" in the IFHS (14AS451) contains an extremely poor copy of a 200pp. TS of this volume, but unfortunately only about a quarter of it is legible.

95.   For a report on one such talk—apparently successful despite much heckling by communists—see *le Libertaire*, 10 June 1921. On the organization of the speaking tour and especially the distribution of the book (of which 2,125 copies were printed), see the "Fonds Mauricius," IFHS, 14AS292/F, Dossier II.

96.   On the pro-bolsheviks' claims, see *le Libertaire*, 12 December 1920 and 28 January 1921. In May the previous year, *Oeuvre* had accused Lepetit of being a police spy, but after public support for Lepetit was forthcoming from leading activists such as François Mayoux and Georges Dumoulin, the paper admitted that its accusation was false. *Le Journal du Peuple*, 13 and 18 May 1919.

97.   See Wayne Thorpe, *"The Workers Themselves". Revolutionary Syndicalism and International Labour, 1913–1923* (Amsterdam: International Institute of Social History & Dordrecht/Boston/London: Kluwer Academic Publishers, 1989), p.148. According to Armando Borghi's autobiography, Vergeat and Lepetit were the most intransigent of the foreign syndicalists in Moscow in 1920 in their opposition to the bolsheviks—Ibid.

98   See *le Libertaire*, 12 December 1920 and 7 January 1921. The 12 December issue also contains an obituary of Lepetit by François; the following issue contains an obituary of both Lepetit and Vergeat by someone signing "C.L." See also Marcel Body's account of his meeting, with them: *Un Piano en bouleau de Carélie. Mes années de Russie (1917–1927)* (Paris: Hachette, 1981), pp.171–80.

99.   The "Fonds Mauricius" contains a newspaper cutting headlined "Mis à Mort par les Soviets." The article suggested that the Cheka arranged the whole episode, that a soviet naval vessel pursued the fishing boat which the French delegates were using, and that the Frenchmen were then thrown overboard. Across the article is written the word "Faux," followed by what seems to be Mauricius' signature. IFHS 14AS292/F.

100.   Extract from *Répression de l'Anarchisme en Russie soviétique*, quoted in *Germinal*, 16 June 1920. According to *le Libertaire*, 22 December 1922, this is a translation of what was the original Russian title of the booklet just cited, published by the Libraire Sociale. For the French edition, a section on the Lepetit/Vergeat/Lefebvre affair was added.

101.   Vilkens, "Souvenirs sur Lepetit, Vergeat et Lefebvre," *le Libertaire*, 11 February 1921.

102.   According to *le Libertaire*, 31 July 1936, which reported his death north of Madrid fighting with an antifascist militia, his real name was in fact Fernandez Alvarez. So why was he referred to by the secretary of his union as "G."? According to Hilarion Arlandis,

in *la Vie ouvrière*, 10 February 1922, his real name was Aimé Salan, who in Russia had written an article under the pseudonym J. Galan. Thorpe, *The Workers Themselves*, p.303, note 50.

103. *Le Libertaire*, 18 February 1921.

104   The first article was published in *le Libertaire*, 14 January 1921—about the same time that "Sur La Dictature" became a regular rubric—and the last in the 29 July issue.

105.   See S. Casteu, "Les Dictateurs à l'oeuvre," *le Libertaire*, 18 February 1921, and *le Libertaire*, 25 March 1921.

106.   Vilkens was eventually expelled by the French authorities. According to *le Libertaire*, 10 February 1922, he had just been escorted to the Belgian border: "We thank him above all for his honest, impartial and courageous study of the Russian revolution, a study which made him many enemies, but which illuminated the darkness in which the bolshevik leaders like to hide their criminal undertaking: the smothering of a movement whose success would have changed the face of the earth and emancipated all workers." The Spanish communist Hilarion Arlandis, while disliking what Wilkens wrote about bolshevik rule, grudgingly admitted that "certainly a great many of the facts cited by Wilkens are objectively correct"—*la Vie ouvrière*, 10 February 1922.

107.   See "Le Congrès Minoritaire," *le Libertaire*, 30 December 1921. For the bolsheviks' opinion of the "ignorant writings of Wilkens and of the other specialists in slander published in profusion in the pages of *le Libertaire*," see Lozovsky's letter of January 1922 to Monatte, in Jean Maitron and Colette Chambelland (eds.), *Syndicalisme révolutionnaire et communisme: Les archives de Pierre Monatte* (Paris: Maspero, 1968), pp.336–43.

108. *Germinal*, 1 November 1924.

109.   Letter of 15 May 1922, in Maitron & Chambelland (eds.), *Archives de Pierre Monatte*, p.344.

110.   See *le Libertaire*, 14 and 21 October 1921. Renato Souvarine was the pseudonym of Renato Siglich, an Italian (born in 1881 in Triest) who had previously been director of *l'Avenire Anarchico*. He had corresponded with Faure over *Ce qu'il faut dire*, and was a friend of Bidault, but appears otherwise not to have been active in the French movement. Reports of Préfet de Police, 28 May and 10 June 1926, F7/13964. Serge was to claim somewhat disingenuously to have published the "Confession"—having found it in the Tsar's archives—out of a concern for disinterested historical knowledge—*Mémoires d'un révolutionnaire 1901–1941* (Paris: Seuil 1951), p.163. The "Confession" was of course used by the bolsheviks—see, for example Yaroslavsky's *History of Anarchism in Russia*, pp.14–15.

111. *Le Libertaire*, 18 October 1924; and Picqueray, *May la réfractaire*, pp.122–5.

112. *Le Libertaire*, 18 October 1924. This assessment of the significance of the January 1924 killings as a watershed in anarchist/communist relations in France was confirmed to me by the prominent anarchist militant Louis Anderson.

5

On the Margins:
the *Temps nouveaux* Group
and the Individualists

We are learning to appreciate, in Russia, how communism must *not* be introduced ...

Peter Kropotkin[1]

As individualists, we are the enemy of all dictatorships.
But we are idealists, not dreamers, and we do not believe
it possible for the men and women of today to live without laws and without gendarmes (red or black).

André Lorulot[2]

JEAN GRAVE AND THE *TEMPS NOUVEAUX* GROUP

Before the Great War, Jean Grave had been central to the anarchist
movement, as were the three newspapers of which he had been the moving force—*le Révolté, la Révolte* and *les Temps nouveaux*. In the words of
Mireille Delfau: "Jean Grave was the incarnation, between 1880 and
1914, of the 'libertarian communist' ideology, such as it emerged pro-
gressively from the confrontation between Marx and Bakunin after the
Commune; hence, in Grave, that vigilance, that acute sense of anarchist
orthodoxy (he was known as the 'high priest' of the rue Mouffetard!)
when illegalism, revolutionary syndicalism and individualism appeared
in the movement."[3] However, the war and Grave's refusal to be "neutral," as he put it, marked a turning point, and from then on he became
increasingly isolated. First there was the split with the "internationalists" in the *Temps nouveaux* group during the war, when Girard, Mignon,
Benoît and others broke with him to found *l'Avenir international*. He retained the support of Dr. Marc Pierrot, Jacques Guérin and Paul Reclus, and this group produced a series of "Bulletins" from 1916 to 1919.
Disagreements then arose over the future of the group's publication,
and eventually there was another split between Grave and a majority of
the others. The review produced by this majority lasted only two years,

and although the "Publications" put out by Grave lasted until 1936, they were produced by a group of only four activists.

All of those associated with the pre-war *Temps nouveaux* who had not actively opposed the war effort were thus thoroughly isolated from the rest of the anarchist movement between the wars: "The war isolated us not just from comrades in other countries, but it also divided the anarchists in this country profoundly enough for them to consider each other enemies and to avoid any further contact."[4] It is clearly not, therefore, because of any representativity that the opinions of this group are worth studying. But their views are worth looking at (i) because of the important rôle these activists played within the movement before the war; (ii) because of the peculiarity of their analysis, a peculiarity deriving from the position they adopted *vis-à-vis* the war; and (iii) because of the group's closeness to Kropotkin, which meant that theirs was the anarchist periodical in France that gave most prominence to Kropotkin's analysis of the Russian revolution.

This group of anarchists were practically the only ones in France to have associated themselves with the notorious "Manifeste des Seize," published early in 1916.[5] This is not the place to discuss the clash between *"défensistes"* (those who supported the national war effort) and *"résistants"* (those who remained true to their "revolutionary antimilitarism" and condemned the war as a conflict between rival imperialisms), but clearly this had an effect on activists' attitudes towards the Russian revolution. Whilst most anarchists had applauded Russia's withdrawal from the war effort, the first thing Kropotkin did on his arrival in Russia was to campaign for the Kerensky government to carry on fighting. There was therefore no welcome for bolshevism in the pages of *les Temps nouveaux*. Indeed, one of the earliest reactions to the Russian revolution to be found in the Bulletins demonstrates a quite astonishing anti-bolshevik feeling and reads more like government propaganda than an anarchist newspaper. Thus whilst the revolution in general was approved of, bolshevism was "a dark reaction"; bolshevik soldiers were selling their rifles to the Germans; they had dug up Tolstoy's grave to steal his jewelry; "expropriation" was merely an excuse for rioting and pillaging: "Reactionaries, tsarists, German agents and Red Guards are colluding in ruining the country in the name of the dictatorship of the proletariat dear to those bourgeois Lenin and Trotsky."[6] In January 1919, the rumour was even repeated that the bolsheviks had murdered Kropotkin.[7]

The group also had little patience with those French comrades who were enthusiastically pro-soviet: "They have ears only for those who speak to them of the establishment of a soviet republic analogous to that of the bolsheviks and they are overcome when they hear a comrade speak ill of bolshevism."[8] In May 1919, when some comrades were announcing their membership of the Moscow International and advocating co-operation with socialists and syndicalists in a communist party or in a national federation of factory committees and workers' councils, the *Temps nouveaux* group were criticizing the soviets as counter-revolutionary and were declaring their support for the Russian anarchists and Left Socialist Revolutionaries against the bolsheviks. Nor does their attitude towards socialists and syndicalists and towards the question of organization seem to have changed at all.[9] In stark contrast to the ambitious revolutionism of other anarchist communists, Grave saw the movement's future in much more modest terms. For him, the only realistic perspective for those who remained true to their anarchist principles was work in single-issue campaigns such as the Tenants' League, the Human Rights League, the Anti-Alcoholism League, and in such organizations as consumer co-operatives.[10]

When the new series of *les Temps nouveaux* started in July 1919, the editorial group made clear their collective position on the Russian revolution and their disagreement with most of the rest of the movement:

> We have no admiration for bolshevism, though we detest no less strongly the parties of reaction who wish its demise. We can see why many revolutionaries, from afar, have idealized this government as a symbol; we understand that workers use the word itself mischievously to frighten the bourgeois. But for us, bolshevism is nothing more than another form of State socialism, very authoritarian, extremely centralized and surviving thanks to violence. It is not part of our programme to make the people happy by decree and against their wishes. We do not believe in the good tyrant. We are not upheld by faith in an infallible gospel which must be applied come what may. Our aspirations come from the aspirations of the masses and not from an *a priori* dogma. Though we believe that revolutions are never made other than by a minority and made no doubt with violence against the tyranny of the privileged and the parasites, such a revolution and such violence must be favoured by the consent of the masses, not by a passive consent, by submission, but by aspiration towards a common ideal: the action of the minority must have as its sole aim the unhindered flowering of the new forms of social life in the process of being developed. Otherwise, it is dictatorship, with all its consequences, including reaction.[11]

The *Temps nouveaux* group did not share the libertarian, sponta-neist interpretation of the Russian revolution common to the sovietists and most other anarchist communists. On the contrary, they saw the revolution as the work of a minority, the bolsheviks. The group seem to have thought that the bolsheviks had little popular support, and that they had simply imposed their will on the Russian people. Consequent-ly, whilst accepting in theory the violent suppression of "the privileged" and of "parasites" by a revolutionary minority, so long as this minority had massive and active popular support, the declaration had then to condemn the bolsheviks' actions as dictatorial.

The *Temps nouveaux* group was, in fact, almost unanimously and without qualification anti-bolshevik, and the attacks became even more bitter and hostile with the launching of Grave's *Publications* in 1920. By 1922, Grave could claim that the activities of the GPU/Cheka put the bolshevik regime on a par with tsarism, and he seems to have been very pessimistic about any possible improvement in the situation: "What is the point of making a revolution?"[12] The most violent attacks were made by a J. Erboville, for whom the Russian revolution was concrete proof of the failure of marxism, and who could even descend to the grossest racism, referring to the "Tartars" and the "Hebrews who have murdered freedom of thought, killed production and sown famine in Russia."[13]

Kropotkin and Rocker

Not all of the interventions published by this group were on this level, though, and not all of them were so one-sided.[14] Having said that, the best examples of intelligent analysis of the Russian situation were pro-duced by Peter Kropotkin and Rudolf Rocker.[15] Rocker was to distin-guish clearly between the soviet system and the bolshevik dictatorship, arguing (as the sovietists were doing at about the same time) that the former was a part of the libertarian tradition, whereas the latter was a bourgeois conception belonging to the jacobin and babouvist tradi-tions.[16]

In 1921, in a special number of *les Temps nouveaux* dedicated to Kropotkin, M. Corn summed up the Russian's attitude thus:

> In the events in Russia, Kropotkin always saw more than just
> a struggle between political parties, more than the bolshevik
> dictatorship: he saw revolution on the march, a new way of
> life being born. He put the interests of the revolution above all
> else, and above all sought to defend it against its enemies: reac-
> tion and the allies' intervention. His attitude could not of course
> have been anything else, and we, his friends here, knew what

it would be before we received a line from him. To everyone
we said in advance: "Kropotkin cannot be with the bolsheviks,
because they represent an extreme expression of the idea of
the state and of dictatorship; but he is above all a socialist and
a revolutionary, and for that reason will defend the revolution
against all its enemies."[17]

In fact, despite Corn's somewhat self-congratulatory gloss, Kropotkin's analysis was far less negative than that of most of the French
comrades around the review. Certainly he disagreed with bolshevik
methods. "The idea of the soviets … is a great idea," he wrote, but totally meaningless when topped with a system which in reality meant the
dictatorship of one party.[18] He was above all concerned to emphasize
the sheer impracticality of trying to undertake such an enormous task,
on the scale of a country like Russia, using an over-centralized system:

> The ways in which to topple a government which is already
> weak are well known from history, both ancient and modern.
> But when it is a question of creating new forms of life — espe-
> cially new forms of production and exchange — without having
> any examples to follow, when everything has to be manufac-
> tured on the spot, when a government undertakes to supply
> every inhabitant with every lamp chimney and even the match
> to go with it, when the government shows itself to be incapable
> of doing it with its civil servants, however many of them there
> are, such a government becomes a hindrance. It develops such
> a formidable bureaucracy that the French bureaucratic system,
> which requires the involvement of 40 civil servants to sell a tree
> uprooted by a storm on a 'route nationale', seems trifling in
> comparison. That is what we are learning in Russia today.[19]

The bolshevik approach, for Kropotkin, paralyzed "the constructive work of the people."[20] In brief, bolshevism was demonstrating just
how not to introduce communism. On the other hand, Kropotkin was
not totally negative. He recognized that the allied intervention and the
civil war had made things much more difficult, and had made the bolsheviks' methods even more authoritarian — hence his insistence that
workers in the west should defend the revolution against its capitalist
and monarchist enemies. He remained optimistic for the future: "One
must recognize that the revolution has already introduced into our daily
work new conceptions of the rights of labour, its true position in society
and the duties of every citizen, and these conceptions will survive."[21]

THE INDIVIDUALIST ANARCHISTS

The individualist anarchists represent another minority within the anarchist movement whose assessment of the Russian revolution was interestingly different. Indeed contrary to both Maitron and Skirda, for whom some individualist pronouncements on bolshevism were "astonishing" or "inexplicable," this author would suggest that these responses, whilst varying with time or on certain specifics or in emphasis, all illuminate a basic attitude common to the individualists.[22] This should become clearer as we look at what was actually said and written.

The earliest responses to the February revolution in the individualist press conspicuously lack the enthusiasm common to the rest of the movement. Albin's *les Glaneurs*, for instance, printed this rather pessimistic piece by Georges Manova in the summer of 1917: "The Russian people have made their Revolution, overthrowing the most odious despotism. That is very good, but I wonder, sometimes, if all this blood so nobly shed will have been shed in vain and if the future of this great people will be one of harmony and freedom ... or, as before, one of slavery and tyranny."[23] Albin himself was even more negative, commenting that "The leaders over there are almost all as tyrannical as ours were in the old days, and the masses just as stupid."[24] Here, already, we see the individualists' disdain for the ignorant masses, and their scorn for the workers' longing for social change: "the imbecilic hope for future barricades."[25] And with Albin the corollary of his contempt for "the masses" who cannot cope without masters was a nietzschean admiration for the heroic, outstanding individual who can act as a master: "The Russian people is nothing without the few terribly courageous individuals who lead them. Yet those individuals act in an authoritarian manner. Indeed they have no choice if they really want to defend the regime which they have established."[26]

Others, taking a stance against the anarchist communists of *Ce qu'il faut dire* and *l'Avenir international*, argued that as anarchists the Russian revolution was not so much to be criticized, but that it was simply of no interest to them. Armand, for instance, attacked Faure:

> I confess that I am still puzzled as to what imp can have provoked Sébastien Faure ... into taking sides with the maximalists and their demands and into defending "the security of the new state of affairs in Russia". I persist in believing: (i) that the differences—or the little schemes—between Korniloff and Kerensky have nothing to do with an-archist [sic] philosophy or the propagation of an-archist ideas; (ii) that an-archism is a philosophy, an anti-authoritarian conception of life—an atti-

tude, an individual activity more or less consistent and rigorous according to the temperament and energy of each individual — which has nothing to do with politics or sociology.[27]

Pierre Chardon took it upon himself to criticize *l'Avenir international* and those who wrote for it — especially Amédée Dunois — for deforming anarchism, for "infecting" it with marxism.[28] For Chardon, anarchism should resist attempts to bring it closer to bolshevist-inspired communism, it ought to rid itself of "the socialistic confusionism in which it sinks more and more every day."[29] Chardon had little admiration for the Russian revolution. This was primarily because the Russians took part in the revolution because of hunger and other material hardship, rather than because they wished to devote themselves, through reading and reflexion, to spiritual self-improvement: "The anarchist is a rebel, but a *cerebral* rebel. ... He understands, but he does not always approve, and he knows that those who, today, are determined to trample the ridiculous symbols of a fallen power would have cried 'Vivat!' if that power had been able to guarantee them 'bread and games'!"[30]

Some individualists took a stand against the Russian revolution, or at least against bolshevism. Han Ryner, for instance, argued against the dictatorship of the proletariat in a public debate with André Lorulot.[31] In late 1922 Armand argued in an open letter to Serge that bolshevism was responsible both for the appearance of fascism and for fascism's brutality: "Mussolinism is a response to the dictatorship of Moscow."[32] But this had not always been Armand's position, and not all individualists changed their earlier opinions in the same way that Armand did. In 1920, *Un* published an article of his which had been written some time before. In it, Armand commented that he did not believe "terrorism" or "dictatorship" could ever be "a factor in the evolution or the development of the human personality."[33] On the other hand, he praised the bolsheviks for what they had achieved in, say, education and adduced the civil war and the intervention as partial explanations for the bolsheviks' failings. He was not, therefore, totally negative: "However repugnant I may find the very word 'dictatorship', no one who has not been corrupted by our base western *arrivisme* can be indifferent to the bolshevists' struggle against capitalism."[34]

Others — like Frédéric Stackelberg, Léon Prouvost, Manuel Devaldès and André Lorulot — were more consistent in their support for the bolsheviks.[35] Lorulot's *l'Idée libre*, especially, printed a whole series of articles about all aspects of the Russian revolution: the system of soviet government, education reforms, the new laws relating to marriage, etc.[36] Lorulot himself campaigned tirelessly in defence of the bolshevik regime, defending it against all its critics, anarchist or otherwise. In November 1918 he declared his support, based as it was at first on a very libertarian understanding of the new governmental structures: "Personally, I am the vassal of no socialist system, I am the slave of no particular programme. I am therefore able to declare, without bias or sectarianism, that the bolshevists' programme represents a decisive step forward—in so far as the ignorance of the Russian masses will allow it to be applied. (Lenin's programme is not in any case a dogmatic programme, it is not even purely marxist.)"[37] There are two interesting things to note here, in relating Lorulot's interpretation to that of the majority of anarchist communists. The first is that in the autumn of 1918 Lorulot was apparently convinced that Lenin was not a dogmatic marxist like the politicians he was used to combatting.[38] In that sense he shared the anarchist communists' libertarian reading of bolshevism. The second is that it was the bolsheviks who were the primary object of Lorulot's admiration: if there had been any progress in Russia, it was thanks to the efforts of the bolsheviks struggling against the backwardness of the masses. This is in total contrast to the anarchist communists' faith in the popular masses and in the spontaneity of revolution, a faith which informed their reading of the Russian revolution and later enabled them to accuse the bolsheviks of "distorting" or "betraying" the revolution.

This belief in the libertarian nature of the early bolshevik system gave way gradually to an unapologetic defence by Lorulot of the dictatorship of the proletariat even though, like other individualists, he often prefaced his defence and justification with a disclaimer protesting his personal dislike of authority and violence.[39] His defence of the bolshevik dictatorship was argued most extensively in a front-page article in *le Réveil de l'Esclave* in March 1921, and this article made very clear how the stance adopted by Lorulot and others, such as Manuel Devaldès, derived from their individualism. There were the familiar reasons: the attacks on the bolsheviks by counter-revolutionaries in the bourgeois press, and Lenin's rôle in taking Russia out of the war: "Indeed they were the first to oppose the world war. How can we not prefer Lenin to someone like Kropotkin or Jean Grave, who associated themselves with the massacres of the world war?"[40] As an individualist, Lorulot's starting-point in considering whether dictatorship was justifiable or not was the question: "Can the people of today live without authority?" His answer was no. The masses never know what they really want, they are very suggestible, easily led: "Whatever the regime (republican, democratic, socialist, anarchist, etc.) the masses will always be led by a minority."[41] Besides, Lorulot believed, people are basically brutes, and need laws and so on to restrain them: "Moreover in a revolutionary period, even a victorious one, the Dictatorship is a lesser evil. Otherwise, it is banditry (when the bolsheviks came to power in Russia people were being murdered on street corners for the slightest thing. The Soviets had great difficulty repressing an 'unimaginable disorder', according to Wells), it is lynchings, it is nonstop murder."[42]

Thus, in brief, an anarchist revolution could not be expected to succeed, because that would require each individual to have perfected themselves beforehand: "So you will understand that Laurent Tailhade's 'radiant anarchy', the 'torch-bearer', is not made for the people of to-day."[43] Authoritarian government was therefore a necessary evil for "the brutes, the ignorant, the alcoholics, the violent" who make up the vast majority of society. But power corrupts, therefore the individualist must refuse to exercise authority him/herself: "Because of our noble individualism, our desire to remain true to ourselves and to live the existence of proud labour and of independence in accord with our personal ideal, we will exercise no function of social authority."[44]

But if the individualist, in order to behave in a civilized manner, does not need to live constrained by laws in the same way as the majority of ordinary mortals; and if s/he wishes, in order not to become sullied, to remain aloof from the exercise of authority necessary to the everyday functioning of society; what is then her/his rôle in society?

> We will continue our task of forming (relatively) better men, of sowing ideas, of encouraging each individual to live their ideal as far as possible, to enhance their lives and those of others, to practice justice and dignity, to do more than just protest against 'bourgeois' society whilst continuing to indulge in all its vices (wine, tobacco, lies, familial authoritarianism, lack of practical solidarity, gossip, and so much more!). And that is worth more than joining the Third International—or being content with criticizing it without doing anything else.[45]

The Nature of Individualist Anarchism

Is the defence of bolshevism by individualist anarchists therefore that surprising? Individualists distinguished themselves by their belief that revolution was not desirable even if it was possible. They insisted that individuals had to make the revolution within themselves, hence the epithet "educationist." They had a generally very low opinion of "the masses" or "the crowd."[46] They saw society as the sum total—and no more—of the individuals who made it up: they rejected the existence of classes. They were not socialists, sharing as they did a Proudhonian insistence on the right to private property as a guarantee of their indi-

vidual freedom. They therefore had little interest in the labour and socialist movements. They were preoccupied to varying degrees with philosophy, the arts and what would today be called "lifestyle" politics. The
outcome was a greater or lesser arrogance and a pretension to the rôle
of educator and guide. Thus the attitude adopted by Marcel Sauvage,
editor of *la Mêlée*, towards the Russian revolution was that he disagreed
with the dictatorial methods of the bolsheviks, without entirely rejecting
the regime as having destroyed the revolution. Instead, he graciously
offered himself as a guide to a doubtless grateful Russian people: "Our
rôle as educators and guides has never been as favoured, as indispensable. Before the Revolution, achieved by the malleable masses under
the influence of a few energetic leaders, we will lay out our ideal, our
systems—our social and individual economy, that which is really new,
really noble in us."[47]

So many individualists continued with this curious position,
whereby their anarchist ideals meant that they disapproved of bolshevism in theory, whilst in practice their individualist pessimism with regard to "human nature" and their elitism led them to accept it and in
certain cases to defend it. Let us conclude our study of the individualist
response with Devaldès' own, revealing conclusion:

> In reality, the differences which the anarchist communists de-
> nounce between their ideal and what has actually been done by
> the dictators must not be put down to the latter, but to human
> nature and the fact that the proletarians were not educated with
> a view to their own emancipation. Let us conclude. The 'yoke'
> of the 'dictatorship of the proletariat' frees the individual, whilst
> the 'freedom' of bourgeois 'democracy' enslaves the individual.
> As for the Freedom of the anarchist communists, it is a bubble
> which bursts at the slightest hint of reality.[48]

The Influence of Individualism

It is doubtful whether the individualists actually had much influence
outside their own circles. It is certainly true that the police paid them
very little attention, so they were presumably considered no threat to
the state. They also had no input into the syndicalist and revolutionary movements: their relations varied from a simple and mutual lack
of interest, to outright mutual hostility. The same could almost be said
of relations between individualists and anarchist communists, although
there were clearly more overlaps, because of a shared anti-statism and
to some extent a shared interest in lifestyle politics. On the other hand,
many individualist periodicals were on the very borderline of what could

be considered anarchism, and no doubt reached an audience in rather more specialized minority markets: naturism, vegetarianism, esperanto, certain artistic and philosophical circles and so on. Individualist periodicals also tended to be shorter and less frequent, and sometimes less well produced (*les Vagabonds*, for instance, was hand-written and duplicated). Having said that, police estimated the print-run of *la Mêlée* to be 5,000 a month, and that of *l'Idée libre* to be 3,000 a month.[49] Equally, we must bear in mind that the major preoccupation of André Lorulot and his review *l'Idée libre* was anti-clericalism. Indeed, the only thing to shake his otherwise consistent support of the bolshevik regime was news of a possible agreement between Moscow and the Vatican.[50] So it would seem reasonable to assume that the individualists were both a minority within the movement, and that they were also ghettoized in a way that the anarchist communists were not. Lorulot was himself rather negative when it came to the vigour and influence of post-war anarchist individualism.[51]

So the individualists, whilst sharing to an extent the same fundamental attitude, also demonstrated a mixed response to the Russian revolution. Prouvost, who seems to have been a contributor to the individualist press, was an exception in that he joined the PC. Others, like Lorulot and Sauvage, out of their disdain for the masses, accepted the necessity for the party dictatorship, but declined to compromise themselves personally. Many were simply uninterested in anything to do with the labour and socialist movements, believing such things totally alien to the lofty and noble concerns of true anarchism. Armand, who had earlier expressed a grudging admiration for the Russian revolutionaries, eventually joined with the vast majority of anarchists in condemning bolshevism as fascistic.

BOLSHEVISM AND FASCISM COMPARED

It is interesting to note Armand's comment that bolshevism was in some way responsible for the appearance and for the brutality of Italian fascism, in view of the continuing historiographical and political debates in this area.[52] The causality argument does not seem to have been developed by Armand or by any other anarchist. The idea of "totalitarianism," however, was one that many on the far left, including anarchists, would have had little objection to, and by the mid-1930s had become something of a commonplace. Pierre Ruff of the UA was to write in 1936: "Hitler's regime is execrable. Stalin's regime is at least as execrable."[53]

But in fact the anarchists did not wait for the well-publicised methods of Stalin's regime before they started comparing bolshevism and fascism. The earliest such comparisons date from the summer of

1922, when Rose of *Germinal* concluded an article about the mass trials of syndicalists and anarchists in Spain and Italy with the following comments:

> In Russia, such a thing is not called 'Fascism'. Here, the true fascists are not the reactionaries; it is the politicians, the red Jesuits, who, through their lies, slanders and denigration poured out onto the working-class militants of this country, have destroyed the trade union movement or at least weakened it to such an extent that the forces of reaction are able to manoeuvre against the working class with complete impunity and with every chance of success.[54]

This notion — that bolshevism was responsible for dividing the labour movement and thus weakening its resistance to fascism — was of course also to become a common one on the far left, particularly with regard to the effects of Stalin's policies on the German labour movement in the early 1930s. But straight comparisons of bolshevik and fascist methods were not uncommon. Bastien, for example, entitled one article "Bolchevisme et Fascisme" and could not have made the point clearer: "In any case, the same disdain of the masses, the same domineering, violent character and the same militaristic mentality can be seen in both parties. They may be opposites as far as their apparent ideology is concerned, but they are the same as regards their means, their practice and their methods."[55]

RELATIONS BETWEEN ANARCHISTS AND COMMUNISTS AFTER 1920

It was by no means as easy for the anarchists to make the break with the communists as it may seem to us with hindsight. Police reports speak of the bitter conflicts within trade unions between anarchists and communists, but also hint at the complexities of relations between individual militants, particularly between friends and even between members of the same family.[56] More than one activist's autobiography stresses the ambivalence of communist/anarchist relations in those days, compared to what we are familiar with in the post-Stalin era. Michaud, for example, recounting his opposition to leninism, added: "Despite everything, in those days, although communists and anarchists confronted each other in the various debates, they still considered each other to be different branches of the same family, and united when faced with a common enemy."[57] May Picqueray would make the same point in her autobiography.[58] And Lecoin, looking back from the 1960s, explained that, despite the anarchists' dislike for bolshevism, circumstances nevertheless meant that they often co-operated with the Communist Party:

> How many times did the Anarchist Union come together with the Communist Party with laudable, revolutionary aims! I would be spoilt for choice if I wanted to reproduce here one of the joint manifestos produced by the two organizations. The anarchists would still stand by those manifestos today; the present-day CP would reject them shamefully. Thus the Communist Party and the Anarchist Union frequently walked the same path together for a while. This was still the heydey of *Poincarisme* and we had to ensure that the country was not thrown straight into another war. The Versailles peace—that latent war—hatched by Wilson, Lloyd George and Clemenceau; the dictatorships of Mussolini and of Primo de Rivera; the conduct of the CGT, first contributing to the war effort and then advocating a servile reformism; the Sacco and Vanzetti affair: these are some examples of the reasons for our *rapprochements* with the Communist Party.[59]

It had in fact always been difficult for the anarchists, especially in the years just after the war. Henri Sirolle had, early on, summed up the attitude of most anarchists then: "The gravity of the situation meant discussions about the appropriateness or the value of bolshevism were not possible: we had to choose to be either with those who revolted against capitalist oppression, or against them."[60] This logic was used by the bolsheviks and their supporters in the west—including Lorulot[61]—from the start of 1921. *Le Libertaire*, for instance, was accused of having the same standpoint as the reactionary *le Temps*.[62] In Bastien's words: "As soon as the anarchists began to fight against the disastrous idea of dictatorship, its supporters began to cry that we were playing into the hands of reaction, that we were fighting against the Russian revolution."[63] The anarchists were very sensitive to this argument, and it represented a great dilemma for them, one which was given voice to many times in the anarchist press: they were, to say the least, loath to "howl with the wolves," to become the bedfellows of reactionaries. The account in *le Libertaire* of the 1921 congress of the UA points out that if, at the previous congress, there had still been lingering doubts about bolshevism, "these must be put down to the revolutionary probity of some comrades who ..., understandably reluctant to harm the Russian revolution, even morally, hesitated to pass judgement."[64] The dilemma—which was not limited to anarchism—was probably expressed most clearly by the Left

Socialist Revolutionary, Maria Spiridinova, in an open letter to workers in the west, published by *les Temps nouveaux* in the spring of 1921:

> This is the situation. If we say the whole truth about what is happening in Russia, the bourgeoisie will take advantage of it to confuse matters and present the crimes committed by the governing parties as those of the revolution itself. If we do not speak out, thus covering with our silence the loss of all our hopes and of all prospects for our revolution, if we hide the horrible crimes committed by the dictators against the Russian workers, if we conceal the fact that the workers of the whole world are being deceived into believing in the socialist revolution which supposedly reigns in Russia, we will be helping push the revolution towards a sad and shameful end and we will be encouraging the world proletariat to make the same mistakes, mistakes which will surely lead to the same failure.[65]

The French anarchists came to the conclusion that defence of the revolution was not the same thing as defence of the bolshevik dictatorship; and that, in the long run, to criticise bolshevism could only be beneficial to the revolution.[66]

Although it would be fair to say that the anarchists' attitude towards the Russian regime was, if anything, to harden, and although their relations with the French communists were likewise to get less, rather than more, comradely, this dilemma was never to be entirely resolved before the second world war. And it must surely have represented a severe handicap for the anarchists in their struggle to hinder the implantation of bolshevism in France. For what was the anarchists' audience to think, when those whom the anarchists condemned as being as evil as the fascists, the anarchists also routinely campaigned with?

Notes

1. "Une Lettre de Pierre Kropotkine," *les Temps nouveaux*, 15 August 1920. Kropotkin had left France for the last time to go and live in England in 1886, and had returned to Russia in the summer of 1917. In June 1920, when he wrote this open letter to workers in the west, he was living at Dmitroff, near Moscow. Brought back from Russia by a British trade unionist and an American journalist, the letter was first published in *The Labour Leader* (weekly paper of the British Independent Labour Party).

2. André Lorulot, "Pour ou contre la dictature," *le Réveil de l'Esclave*, March 1921.

3. Introduction to Jean Grave, *Quarante ans de propagande anarchiste* (Paris: Flammarion, 1973), p.25.

4.   Grave in *Publications de "La Révolte" et "Temps Nouveaux,"* May 1922. See René Michaud's account of how "Dr P..." (Pierrot) was obliged to leave a public meeting being addressed by Lecoin, before the latter would agree to continue. *J'avais vingt ans* (Paris: Syros, 1983), p.137.

5.   See Maitron, vol.II, pp.12–23.

6.   *Les Temps nouveaux*, September 1918.

7.   According to a leaflet entitled "Le Sort de Pierre Kropotkine" inserted in *les Temps nouveaux*, January 1919. The leaflet ended with the cry: "Down with bolshevik tyranny! Long live socialism!"

8.   *Les Temps nouveaux*, 1 May 1919.

9.   The UA was not to be spared criticism either: see F. Fichard, "Un Congrès, dit Anarchiste," *Publications de "La Révolte" et "Temps Nouveaux,"* no.11 (1922).

10.   See various articles by Grave: for instance, "Ce que l'on peut faire," *Publications du "Groupe de Propagande par l'Ecrit,"* no.2 (1920), and "Pour préparer la société future," *Publications de "La Révolte" et "Temps Nouveaux,"* no.9 (1921).

11.   *Les Temps nouveaux. Revue internationale des Idées Communistes,* 15 July 1919.

12.   *Publications de "La Révolte" et "Temps Nouveaux"* no.12 (April 1922).

13.   See "Les Moscovites," *Publications de "La Révolte" et "Temps Nouveaux"* no.16 (October 1922).

14.   Only one article attempted a justification of the bolshevik dictatorship: F. David in *les Temps nouveaux*, 15 August 1920.

15.   Rocker was German and a bookbinder by trade. Forced to leave Germany for political reasons, he arrived in Paris in 1893 and in London two years later. It was there that he became involved with Jewish immigrant workers. He was interned by the British authorities in 1914, and returned to Berlin in 1919 to help organize the revolutionary syndicalist *Freie Arbeiter Union Deutschlands.*

16.   See "Le Système des Soviets ou la Dictature?," *les Temps nouveaux*, 15 August and 15 September 1920. The article has been republished in Nikolai Bukharin, Luigi Fabbri, Rudolf Rocker, *The Poverty of Statism* (Orkney: Cienfuegos Press, 1981), pp.63–74.

17.   M. Corn, "Kropotkine et la Russie," *les Temps nouveaux*, March 1921: "Numéro spécial consacé à Pierre Kropotkine, l'ami, l'homme, l'anarchiste, le savant, son oeuvre, souvenirs personnels et hommages posthumes."

18.   "Une Lettre de Pierre Kropotkine," *les Temps nouveaux*, 15 August 1920.

19.   Ibid.

20.   "Une Lettre de Pierre Kropotkine," *les Temps nouveaux*, 15 October 1919.

21.   "Une Lettre de Pierre Kropotkine," *les Temps nouveaux*, 15 August 1920.

22.   Alexandre Skirda, *Autonomie Individuelle et Force Collective: Les anarchistes et l'organisation de Proudhon à nos jours* (Paris: Alexandre Skirda, 1987), p.154: "One of the most astonishing things is to see ex-individualists becoming fervent followers of bolshevism." All the "ex-individualists" cited in fact remained individualists. Jean Maitron (vol. II, p.54) found the case of such individualists "quite inexplicable."

23.   *Les Glaneurs*, June 1917.

24.   *Les Glaneurs*, September 1917.

25.   Ibid. See also Albin, "Epis Mûrs," *les Glaneurs*, January 1918: "The peoples of today are in no state to govern themselves."

26.   *Les Glaneurs*, January 1918.

27.   *Par-delà la Mêlée*, 15 September 1917.

28. Chardon embraced the economic theories of Proudhon, criticized Kropotkin's communism as naïve and unworkable and insisted that Dunois "has always been drenched with marxism." *La Mêlée*, 15 July and 1 October 1918.

29. *La Mêlée*, 15 December 1918.

30. Ibid.

31. *Le Réveil de l'Esclave*, March 1921.

32. *L'en dehors*, November 1922.

33. *Un*, December 1920.

34. Ibid.

35. See for example: Prouvost and Stackelberg in *le Réveil de l'Esclave*, March 1921.

36. See for instance "La Faillite du Parlementarisme," *l'Idée libre*, October 1919; J.-L. Delvy, "L'Education au Pays des Soviets," July 1920; Léon Prouvost, "Le code bolchevik du mariage," July 1921.

37. *L'Idée libre*, November 1918. At this early stage, Lorulot believed the soviet system to represent a "free, harmonious federalism."

38. Lorulot thought that even if there were structural dangers in the bolshevik system, it was possible to rely on the "morality and probity of Lenin and his friends," Ibid. Cf. Bergeron's much later review of Gorky's study of Lenin: "Needless to say that the Lenin seen by Maxim Gorky (and who would question the probity and psychological sensitivity of Gorky?) is not the autocratic and bloodthirsty Lenin presented to us by the so-called anarchist elements and the so-called reactionaries; it is a noble-hearted and self-sacrificing Lenin." *Lueurs*, 15 April 1925. Gorky was much admired by the French individualists both as a writer and as a privileged interpreter of social and political developments.

39. For example in *le Réveil de l'Esclave*, March 1921: "I repeat, I am not a supporter of Dictatorship. But I feel a certain sympathy for the Russian bolshevists."

40. *Le Réveil de l'Esclave*, March 1921.

41. Ibid.. Cf. J.-L. Delvy's reference to "an impulsive and sentimental mass always on the side of whoever gives it something to eat." *L'Idée Libre*, July 1920.

42. *Le Réveil de l'Esclave*, March 1921.

43. Ibid. On the anarchist poet Tailhade (1854–1919) see Thierry Maricourt, *Histoire de la littérature libertaire* (Paris: Albin Michel, 1990), pp.222–9.

44. *Le Réveil de l'Esclave*, March 1921.

45. Ibid.

46. Victor Serge, who before the war had himself been associated with the individualists more than with the anarchist communists, now criticized the individualists for their arrogance in this respect: "But what is this 'mass' which you so scorn? Where can it be found? Is it not also you and I?" *La Mêlée*, 15 November 1918. Serge was at that time being held in a concentration camp at Précigné (Sarthe), but was soon to be sent back to Russia with others, in exchange for French hostages held by the bolsheviks. See his *Mémoires d'un révolutionnaire 1901–1941* (Paris: Seuil, 1951), ch.2; and Jean Maitron, "De Kibaltchiche à Victor Serge. Le Rétif (1909–1919)," in *Mouvement social* no.47 (April–June 1964), pp.45–78.

47. *La Mêlée*, 15 August 1919.

48. *Le Réveil de l'Esclave*, April 1921.

49. Undated Sûreté report [1920?]. F7/13090.

50. See the *Bulletin mensuel de la Ligue d'Action Anticatholique*, May 1922, supplement to *l'Idée libre*, May 1922: "Here at 'l'Idée Libre' we have always supported with the greatest sympathy the difficult work of the Soviets. But today, if the reports of the treaty between

the bolsheviks and the pope are correct, we are bound to declare that the bolsheviks have made a very big mistake."

51.   *Le Réveil de l'Esclave*, January 1922.

52.   It is interesting because such an interpretation tends to be favoured by extreme-right sympathizers. See S. Payne, *A History of Fascism, 1914–45* (London: 1995); R. Griffin, *The Nature of Fascism* (London: 1991); R. Griffin (ed.), *International Fascism. Theories, Causes and the New Consensus* (London: Arnold, 1998).

53.   *Le Libertaire*, 28 August 1936;. Ruff was born of wealthy Jewish parents in 1877. Having broken with his family when still young, he made his living as a proof-reader. Arrested in 1942, he was to die in deportation in Germany. See *DBMOF*, vol.15.

54.   "Les Fascismes," *Germinal*, 12 August 1922.

55.   *Germinal*, 13 March 1926. For other early examples, see *Germinal*, 22 September 1923 and *le Libertaire*, 15 December 1922.

56.   Daniel Colson, *Anarcho-syndicalisme et communisme. Saint-Etienne 1920–1925* (Saint-Etienne: Université de Saint-Etienne/Centre d'Etudes Foréziennes/Atelier de Création Libertaire, 1986), p.73, note 79.

57.   Michaud, *J'avais vingt ans*, p.242.

58.   May Picqueray, *May la réfractaire* (Paris: Atelier Marcel Jullian, 1979), p.92.

59.   Louis Lecoin, *Le Cours d'une vie* (Paris: Louis Lecoin, 1965), p. 98. Raymond Poincaré was President of the Republic 1913–20, Prime Minister and Foreign Minister 1922–24; in favour of a policy of "firmness" towards Germany since before the war, he was responsible for the occupation of the Ruhr.

60.   *Le Libertaire*, 29 June 1919.

61.   *Le Réveil de l'Esclave*, March and April 1921.

62.   *Germinal*, 23 July 1921.

63.   *Germinal*, 22 January 1921.

64.   *Le Libertaire*, 2 December 1921.

65.   *Les Temps nouveaux*, April-May 1921.

66.   See Sébastien Faure's explanations of why he waited for so long before becoming openly critical of the bolshevik regime: the three-part article "Mon opinion sur la dictature," *le Libertaire*, 15, 22 and 29 April 1921; see also his article "Claire et logique: Telle est, comme toujours, notre attitude," *Germinal*, 5 February 1921.

6

The Anarchists and the Revolutionary Syndicalist Movement

The war has revolutionized all the theories we believed to be inviolable.

Executive Commission of the Revolutionary Syndicalist Committee, 1921[1]

If on a political level the anarchists were in an ambivalent or contradictory position as regards their relations with the communists in day-to-day campaigning activities, the situation in the syndicalist movement was certainly no clearer.[2] The revolutionary minority within the CGT at the end of the Great War was heterogeneous, but—represented by the Comité de défense syndicaliste (CDS), with Raymond Péricat as its secretary—it was united in its opposition to the "reformist" majority because of what was perceived as the betrayal by Léon Jouhaux and the CGT leadership of the organization's revolutionary, antimilitarist and internationalist principles in 1914–18—not just because of the leadership's embracing of the national war effort, but also because of its involvement with government.[3] In the words of the anarchist coal-miners' leader Benoît Broutchoux, such participation was "antisyndicalist in the sense that the CGT has to stay in the background or play the rôle of servant, which is a violation of the Confederation's decisions."[4] The CGT's continuation of this policy of co-operative engagement with the state (the policy of "maintaining a presence" implied by its "Minimum Programme" of December 1918) after the war was seen as corporatist and class collaborationist; its performance during the (arguably) potentially revolutionary period of 1919–20 as irredeemably and unforgivably feeble and reformist. In both respects, the CGT leadership and majority were condemned as having betrayed the principles of revolutionary syndicalism as enshrined in the founding statutes of 1895 and the Amiens Charter of 1906.

The revolutionary syndicalist minority was also initially united in its admiration for the Russian revolution, "inspirational and pure in its

Table 2

A Chronology of Revolutionary Syndicalism, 1916–1926

	CGT congresses	CGT minority	"Anarcho-syndicalist" tendency within the minority	International Communist Organizations	Revolutionary Syndicalist International
1916		CDS (Péricat) (Aug.)			
1917	Clermont-Ferrand conference (Dec)				
1918	19th National Congress, Paris-Versaille (July)	Minority conference, St-Etienne (May)			
1919	20th National Congress, Lyon (Sept.)	CSR (Dec.) *Vie ouvrière* relaunch (April)		Comintern (March)	
1920	21st National Congress, Orléans (Sept.–Oct.)			2nd Comintern conference (July–Aug.)	Berlin conference, (Dec.)
1921	22nd National Congress, Lille (July)	CSR conference, Paris (Dec.)		Profintern (July)	
1922		CGTU founding congress, St-Etienne (June-July)	CDS (Besnard) (July)	2nd Profintern conference (Nov.)	2nd Berlin conference (June)
1923	23d National Congress, Paris (Jan.–Feb.)	2nd National Congress CGTU, Bourges (Nov.)			IWMA founding congress, Berlin (Dec. 22–Jan. 23)
1924					
1925			UFSA Founding congress, St-Ouen (July)		
1926			CGTSR Founding congress, Lyon (Nov.)		

Notes: CGT and CGTU congresses are shown only up to 1923. Underlining indicates the creation of a group or organization.

early days."[5] After the creation of the SFIC at the end of 1920, the situation in the syndicalist ranks would be rendered more complicated by the appearance of a new kind of activist: the Communist Party member. From then on, although Jouhaux's two-fold treachery would never be forgotten and would still occasionally serve to unite revolutionaries of all tendencies, debate tended to hinge more on the question of relations between the unions and political parties, hence the importance of the debate regarding international affiliation and the true nature of the Profintern, created under the auspices of the Comintern in 1921.[6]

THE CGT'S LYON CONGRESS, 1919: "THE ADMINISTRATOR IS KILLING THE APOSTLE"

As the veteran anarchist and syndicalist Georges Yvetot put it just before the CGT's Lyon congress of September 1919, the first since the Armistice: "There can be no doubt: there will be a sharp struggle at the Confederal Congress in Lyon. It is unavoidable and it will be useful."[7] It was indeed a tumultuous one in comparison with the two previous national congresses. (Despite the existence of a growing and increasingly well-organized revolutionary opposition, the military situation meant that the CGT congresses of 1917 and 1918 were in fact characterized by a certain restraint and willingness to compromise on both sides.) In 1919, the minority was also now able to add its objection to Jouhaux's continuing "class collaboration" after the armistice to its critique of his war-time policy and his about-turn in 1914.

Behind such strategic changes lay the CGT leadership's proposals for "rationalizing" the CGT. At Lyon, Pierre Monatte attacked the proposed administrative reorganization, arguing that it took all influence away from the UDs (Departmental Unions), "more idealistic," and gave more power to the Industrial Federations, which, he claimed, were "sectional and centralist."[8] At the same congress, Guillaume Verdier of the Metalworkers also insisted, with reference to the strikes of that year: "It was we, the secretaries and representatives of the UDs who were most strongly in favour of action. ... We felt that in the National Council we represented the class spirit of the workers, a spirit which clashed with the sectional spirit of the Federation secretaries."[9] Yvetot, who had succeeded Pelloutier at the Fédération des Bourses in 1901 and who had been given the task of establishing UDs across France in 1913, wrote in *le Journal du Peuple* in support of Monatte's speech at Lyon, underlining the revolutionary rôle of the UDs:

> The rôle of the Departemental Union is not to develop sectionalism, as the Industrial Federations develop sectionalism. On

the contrary, the *raison d'être* of the UDs is the development of syndicalism. The propaganda carried out by the UDs, by virtue of the fact that it is broader and more general, relating to the cause of the working class rather than to the cause of a particular trade or industry, tends to make *trade unionists* of those who were merely *unionized*, whatever their trade. On the other hand, the federations direct their efforts at gaining a greater number of members whose sectional interests they then defend and protect and often do no more than that.

Federations, Yvetot went on, inevitably centralise, whereas the Departmental Union inevitably decentralises: "So one can see how easy it is for activists who are courageous, intelligent and enthusiastic to sow everywhere and for everybody the beneficial and fertile seed of the idea of social revolution. Within the Departmental Unions and everywhere in the name of the Departmental Unions, all the economic and social problems of production, distribution and consumption are discussed and will one day be resolved. They are our Soviets!"[10]

Criticisms of the CGT leadership on the grounds of bureaucracy and over-centralization were widespread among anarchists and revolutionary syndicalists.[11] As one Parisian railworker and union branch secretary put it:

The cause of syndicalism, to our mind, is not promoted by excessive centralizations which wrench control of trade union affairs out of the hands of the rank and file in order to place it in the hands of a few individuals who lose no time in transforming themselves from mandated delegates into leaders; on the contrary, if we want syndicalism to develop, we should firstly be trying to interest and involve the masses in the life of their organization, and secondly in the life of the working class as a whole.[12]

Three years after these remarks were made, the September 1920 congress of the revolutionary minority would pass a motion which also stressed this concern regarding the CGT's lack of connection with ordinary trade unionists and arguing that the revitalization of the CGT would have to involve the establishment of "more direct links with the workers in their workshops, building sites, offices and fields."[13] These are concerns which still have a resonance today, and we shall return to the anarchist syndicalists' views on trade union organization when we come to examine certain aspects of the debates at the CGTU's Saint-Etienne congress of 1922, the creation of the "anarcho-syndicalist"

CGTSR in 1926 and the decision of some union organizations to remain or become independent of any national confederation.

But it is clear that feelings about internal democracy in the CGT were already running high at the end of the war and that such concerns contributed to opposition to the leadership of Jouhaux and his reformist colleagues. By 1919, the revolutionaries were becoming stronger and voices calling for an immediate split from the CGT were becoming more numerous. The minority's motion—condemning the CGT leadership's policy of the previous five years, rejecting further class collaboration and calling for the "generalized expropriation of the capitalist class" after the example of the Russian revolution—gained 588 votes against 1,393 for the leadership and 42 abstentions.[14]

THE CREATION OF THE REVOLUTIONARY SYNDICALIST COMMITTEES, 1919–20

In October 1919, immediately after the CGT Congress, the revolutionary minority formed a provisional committee of which Monatte became secretary and which included Bertho Lepetit, Gaston Monmousseau, Raymond Péricat, Henri Sirolle and Joseph Tommasi. Two months later, Marie Guillot and the syndicalists around L'Ecole émancipée called for the creation of a Comité Syndicaliste Révolutionnaire (CSR, Revolutionary Syndicalist Committee) and the creation of local committees throughout the country in an attempt to organize all those who "accept as an organizational basis the régime of direct proletarian sovereignty" as well as "violent struggle if necessary" in order to take control of the means of production and exchange, a control which would be ensured "temporarily by the dictatorship of the proletariat."[15]

In September 1920, a congress of the CSRs decided on organizational structures were decided on.[16] A Central Committee was also elected, with Monatte as secretary general.[17] In Moscow, in July 1920, just before the opening of the second conference of the Comintern, a series of meetings of trade unionists from various countries had led to the creation of a "Provisional International Trade Union Council," which called for the creation of a Red International of Labour Unions.[18] A vote at the CSR congress on affiliation to this new trade union international was virtually unanimous.[19]

THE CGT'S ORLÉANS CONGRESS, 1920

At the CGT's Orléans congress in October 1920, the debates continued to centre on the Jouhaux leadership's "collaborationist" policies, but increasingly importance was also attached to the question of international affiliation. Jouhaux attempted to woo the anarchists by invoking the Amiens Charter and emphasizing the question of freedom from party political interference. At this stage, however, the revolutionaries' passionate opposition to the majority's record was enough to overcome their own divisions.

Between Orléans and the CGT's next congress, held in Lille in July 1921, the revolutionaries' influence grew considerably, the CSRs now having established a parallel organization including 11 Regional Unions and 17 Federations and representing about 45% of the total vote. It has been calculated that between 300,000 and 400,000 workers were voting for "anarcho-syndicalist" positions in 1920–21 — more, in absolute terms, than ever before, even at the height of anarchist influence within the CGT around 1909.[20]

January 1921 also saw the creation by the UA of a Club Ouvrier, Anarchiste, Syndicaliste, Fédéraliste which held a series of meetings addressed by UA militants, CSR representatives, R. Péricat (for the Confédération des travailleurs du monde[21]) and others on all the major questions facing the syndicalist movement.[22] One militant, reflecting a widespread anarchist suspicion of the CSRs because of the rôle within them of many militants perceived to be too close to the bolsheviks, argued as late as May 1921 that the Club ought to be developed into an alternative to the CSRs, "too influenced by the politicians."[23]

But in fact from May 1921, the CSRs were led by anarchists and by syndicalists whose conception of syndicalism was very similar to the anarchists': Pierre Besnard was elected secretary general, with Pierre Fargues and Augustin Quinton as the two assistant secretaries. The prospect of the CGT's soon being led by Besnard and the anarchists around him was, then, not unrealistic. That the Besnard group was determined to take control of the CGT is indicated by the fact that Besnard and 17 of his closest allies were involved in a secret "Pact" between February and July 1921 to ensure their dominance of the CSR and, ultimately, of the CGT and to prevent bolshevism from destroying the revolutionary syndicalist movement.[24] This was to be done by ensuring the election of comrades who were "exclusively federalist and autonomist revolutionary syndicalist" to as many positions of responsibility as possible. The Pact's existence is perhaps indicative of the effect on syndicalists in France of the eye-witness accounts of the realities of bolshevism provided by syndicalists such as Lepetit, Vergeat and Wilkens. And it certainly tells us something about the atmosphere in the CGT at the time. As the UA's Content wrote in *le Libertaire* in the spring of 1922: "The syndicalist movement ... at present resembles bedlam, with everyone protesting their good intentions whilst accusing others of the worst."[25]

THE CGT'S LILLE CONGRESS, 1921: THE PARTING OF THE WAYS

Hopes of anarchist syndicalists once again dominating the CGT would, however, soon be dashed. By the time of the Lille congress of July 1921, the CGT had already begun moves to expel unions that had affiliated to the CSR.[26] In these circumstances, it is not surprising that barely had the Lille congress begun than trouble broke out, apparently provoked by physical intimidation on the part of stewards and by attempts to exclude delegates belonging to the minority. The fighting was only stopped by Lecoin firing two shots in the air.[27] The revolutionary minority were so incensed by these provocations that many of them joined the calls for an immediate split, thus adding to divisions that already existed among the revolutionaries because of the debate over the Profintern.

On the second day of the congress, Lecoin spoke with passion on the leadership's record:[28]

> If, as was the case in the old days, we could face each other with sincerity on both sides, we would be able to get a result. But as long as we have at the head of our organization men who are the shame of the entire working class, it will not be possible. The first thing you have to do is to reject them, throw them out.
>
> Jouhaux and his accomplices have sometimes expressed regret that those who made accusations against them in the press did not make those accusations to their face, here at congress. Well, I for one am happy to repeat to Jouhaux' face everything I have ever written about him!

Lecoin went on to quote at length a rousing revolutionary and antimilitarist speech made by Jouhaux in 1912 and to contrast this with his attitude in 1914 and during the war: "I suppose Jouhaux personally had the right to change his mind, pack his bag and leave. But he did not have the right to drag with him the whole of the CGT and to sound off in support of the massacres of the war in the name of the organization."[29] He ended by accusing Jouhaux and Dumoulin of cowardice, of having capitulated in 1914 for fear of being held personally responsible by the state for any revolutionary activity by the CGT, and because they had been promised by Louis Malvy, the Minister of the Interior, that they would be left in peace if they prevented the CGT from disrupting the mobilisation.[30]

Such impassioned denunciations give an idea of the depth of feeling shared by many delegates. It was largely thanks to Lecoin's efforts that the minority managed to unite around a single resolution. This reaffirmed the complete independence of syndicalism from all political groups and demanded that the CGT leave both the IFTU (the reformist International Federation of Trade Unions, which had been reconstituted at the Amsterdam congress of July–August 1919) and the International Labour Office (created in Geneva by the League of Nations); it suggested that the CGT affiliate to the Profintern only on condition that the latter respect syndicalist autonomy. Support for the minority had been growing and came close to matching the majority, despite the uses to which the majority had put fears of subordination of the unions to the Comintern. In the vote on general orientation at the end of the Lille congress, the majority won by only 1,556 to 1,348 and on international affiliation, the majority (affiliation to the IFTU) gained 1,572 votes to the revolutionaries' 1,325 (affiliation to the new Moscow-based International), with 66 abstentions.[31]

The CSR central committee called an extraordinary congress—a "unity congress"—for December 1921, protesting that the expulsions were contrary to the CGT's statutes, and the autumn of 1921 saw the continuation of negotiations aimed at enabling the re-admission of the expelled organizations. But to no avail. By the time the "unity congress" took place in December, all it could do—apart from sending a delegation to the CGT headquarters in a last-ditch effort which nobody really believed would work—was acknowledge the expulsion of the CSRs by the CGT leadership and the effective split of the organization. Already, the minority had begun to refer to itself as the "CGT Révolutionnaire."

RESPONSIBILITY FOR THE SPLIT OF 1921

The division of the CGT inevitably had serious repercussions, and both organizations (the CGT and what would become the CGTU) were bound to suffer. A contemporary, writing in 1923, insisted: "There is no doubt that for three years now syndicalism has been going through a serious crisis: a crisis of recruitment, a crisis of confidence, a crisis of will."[32] The working class was becoming tired of watching the different factions tearing into each other. The gradual decline in membership, which began with the repression of the 1920 strikes, continued and was exacerbated. An exhausted and demoralized working class would not regain its combativity for over a decade.

Who to hold responsible for the split was a matter for debate then and still is today. Maitron quotes a comrade of Besnard's, the Loire metal-worker Théo Argence, for whom it was Besnard's doctrinaire and stubborn character that led him to create new organizations that he could shape according to his own opinions.[33] Quinton, Fargues and

Besnard insisted in their motion to the CSR congress of December 1921 that they believed the split to have been "wanted, calculated and premeditated" by the CGT leadership.[34] The UA's André Colomer held the communists responsible: "Nothing the revolutionary syndicalist movement is suffering from at the moment is worse than the ills caused by the communist's policies. By creating confusion between the union and the party, by clouding the issues in the International, by systematically installing its supporters at the head of the workers' organizations, Moscow is just as responsible as Jouhaux and his accomplices for the mess the movement is now in and which we are trying to get out of."[35]

Monatte, for his part, denied that the communists were responsible and pointed the finger at the reformist majority and blamed the "so-called pure syndicalists" around Besnard (including several who at the time were members of the SFIC but rejected the Comintern's policy) for being so naïve and hot-headed.[36] The differences between Monatte and the VO group on the one hand and the anarchists and "pure syndicalists" on the other were certainly profound; if the former had cautioned patience and advocated gradually undermining the leadership's support in the Federations and UDs, the latter were visibly less patient. The great majority of members of the revolutionary minority were still remarkably determined to avoid a split if at all possible, but a few had been calling for a break away from the CGT since 1919. The UA's Content, for instance, wrote in July 1919 attacking the "renegades" Jouhaux and Dumoulin and insisting that the time had come for a clarification of the conflict between the majority and the minority: "Following the example of our Italian, Spanish and American comrades ... let us create more flexible and less hierarchical organizations, impregnated with the idealist and revolutionary spirit ... That is the urgent task of the moment: the organization of the workers on a new basis, with new methods; the organization of idealistic, anarchist and revolutionary minorities, as a ferment, as pioneers, as an inspiration to others."[37] Such demands were expressed more forcefully after Lille. André Colomer, secretary of the Paris Inter-Union Committee for Entertainment Industry Workers and another leading figure amongst UA members in the CGT, wrote in *le Libertaire*, "Before Lille, I believed unity possible, indispensible ... At Lille, I was afraid of a split. .... Today, two months after Lille, not only do I see a split as inevitable, but I also think it indispensible. ... In fact, the division exists already: we are already effectively split."[38] Colomer's argument was that coexistence was favourable only to the reformists and was demotivating for the mass of militants. The revolutionary syndicalist movement had to act clearly and decisively, giving the lead by creating a new organization free of centralization and bureaucracy: "Let us prepare resolutely, let us organize, let us create today the CGT we want: the revolutionary CGT."

CONFLICT WITHIN THE "CGT RÉVOLUTIONNAIRE," 1921–22

The CSR's December 1921 congress in Paris was thus held in a tense, heady atmosphere, and on the second day came confirmation of the expulsion of the CSRs. During late 1921 and until the summer of 1922, the revolutionaries' own divisions became more visible as they were no longer united against the common enemy of reformism and as they came to be faced with major tactical and strategic decisions with far-reaching consequences for the whole of the French left and labour movement.

There was a small minority of syndicalists in the CSRs who were members of the SFIC and faithful to the Comintern line, and who were thus unreservedly in favour of membership of the Profintern and in favour of close links between the syndicalist organization and the communist organization, both nationally and internationally. Given the ideologically chaotic state of the nascent SFIC, however, many other syndicalists who were simultaneously members of the party nevertheless continued to assert the traditional syndicalist demand for complete autonomy from all political parties. Such communists thus found themselves among the "pure syndicalists" allied with the anarchists.[39] Pierre Besnard himself totally rejected any links with political parties and, unlike the UA militants, believed in the self-sufficiency of syndicalism.[40] It is worth quoting at some length the resolution put forward by Quinton, Fargues and Besnard, secretaries of the CSR Central Committee in December 1921:

> Syndicalism must live and develop in absolute independence, and … it must enjoy the complete autonomy which is appropriate to its character as a true revolutionary force.
>
> This does not mean that syndicalists intend to ignore the other forces which, acting in other domains and in different ways, also have as their objective the disappearance of Capitalism and the State; but they declare that all the revolutionary forces have as their mission to interpret the aspirations of a proletariat whom it is their duty to serve and not to command. …
>
> Consequently, … although the CGTR refuses any idea of subordination or permanent linkage between one organization and another, it will always be ready to accept all honest proposals of sincere and disinterested co-operation.
>
> … In the pre-revolutionary period, each grouping must work in its own domain, motivated by the general interest of the work-

ing class. ... Alliances freely entered into, of limited and vari-
able duration, may be concluded between the various revolutionary forces in order to achieve pre-defined, shared objectives
and employing means which are clearly established by those
concerned.[41]

The position of syndicalists such as Monatte and Monmousseau,
grouped around *la Vie ouvrière*, was that co-operation between the CGT
and the SFIC, as equal partners, would give the revolutionary movement a much needed cohesion and would actually strengthen syndicalism rather than weaken it. The lesson of recent years was, for most of
them, that the Amiens Charter and pre-war revolutionary syndicalism
were in need of revision. Many VO supporters were nevertheless distrustful of the SFIC, and Monmousseau, for instance, wrote in September 1920 in response to concerns expressed by the "pure syndicalist"
Verdier: "We remain convinced autonomists."[42] Indeed, when two of
the French CSR delegates to the founding conference of the Profintern
(July 1921) agreed to sign the final motion on close organic links between all sections of the revolutionary movement, such was the almost
universal disapproval with which they were greeted by other CSR militants on their return to France, that one of them, Victor Godonnèche,
felt obliged to resign from the *Vie ouvrière* group and the other, Tommasi,
resigned from his UD post.[43] In fact, although Monatte and those close
to him were, in general, hostile to the anarchists, such were their differences with the SFIC and the Russian revolutionaries at this stage, that
in late 1921 they found themselves quite close to the so-called "pure
syndicalists." This would change in the spring of 1922.

Right from the very start of the December 1921 congress, then,
two main tendencies had appeared. The anarchists and the "pure syndicalists" (Besnard, Barthes, Veber, Boudoux *et al*) were in favour of
an immediate break away from the CGT.[44] Another tendency, led by
Monatte, was more cautious and drew a distinction between the hated
CGT leadership and the rank and file at present still in the majority, arguing that the latter, not represented at the minority's congress, should
be given more time to join them, and that the revolutionaries as a whole
should fight tooth and nail to stay in the CGT and gain control of it from
within.

In the end, a compromise resolution was passed unanimously, reaffirming the unity of those present on the basis of the Amiens Charter,
and demanding that an extraordinary congress of the CGT be held in
the first quarter of 1922. The CGT leadership was given until 31 January to come to a decision. In the meantime, a provisional Administrative

Commission and Confederal Bureau were created to act as a link between the organizations present. There are doubts as to how democratic the following elections were, given the haste and state of confusion in which the list of candidates was drawn up and the elections carried out, and Marie Guillot for one would write about this to the CA afterwards, complaining in particular of intimidation by certain anarchist militants.[45] But the result was an overwhelming victory for the anarchists and "pure syndicalists," and a clear defeat for Monatte and for those communists faithful to the International's line. The remainder of the congress was even more dominated by the anarchists and their allies, the debates devoted to attacks on bolshevik Russia and the "dictatorship of the politicians" allegedly proposed by the Profintern. The verdict of a triumphant *le Libertaire* was that "the revolutionary syndicalists have understood clearly that Jouhaux and his friends betrayed them during the war, and they understand equally well that Monatte and his friends were betraying true syndicalism by agreeing to be the agents of party politics in the trade unions."[46]

ANARCHO-SYNDICALIST DOMINANCE IN THE CGTR

The period between the split in December 1921 and the founding congress of the CGTU at Saint-Etienne in June 1922 represents the highpoint of the anarchists' influence, an influence made possible to a large extent by the other revolutionaries' divisions and uncertainties. As Rosmer put it in a letter to the Profintern Executive: "The anarchists have quite a lot of influence. Their theoretical baggage and their taste for organization are not great; but in the midst of the indecision, they give the impression of knowing what they want and where they want to go, and they are carrying the undecided along with them."[47] The CSR's 14-strong provisional Administrative Committee included 5 of the signatories of the "Pact" (Besnard, Verdier, Quinton, Pothion and Bisch) and three leading UA members (Colomer, Lecoin, Barthes); the Bureau consisted of three anarchists: Labrousse (a building-worker), Paul Cadeau and Henri Totti (a railway-worker from Marseille). From December 1921 to April 1922, the CSRs had their own weekly organ, *le Syndicaliste Révolutionnaire* (managing editor J. B. Vallet of the Building-workers), succeeded by *la Bataille Syndicaliste* in May–June 1922. Both papers were predominantly anarchistic in tone. The first issue of *le Syndicaliste révolutionnaire* declared the CSRs to be "federalist," "autonomist" and "independent," the heirs of Bakunin, Proudhon, Pelloutier and the pre-war CGT; the CSRs were to be distinguished from the "new right-wing syndicalism" (the reformists) and from the "new left-wing syndicalism" (who wanted links with the parties of the Left).[48]

Such was the extent of anarchist domination of the CGTU in the first months of 1922, that the communists who had got themselves elected to the CA stopped attending meetings after the spring of that year, and the Russians were so worried they launched a propaganda campaign and redoubled their efforts to organize an opposition to the anarchists. The turning point, however, was the return to the fray of Pierre Monatte, who, after remaining silent since the previous December, wrote in *l'Humanité* in April 1922, accusing the "pure syndicalists" of being responsible for splitting the CGT, and attacking the growing anarchist domination of the CGTU and the organization's increasingly anti-soviet stance.[49] Soon afterwards, Monatte would join the editorial team of *l'Humanité*, thus lending valuable working-class credibility to the SFIC.

THE FOUNDING CONFERENCE OF THE CGTU, SAINT-ETIENNE, 1922

So the Saint-Etienne congress of June 1922 represented the culmination of the conflicts between the different revolutionary syndicalist tendencies which had been going on more or less openly since 1918. The different tendencies clashed over five questions: (i) the behaviour of the Provisional Administrative Committee and Bureau since December 1921; (ii) the future structure of the CGTU; (iii) relations between the CGTU and "outside organizations"; (iv) the aims of revolutionary syndicalism; and (v) international affiliation.[50]

The anarcho-syndicalists: domineering conspirators?

Firstly, then, having accused the communist members of the CA of having "deserted their posts" for having failed to attend meetings, the anarchists and "pure syndicalists" were themselves accused by the former of having effectively excluded those with different opinions through a combination of hostile, insulting and intimidatory behaviour and by the undemocratic imposition of decisions prior to any real debate. Further, the provisional CA and Bureau had been mandated the previous December to invite all syndicalists to the Saint-Etienne congress, whereas they had only invited those unions which had already joined the revolutionary minority in December 1921, thus reinforcing their own position. They had also exceeded their mandate by effectively establishing policy, which was the prerogative of congress. It was difficult for the anarchists and their allies to answer these allegations, particularly after the revelation of the existence of the Besnard group's Pact, which it had been easy for Monatte to portray as a conspiracy to ensure the domination of an unelected clique.[51] In the light of this, warnings coming from those involved in the Pact of the dangers of interference, underhand manipulation and undue influence by the communists were somewhat undermined.

The structure of the CGTU

The CA was proposing four main changes, whose overarching aim was to "place the entire confederal organization under the constant and direct control of its members":[52] (i) the Departmental Unions (based on bourgeois political structures) would be replaced by Regional Unions (which would be based on the economic and social realities of the country); (ii) the Federations would lose all power; (iii) no member of the Confederal Bureau would be eligible for re-election for a period of three years; (iv) responsibility for propaganda and thus the allocations of financial resources would be shifted from the Confederation to the URs. The communist syndicalists argued against these proposals for a series of reasons: (i) the practical administrative difficulties of abolishing the familiar UDs and replacing them with completely new bodies; (ii) replacing 90 UDs with only 20 URs would both produce more distant bureaucracies and signifcantly reduce the representation of member unions, effectively centralizing rather than decentralizing; (iii) if it was a good idea to reduce the power of the Federations, their exclusion from the CCN and CA would render the co-ordination of a national industrial strike impossible; (iv) there simply were not enough good militants for mandates not to be renewed; (v) in a country which was increasingly centralized both politically and economically, how could the working class fight back if it was effectively prevented from organizing coherently at a national level?

The CGTU's relations with political organizations

When it came to the question of relations with "outside groups," the anarchists inveighed of course against the Comintern's policy of "organic links" between syndicalists and communists at both national and international levels. The communists replied that the anarchists were also guilty of attempting to impose their own political and philosophical views on the CGTU. Again, this was an accusation which was difficult to answer and highlights a certain ambiguity in the position adopted in this period by many anarchists.

The aims of revolutionary syndicalism

The ultimate aim of all present at Saint-Etienne was revolution, and most judged it to be imminent: the text put by Quinton, Fargues and Besnard to the December 1921 congress had taken as its premiss that "our country is moving chaotically but surely towards the destruction of its present foundations," and the debates must be understood in this context.[53] Beyond this, analyses diverged. For the anarchists, the aim of the revolution must be to destroy not just capitalism but also the State. A "proletarian" State was a utopia, and the example of what had happened in Russia was proof of this. If some kind of transitional period—during which capital would defend its interests with violence—was inevitable, only the unions themselves were capable of ensuring the defence of the revolution, both against bourgeois reaction and against any political party that attempted to profit from the workers' revolutionary movement.

The communist syndicalists found this view of the situation of the French working class rather idyllic: the majority of French workers were not unionized; it was difficult to imagine the CGTU's administrative structure being able to cope with co-ordinating every aspect of the country's social and economic life, as well organizing the armed defence of the revolution; if the French proletariat was so "mature" and class conscious, what had gone wrong in 1914 and 1920? The revolutionary movement had to be careful not to separate itself from non-proletarians; and within the working class, the revolutionaries must not isolate themselves from the more "backward" masses. At the same time as the "economic" revolution, the State apparatus had to be conquered and some form of repressive force had to be created to deal with counter-revolutionaries: anything else was simply utopian.

The CGTU's international affiliation

This was the only debate on which the alliance between anarchists and "pure syndicalists" was broken: only the anarchists argued unambiguously against affiliation to the Moscow-based international. The Profintern had held its constitutive congress in July 1921, in parallel with the third congress of the Comintern and just days before the CGT's Lille congress. The French CSR delegation consisted of Jean Gaudeaux, Henri Sirolle, Michel Kneller, Victor Godonnèche, Joseph Tommasi, Victor Labonne, Georges Gaye and Claudine and Albert Lemoine.[54] Sirolle made contact with the Russian anarchists around *Golos Truda* (The Voice of Labour) as soon as the delegation arrived in Moscow, and so had access to detailed information regarding the repression of dissident revolutionaries. The French anarchist syndicalists seem to have been isolated at the congress, and because of their insistence on traditional syndicalist autonomism were perceived by the bolsheviks and those close to them as being obstructive—although it is debatable how real this isolation was, given the ways in which the bolsheviks fabricated majorities at the conference for their own positions.[55]

The congress' final resolution concerning relations between the Comintern and the Profintern argued—despite protests and a counter-proposal put forward by Lemoine—that in the face of the "united forces of the bourgeoisie," it was necessary for the revolutionary movement to have "close contacts and organic links" between the Comintern and the Profintern and that it was "highly desirable" that there be similar co-operation at the national level between syndicalist organizations and their respective Communist Parties.[56]

As soon as this resolution became known in France, it caused a stir. The Central Committee of the CSRs immediately published a declaration rejecting the resolution on the grounds that it was contrary to syndicalist autonomy and that it would be incapable of rallying the international syndicalist movement to the new International. Close liaison with the French PC, it argued, would effectively prevent the revolutionary CGT from being open to all workers and would reduce the organization to the status of a political sect. The CSRs were also of the opinion, however, that Godonnèche and Tommasi had exceeded their mandate in signing the Profintern resolution.

By the time of the CSR's December 1921 congress, not much progress had been made. The Central Committee's resolution (signed by Quinton, Fargues and Besnard) "regretted that the decisions taken by the Moscow congress make it impossible for the CGTR to affiliate to the Profintern" but nevertheless went on to assert that "the axis of revolutionary action remains in Moscow" and that "the Russian Revolution is still the only force of attraction for World Revolution."[57] It was still hoped that an agreement could be reached with the Profintern that would enable the CGTR to join, but prior to this, the CSRs wished to organize a conference of representatives of "all the proletariats which share, partially or totally, the French point of view." Having established a common position, this conference should then request an extraordinary congress of the Profintern.

The reason for anarchist hostility was that Article 14 of the Comintern's statutes, according to which the syndicalist organization was the syndicalist section of the Comintern, looked to them very much like a replay of the attempt by the marxist socialist Jules Guesde to subordinate the unions to the politicians in the early days of the CGT. As the anarchist syndicalist J.-S. Boudoux put it in the "Tribune Syndicaliste" of *le Libertaire* at the time of the Profintern's founding conference: "We are convinced that Russian syndicalism is a creature of the State, not sovietic, but centralist. ... We know that we must, in the interests of syndicalism both nationally and internationally, break with Amsterdam, seat of the *political and governmental* trade union International. But is that a reason, despite our great sympathies for the Russian Revolution, to throw ourselves into the arms of the *Bolsheviks*, a Russian governmental political party?"[58] The essential point here was the old one of syndicalist autonomy (and therefore working-class unity) *versus* links with political parties: "This dilemma, communism and syndicalism, is not a new one! It is a new version of an old cliché. The first time around, it was called socialism and syndicalism, now and since Tours it is called communism and syndicalism. Jokers! because for us it will always be politicking and syndicalism."[59] Two years later, as the SFIC was increasing its control of the unions, P. Laccord would make similar points:

> It is the Guesde saga all over again. It is the continuation of the struggle between authoritarian communism and syndicalism. A party organization on the one hand, a class organization on the other. The communist party wants to pass itself off as a class party and to substitute itself for revolutionary syndicalism. But *it is not a class party*: it brings together individuals who have contradictory interests, it flatters both workers and petty-bourgeois. It is a party like any other, with its politicians and its careerists.[60]

The bolsheviks' counterargument was that the Amiens Charter's principal function had been to maintain the CGT on a revolutionary course and to prevent it from being tied to the coat-tails of the reformist SFIO. The main reason for the hostility of that era to political parties was that there had been no truly revolutionary party. With the creation of a Communist Party, that had now changed, and to maintain the Charter's opposition to political parties as an abstract principle was ahistorical and represented a misunderstanding of the real meaning of Amiens. To accept co-operation between syndicalists and communists was not to accept the subordination of one to the other; acceptable forms of co-ordination which best suited the revolutionary movement of each country simply had to be worked out.

Thus at Saint-Etienne, Besnard and the "pure syndicalists" were in favour of joining the Profintern on condition that there would be no organic links between the two internationals, and that there should be absolute autonomy for different national sections. The communists at Saint-Etienne were themselves divided. The motion which would eventually be successful, proposed by Pierre Semard and Monmousseau, argued that the CGTU should join if they were independent of the SFIC, and that, once members, they should argue within the organization for independence of the Comintern and should stay members whether or not they achieved this.

In the end, the Monmousseau motion won out over the Besnard motion by 743 votes to 406. On the resolution concerning national strategy, the communist syndicalists also won and by a similarly convincing majority: 729 to 391.[61] Maitron estimated that at this stage, therefore, syndicalists supporting anarchist motions amounted to about a third of the CGTU, about a sixth of all organized labour (CGTU and CGT together), in other words around 120,000 syndicalists. (This is not of course to say that all those syndicalists were anarchists.)

The underlying cause of the anarchists' failure at Saint-Etienne was doubtless the continuing prestige of the Russian revolution and of its leaders and the refusal of many sympathizers with Moscow to face facts when it came to hard evidence of the realities of political repression. The surprise visit of Lozovsky and his speech to the delegates were crucial in this respect.[62] The anarchists, on the other hand, were perceived by many to be criticizing the only revolution that had succeeded. Berlin, as one delegate scornfully pointed out, was an attempt to create "a revolutionary International excluding the only people who have so far actually succeeded in making a revolution."[63]

THE SECOND COMMITTEE FOR THE DEFENCE OF SYNDICALISM, 1922–23

The composition of the new Bureau meant that the CGTU was now under the control of the VO group. For the anarchists, this was the triumph of Guesdism: "The attempt which failed in 1906 has just succeeded in 1922."[64] Besnard declared in the pages of *le Libertaire*: "Syndicalism is in danger," and those who were concerned at what they perceived to be the danger of Communist Party control over the syndicalist organization rallied to the Comité de Défense Syndicaliste (CDS, Committee for the Defence of Syndicalism) which Besnard created immediately after Saint-Etienne.[65]

But the problem for the anti-communist minority in the CGTU, quite apart from the fact that the syndicalist movement generally was in a lamentable state by this point, was its lack of a unified strategy (some revolutionary syndicalists, for instance, being in favour of joining the Profintern but opposed to the growing and increasingly undemocratic communist influence over the CGTU), and even amongst the anarchists there was serious disagreement as to what to do. Some anarchists, in-cluding Sirolle, Relenque, Cadeau, Gaudeaux and Jules Teulade, even refused to join the CDS.[66] They wanted only the abandonment of the article in the Profintern's statutes on close links between it and the Co-mintern, although they were also unhappy with increasing Communist Party domination. The CDS was also divided over the question of unity with the CGT. Besnard wanted unity to be recreated "by the rank and file"—in other words, through appealing for reunification directly to all syndicalists, including CGT members, bypassing the union leadership. This was what the Executive Committee tried to do in the autumn of 1922, but a minority of the Executive (including Colomer and Lecoin) and a majority of the Paris region CDS wanted to maintain the unity of all revolutionary tendencies within the CGTU.[67]

THE CREATION OF THE IWMA, 1920–23

Besnard and the CDS now began to campaign in favour of affiliation to the AIT (Association internationale des travailleurs, or IWMA, In-ternational Working-Mens' Association), founded in Berlin at the end of 1922 as a revolutionary syndicalist alternative to both the IFTU and the Profintern.[68]

The IWMA had its origins in an international conference of revo-lutionary syndicalists held in Berlin in December 1920 in response to the Comintern's decision in July of that year to create a new trade union international—although the conference also saw itself as a continuation of the work of the international syndicalist conference held in London in 1913.[69] The conference delegates represented around a million syndical-ists from seven countries, and included French CSR delegates (Godon-nèche and Jean Ceppe).[70] All but the French agreed that the western syndicalists nevertheless needed to meet separately first to elaborate a common platform. The syndicalists' aim at this stage was therefore not to create a separate "anarcho-syndicalist" international, but to discuss their shared objectives as revolutionary syndicalists within the future Profintern. In contrast, Godonnèche and Ceppe spoke firmly in favour of declaring for the Profintern without further ado and wished only that the organizations present in Berlin should also attend the creation of the Profintern in Moscow. As all the delegates agreed with this, the French then left Berlin. The remaining delegations thus set about formulating a joint statement. This led to the adoption of five resolutions regarding what the delegates felt should be the characteristics of the International to be created at Moscow. These resolutions reiterated the usual syndicalist tenets: revolutionism, direct action, anti-parliamentarism, working-class autonomy, independence of the syndicalist organization.

The failure of the 1921 Profintern congress to produce a revolutionary syndicalist organization prompted German and other anarchist syndicalists to call for a second international syndicalist conference in Berlin, this time with the explicit intention of creating a third trade union international.[71] It was proposed to take the five substantive resolutions adopted at the previous Berlin conference as a basis.

This decision by those present at the Düsseldorf conference (October 1921) — at which there were no French delegates — coincided with the complex period following the CGT's Lille congress at the end of which (in December) the CSRs would be expelled. The French syndicalists seem to have been less quick than their counterparts in other countries to conclude that the Profintern was a completely hopeless cause, and the debate was still going on about the Profintern's statutes.

The second international syndicalist conference, Berlin, 1922

This conference took place in June 1922, just before the founding conference of the CGTU at Saint-Etienne, with delegates from six countries representing over 1,400,000 workers.[72] The CGTU sent a delegation consisting of Besnard, Lecoin and Totti mandated to act purely as observers: it would be up to the Saint-Etienne congress to make decisions regarding, notably, international affiliation.[73] The French delegation were the only ones who supported continued contact with the Profintern, in line, as Lecoin informed the conference, with the CGTU's policy, namely that a congress should be called of all syndicalist organizations not belonging to the Amsterdam International which should produce new statutes to be put to the Profintern.[74]

Wayne Thorpe argues convincingly that the June 1922 conference marks the turning-point in relations between the international revolutionary syndicalist movement and the bolsheviks. At the conference held in December 1920, such had been enthusiasm for the Russian revolution and the desire to unite the international revolutionary movement, that it was only thanks to the Germans and Swedes that the bolshevik policies of political links and centralised control were challenged. In the meantime, western syndicalists had witnessed the bolsheviks' undemocratic behaviour at the Profintern congress, their stance on political prisoners and their subsequent deportation of dissident revolutionaries. The declaration of principles adopted in Berlin in June 1922 was not only a clear reaffirmation of libertarian syndicalist principles, it included a stark and explicit rejection of bolshevism, of the dictatorship of the proletariat and of the idea that the State would wither away after the Revolution—"nothing more than a sophism masking the facts," according to Rocker. Experience had now shown that such a dictatorship could serve to create a new privileged class in society and that it was therefore inimical to the Revolution. Syndicalists, according to Rocker's declaration, were opposed to dictatorship precisely because they were revolutionaries.[75] The French delegation abstained in an otherwise unanimous vote on this declaration of principles, but declared it their duty to defend those principles at Saint-Etienne.

The founding congress of the IWMA, Berlin, 1922–23

The conference which would become the founding congress of the IWMA took place in Berlin between 25 December 1922 and 2 January 1923, with no Profintern representatives present. There were over 30 delegates at the Berlin conference claiming to represent over 2,000,000 workers (but actually probably representing nearer 1,500,000), and 15 countries were represented directly or indirectly.[76] France was represented in the form of Besnard and Claudine Lemoine for the CDS (representing 100,000 members), Couture from the Building-Workers' Federation (32,000 members) and a delegate from the Seine Syndicalist Youth Federation (750 members). All the French delegates were present only in an advisory capacity.

The conference had been postponed until December to see what would happen at the second Profintern congress. Although the congress decisions had not yet been officially published, it was clear from Russian and other articles that the changes which had been made to Article 11 of the Profintern statutes governing its relations with the Comintern had only been modified in a purely cosmetic fashion in order to appease sceptical syndicalists from outside Russia.[77] All but the CDS and NAS delegates were in favour of proceeding to the creation a new International on revolutionary syndicalist lines.

Besnard and Lemoine were in a difficult situation in that a majority in the CGTU, of which the CDS was of course only a small part, had voted to affiliate to the Profintern on condition that Article 11 was modified. They were wary of appearing to be in favour of further schism within the labour movement, especially at a time when the Comintern and the French Communists were arguing for a united workers' front. So although all the delegates agreed unanimously (after the NAS delegation had withdrawn) that a new, independent International had now to be formed, it was at the insistence of the French delegates—and despite strong opposition from several delegations—that a resolution was adopted instructing the secretariat to make a last attempt at unity or co-operation with the Profintern.[78] Besnard declared that the CDS was "morally attached" to the Berlin International, but was adamant that the International should do its utmost to create a united front with all revolutionary organizations outside it.[79] The statutes of the new International were based on the ten-point declaration of the June conference.[80]

The IWMA Secretariat accordingly approached the Profintern regarding further discussions about a unitary international organization, but was rejected. As Thorpe has commented: "As eager as the Bolsheviks were to secure the support of all revolutionary groups, particularly that of the syndicalists, they would nevertheless insist that the desired collaboration be on Bolshevik terms."[81] And Augustin Souchy's gloss: "The division within the revolutionary labour movement, introduced into the First International through the authoritarian behaviour of Karl Marx, was perpetuated by Marx' Muscovite heirs."[82]

THE CGTU'S BOURGES CONGRESS, 1923

But the communists together with the revolutionary syndicalists who were moving closer to the SFIC were increasing their control of the CGTU, to some extent because of the modification made to Article 11 of the Profintern's statutes. When an attempt was made in March 1923 to call for an extraordinary congress in order to challenge the international affiliation, only about a quarter of the CGTU supported the call.

At the Bourges congress of November 1923, the CDS, led by Besnard, unequivocally opposed the policy of the CGTU leadership with regard both to affiliation to the Profintern and to the growing influence of the SFIC on the organization. Besnard read to the congress a message from the IWMA Bureau explaining the reasons for its creation and informing it of the Profintern's refusal to co-operate with the IWMA in joint campaigns against Italian fascism or against the occupation of the Ruhr. The CDS was strongly opposed at this stage to dividing the CGTU, believing that it might still be possible to win the organization over to revolutionary syndicalist principles. However, the communists' control of the CGTU was by this stage too strong to be affected by the CDS' arguments, and motions regarding affiliation to the Profintern and the IWMA won 962 and 219 votes respectively.[83] The extent of anarchist influence, therefore, seems to have fallen by this point to below 100,000 syndicalists.[84] After Saint-Etienne, the SFIC had consolidated its hold on most UDs, and after Bourges communist control of all the CGTU's activities was gradually to increase. The supreme guiding rôle of the PC would be formally acknowledged at the CGTU's 1929 Paris congress.

This increase of communist control hardened opposition among significant numbers of revolutionary syndicalists and even before Bourges was seen by some as a deliberate attempt to rid the CGTU of its dissident minorities.[85] Many left the CGTU and either joined or formed independent unions, or, after 1926, went to the "anarcho-syndicalist" CGTSR (to be discussed below). Some unions were expelled from the CGTU. Many who previously had supported affiliation to the Profintern, but who were angered by the party's pretensions to lead the unions, joined the newly created dissident Groupes syndicalistes révolutionnaires (GSR) led by Guillot. After Monatte was expelled from the PC in 1924, he and the small circle around him (such as Maurice Chambelland) would also join the internal opposition within the CGTU, creating a Ligue syndicaliste alongside the GSRs and launching the journal *la Révolution prolétarienne* (to which many anarchists, in coming years, would contribute[86]). The Ligue would later merge with another dissident syndicalist group, the Comité pour l'indépendance du syndicalisme (CIS), which from 1929 had its own newspaper, *le Cri du Peuple*, which would also carry articles by anarchist militants.

TOWARDS A THIRD CONFEDERATION, 1923–26

In June 1923, after a year as secretary of the CDS, Besnard resigned from his post. At the same time, he also stepped down as a delegate to the Executive Bureau of the IWMA.[87] The failure of the overtures to the CGT which he had secretly made early in 1924 in the hope of reuniting the entire syndicalist movement (and thus isolating the communists), coupled no doubt with the serious deterioration of relations with the communists in the CGTU (symbolized by the shooting dead of Poncet and Clot in January of that year), was what finally persuaded Besnard to work for a third confederation.[88] Since the 1923 Bourges congress, some trade unions had left the CGTU, as had the Buildingworkers' Federation and certain UDs (including the Rhône and the Oise, for instance).[89] Besnard decided to organize a meeting of the minority within the CGTU in November 1924, and the outcome was the creation of an Union fédérative des syndicats autonomes de France (UFSA, Federal Union of Autonomous Trade Unions of France), with a *Commission Exécutive* of which Besnard was a member. At its first congress at Saint-Ouen in July 1925, Besnard was elected secretary general. The declared aim of the UFSA was to highlight the widespread disaffection among militants in both the CGT and the CGTU, to encourage the two CGTs to abandon their sectarianism and to lead them to reconsider the unity of the labour movement.

But the reunification envisaged was to be strictly on the basis of the complete autonomy of the unions. A leaflet put out by the UFSA's provisional *Commission Exécutive* thus rejected the CGTU's subsequent unity campaign, arguing that the aim of the Profintern was the total domination of French syndicalism by the SFIC, "for the ends of a Party exercising its dictatorship despotically over the proletariat."[90] The Syndicat Autonome des Ouvriers Métallurgistes de la Seine was similarly uncompromising in its rejection of the Comintern and the Profintern whose fundamental belief was, it claimed, that: "only the Communist Politicians possessed the requisite qualities for counselling, directing, and imposing on the syndicalists ... the tactics, methods, demands and strikes judged by them to be necessary for their policy, whose objective is to take Power—supposedly for the benefit of the working class, but in reality, just as in Russia, against the working class, by the application of the dictatorship over the working class of the country."[91]

By 1926, it was becoming clear that the UFSA was not achieving its aims, and that it was actually losing members rather than gaining them. In August 1926, *la Voix du Travail*, a new monthly paper, was launched by an IWMA Action Committee in Paris as an organ for those in the UFSA who shared the IWMA's view—namely, that the quest for unity at all costs would mean the destruction of syndicalism.[92] In Lyon in September–October 1926, an autonomous building-workers' federation was created, the Syndicat Unique du Bâtiment (SUB) with the anarchist Koch as its secretary.[93] Just weeks later, 31 October–1 November, the congress of the Union des syndicats autonomes du Rhône, chaired by Besnard, passed a resolution calling for a new CGT which would be "revolutionary syndicalist, federalist and anti-statist."[94] A fortnight later, the new Building-workers' Federation held an extraordinary national congress, also in Lyon, at which delegates voted by 52 to 3 (with 2 abstentions) to create a third confederation to rival the CGT and CGTU.[95] Immediately after this SUB congress, a further congress in Lyon, this time called by the UFSA, the SUB and the Autonomous Barbers' Union, brought together 69 delegates representing 89 unions. This congress voted by 84 votes to 3 with 2 abstentions to found the Confédération Générale du Travail Syndicaliste Révolutionnaire, to be based in Lyon and affiliated to the Berlin IWMA. The statutes of the CGTSR, presented by Lucien Huart on the second day of the congress, were adopted unanimously, and were characterized by strict limits imposed on the functions and powers of each office-holder and of each part of the organization, with no officer of the union having the right to be re-elected or to hold two posts concurrently. On the third day of the congress, a revolutionary syndicalist manifesto produced by Besnard was adopted.[96]

Eighty unions had joined the CGTSR at its founding congress, and it had support primarily in *"la petite industrie,"* in industries with artisanal traditions, especially among the building-workers and in some metal-working trades, but also in leather, clothing, hair-dressing and in transport. Geographically speaking, it was strongest in the Seine, Seine-et-Oise and Seine-et-Marne, and its most important centres were Lyon, Saint-Etienne, Clermont-Ferrand, Bordeaux, Toulouse, Limoges, Trélazé and Marseille.[97] A year after the CGTSR's creation, a reformist paper commented: "Up until now, not much has been heard of the CGTSR. It is doubtful whether much will be heard of it in the future."[98] In November 1928, Besnard had informed the CGTSR's second congress that membership had not increased since 1926, but that it had not declined either.[99] The only exception to this stagnation would be the general upturn in militancy of 1936: according to the prominent anarchist and CGTSR militant Paul Lapeyre, membership of the CGTSR rose from 3,000 to 5,000 at the time of the Popular Front and the Spanish revolution.[100] Other estimates of CGTSR membership have varied between 1,000 and 20,000.[101] The print-run of *le Combat Syndicaliste*, the confederation's organ launched in 1928, hovered around 6,000, but the paper may have actually been read by two or three times that number.[102]

A NEW DOCTRINE: "ANARCHO-SYNDICALISM"

The "Lyon Charter" of 1926 was seen by Besnard as the updating of the Amiens Charter. It included reference to fascism ("the new governmental doctrine of finance capital, who direct the entire capitalist system"[103]) and discussion of the need to integrate the new castes of scientists and technicians into the labour movement in preparation for the revolution.[104] It was also very insistent on the need to bring together urban workers and their "peasant brothers" (a lesson of the Russian revolution often emphasized in the post-war years).[105] The Charter reasserted the traditional idea of the self-sufficiency of syndicalism, whilst emphasizing that the movement is fully aware of "the extreme complexity of the problems which will be posed by the destruction of capitalism."[106]

Whereas these points could all be seen as a "modernization" of Amiens, the Lyon Charter differs fundamentally from Amiens in its emphatic and repeated assertions that political parties are harmful and to be actively opposed, rather than merely ignored and excluded from the life of the trade unions; and that not only political parties but also the other trade union organizations have aims that are "fundamentally opposed" to those of the CGTSR.[107] Co-operation with the CGT or CGTU was thus only to be envisaged in the case of limited demands and campaigns

around wages and working-conditions. Anything beyond that was condemned as useless, although the demands around which the CGTSR
campaigned over the coming years differed relatively little from those
pursued by the other two confederations (working hours, sick pay, a
rôle for "works committees," the abolition of the military tribunals and
a total amnesty, the repeal of the 1920 laws against contraception and
abortion, etc.). The only campaign which was distinctive of the CGTSR
was for the "*salaire unique,*" an egalitarian single wage.[108]

Colson has pointed out that until 1937 the CGTSR always referred to itself as "revolutionary syndicalist" (often qualified with "federalist and antistatist"), not "anarcho-syndicalist." Nor was the term
ever used by Besnard in any of his books.[109] The term "anarcho-syndicalist" only came into wide use in 1921–22 when it was applied po-
lemically as a pejorative term by communists to any syndicalists—even
members of the SFIC—who opposed increased control of syndicalism
by the Communist Parties.[110] Although the label began to be taken
up and used positively of their own position by some revolutionary
syndicalists from 1922, Besnard himself first used the term to describe
the ideology of the CGTSR and IWMA in his planned address to the
international anarchist congress of 1937: anarcho-syndicalism "takes
its doctrine from anarchism and its form of organization from revolutionary syndicalism."[111]

As Colson remarks: "Contrary to all the historical periodizations
which have been imposed since then, we can say that anarcho-syndicalism, as a definable ideological current within the working-class movement, postdates the communist movement which allegedly succeeded
it."[112] Pre-war "revolutionary syndicalism" was itself a theorization, after the event, of a set of attitudes and practices shared by a very large
proportion of the labour movement during the vigorous growth years
of the labour movement around the turn of the century. By the time of
the vote on strategy at the CGT's Amiens Congress of 1906 and by the
time of the creation of Monatte's *la Vie ouvrière* three years later, these
attitudes and practices were already in decline and the CGT's "crisis"
had already begun. A similar process occurred in the early 1920s, as
this crisis was aggravated—but not initiated—by the Great War and the
bolshevik revolution. The CGT Syndicaliste Révolutionnaire founded
in 1926 bore little resemblance to the CGT in its "heroic" revolutionary
syndicalist days. "Revolutionary syndicalism" had been a very vague
and general reference and one to which syndicalists of all or no political
allegiance could rally, even moderates and reformists: the Amiens congress vote, it is worth reminding ourselves, had been passed virtually
unanimously. The whole point of revolutionary syndicalism and Amiens

was that they were inclusive, they were based on the felt reality of shared class interests, not on ideological positioning. Only in 1920, with the creation of the CSRs, did "revolutionary syndicalist" become a label attached to a specific organization, and even then it was an organization that attempted to rally to itself all those—whether anarchist, communist or whatever—who were opposed to the CGT leadership. By the time the CGTSR was created, the label was being used of a minority organization with a very specific and therefore exclusive ideological orientation and at a time when, as Mercier-Vega has emphasized, its explicitly *anti*-political stance was becoming less attractive amongst unionized workers.[113] Any pretension on the part of the CGTSR to provide the "syndicat unique"—the single, all-inclusive union per trade or industry or locality (as opposed to the fragmentation of the trade union movement into "*syndicats d'opinion*")—deemed so essential by both Monatte and Malatesta in their famous confrontation in 1907, was rather ironic.

DISSENTERS: AUTONOMISM AND LOCALISM

Those most strongly in favour of creating a third confederation at the 1926 Lyon congress were those militants closest to Besnard: Huart (Shoemakers' Union, Paris), Henri Fourcade (Rhône UD), Clément (Pipe-makers, Saint-Claude), Raitzon (Lyon metal-workers), Marius Boisson (Building-workers' Federation), Boudoux (Paris SUB), Georges Leroy (Hairdressers, Paris), Jean Aigueperse (Leatherworkers, Saint-Etienne), Garros (Lyon electricity industry workers) and Edouard Demonsais (Toulon Council workers).[114] Many others were less enthusiastic. Some preferred to stay in the CGTU in spite of everything, some returned to the CGT, others preferred to remain independent. The two main arguments against a third confederation were, firstly, that the labour movement would be even more divided and weakened; and, secondly, that the CGTSR, although not linked to a political party as such, was none the less "politicized" through its very close connections with a particular ideology, and would therefore alienate many non-anarchist workers who nevertheless remained revolutionary syndicalist. Several prominent activists, including Bastien (Syndicats autonomes d'Amiens), Albert Guigui (Métaux de Paris) and Julien Le Pen (Syndicat Unique du Bâtiment) spoke out against the creation of the CGTSR. As the latter put it, "If we have a third confederation, we'll have two too many."[115] For Guigui, it was, by 1926, simply too late to create a third confederation with any hope of success.

In certain towns, then, some trade unions, dominated by anarchists, ignored the CGTSR, created an Union des syndicats autonomes and remained independent until the reunification of the CGT in 1936.[116] As Georges Bastien argued: "Once they have become autonomous, the unions would do well to stay that way and, when they reorganize links in order to develop solidarity, the exchange of information, mutual aid and so on, let them not reconstitute in any way another CGT, a copy of a State in the other State."[117]

Indeed it was about this time that Bastien produced a pamphlet published by the Amiens Autonomous Weavers' Union of which he was the secretary: "Pour la Rénovation du Syndicalisme."[118] His autonomist argument went far beyond the critique of the rôle of the industrial federations (as compared to that of the UDs) which we have already examined. Bastien argued that "the present crisis of syndicalism" was not due to the bad leadership of a few individuals. If the syndicalist movement had fallen prey to the "*manœuvres*" of such individuals, it was because the movement no longer had any vitality: "it is above all because the membership as a whole has lost the habit of making its own decisions."[119] This he put down to the fact that ordinary grass-roots members had lost the habit of thinking and acting for themselves, because everything was done for them by "a caste of functionaries."

Centralism, "*fonctionnarisme,*" bureaucratization, even parliamentarism are all curses which were laid by Bastien at the door of the structural reforms of the CGT. Lamenting the eclipse of the Bourse du Travail "which were at the origin of the syndicalist movement," he accused the Federations and UDs of being expensive, over-staffed, inefficient, complicated and distant from ordinary members: "99% of union members understand nothing about how the unions are organized and they do not even know what happens to their subscriptions."[120] The effect was to alienate workers in the same way as bourgeois parliamentary democracy alienates and produces apathy amongst the working class. The corollary of such alienation at the grass-roots was a flourishing cast of professional functionaries at the top—and this, according to Bastien, was all that was seen of the life of the CGT by those who were not familiar with life at the bottom of the hierarchy:

> Rather than having all workers inspired by the spirit of struggle and the will to achieve emancipation, we have fallen into the basest practices: electoral bargaining, Congress manœuvres, the quest for a majority by any means (clean or not), in a word the conquest of power at the departmental, federal or national level.
>
> Where in all that is the great spirit of initiative and of combativity which syndicalism was supposed to develop in the mass

of the workers? It has been replaced by politicking, bickering, infighting between tendencies (or rather between personalities in pursuit of positions) and between parties wanting to widen their influence.[121]

Inevitably, such a system gravitates against revolutionary action, creating a leadership that prefers to negotiate with employers and politicians rather than do anything to rock the boat: "Apart from a few honourable exceptions, paid officials do not like trouble, because that might harm the organization and thus endanger their positions. They therefore automatically endeavour to smooth over any difficulties. Bureaucracy and centralism are diverting revolutionary syndicalism and leading it to compromise with the existing social order."[122]

Furthermore, Bastien insisted, if the CGT — in its new, centralised form — were to attempt to fulfil what had always been, according to syndicalist doctrine, its rôle in the revolutionary period, the result would be a centralizing dictatorship: "The confederation and the federations will organize production, directing industry, agriculture and transport from above? How? ... That sounds very much like the assertions of those who are in favour of a dictatorship. Whether it is labelled communist or syndicalist, it would come to the same."[123]

Hence the importance of the "local interprofessional organization" (the Local Union or the Bourse du Travail, whatever the label[124]), with the emphasis on the involvement of grass-roots activists, direct control, mandated delegation, transparency, the fostering of working-class solidarity, the "social and technical education" of each worker to make of them "an emancipated individual" — all in contrast with the "poor copies of the parliamentary regime that are the CGT and CGTU."[125]

Such "localism," as Amdur's study of the movement in the Loire and Haute-Vienne has shown, was inherent in the attitude of many syndicalists — not necessarily anarchists — who were suspicious of central bureaucracies, who in the early to mid-1920s rejected all outside control, whether by Paris or by Moscow, and who put the emphasis on the needs of the unions' local members. A rejection of the CGT and of the CGTU thus often derived not from an absence of political consciousness, not from an absence of revolutionism, but from a concern even on the part of revolutionaries with bread-and-butter issues which, it was felt, could best be handled by local militants familiar with local needs and preoccupations: "Anarchist theory seemed at most to reinforce a sense of localism that most syndicalists had reached on other, more practical grounds."[126]

ANARCHISM AND SYNDICALISM AFTER 1922

By the end of 1926 not only was the labour movement divided between three national confederations, with many unions remaining independent, but anarchist syndicalists were to be found in all three confederations, as well as in independent unions. The UA and *le Libertaire* were to remain very reserved towards the third confederation and as we shall see, the hostility (at least at the level of the national leadership) would be fully reciprocated, and would contribute to later disunity within the anarchist movement. A motion passed by the UA's 1931 congress declared: "In the present state of the French trade union movement, it is just as necessary for anarchists to work in the unions still under the influence of the politicians as to join the CGTSR."[127]

But as one militant said of his fellow UA members in 1922, "*all* the anarchists—for if there are a few exceptions, they merely confirm the rule—are unionized."[128] Trade unions continued to be regarded by anarchists as the primary site for revolutionary activism, however much they might disapprove of the programmes of their confederations. As Lecoin said of the 1920 strikes, one of whose major aims was the nationalization of the railways: "The anarchists, who work among the mass of workers on every occasion and who support every action which represent a potential threat to the established order, have followed this strike movement with sympathy and have participated as best they could. That does not necessarily mean they are particularly enthusiastic about the strikes' declared objectives."[129] But if for a majority of anarchists the labour movement was their natural focus, the struggle would nevertheless be a difficult one in more ways than one. Mercier-Vega has pointed out, for instance, that the anarchists, who, in the 1930s, set up factory groups and, along with various oppositional communists, formed the Cercles syndicalistes lutte de classe (Class Struggle Syndicalist Groups) were not only faced with a very difficult struggle against employers (with the ever present threat of the sack and the blacklist), but were at the same time squeezed between the reformists of the CGT and the stalinists of the CGTU.[130] Despite all this, for the UA, class solidarity had its obligations: "We anarchists must not forget, comrades, that we are also trade unionists, and that, despite our critical sense which we must exercise at all times because we are anarchists first of all, we must be in close community of interests with the world of the working class organized against all capitalist exploitation."[131]

Notes

1. Quinton, Fargues and Besnard, "Résolutions présentées par la Commission Exécutive du Comité Central des CSR au Congrès de la Minorité Révolutionnaire," in J. Maitron and C. Chambelland (eds.), *Syndicalisme révolutionnaire et communisme: Les archives de Pierre Monatte* (Paris: Maspero, 1968), p.283.

2. For a more detailed treatment, see my *Anarchism, Syndicalism and the Bolshevik Challenge in France, 1918–1926* (forthcoming).

3. See John Horne, *Labour at War, France and Britain, 1914–1918* (Oxford: Clarendon Press, 1991).

4. *La Plèbe*, 4 May 1918.

5. Syndicat Autonome des Ouvriers Métallurgistes de la Seine, "Manifeste — Aux Métallurgistes!" — IISG, Fedeli Archive.

6. The Profintern was known as the Internationale syndicale rouge (ISR) in French and the Red International of Labour Unions (RILU) in English.

7. *Le Journal du Peuple*, 15 September 1919.

8. *Le Journal du Peuple*, 18 September 1919.

9. Quoted in Jean-Louis Robert, *La Scission Syndicale de 1921. Essai de reconnaissance des formes* (Paris: Publications de la Sorbonne, 1980), p.175, note 4.

10. G. Yvetot, "Le Fédéralisme Ouvrier. Les Unions Départementales," *Le Journal du Peuple*, 22 September 1919. Jean Charles' analysis of the revolutionary minority's support in the different constituent organizations of the CGT led him to the same conclusion: "La CGTU et la greffe du communisme sur le mouvement syndical français, 1920–1929" (Unpublished and unfinished thesis, University of Besançon, 1969), vol.I, p.58.

11. See for example: *le Journal du Peuple*, 9 and 16 August 1916, 24 August 1921; 1 February 1917 and *le Syndicaliste révolutionnaire*, 12 and 19 January, 16 February 1922; *le Libertaire* also carried innumerable articles on these themes, e.g. one by J.S. Boudoux, 13 April 1919, which referred to the full-time officers of the CGT as "the eunuchs of syndicalism," "the leeches of the workers' organization" and "fleas on the body of the unionized proletariat." See also Kathryn E. Amdur, *Syndicalist Legacy: Trade Unions and Politics in Two French Cities in the Era of World War I* (Urbana & Chicago: University of Illinois Press, 1986), p.64.

12. *Le Journal du Peuple*, 16 February 1917.

13. *Le Journal du Peuple*, 28 September 1920.

14. Michel Dreyfus, *Histoire de la CGT. Cent ans de syndicalisme en France* (Brussels: Complexe, 1995), p.104.

15. Quoted in Dreyfus, *CGT*, pp.113–4.

16. *Le Journal du Peuple*, 27 September 1920.

17. In May 1920, various activists had been arrested and imprisoned on charges of plotting against the internal security of the State. These included Pierre Monatte, Boris Souvarine, Fernand Loriot, Gaston Monmousseau and, from the FCS and PC, Jacques Sigrand, Henri Bott, Marius Hanot and Alexandre Lebourg. Victor Godonnèche, a comrade of Monatte's from the Vie ouvrière group, temporarily replaced the latter as secretary general of the CSRs while he was in gaol (from May 1920 to March 1921).

18. See the "Declaration of the 'International Soviet of Labour Unions,'" including Provisional Statutes, in Maitron and Chambelland (eds.), *Archives de Pierre Monatte*, pp.286–90.

19. The CSR congress vote was unanimous except for one delegate who voted against the motion: Marseille (pseudonym of Henri Lacrosille, who would eventually join the CGTSR). *Le Journal du Peuple*, 27 September 1920.

20. Groupe Louis Bertho-Lepetit de la Fédération Anarchiste, *L'Influence anarcho-syndicaliste dans la CGT 1902–1923* (n.d.), p.6. See also Annie Kriegel, *La Croissance de la CGT 1918–1921. Essai statistique* (Paris & La Haye: Mouton, 1966) and Robert, *La Scission Syndicale*.

21. *Le Libertaire*, 21 January 1921. Péricat, despairing of transforming the CGT from within, founded the CTM in the summer of 1920, taking the already autonomous Marseille building-workers' union as its basis. It had around 400–500 members. Maitron, vol. II, p.59.

22. A meeting of 13 February 1921, for instance, was a debate on the subject: "Is dictatorship compatible with revolutionary syndicalism?" and included readings from and discussion of the latest writings of Lenin and Trotsky. *Le Libertaire*, 11 February 1921. The club's manifesto, reflecting the final resolutions of the international syndicalist conference in Berlin, December 1920, was published in *le Libertaire*, 29 April 1921.

23. E. Joret in *le Libertaire*, 27 May 1921.

24. The Pact's signatories were Verdier, Besnard, Marie, Bische, Michel Relenque (or Relenk, pseudonym of Kneller), Churin, Macheboeuf, Scheiber, Pothion, Jouve, Ferrand, Daguerre, Maison (or Maisot), Jean Gaudeaux, Henri Sirolle, Vallet (or Varlet), Henri Totti, Fourcade. For the text of the Pact, see Maitron & Chambelland (eds.), *Archives de Pierre Monatte*, pp.277–8. The Pact's existence was disclosed in *La Bataille syndicaliste*, 15 June 1922 and explained by Besnard in *Le Journal du Peuple*, 23 July 1922.

25. *Le Libertaire*, 26 May 1922.

26. *Le Journal du Peuple*, 21 September 1921.

27. Louis Lecoin, *Le cours d'une vie* (Paris: Lecoin, 1965), p.99; Stéphane Manier, "Le Bureau Confédéral se défend à coups de revolver et de matraque," *le Journal du Peuple*, 26 July 1921; Richetta (Fédération textile), "Aux camarades de la Commission d'enquête sur les bagarres du lundi, 25 juillet," in Maitron and Chambelland (eds.), *Archives de Pierre Monatte*, pp.278–9.

28. No other speaker caused as much displeasure to the majority, apparently, and Lecoin was much applauded by the minority. *Le Journal du Peuple*, 29 July 1921.

29. Lecoin, *Cours d'une vie*, p.99–101. The full version of the speech as taken down by CGT stenographers and reproduced in *le Libertaire*, 26 August 1921, is slightly different, but not significantly.

30. Monatte made similar accusations in "La scission syndicale de 1921" in his *Trois scissions syndicales* (Paris: Les Editions Ouvrières, 1958), pp.138–75.

31. M. Labi, *La grande division des travailleurs. Première scission de la CGT (1914–1921)* (Paris: Edns. ouvrières, 1964), p.69; *Le Journal du Peuple*, 31 July 1921; Wayne Thorpe, *"The Workers Themselves". Revolutionary Syndicalism and International Labour, 1913–1923* (Amsterdam: International Institute of Social History & Dordrecht/Boston/London: Kluwer Academic Publishers, 1989), pp.206–7.

32. Etienne Martin-Saint-Léon, *Les deux CGT. Syndicalisme et communisme* (Paris: Plon, 1923), quoted in Guy Groux and René Mouriaux, *La CGT. Crises et alternatives* (Paris: Economica, 1992), p.56.

33. See Maitron, vol.II, pp.59–60 and Kathryn E. Amdur, "La tradition révolutionnaire entre syndicalisme et communisme dans la France de l'entre-deux-guerres," in *Mouvement social* no.139 (April-June 1987), p.35.

34. Quinton, Fargues and Besnard, "Résolutions présentées par la Commission Exécutive du Comité Central des CSR au Congrès de la Minorité Révolutionnaire" in Maitron and Chambelland (eds.), *Archives de Pierre Monatte*, p.281.

35. *Le Libertaire*, 6 January 1922.

36. Quoted partially in Maitron and Chambelland (eds), *Archives de Pierre Monatte*, p.273, and fully in Laurent Batsch and Michel Bouvet, *CGT—Autour de la scission de 1921* (Paris: Editions La Brèche, 1983), p.34. See also Colette Chambelland, *Pierre Monatte, une autre voix syndicaliste* (Paris: Les Editions de l'atelier/Editions ouvrières, 1999), p.128, on Monatte's declared (and reciprocated) hostility towards the anarchists; and Monatte's impassioned and bitter attack on the reformists in "La scission syndicale de 1921," pp.138–75.

37. *Le Libertaire*, 27 July 1919. The Italian USI, the Spanish CNT and the American IWW had all been created as separate revolutionary syndicalist unions in opposition to existing reformist unions in those countries (the CGL, UGT and AFL respectively). Other anarchist syndicalists argued against splitting the CGT—Sirolle, Lepetit and Lecoin, for instance. See *le Libertaire*, 28 September, 12 October, 14 December 1919.

38. *Le Libertaire*, 14 October 1921.

39. The "pure syndicalists" and particularly the communists amongst them wrote frequently in the pages of Henri Fabre's daily, *le Journal du Peuple*, which would make Fabre very unpopular in Moscow and for which he would pay in May 1922 with his expulsion from the party at the insistence of the Comintern Executive.

40. See Amdur, "La tradition révolutionnaire," pp.34–5; Maitron, vol.II, pp.59–60; *DBMOF* vol.19. Born in 1886, Besnard was a leading member of the railway workers' union and had been sacked during the strikes of May 1920.

41. Maitron and Chambelland (eds.), *Archives de Pierre Monatte*, p.284.

42. *Le Journal du Peuple*, 28 September 1920.

43. See Charles, "La CGTU," pp.15–17; Pierre Broué, *Histoire de l'Internationale Communiste, 1919–1943* (Paris: Fayard, 1997), pp.234–5; and Pierre Besnard, "Die IAA und die RGI" [first published c.1933] in Augustin Souchy, Rudolf Rocker, Alexander Schapiro, Pierre Besnard *et al*, *Die IAA—Geschichte der Internationalen Arbeiter-Assoziation* (Berlin: Libertad Verlag, 1980), pp.29–31.

44. J.S. Boudoux was a steel fitter and an anarchist. Paul Veber (1892?–1928?) was an anarchist and a member of the Executive Committee of the Metalworkers' federation in 1915.

45. Archives Monatte, Dossier décembre 1921, quoted in Charles, "La CGTU," p.87, note 3.

46. *Le Libertaire*, 30 December 1921. A weary Monatte would resign from the Provisional CA at the end of December, and abandon *la Vie ouvrière* the following month.

47. Quoted in Charles, "La CGTU," p.21.

48. *Le Syndicaliste révolutionnaire* no.1, 22 December 1921.

49. Chambelland, *Pierre Monatte*, pp.131–2; Charles, "La CGTU," p.121, note 3; and in Maitron and Chambelland (eds.), *Archives de Pierre Monatte*, pp.343–7.

50. See Charles, "La CGTU," pp.139–82.

51. See *l'Humanité*, 22 June 1921.

52. Proposed statutes in Maitron and Chambelland (eds.), *Archives de Pierre Monatte*, pp.328–34.

53. Maitron and Chambelland (eds.), *Archives de Pierre Monatte*, p.282.

54.   Henri Sirolle was secretary of the Railwayworkers' federation in 1920. Michel Kneller, also known as Relenque, was a building worker. Gaudeaux was a travelling salesman.

55.   See Maitron and Chambelland (eds.), *Archives de Pierre Monatte*, pp.290–321, and Thorpe, *The Workers Themselves*, pp.181–8. Lozovsky was not above describing mass dissent involving the delegates of some of the biggest unions in Europe as being the work of "a few mischief-making souls."

56.   Lemoine's counter-proposal affirmed the autonomy of the Profintern, denied the "moral leadership" of the Comintern and urged for modes of co-ordination to be established which precluded any relationship of subordination. Maitron and Chambelland (eds.), *Archives de Pierre Monatte*, p.298; Thorpe, *The Workers Themselves*, pp.186–7.

57.   *Le Syndicaliste Révolutionnaire*, 22 December 1921. Quinton was a metalworker and an anarchist.

58.   *Le Libertaire*, 1 July 1921.

59.   Fernand Jack in *Le Libertaire*, 1 July 1921.

60.   *Le Libertaire*, 3 August 1923.

61.   Maitron, vol.II, p.62.

62.   Lozovsky's visit to the congress had to be kept secret in order to prevent his arrest. The Rhône UD was given responsibility for arranging everything, but the Saint-Etienne militant Arnaud felt justified in betraying this confidence in order to warn the Besnard group of Lozovsky's visit so that they could prepare for it. See Colson, *Anarcho-syndicalisme*, pp.128–9, on the trouble this caused.

63.   Julienne, quoted in Charles, "La CGTU," p.171.

64.   E. Demonsais, treasurer of the Minority's Var UD, in *le Libertaire*, 21 July 1922.

65.   Amdur, "La tradition révolutionnaire," p.36.

66.   Jules Teulade, a steel fitter and secretary of the Paris Steel fitters union in 1922, would join the Communist Party in 1923. See Sirolle's argument in favour of joining the Profintern in *le Libertaire*, 4 August 1922, and Le Meillour's criticisms of him for being in favour of the Profintern and still calling himself an anarchist in *le Libertaire*, 8 September 1922.

67.   Maitron, vol.II, p.66 and *le Libertaire*, 13 October 1922.

68.   See Thorpe, *The Workers Themselves* and Souchy *et al*, *Die IAA*.

69.   See Thorpe, *The Workers Themselves*, pp. 66–86.

70.   Augustin Souchy, "Die Gründung der Internatinalen Arbeiter-Assoziation" [first published c.1933] in Souchy *et al*, *Die IAA*, pp.3–10; Thorpe, *The Workers Themselves*, pp.150–60. The delegates were from the USA (IWW), Argentina (FORA), Germany (FAUD), Britain (Shop Stewards' and Workers' Committee Movement), Holland (NAS) and Sweden (SAC). The German delegates also held a mandate from a small Czechoslovakian syndicalist organization. The Spanish CNT, the Italian USI and syndicalist organizations from Denmark, Norway and Portugal were unable to send delegates but declared their support for the conference. The British delegation was the only one, apart from the French, whose organization had already affiliated to the International Trade Union Council created in Moscow during the 2nd Comintern congress in July 1920.

71.   The call was made at the end of the October 1921 Düsseldorf congress of the Freie Arbeiter Union Deutschlands, which was also attended by syndicalist delegates from Holland, Sweden, Czechoslovakia and the US. The Italian USI associated themselves with the call by telegramme.

72.   Apart from the CGTU, there were delegates from the German FAUD, the Italian USI, the Spanish CNT, the Swedish SAC and the Norwegian NSF. Thorpe, *The Workers Themselves*, p.219.

73.   Délégation de la CA de la CGTU (P. Besnard, L. Lecoin and H. Totti), *Rapport sur la conférence préalable internationale syndicaliste révolutionnaire qui s'est tenue à Berlin les 16, 17, 18 et 19 Juin 1922* (Paris: CGTU, n.d.), 4pp.

74.   Maitron and Chambelland (eds.), *Archives de Pierre Monatte*, p.335.

75.   Quoted in Thorpe, *The Workers Themselves*, pp.224–5.

76.   Deliberative votes were allocated to the German FAUD (120,000 members), the Italian USI (500,000), the Swedish SAC (32,000), the Dutch NAS (22,500), the Norwegian NSF (3,000), the Danish Syndikalistik Propagandaforbund (600), the Argentinian FORA (200,000), the Mexican CGT (30,000). The Portugese CGT (150,000) had sent its consent was recongized as a full member. Delegates of the Chilean IWW (20,000) and the Uruguayan FORU arrived too late to take part. The Spanish CNT delegates were arrested before they got to Berlin. The French CDS, the German AAUE (75,000), the Russian Syndicalist Minority and the Czechoslovakian FAU were granted consultative votes. Thorpe, *The Workers Themselves*, p.244–5; Souchy, "Gründung der IAA," p.9.

77.   See Thorpe, *The Workers Themselves*, p.245.

78.   Souchy, "Gründung der IAA," p.10.

79.   Thorpe, *The Workers Themselves*, p.251.

80.   See Thorpe, *The Workers Themselves*, pp.253–6.

81.   Thorpe, *The Workers Themselves*, p.139.

82.   Souchy, "Gründung der IAA," p.10.

83.   See Amdur, *Syndicalist Legacy*, p.237, for details of the dwindling dissident vote in the CGTU, 1922–27.

84.   Groupe Louis Bertho-Lepetit, *L'Influence anarcho-syndicaliste*, p.6.

85.   See *le Libertaire*, 20 April 1923.

86.   The sub-title of *Révolution prolétarienne* was initially *Syndicaliste communiste*; this was changed in 1930 to *Syndicaliste révolutionnaire*.

87.   Besnard, "A bas le fonctionnarisme!," *le Libertaire*, 8 June 1923: "I have myself fought for too long against the running sore which is trade union bureaucracy to tolerate in this respect a clear violation of the spirit of our statutes."

88.   Maitron, vol.II, pp.66–9. Maitron reproduces the text of a letter sent by Besnard to Argence outlining his plans. Besnard seems to have been supported in this venture by Fourcade and Monier.

89.   For a detailed examination of the complex and often messy processes by which particular unions came to affiliate to the CGT, the CGTU or the CGTSR or to remain independent, see Amdur, *Syndicalist Legacy*, ch.9.

90.   UFSA leaflet, "Le Chantage de l'Unité"—IISG, Fedeli Archive.

91.   "Manifeste—Aux Métallurgistes!"—IISG, Fedeli Archive. This leaflet is a good example of the way in which the killings of 11 January 1924—"the consequence of political interference in the unions"—were already attaining the status of an unhappy milestone in French labour history and contributed to the widening gap between communists and anarchists.

92.   15 nos. would appear: no.1 in August 1926, no.15 in October 1927. From April 1927 it would become the bulletin of the CGTSR.

93.   On the SUB, see Claire Auzias, "La CGTSR, 1926–1928; un épisode de décentralisation syndicale" in *Mouvement social*, supplement to no.144 (October–November 1988),

special no.: "Avec Jean Maitron," pp.55–65; Stéphane Sirot, "Les syndicalistes du bâtiment entre les deux guerres: origines et trajectoires" in Michel Dreyfus, Claude Pennetier and Nathalie Viet-Depaule (eds.), *La Part des militants. Biographie et mouvement ouvrier: Autour du Maitron, Dictionnaire biographique du mouvement ouvrier français* (Paris: Edns. de l'Atelier/Edns. ouvrières, 1996), pp.145–56; and Paul Sharkey, "French Anarchist Syndicalists and Federal Syndicalism, and the Supercession of Revolutionary Syndicalism in the French General Confederation of Labour between 1919 and 1926, as reflected in the columns of *Le Libertaire*" (unpublished MA Dissertation, University of Belfast, 1994), 140pp. The Lyon buiding-workers were to be the mainstay of anarchist syndicalism in the region, and after the CGTSR's national headquarters were moved from Lyon to Paris at the end of 1928, it was the only CGTSR union in the area whose membership did not go into a slow decline.

94.   Auzias, "La CGTSR," pp.57–7.

95.   They also passed resolutions saluting Sacco and Vanzetti and appealing for insurrectionary general strike if necessary to counter the fascist threat. Auzias, "La CGTSR," p.58.

96.   The manifesto was reproduced as an appendix to Besnard's *L'Ethique du syndicalisme* (Paris: CGTSR, 1938; republished by Edition CNT Région parisienne, 1990), pp.127–39. Prefatory remarks by Besnard include an interesting history of the "Lyon Charter," as this document became known. The first version of the Charter was apparently written by Victor Griffuelhes (author of the Amiens Charter) and given to Besnard in 1921, in order to help protect syndicalism "against invasion by the Communist Party." The Charter, however, remained secret until 1922, when it provided the basis of Besnard's motion to the Saint-Etienne congress. This "charter of the minority" then became the manifesto of the second CDS and, re-drafted yet again, of the UFSA. Rewritten once more by Besnard, it finally came to be presented to the CGTSR's constitutive congress of 1926 in Lyon.

97.   Maitron, vol.II, p.72, Jacques Kergoat; *La France du Front Populaire* (Paris: La Découverte, 1986), p.167; Jérémie Berthuin, *De l'espoir à la désillusion. La CGT-SR et la Révolution espagnole, Juillet 1936 – décembre 1937* (Paris: CNT-Région parisienne, 2000), p.25; Samuel Jospin, "La CGTSR à travers son journal *Le Combat Syndicaliste* (1926–1937)" (Unpublished MA Dissertation, Paris I, 1974), pp.117–21.

98.   *L'Information ouvrière et sociale*, 20 January 1927, quoted in Berthuin, *La CGT-SR*, p.27.

99.   Auzias, "La CGTSR," p.63.

100.   Letter to the author.

101.   Kergoat claims that the CGTSR had barely 1,000 members at the time of the 1936 strikes, but gives no source—*La France du Front Populaire*, p.167. Jospin suggests figures between 1,000 and 6,000, but gives no source—"La CGTSR," p.116. Berthuin says at first 8,000 in 1936–7, then 8,000–10,000, but gives no source on either occasion—*La CGT-SR*, pp.21 and 25. Jean Rabaut suggests 4,000–20,000—*Tout est possible! Les 'gauchistes' français, 1929–1944* (Paris: Denoël/Gonthier, 1974), p.224. Claire Auzias says 5,000–6,000—*Mémoires libertaires: Lyon 1919–1939* (Doctoral thesis, University of Lyon, 1980), p.158. The CGTSR and the autonomous unions did not publish national membership figures.

102.   "*Le Combat Syndicaliste* ... was sold through its member unions and for financial reasons we tried to limit the number of unsold copies. Every copy ordered was paid for. A small publisher we knew agreed to review the print-run every week to within a hundred. It varied between 5,700 and 6,200. ... Given the level of unemployment, two or three militants would get together to buy a paper between them." Lapeyre, letter to the author.

103.   Besnard, *Ethique*, p.130.

104. This was a theme developed by Besnard previously. See, for instance, the proposed resolutions of the Executive Commission of the CGTR to the minority's December 1921 congress, Maitron and Chambelland (eds.), *Archives de Pierre Monatte*, p.283. Besnard was not the only supposedly backward-looking "anarcho-syndicalist" who embraced modern technology and industrial rationalization. See also, for example, Péricat, "La Surproduction" in *Le Journal du Peuple*, 7 December 1918, in favour of mechanization and rationalization, but opposed to its making human work harder. See also Besnard's speech on the "programme technique" of the minority at the CGT's Lille congress (which surprised the majority, as they thought only they had one), in *Le Journal du Peuple*, 30 July 1921.

105. Besnard, *Ethique*, p.132.

106. Besnard, *Ethique*, p.131.

107. Besnard, *Ethique*, p.136–7.

108. See Wayne Thorpe, "Anarcho-syndicalism in Inter-War France: The Vision of Pierre Besnard" in *European History Quarterly* vol.26, no.4 (1996), pp.559–90. Thorpe shows clearly that Besnard's views in no way conformed to the stereotypical representation of revolutionary syndicalism as anachronistic, defensive and backward-looking.

109. Pierre Besnard, *Les syndicats ouvriers et la révolution sociale* (Paris: Le Monde nouveau, 1930); *Le Monde nouveau* (Paris: CGTSR, 1936); *L'Ethique du syndicalisme* (Paris: CGTSR, 1938).

110. Thorpe and Mercier-Vega both provide examples of the use of the label "anarcho-syndicaliste" around the time of the debate over syndicalist strategy and the crisis of the CGT (1907–8) — "The Vision of P. Besnard," p.589, note 74; *Le Syndicalisme révolutionnaire*, p.9. This does not, however, invalidate Colson's point that the term only came to be used widely from the 1920s.

111. Pierre Besnard, *L'Anarcho-Syndicalisme et l'Anarchisme, Rapport de Pierre Besnard, Secretaire de l'A.I.T. au Congrès Anarchiste International de 1937* (dated 30 May 1937; Republished as supplement to *le Monde Libertaire*, 1963; Preface by A. Schapiro), p.3.

112. Colson, *Anarcho-syndicalisme*, p.20; see ch.2, "Le mythe de l'anarcho-syndicalisme," pp.19–27.

113. See Mercier-Vega, *Le Syndicalisme révolutionnaire*, pp.39–47, on the CGTSR and IWMA.

114. Auzias, "La CGTSR," p.59.

115. Quoted in Auzias, "La CGTSR," p.57.

116. This included, for example, in Limoges, pottery, shoe-making, furniture and garment industry workers. Maitron, vol.II, p.70. Most unions that went independent in the early 1920s stayed independent into the 1930s, when many rejoined the CGT or went to the CGTSR — Amdur, *Syndicalist Legacy*, pp.238–9.

117. Georges Bastien, *Pour la Rénovation du Syndicalisme* (Amiens: Syndicat autonome des Tisseurs d'Amiens, n.d. [1922–26]), p.6.

118. Bastien, *Rénovation*.

119. Bastien, *Rénovation*, p.1. Cf. Sébastien Faure's remark in a speech on syndicalism reported in *le Libertaire*, 4 February 1921: "It is not the personnel which must be changed, it is the methods. Syndicalism has adopted a centralism which is killing it." Malatesta used a similar argument at the Amsterdam conference of 1907 in his debate with Monatte, whom he criticized for believing the problem lay with the failings of individuals. Malatesta compared the corruption of the syndicalist who became a full-time officer with that of the socialist who became a member of parliament. See the full text in Louis Mercier-Vega, *Le syndicalisme révolutionnaire: Une pratique qui cherche une doctrine*, pp.18–19; published in L. Mercier-Vega and V. Griffuelhes, *Anarcho-syndicalisme et syndicalisme révolutionnaire* (Paris:

Cahiers Spartacus, Série B, no.97, September–October 1978), pp.5–86. I know of little that has been published on this question other than Rolande Trempé *et al*, "Sur le permanent dans le mouvement ouvrier français" in *Mouvement social* no.99 (April–June 1977), pp.39–46.

120.   Bastien, *Rénovation*, p.4.

121.   Ibid, p.5.

122.   Ibid, p.6.

123.   Ibid, p.9.

124.   The CGT decided to replace the "Bourses du Travail" with a network of "Unions Locales"—which tended to be intermediaries or representatives of the UD, rather than the autonomous organization of the grass-roots—in December 1921. This was a continuation of the process of organizational "integration" launched by the CGT before the war.

125.   Bastien, *Rénovation*, p.16.

126.   Amdur, *Syndicalist Legacy*, p.233. Amdur writes that a big proportion of Limoges syndicalists were "ardent localists"—p.232.

127.   *Le Libertaire*, 23 October 1931.

128.   Léon Rouget in *le Libertaire*, 10 February 1922.

129.   *Le Libertaire*, 6 June 1920.

130.   Mercier-Vega, *Le Syndicalisme révolutionnaire*, p.45. Mercier-Vega was, in the 1930s, known as Charles Ridel.

131.   *Le Libertaire*, 17 January 1914.

7

The Crisis of Anarchism, 1924–34

Will the 'good times' return? I do not believe so. Those
days are gone.

André Lorulot[1]

CRISIS

At the risk of being too neat in our periodization, we can say that the decade 1924–34 represented a major downswing for the anarchist movement. Internationally, the anarchist movement recognized it was in crisis
in the sense that it was faced with the new challenge of communism.[2] In
France, however, the downturn in this period was not limited to anarchism: the syndicalist movement was profoundly weakened by the splits
of 1921–22 and after; the rump of the SFIO, following the majority decision to affiliate to the Comintern, was racked with internal dissensions;
the membership of the SFIC fell from around 100,000 just after Tours,
to less than 30,000 by 1932–33.[3] But it seems nevertheless true to say, as
Maitron has put it, that "A certain kind of anarchism, full of ingenuous-
ness and faith in the future, died with the century in which it was born
and first flourished."[4] The catastrophe of 1914–18; the brief rekindling
of hope represented by the revolution of 1917, followed by bitter disillusion; the failure of the strike movements of 1919 and 1920—these produced a deep pessimism in the anarchist movement, "that disheartening
pessimism which is causing so much damage in our movement," as one
activist put it in 1925.[5] Lorulot had already registered the change in
mood by the end of 1921: "The heavy blows suffered by the syndicalist
and revolutionary movement—the failure of the rail strike …, the electoral victory of the 'National Bloc', schism tearing apart the Socialists
and the CGT—all that has not failed to cause a sense of decline and of
apathy, a malaise (aggravated by the economic crisis, which is producing resignation rather than revolt!) which all our comrades are aware
of."[6] Dolcino, arguing in particular that the cause of anarchism's lack
of success was a neglect of economic realities, talked in 1922 of "how

little anarchist ideas have spread over the last 30 years or so, despite the boundless efforts of thousands of militants." He went on:

> We are, quite evidently, stagnating. The source from which sprang the marvellous burgeoning of anarchist publications towards the end of the 19th century has dried up. The older militants are gradually disappearing, a few youngsters are coming to us and end up filling the gaps, but rare are those who are still active once they get past the age of 30. That fact alone should make us think. But what is even more serious is that the masses continue to be completely uninterested in our philosophical and aesthetic quarrels, which seem to be our sole *raison d'être*, our only occupation.[7]

It is indicative of the disillusion and despair of the anarchists that the *"Grand Soir"* — the eschatological vision of the destruction of bourgeois society, an image common in anarchist discourse from the 1880s — was referred to only ironically in *le Libertaire* after 1924, not to reappear until the summer of 1936.[8]

As was also the case with the CGT and the SFIO, the immediate post-war period had seen a certain resurgence of support for the anarchists. "After the 1914–18 war," wrote Nicolas Faucier, who was to be in charge of the administration of *le Libertaire* 1927–29, "anarchism, as a tendency within the wider socialist movement, experienced a noticeable growth due in large part to the enthusiasm caused by the Russian revolution."[9] Jean Grave agreed that many joined the movement after the war, adding that he doubted whether many of them knew much about anarchism.[10] Nevertheless, once the potentially revolutionary upheavals of 1917–20 faded away, decline set in. Many activists ceased to be active, regional federations disappeared, many groups disaffiliated from the UA amid accusations of domination by Paris: "And so the local groups, with little cohesion, vegetated, enlivened occasionally by infrequent propaganda tours, the odd public talk or discussion meetings among friends."[11] Bidault, another prominent Parisian activist and responsible in these years for the production of the *Brochure mensuelle* series, wrote in 1932 that: "The French anarchist movement seems dead. 'Le Lib' is living from hand to mouth and its print-run is in decline."[12] Louis Anderson was even briefer: for him the movement at that time was "zero."[13] Anderson in fact was typical of those many activists who disappeared from political life after the early 1920s to reappear only in the mid-30s: he was to be editor of *le Libertaire* 1936–39. Many others did not cease activism altogether, but limited themselves to more specific campaigns: anticlericalism, antimilitarism, naturism, sexual liberation

… A concern with "lifestyle" politics was not absent from mainstream anarchist-communism, though. Vegetarianism, veganism and abstinence from alcohol and caffeine were common. And Faucier has related how widespread was propaganda to do with contraception and abortion, made illegal in 1920: "In the various companies where I worked — Renault, Farman, Chenard et Walcker and later in the press — I made our propaganda more attractive to many workers delighted to find in the appropriate books and pamphlets details of the methods for limiting the size of their families."[14]

SENSATIONAL HEADLINES: COTTIN, DAUDET AND BERTON

It is true that *le Libertaire* became a daily from December 1923 to March 1925, but that was mainly because of privileged access to information concerning the mysterious death of Philippe Daudet, son of the leader of the extreme-right Action Française. And it also provoked Haussard and Anderson into leaving *le Libertaire* and founding their own paper, *l'Idée anarchiste*, disgusted at what they saw as the sensationalist and unprincipled exploitation of the young Daudet's death by Lecoin, Georges Vidal and Colomer.[15] The Daudet affair certainly put anarchism back in the headlines, though — as had Emile Cottin's attempted assassination of Prime Minister Clemenceau in 1919 and as did Germaine Berton's successful assassination of the *Action Française* general secretary Marius Plateau in 1923.[16]

Whether such sensational events contributed, as Faucier claims, to the maintenance of "a climate favourable to the dissemination of anarchist ideas" is surely questionable.[17] Faucier himself was of the opinion that the terrorist and illegalist phases of the movement's history had done it only harm, and it seems likely that if the Cottin, Daudet and Berton affairs kept anarchism in the news, they will also have helped to maintain for anarchism precisely the kind of image that many activists, from Fernand Pelloutier onwards, have wished to cast off.

SOLIDARITY: SACCO AND VANZETTI AND OTHER CAMPAIGNS

Fortunately for the movement, the UA was involved in campaigns other than that for the release of Cottin. It achieved a high profile for a while when Louis Lecoin headed the "Sacco and Vanzetti Committee," which organized the massive popular campaign for the release of the two Italian anarchists.[18] During the summer of 1927, the print-run of *le Libertaire* rose from its more usual 6,000–10,000 to around 20,000–30,000: and for the number that finally had to announce the execution of Sacco and Vanzetti, and that advertized a demonstration called by the Committee,

50,000 copies were printed.[19] But again, was this an unequivocal success? It has been argued that politically it was the SFIC that benefitted most from this campaign, making every effort to make political capital out of the issues involved, whereas the anarchists adopted a more disinterested, humanitarian approach.[20] Maurice Joyeux has questioned whether Lecoin was not more of a liberal humanist than a revolutionary anarchist: his technique was to establish an unelected committee concerning itself with a single *cause célèbre*, and to solicit the support of as many "personalities" as possible, whatever their political position on other matters.[21] A similar method was used by Lecoin and his collaborators in ensuring the release from a French gaol of the Spanish anarchists Joaquin Ascaso, Gregorio Jover and Buenaventura Durruti in 1927, and, as we shall see below, during the Spanish civil war.[22] Campaigns of this sort seem indeed to have taken up a considerable proportion of the anarchists' time, energy and financial resources in this period. There was a plethora of organizations that, on occasion, competed not only with the communists' Solidarité rouge internationale (SRI, International Red Solidarity), but also with each other: there was a Comité du Droit d'Asile (Right of Asylum Committee), the old Comité de Défense Sociale (Workers' Defence Committee), the UA's own Entr'aide (Mutual Aid), the Comité International de Défense Anarchiste (International Anarchist Defence Committee), and then specific committees for each campaign undertaken, specific committees for Spanish exiles and for Italian exiles...[23]

A CONTRADICTORY ANTI-COMMUNISM

Throughout this period, the campaign against Russian bolshevism and French communism continued apace. It was an uphill struggle. "It has to be said," Faucier would write, "that the struggle was far from even, since we were working both against capitalist reaction and against the gravediggers of the revolution—the latter having at their disposal enormous resources with which to blinker the mass of workers fooled by the soviet mirage. Inevitably many militants burned out."[24] UA militants helped by the exiled Russian syndicalist Nicholas Lazarevitch toured the country in the late 1920s. Audiences were usually between 100 and 400, but Faure's reputation as an orator often drew more—over 1,000 on one occasion in Amiens, according to the police.[25] After the killing of Plateau in 1925, and worried by a hate campaign directed at the Prime Minister, Poincaré, the police conducted an investigation of anarchist circles, only to conclude that: "The anarchist milieux are quieter than ever. They make a lot of speeches, but they are inspired above all by the disagreements dividing anarchists and communists."[26] A similar though more localized report of 1932, this time investigating rumours of an international terrorist ring, concluded that anarchists and communists, though active, were no serious threat, since they were at loggerheads with each other: "We have noticed that at virtually every meeting organized by the communists in Béziers, that the anarchists put up a consistent and ardent opposition to muscovite theories by delegating one of their speakers who always delivers a violent indictment of the acts of the Soviet Government. This often provokes disturbances amongst the audience and scuffles between supporters and adversaries of whichever speaker is on the platform."[27]

But to go away just with an impression of fierce and sometimes physically violent opposition would be simplistic and would not, as we have already stressed, do justice to a complex and paradoxical situation. Despite the resolution of the UA's 1921 Lyon congress never to co-operate again with political parties, even in specific and short-term campaigns, the practice did in fact continue.[28] Campaigns for political prisoners (unless in the USSR, of course) were often run together; the General Amnesty Committee brought together the UA, the SFIC, the ARAC, the Union socialiste communiste, the Comité de défense sociale and other groups.[29] Joint meetings on particular topics took place in an atmosphere of peaceful co-operation.[30]

Having said that, the anarchists remained very distrustful of communist-initiated "action committees," even whilst participating for the sake of revolutionary solidarity. Commenting on the effective abandonment of the Lyon congress decision in the face of the necessity to organize wide opposition to the occupation of the Ruhr, Louis Descarsins and Eugène Haussard provided the following summary of the problem from the anarchist point of view:

> What, we believe, has above all prevented more anarchists from taking part in the majority of Action Committees is the repugnance—the word is not too strong—which many of our comrades feel at the idea of associating with communist politicians. Such association is obviously hardly pleasant. Quite apart from the disagreeable nature of having to have contact with people for whom we feel little respect, there is the even more unpleasant diplomacy which we feel almost obliged to adopt, in spite of ourselves, in order to prevent or frustrate the clever manœuvres of these experienced twisters whose sole method—in all circumstances—seems to be to take their partners for a ride to the greater profit of their own party without giving a thought to the agreed common objectives. And then the other thing is

that in nearly all cases where the communists have initiated an Action Committee they of course make sure they dominate it. With them this is more than a tactic, it is a policy. A policy which consists of taking control of all movements in order to maintain the illusion amongst the workers that they are the only, unquestionable revolutionaries.[31]

Of course some anarchists abandoned the movement to join the SFIC. The claims made by the SFIC itself, through the ex-anarchist Girault, that the great majority of anarchist communists and anarchist syndicalists joined the SFIC are however clearly untrue.[32] *Le Libertaire* itself referred to "Girault who thinks that, because he has become a communist, *all* the anarchists have joined the CP."[33] Very few prominent anarchists seem to have joined the SFIC. Apart from Girault and Serge, both of whom the SFIC frequently cited in an attempt to persuade other anarchists to join, only two others stand out: Mignon and Colomer.[34] Indeed, the very fact that Serge and Girault were the only ones cited by the communists would suggest there were no other examples of "prestigious" desertions. It is more likely that, as Grave suggested, many new young activists with no real knowledge of anarchism joined the movement after the 14–18 war at the height of what seemed to be a revolutionary situation, but that they soon left again, disgusted, as Grave insisted, at the anarchists' inability to organize, at their failure to make an impact during the strike movements of 1919–20, at their perceived turning away from the Russian revolution.[35] Charles Ridel (Louis Mercier-Vega) would make a similar critical comment regarding the fate of new recruits to the movement in the mid-1930s: "The 'firm' had never changed, and newcomers usually stood amazed when they saw what it was like inside and how it operated."[36]

THE ORGANIZATIONAL DEBATE AFTER 1920

Having once re-affirmed itself at the UA's 1920 congress as a distinct ideological current, anarchist communism in France was to turn itself with a hitherto unknown zeal to the vexed and complex question of organization. To a large extent this was a continuation of the pre-war debate. There had at that time been a great awareness that many potential militants, looking for more cohesiveness, were lost to better organized sectors of the socialist movement (syndicalism and/or the SFIO); and that simultaneously, the looseness of the anarchist movement meant that many militants devoted themselves to more specific or marginal causes (co-operatism, for instance, or communalism) to such an extent that they were lost to anarchism proper. But clearly, as we have already seen, the

Great War and the Russian revolution provoked a much deeper questioning of the anarchist emphasis on autonomy and anti-dogmatism. By 1920–21, recoiling from the perceived excesses of bolshevism, French anarchist communism had taken itself in hand to a certain extent, and revisionist tendencies in the movement were halted. But not entirely. And whilst a clear line had been drawn between authoritarian communism and anarchist communism, the 1921 congress of the UA made clear its will to change:

> There is clearly a strong desire on the part of the French anarchists to leave behind their state of non-coordination. There are many anarchists in France. If we were to count all those who agree with our ideal as the only logical one and the only one which can give humanity freedom and well-being, there would probably be more of us than of any other school of thought. Unfortunately, for too long we anarchists have failed to organize ourselves and to co-ordinate our efforts in working for the achievement of our ideal. As a result, we have been weakened when faced with the political parties who ... have been better able to gain the confidence of many and to organize themselves.[37]

An earlier congress bringing together 60 or so delegates in Lyon had been unanimous on the need for tighter organization and for collective work. Bastien believed the removal of both "the elements of extreme individualism and those which are more bourgeois than anarchist," and "the supporters of confusionism" had strengthened anarchist communism, since success demanded "clarity of objective and unity of view with regard to the methods to be utilized in achieving that objective."[38] But the concrete results of this determination to "organize" were to be minimal. The UA was to "stimulate" activities and propaganda of a national nature; regional federations and local groups were left in complete freedom to organize their activities and to administer themselves "in whatever way best reflects the temperament of their members"; groups were free to fix subscriptions at whatever level they wished, or to have no regular subscriptions at all; money could be raised in any way a local group saw fit.[39]

Activists like Bastien who were in favour of much more cohesive organization were disappointed. Writing in *le Libertaire* in 1921, Bastien stressed how many activists had made clear to him that they felt closest to anarchism, but that their local SFIO or SFIC groups were the only ones organized enough to undertake anything in a sustained way: "We ploughed and sowed. They have reaped the harvest."[40] The principal aim of the Levallois-Perret congress of 1922 was to study practical ways of strengthening the organization of anarchists. In fact, the only advance to come out of the congress was to make the financing of the UA a little more reliable: although the level of subscriptions was still to be set freely by each group, the groups had now to guarantee that a subscription would be paid. It was also decided that an organizing committee (*comité d'initiative*) would be composed of two delegates from each regional federation. Despite signs that a desire for tighter organization was still there in some quarters, the immediate post-war impulse seems to have been fading, and Bastien inveighed against the *"inorganisables."*[41] His assessment in this regard of the two basic currents within anarchist-communism is enlightening:

> It struck me that this Congress produced a clear differentiation of the tendencies in the movement, a differentiation which is becoming clearer and clearer. On the one hand, a tendency which is purely critical, destructive, negative; on the other, the positive, constructive tendency which wants to organize more seriously and is interested in studying the important question of the rebuilding of society and wishes to find some practical solutions. The first group tends to distance itself from working people and to talk about Nietzschean 'supermen', while the second group, on the contrary, is close to the class of producers, seeking to urge them into revolutionary, antiauthoritarian and federalist action. I am quite convinced that this second anarchist current will find its way, will organize its forces and play a rôle in the class struggles.[42]

The Rôle of Exiled Anarchist Communities in France

The debate about organization did not really develop further until 1926, and that new development was provoked by exiles from other countries. With the advent of the Mussolini and Primo de Rivera dictatorships in 1922–23, the already sizeable Italian and Spanish communities in France were further enlarged by the advent of anti-fascist exiles, many of them anarchists. These were strongest, not surprisingly, in the south-east and south-west of France, and also in Paris. The capital also played host in the inter-war years to a considerable number of anarchists originating from Hungary, Bulgaria, Poland, Russia and the Ukraine.[43] It was the East Europeans who opened the debate, initially in the pages of the Russian-language *Dielo Trouda* (The Cause of Labour), founded in Paris in 1925.[44] The argument revolved around the reasons for the anarchists' defeat in Russia. Was it caused by bolshevik repression and by the "immaturity" of the Russian people? Or was it caused by the internal weaknesses of the anarchist movement? The latter argument, with concrete proposals for remedying the situation, was put by Makhno, Piotr Arshinov and others in their *Plate-forme d'organisation de l'Union Générale des Anarchistes (Projet)*, published in Paris in 1926, and the debate soon acquired international dimensions.[45]

Plate-forme or Synthèse?

The main points of the *Plate-forme* were that the success of the revolution demands that the traditionally absolute freedom of individuals and groups in the choice of tactics must be limited; that an anarchist organization with a much greater degree of ideological and tactical unity must therefore be built immediately; that this organization must be responsible for the political and social activities of each of its members, and that members must be responsible for the activities of the organization; and that it was essential for anarchists to prepare themselves well in advance both for fighting the unavoidable revolutionary war and for organizing post-revolutionary social and economic structures. The platformists saw themselves as Bakuninists, as libertarian communists. For them, anarchism was not a humanitarian theory or philosophy, but a revolutionary practice deriving from the experiences in struggle of the urban and rural working classes. Arshinov defined the platformists' aim as "organizing the ideological influence of anarchism on the masses not as a weak and intermittent factor, but as a constant in the workers' revolutionary class struggle."[46]

The whole debate around the *Plate-forme* was distorted by personal enmities (particularly between Voline and Makhno); by misunderstandings (some genuine, some apparently deliberate, some based on bad translations from the Russian of words to do with leadership, guidance and so on);[47] and by the long-standing, sometimes profound, hostility between anarchist communists and those nearer to the individualists—the platformist Maxime Ranko attacked what he called the individualists' "anarcho-sexualism," Voline and others complained of the platformists' excessive workerism, anti-intellectualism and "anarcho-hooliganism."[48]

However, the basis of the argument against the *Plate-forme* was that the proposals for re-organization were too centralist and too authoritarian, that they represented a "bolshevization" of anarchism.[49] The Paris congress of the UA in 1927 nevertheless saw the triumph of the platformist position, and part of the opposition left the UA—now judged to be "anti-anarchist"—to found the Association des fédéralistes anarchistes (AFA, Association of Anarchist Federalists). The AFA's most prominent member, Sébastien Faure, published his response to the *Plate-forme* in 1928. *La Synthèse anarchiste* argued that the anarchist movement consisted of three tendencies: communist, syndicalist and individualist; that, far from being in conflict, they complemented each other; and that all anarchists should therefore stop being sectarian and work together in one organization.[50] This was a sentimental appeal to a mutual goodwill that never really existed between the different tendencies, and the hostility between the factions persisted.

The Platformist UACR, 1927–30

The Union anarchiste (UA, Anarchist Union) had become the UAC (Union anarchiste communiste, Anarchist Communist Union) at the Orléans congress of 1926 in an attempt to placate the platformists without going too far. At Paris in 1927, with the platformists in the majority, it became the Union anarchiste communiste révolutionnaire (UACR, Revolutionary Anarchist Communist Union). The majority vote was now accepted as binding; no criticism by members of UACR policy was allowed outside the organization; positions adopted by the annual congress could not be the subject of criticisms within the pages of the Union's organ, *le Libertaire*, apart from during a three-month period immediately prior to the congress; membership was possible only through a group (in other words it was no longer open to isolated individuals), and involved subscriptions and membership cards. According to Faucier, himself a supporter of the *Plate-forme*, this "revisionism"—as he called it—had its strongest support in the *Germinal* group (which was one reason the 1928 congress was held in Amiens), among several groups in the west of France, and above all in the Languedoc Federation. This was due in large part to the fact that the latter's member groups (Montpellier, Béziers, Narbonne, Coursan, Lézignan and others) included many Spanish exiles "who had adopted clear positions in favour of the idea of the armed defence of the revolution and the need to plan for a more or less lengthy transitional period preceding the achievement of true libertarian communism."[51] Faucier was also ready to admit that such questions "hardly interested anyone but the leaders of the different tendencies and a minority of militants, particularly among the young and also some intellectuals, practically all in the Paris region."[52]

The loss of a number of militants to a rival organization (the AFA) and the simple disaffiliation of other groups was bound to cause the UACR financial as well as organizational problems. With the passing of time, it also became clear that most French anarchists "rebelled against the discipline of such a strict organization."[53] The UACR did not manage to hold a congress in 1929, and the following year, in Paris, they

Table 3

The Evolution of National Anarchist Organizations, 1913–1939

Fédération communiste
révolutionnaire anarchiste
(1913)

Union anarchiste
(1920)

Union anarchiste
communiste
(1926)

Union anarchiste
communiste révolutionnaire
(1927)

Association des
fédéralistes anarchistes
(1927-30)

Union anarchiste
(1934)

Fédération communiste
libertaire
(1934-36)

Union anarchiste
(1936)

Fédération anarchiste
française
(1936)

(1939)   (1939)

were voted out. The "synthesists" gained control, and the revisionist organizational principles were abandoned. In 1931, the Languedoc Federation was expelled for "marxist deviations copied from the political parties," because at its congress it had accepted the unavoidability of some kind of "period of adaptation" immediately after the revolution.[54] At a so-called "unity congress" in 1934 in Paris, the UACR again became the simple UA. Because more traditional structures were re-adopted, Faure and most of the AFA's members had returned to the fold. As a consequence, those who insisted on more workerist and more organizationalist policies split off to form a Fédération communiste libertaire (FCL, Libertarian Communist Federation). The FCL was to re-join the UA in 1936, whilst continuing to exist as a tendency.

After the platformists had been replaced as the majority in 1930, the positions of responsibility in the UA, *le Libertaire* and the Librairie Sociale (the UA's bookshop) had been filled by supporters of the "synthesis." According to Faucier, the platformists at first maintained a certain distance, but very soon their contribution began to be missed, because they were among the most active:

> So it was that because of the wishes of both sides and because of the practicalities of running the organization, there was a *rapprochement*. For some, the platformists' return was dictated by the needs of our campaigns, which had been weakened; others could simply no longer bear to be inactive. It is true that among the latter, some did not hide their intention of progressively regaining the positions they had occupied before and had been forced to abandon by the vote of what they saw as a fragmentary and artificial majority. That is in fact what soon happened. After a few months, they were again in the secretariat of the UA and in the administration and editorial committee of *le Libertaire*, where, imperceptibly, their positions began to show through, though because they were in a more moderate form they were more readily accepted.[55]

Thus it was that in 1934–36—when the organizational debate was pushed off centre stage by the increasing fascist threat—the UA, though not technically "platformist," was in fact once more dominated by activists whose instinct was to organize for a workers' front.

Notes

1   *Le Réveil de l'Esclave*, 1 January 1922.

2.   Luigi Fabbri, *Crise de l'anarchisme* (Paris: Groupe Malatesta de la Fédération anarchiste, n.d. [first published in Italy 1918–1920]).

3.   Estimates vary but the consensus among historians is 20,000–30,000. See Henri Dubief, *Le déclin de la IIIe République 1929–1938* (Paris: Seuil, 1976), p.195; Jean Bron, *Histoire du Mouvement ouvrier français* (Paris: Editions Ouvrières, 1970), vol.II, pp 188–9; Philippe Robrieux, *Histoire intérieure du Parti communiste* (Paris: Arthème Fayard, 1980), vol I: *1920–1945* pp.48–50 and 309–10; Jacques Fauvet, *Histoire du Parti communiste français de 1920 à 1976* (Paris: Fayard, 1977), p.55.

4.   Maitron, vol.I, p.481.

5.   Albin Cantone contrasting the ardour of the Italian anarchist movement with the state of affairs in France. *Lueurs*, 10 January 1925.

6.   *Le Réveil de l'Esclave*, 1 December 1921.

7.   *Le Libertaire*, 24 February 1922.

8.   See D. Steenhuyse, "Quelques jalons dans l'étude du thème du 'Grand Soir' jusqu'en 1900," *Mouvement social* no.75 (April–June 1971), pp.63–76.

9.   Nicolas Faucier, "Rapport sur le mouvement anarchiste en France, sa composition, son comportement durant la période 1930–1940," 13pp. TS, p.1.

10.   Grave, "La situation anarchiste actuelle. Que faire?," 8pp. TS, pp.1–2. Nettlau Archive, IISG.

11.   Faucier, "Rapport," p.2. Ironically, the "Police Générale" files (F713059) are much richer in information concerning the daily activities of local anarchist groups in the late 1920s and early 1930s than they are in the earlier, more volatile period or in the late 1930s.

12.   Letter dated 8 July 1932 to Hugo Treni (pseudonym of the Italian anarchist Fedeli) in Uruguay. Fedeli Archive, IISG.

13.   In conversation with the author.

14.   Nicolas Faucier, "Souvenirs d'un permanent anarchiste (1927–1929)," in *Mouvement social* no.83 (April–June 1973), pp.47–56, p.55.

15.   Information supplied by Anderson. *L'Idée anarchiste* survived 13 numbers, March to November 1924. P. Daudet was found shot dead in the back of a taxi, apparently having committed suicide. He seems to have acquired the gun from an anarchist. His intentions and the way he met his death were never established satisfactorily.

16.   See the UA pamphlet *Emile Cottin: son geste, sa condamnation, son supplice* (n.d.), a copy of which may be found in F7/13054. On Berton and Plateau, see Charles Maurras, *La Violence et la Mesure* (Paris, 1924) and Iwan Goll, *Germaine Berton, die rote Jungfrau* (Berlin, 1925). Berton seems to have been romantically linked, as they say, with P. Daudet. A book to be entitled *De Germaine Berton à Philippe Daudet. Chronique sanglante des années 1920–1925* was advertized in the late 1920s as being "about to appear," but I have been unable to find a copy.

17.   Faucier, "Rapport," p.2.

18.   See Lecoin's autobiography, *Le cours d'une vie* (Paris: Louis Lecoin, 1965).

19.   Faucier, "Souvenirs," p.48.

20.   Anne Rebeyrol and Jean-Paul Roux-Fouillet, "L'affaire Sacco-Vanzetti vue par *l'Humanité* et *le Libertaire*" (Unpublished *Mémoire de Maîtrise*, supervised by J. Maitron and J. Droz, Université de Paris I, 1971).

21.   Maurice Joyeux, "Louis Lecoin" in *la Rue (Revue culturelle et littéraire d'expression anarchiste)* no.11 (1971), pp.4–17. On Lecoin, see also Sylvain Garel, *Louis Lecoin et le mouvement anarchiste* (Fresnes-Antony: Editions du Groupe Fresnes-Antony de la Fédération Anarchiste, 1982), translated as *Louis Lecoin. An Anarchist Life* (London: KSL Publications, 2000).

22.   Durruti, Francisco Ascaso and Gregorio Jover were arrested in Paris in June 1926, just before they could carry out their plan to assassinate King Alfonso XIII and Miguel Primo de Rivera, who were on a state visit to Paris. Both Spain and Argentina requested that they be extradited to face charges arising from alleged bank robberies and assassinations. It was thanks to a massive campaign animated primarily by Louis Lecoin of the UA that they were released the following month. Lecoin, *Le cours d'une vie*, pp.121–30; Abel Paz, *Durruti: The People Armed* (New York: Black Rose Books/Free Life Editions, 1977), pp.81–7.

23.   See the many reports in F7/13061 and 13062. These files also contain leaflets relating to the different campaigns undertaken by these groups.

24.   Faucier, "Rapport," p.2.

25.   See numerous police reports, F7/1306O and 13061.

26.   Report on "Les bruits d'un attentat possible contre M. Poincaré," 28 November 1923, F7/12907.

27.   Report of "Sous-préfet" of Béziers to "Préfet" of the Hérault, 8 April 1932, F7/13964.

28.   "Les Résolutions du Congrès Anarchiste," *Germinal*, 10 December 1921.

29.   Sûreté Générale report of 16 October 1923, BB18/6466. The *Union socialiste communiste* (USC) was created in 1923 by Frossard and others forced out of the SFIC in the first wave of "bolshevization" of the party.

30.   A typical example was reported by the Angers police, 20 January 1932. A meeting on the 19th had attracted a crowd of about 100, 75% of whom were members or supporters of the SFIC, the Communist Youth, or the SRI. The main speaker was Jeanne Humbert, who was an anarchist even though her major area of activity was "neo-malthusianism" (family planning). That was the topic for the meeting, which had been organized by the "Groupe d'études sociales," i.e. most probably the local anarchist group. The chair was a joiner/carpenter called Bonneau/Bonnaud, who had previously been secretary of the Angers SFIC, but had now become an anarchist. The other speakers were a Mme Lucas of the SRI and a M. Gilet of the SFIC. The meeting was perfectly calm.

31.   "Les Anarchistes et les Comités d'Action," *le Libertaire*, 6 April 1923.

32.   See Ernest Girault, *Pourquoi les Anarchistes-Communistes français ont rallié la IIIe Internationale* (Paris: Librairie de l'Humanité, 1926). Girault saw bolshevism as a logical development out of bakuninist anarchism and revolutionary syndicalism.

33.   "Girault-Girouette," *le Libertaire*, 10 September 1926.

34.   Mignon, a doctor, joined the SFIC in 1921, and was expelled in 1923 for demanding more direct decision-making structures within the party. *DBMOF*, vol.14. According to the *DBMOF*, vol.23, Colomer (1886–1931) did not actually join the SFIC until 1927, but between 1924 and 1927 he was certainly moving gradually closer to communism and he features on a list of SFIC members produced by the police in 1924 (F7/13091). He visited the USSR in 1927 for the 10th anniversary celebrations as a member of a delegation sent by the *Comité des Amis de l'URSS* (police reports of 29 December 1927 and 9 January 1928, and Commissariat Spécial report, Lorient, 26 January 1928, F7/13060). Lecoin was to say of Colomer: "The secretary of our editorial committee, André Colomer, was a nice fellow, too easy-going, and liked to play to the gallery. He loved applause and preferred

to run from meeting to meeting rather than to get on with producing the newspaper. He was a poet of the aesthetic type, capable of making a valuable contribution to the paper but not of producing an issue from start to finish. ... He quickly became the darling of the UA. He was very charming. Extreme, vehement, chaotic, his analyses suffered because of his inconsistencies and his childlike character. And after having accused the bolsheviks of being murderers, he joined the party. It is not true to say that this about-turn was motivated by self-interest. It was his vanity which pushed this individualist into siding with the authoritarians — it was not for nothing that he was secretary of the Entertainment Workers' Federation!" *Cours d'une vie*, pp.114–5.

35.   Grave, "La situation anarchiste actuelle," p.2, IISG, Nettlau Archive.

36.   *Révision*, February 1938.

37.   Georges Bastien, *Germinal*, 3 December 1921.

38.   Ibid. It will be remembered that the individualists got their own newspaper around which to group with the appearance of *l'Anarchie* in 1905, and that they were expelled from the founding congress of the FCRA, precursor of the UA, in 1913.

39.   "Les Résolutions du Congrès Anarchiste," *Germinal*, 10 December 1921.

40.   *Le Libertaire*, 16 September 1921.

41.   See for example "L'Organisation Pratique des Anarchistes. Rapport et Projet présentés par le Groupe Anarchiste du 20e," *le Libertaire*, 3 November 1922. This local group insisted on the need for "method, cohesion and unity."

42.   *Germinal*, 8 December 1922.

43.   These communities of exiled anarchists living in France have, to my knowledge, never been researched. It would be interesting to know to what extent the Spanish and Italians in particular merged with the French movement, and to what extent they met only in their own organizations, of which there seem to have been a great deal in France. Faucier mentions the many foreign militants — "some of whom had created their own cultural or mutual aid groups" — who used to meet at the UA premises in Paris, and adds: "The Spanish especially had a well established networks of groups throughout their adopted country, with their own press supported financially by the activities of artistic groups, which would at every possible opportunity organize Sunday performances at which everybody liked to get together again socially." — "Souvenirs," pp.55–6. A report about antifascists from the Prefect of Alpes-Maritimes talked about "several tens of thousands of foreigners with worrying opinions and personal histories." Report of 5 October 1927, F7/13964. See Gérard Noiriel, *Le Creuset Français: Histoire de l'immigration XIXe-XXe siècles* (Paris: Seuil, 1988); Nancy L. Green *The Pletzl of Paris. Jewish Immigrant Workers in the Belle Epoque* (New York: Holmes and Meier, 1986); Louis Stein, *Beyond Death and Exile. The Spanish Republicans in France, 1939–1955* (Cambridge, Mass.: Harvard University Press, 1979).

44.   Alexandre Skirda, *Autonomie Individuelle et Force Collective: Les anarchistes et l'organisation de Proudhon à nos jours* (Paris: Alexandre Skirda, 1987), ch.15.

45.   Groupe d'anarchistes russes à l'étranger, *Plate-forme d'organisation de l'Union Générale des Anarchistes (Projet); Supplément à la Plate-forme d'organisation de l'Union Générale des Anarchistes (Questions et Réponses)* (Paris: Librairie Internationale, 1926). On the debate, see Skirda, *Autonomie Individuelle*, ch.15; Maitron, vol.II, pp.80–85; Faucier, "Rapport."

46.   Quoted in Skirda, *Autonomie Individuelle*, p.167.

47.   According to Skirda, *Autonomie Individuelle*, p.173.

48.   Maxime Ranko in *le Libertaire*, 28 January 1927 and Voline in Skirda, *Autonomie Individuelle*, p.177.

49.   See Eugène Maldent, "Bolchevisation de l'anarchisme," *le Libertaire*, 10 February 1927.

50.   Sébastien Faure, *La Synthèse anarchiste* (Paris, n d. [1928]). The text was re-printed in *Mouvement social* no.83 (April–June 1973), pp. 64–72; and, together with the *Plate-forme*, in *L'Organisation*, no.12 in the "Volonté Anarchiste" series of pamphlets (Fresnes-Antony: Editions du Groupe Fresnes-Antony de la Féderation Anarchiste, 1980). The *Plate-forme* and other related organizationalist texts have been included as appendices in Skirda, *Autonomie Individuelle*.

51.   Faucier, "Rapport." p.4.

52.   Ibid, p.5.

53.   Ibid, p.5.

54.   Ibid, p.4; Maitron, vol.II, p.87. The Livry-Gargan group was also expelled, but both it and the Languedoc Federation were re-admitted at the 1933 congress.

55.   Faucier, "Rapport," p.8.

Part II

Antifascism, the Spanish Revolution and War, 1934–1945

8

Popular Front or Revolutionary Front? Anarchist Antifascism

[The Popular Front] experiment will be the greatest confirmation of our ideas on the incapacity of political parties to lead the proletariat to its complete emancipation
                                        Le Libertaire, *April 1936*

We are faced more and more with the dilemma: fascism
or revolution.
                                        Le Libertaire, *August 1936*

When examining the anarchists' engagement with 1930s "antifascism"
and when analysing their apparently equivocal attitude towards the *Front
populaire*, we have to bear in mind Daniel Guérin's distinction between
what he calls the "Popular Front no.1"—an electoral alliance between
social democracy, stalinism and bourgeois liberalism—and the "Popular Front no.2"—a powerful, extra-parliamentary movement, the initiative for which came from the working class: "the true popular front, the
popular front of the streets and not of the politicians."[1] The anarchists
were careful to distinguish between the Popular Front's leaders—the
politicians—and its working-class supporters, and they enthused over
"the fraternity, the solidarity and the strength of the working class"
manifested in the extra-parliamentary antifascist movement of 1934–35.
They also took an active part in that movement, and in some respects a
leading part.

TOWARDS ANTIFASCIST UNITY, 1933–35: THE UNITED FRONT

For some time after the emergence of fascist movements across Europe,
many revolutionaries failed to understand the true significance of the

Earlier versions of this chapter appeared as "The other Popular Front: French anarchism
and the Front Revolutionnaire" in Martin Alexander and Helen Graham (eds.), *The French
and Spanish Popular Fronts: Comparative Perspectives* (Cambridge: Cambridge University
Press, 1989), pp. 131–144; and "'Fascism or Revolution!' Anarchism and Antifascism in
France, 1933–1939," in *Contemporary European History* vol. 8, no. 1 (1999), pp. 51–71.

danger. It was seen as a localised phenomenon, limited to countries—like postwar Italy—with "fragile institutions." The triumph of nazism in Germany, the home of one of the "strongest" labour movements in Europe, marked something of a turning-point in terms of French revolutionaries' attitude. Clearly circumstances in Italy and in Weimar Germany were not the same as those prevailing in France, but the conditions for the growth of a mass fascist movement were nonetheless beginning to be apparent here too: ministerial instability, political-financial scandals, persistent and widespread questioning of the legitimacy of the Republic, resurgence of the extreme right, economic crisis and growing unemployment. The Comintern's 1931 analysis of the social effects of the crisis predicted a clarification of the fundamental class conflict between workers and capital, with workers being pushed towards revolutionary socialist positions. For the anarchist Maurice Joyeux, this betrayed great complacency regarding the political consciousness of the working class: "From 1934, some militants began to understand that the proletarianization of the unemployed did not necessarily contribute to their combativity. People rejected by society in that way are ready to serve any master who promises them bread."[2] Revolutionaries began to fear the defection to fascism of significant sections of the middle classes and even of the proletariat. The lessons of Italy and Germany seemed to be that the extreme right could only be halted by a strong and above all united working-class front.

Unity of action within the labour movement thus became one of the principal objectives of anarchist campaigning. At least, this was the case with the UA, most of whose members seem to have been members of the CGT—the CGTSR continued to preclude cooperation with the CGT. Soon after the nazi takeover in Germany, leading members of the UA such as Lashortes and René Frémont thus began to call for a "united front" that would bring together all the labour and political organisations opposed to fascism: "In the face of the political parties' failure to act, it is up to the Anarchist Union to take responsibility for launching an action committee in which all organisations would be represented in a powerful United Front. It must be the union, in good faith and for a clearly determined objective, of all those who do not wish to see the gangrene of fascism triumph in France."[3] Manfredonia has argued that this proposal was at best ambiguous, and at worst—if it was meant to be taken as a call for unity of action agreed "at the top" with the PS and the PC leadership—optimistic to the point of naivety.[4] It had its critics among anarchists at the time. The "revolutionary individualist" Fernand Fortin, in an article in *la Revue anarchiste* entitled "From unity of action to *Union sacrée*," exclaimed incredulously: "Are we to make common cause with the political parties, even if only with those which claim to be 'extreme-left'? Are we to work for the Socialist and Communist Parties? That really would be the limit."[5]

The united front proposal certainly seems to have contributed to the haemorrhage of activists from which the UACR was suffering at that time. This worrying situation, plus mounting concern after the events of 6 February 1934 (when extreme-right demonstrators attacked the National Assembly), would lead a group of prominent anarchists (Louis Lecoin, Sébastien Faure, Georges Bastien and Pierre Le Meillour) to call for a special conference to resolve the movement's tactical differences and produce a more united national organisation. This would be the "unity congress" of May 1934 in Paris, which as we have seen resulted in the abandoning of some of the more "organizationalist" principles of the UACR, as well as in a reversion to the old name of "Union anarchiste." As for the united front policy, the Paris congress reaffirmed its fundamental distrust of politicians and declared itself "opposed in principle to contact with political parties," but added that at the local level and for "clearly defined aims," anarchists could participate in unitary committees. In other words, local groups were left free to do more or less as they wished at that level, whilst contact between the UA and political parties at the national level was ruled out. The reference to the "united front" was maintained, but only in the sense of a "means of preparing the unity of the working class."[6] As Manfredonia has pointed out, however, whilst eliminating a certain ambiguity regarding relations between the anarchists' organization and political parties, this new line contained no fresh, alternative proposals for the coordinated creation of a working-class front "from below." The movement continued therefore to be divided: some persisted in rejecting all cooperation with other left-wing groups and in presenting stalinists and fascists as equivalent; whilst others such as René Frémont, the platformists and probably the majority of UA members continued to see cooperation within the broader labour movement and with other left-wing groups as the only possible way forward. The parallels with the debate which was being carried on within the leadership of the Comintern at the same time are striking.

The effect of the fascists' attack on the Assemblée nationale on 6 February 1934 was a groundswell of support for labour unity. The UA was one of the eight organizations represented at the meeting held in the offices of the CGT the next day.[7] According to Lefranc, Jouhaux particularly wanted the anarchists to be associated with the CGT's call for a general strike: "fidelity to the ideals of his youth and the desire to cover himself against accusations of having sold out to the government."[8] UA members took part in the strike, held on 12 February and supported by the CGTU as well as by the CGT. Its success was imm-mensely encouraging to the anarchists, though they were less pleased with its "co-option" by the PC and PS pact of that July, which would lead to the launching of the Front populaire a year later: "We rejoice at the unity of action which has now been realised, having been among the first to call for it. If fascism has taken a step back, it is thanks to that unity. We believe it necessary, however, to oppose the so-called Popular Front, which is a distortion of that unity."[9] During the summer of 1934, the anarchists were involved in the setting-up of a *Centre de liaison et de coordination des forces antifascistes de la région parisienne* — a non-communist rival, more or less, to the communist-dominated Comité Amsterdam-Pleyel.[10] Some felt a "profound distaste at having to associate with cer-tain elements."[11] Nonetheless, they decided that, as Sébastien Faure put it, "for the time being, the most important thing is to halt the progress of fascism" and agreed to take part in the demonstration of 14 July, 1935.[12] As the prefect of police refused to allow the anarchist black flag on the demonstration, they took part with their respective trade unions rather than as a separate anarchist contingent.[13]

At its Easter congress, 12–13 April 1936, this tactic was confirmed as policy: the UA could not remain on the touch-line. Anarchists must ally themselves with the non-anarchist left and take part in the mass antifascist movement — albeit whilst trying to exert a revolutionary in-fluence.[14] It is no coincidence that it was at this conference that the FCL rejoined the UA.[15] Nor was it unconnected that the following August the opposite faction left the UA to found the FAF (Fédération anarchiste de langue française), condemning the UA for being centralist, dominated by a Parisian clique, authoritarian and too conciliatory towards the non-anarchist left.[16] The Nîmes-based *Terre libre*, which had existed since 1934, would become the organ of the FAF in February 1937.

THE STRIKE MOVEMENT OF 1936

After the reunification of the CGT in February 1936 — welcomed by all except the CGTSR, for whom the CGT was incorrigibly passive, reform-ist and compromised by its links with the Socialist Party — came the sum-mer strike-wave. The anarchists were overjoyed. "Let us salute this mag-nificent dawn!," declaimed *le Combat syndicaliste*.[17] The strikes were "an outstanding and unprecedented triumph": "For the first time in history, the whole of the working class has risen up and imposed its will on its oppressors, the bosses."[18] But the greatest value of the strikes lay not so much in the concessions won, as in the way in which they were won. The occupations, in particular, were a new strike form which corresponded closely to what anarchists had been proposing for many years: "Attacking both the right to property and the principle of authority, the workers have taken control of the means of production, which are their means of work; for a moment, they have stopped the source of profit and exerted their right of occupation, proving in the process their capacity for organisation and self-management. They have proved the value of direct action."[19]

Thus, whilst not undervaluing the gains made by workers in 1936, the strikes, for the anarchists, did not represent a situation which needed to be "normalised" by a few concessions from the employers: they were just the beginning. This could have been the first stage of an ever wider, ever deeper movement on the part of a class which had at last refound its unity, its strength and its self-confidence. The Matignon Agreement and the attitude of Maurice Thorez, Léon Blum and Jouhaux were seen as the betrayal of a movement that was still at its height and had not yet fulfilled its true potential: "For some, hope has been destroyed; for others, a danger avoided; an opportunity to emancipate labour has perhaps been lost."[20] Two years later, when the euphoria in France had evaporated and when the Spanish revolution had effectively also been destroyed, the young and disillusioned revolutionaries around the new monthly journal *Révision* provided an even more negative appraisal:

> Not only did the Matignon Agreement, a treaty concluded under the auspices of the Socialist government between the big employers and the leadership of the CGT, fail to limit profits or restrict the power of capital. It has actually forced capital to organise itself more seriously than in the past and has reinforced the influence of the most powerful capitalists over the capitalist class as a whole. The working class is deluding itself as to the value of the reforms it won.[21]

As for the extent of the anarchists' own involvement in the strikes, it is difficult to ascertain with any precision. It seems that when the Paris Federation of the UA called an extraordinary congress for 4 June in order to discuss tactics, hardly anyone was able to attend as activists were already too involved in the strikes they were supposed to be discussing. We also know that after the CGT's reunification congress of March 1936, the more workerist of the anarchists fought hard to establish factory committees in an attempt to nurture the "syndicalist spirit"[22] whose reassertion they perceived in the mass support for reunification and to fight against PS or PC manipulation of the unions for party political purposes. These factory committees had three objectives: to disseminate anarchist ideas; to encourage direct action; to work in and foster the revolutionary militias some socialists were setting up.[23] Factory committees were established in various of the bigger companies in the Paris region, although estimates of how successful they were vary.[24] But when their representation at the UA congress of October–November 1937 was discussed, it was rejected for fear that the organization might be "diverted into the domain of workplace affairs," as Fernand Vintrigner put it.[25] A referendum on the factory committees that was supposed to be organized within a month of the congress seems never to have happened, and the policy was abandoned by the UA.

First-hand accounts of the spring and summer of 1936 by anarchist activists also vary in the impressions they give. Joyeux writes that his UA group in the 17th *arrondissement* failed to exploit the opportunities afforded anarchists by the Popular Front, being subsumed instead in the general enthusiasm for political reform.[26] Léo Eichenbaum-Voline suggests that "apart from a few isolated individuals lost in the crowd," the anarchists did nothing but argue about their differences.[27] Nicolas Faucier, in contrast, claims far more involvement and commitment on the part of the anarchist movement: "The anarchists were at the heart of the struggle. At the offices of the *Union anarchiste*, there was a constant toing and froing of militants and sympathisers wanting propaganda material for solidarity work with the strikers."[28] The veteran activist André Senez specifies that the anarchists who were most involved in the strike movement were those who were members of both the UA and the CGT, and especially ex-FCL militants.[29] Henri Bouyé admits that "our movement was not equal to the situation," but also distinguishes between the different tendencies: the greatest offenders, in his eyes, were the individualists—who were interested neither in the labour movement nor in social revolution—and the CGTSR—which was too isolated.[30]

Although information is sparse and impressionistic, some anarchists did play an important rôle in their unions: Pierre-Valentin Berthier and Bernard Bouquereau, for instance, fomented and organised strikes in the tanneries of Issoudun;[31] Bouyé organised a strike of florists in the shop where he worked, drew up their list of demands and created the Syndicat des employés et travailleurs fleuristes de la région parisienne *(CGT)* (Florist Workers' Union)[32]; Patat created the Syndicat de l'alimentation (Food Industry Workers' Union); Felix Guyard was a prominent activist at the Sautter-Harlé engineering works; Roger Caron of the JAC (Jeunesses anarchistes-communistes, the UA's youth organisation) was elected to the bureau of the metal-workers' union.[33] Among CGTSR militants, Clément Snappe played a leading rôle in the La Villette steel works; Basson in the charcoal plant in Saint-Etienne; H. Boucharel amongst the building-workers of Limoges.[34] By all accounts, one of the greatest obstacles in the way of anarchist involvement in syndicalist activities at this time was the determination of the PCF to maintain its authority within the trade union hierarchies.

ANTIMILITARISM, ANTISTALINISM

The anarchists were also an integral part of that sector of the labour movement that, throughout this period, adopted a resolutely antimilitarist—and consequently antistalinist—stance. They took part in the Centre de liaison contre la guerre et l'Union sacrée, established in opposition to the Stalin-Laval Pact of May 1935.[35] Organised by the syndicalists of the Révolution prolétarienne group and the Ligue syndicaliste, the centre's manifesto and two conferences were supported by the UA, the FCL and even the CGTSR, as well as by other groups and individuals closely associated with the anarchist movement: the pacifists around la Patrie humaine and le Barrage, the Ligue internationale des combattants de la paix (whose president was Sébastien Faure), Henri Poulaille, Ernestan and Simone Weil. In January 1937, anarchists also joined with the Gauche révolutionnaire, the Monatte-Louzon group and others to create the Cercle syndicaliste lutte de classes—an attempt to regroup the revolutionary opposition to the policies of Jouhaux and Benoit Frachon.[36] Many of those involved with Révolution prolétarienne and the Ligue syndicaliste were of course themselves very close to anarchism.

DIRECT ACTION AND THE CRITIQUE OF THE POPULAR FRONT

"Popular Frontism," then, was clearly welcomed by the anarchists, but only in the sense of a united working-class front created from the bottom up. The "so-called Popular Front" created by the parties was "a distortion of that unity," linked as it was to the Stalin-Laval Pact.[37] For the anarchists, this pact was a new *Union sacrée* intended, "through an alliance of French and Russian imperialism," to maintain "the *status quo* established at Versailles."[38] In March 1936, *le Libertaire* declared in banner headlines that "Popular Front means *Union sacrée*, and *Union sacrée* means war."[39] The pact cemented their hostility to the Communists— or "*nacos*" (*nationaux-communistes*, national-communists), as they were coming to be known—and, of course, encouraged them in their belief that the Communists' primary motive in promoting the Popular Front was what they saw as Stalin's bellicose and reactionary foreign policy. The threat of war was looming on the horizon, and the false conflict between fascism and "democracy" was preparing minds by making war seem acceptable: "It is time the working class separated itself from all these traitors and that it defined its *own* anti-war policy. It is not a matter of choosing between German and French imperialism. … The working class must fight them *both*."[40] A year later, in the spring of 1936, Attruia summed up the anarchists' attitude to communist strategy: "It is not the task of true revolutionaries to defend this State against another State — even a fascist one — but to destroy the State through revolution. Their duty is not, as Vaillant-Couturier has written in *l'Humanité*, to oppose 'the permanent threat of a fascist putsch with the barrier of republican feeling in the country and among the forces of law and order' (sic), but actively to prepare a revolutionary response."[41]

But the anarchists also attacked what they saw as the fundamental deceptiveness of the Popular Front policy, the naïvety of believing that anything significant could be achieved by electing a Popular Front government: "make the rich pay" was a seductive but misleading slogan.[42] This was, of course, a matter of very basic anarchist principle, as the UA's manifesto (adopted at the Paris congress in April 1936)[43] made clear. Parliamentarism was the gravest danger to the working class, being no more than an anaesthetic. An electoral alliance with the bourgeoisie was a trick, because it had the working class believe that their interests were the same as their rulers', and a century's experience showed that it was "always the working class that pays the cost of such alliances." It was therefore foolish to believe that a Popular Front government would or could achieve what the working class needed: "Will it expropriate the industrialists and the financiers? No. That is not its aim — our nice republican Radicals could never subscribe to such a thing."[44] Popular Front governments in France or Spain would not be able to achieve what the working class wanted without going beyond the legal framework of a bourgeois parliament, and they would not be able to do that without destroying themselves as coalition governments. Anarchists wondered what would happen then: "Parliamentary resistance? Capitalism has shown in several countries that it is quite capable of overcoming such opposition without lifting a finger. The Popular Front, if it wishes to hold on to power, will have to protect itself by adopting a 'neutrality' which will be greatly appreciated by capital. Otherwise, it will be forced to step down. There is no other possible solution."[45] In the spring of 1936, the UA was already forecasting total disillusion on the part of the working class: "This experiment will be the greatest confirmation of our ideas on the incapacity of political parties to lead the proletariat to its complete emancipation."[46] They were also suggesting that this disappointment might well result in "a new revolutionary upsurge" (*le Libertaire*, 21 February 1936).

For the UA, those things that were achieved — from the amnesty accorded political prisoners by the new Republican government in Spain to paid holidays in France — were won not by the Popular Front governments, but forced upon these by the direct action of the working class itself.[47] For the anarchists, the direct intervention of the labour movement, unmediated and unrestricted by electoralism, had more progressive potential than the coalition between the Socialist, Communist and Radical Party hierarchies — a coalition that a *le Libertaire* editorial insisted was a product and not a cause of the spontaneous popular movement: "In Spain as in France, all the parliamentary hubbub surrounding the Popular Front, the shifts in parliamentary majorities and so on — which are persistently taken for causes by commentators who are either blinkered or who have an interest in such misunderstanding — are nothing but the effect of the tremendous dissatisfaction of the masses who have a direct interest in real change."[48]

SPAIN AND NON-INTERVENTIONISM

But it was the Spanish revolution that, more than anything, aroused the imagination and enthusiasm of the French anarchists. Again, when it came to the question of "non-intervention," they were clear on the rôle of the French government. The anarchists certainly did not want the Blum government to intervene militarily, but the prime minister was branded a Pontius Pilate for his refusal to allow normal trade relations with Republican Spain to continue or to turn a blind eye to the export of munitions even if it was technically prohibited. The working class could and should rely only on itself: "The defence of Spain in revolutionary struggle must be assured by the French working class, and not by the French nation. The neutrality of the latter must not lead to the passivity of the former."[49] It must act to destroy pro-fascist forces in France, and constitute "the revolutionary front of solidarity with Spain."[50] Thus the campaign of solidarity for Spain was not a humanitarian effort sealed off from revolutionary politics in France — the two were closely linked.

So, in analysing the tasks facing the revolutionary left, concerning both domestic politics and the Spanish problem, the UA rejected reliance on a Popular Front government in favour of direct and autonomous action by the labour movement. This was the basis of what the UA began to call the "revolutionary front" — basically a return to the "united front" policy, but with a new emphasis to distinguish this front from the reformist Popular Front.[51]

IMPERIALISM AND THE MYTH OF "DEMOCRACY V. FASCISM"

These two underlying principles — working-class autonomy and revolutionary class struggle — implied opposition to the "neo-reformism" that, according to the anarchist analysis, was basically a more insidious form of fascism, trying to integrate the trade union movement into an increasingly corporate state.[52] As Séchaud put it: "We are faced more and more with the dilemma: fascism or revolution."[53] Therefore as far as international politics were concerned, the UA's call for a revolutionary front clearly espoused traditional proletarian internationalism, denouncing the myth of the struggle between fascism and democracy, and rejecting national defence, whether in a capitalist or a "state capitalist" country. The implications for the campaign around Spain were clear. One of the UA's main aims in that respect was to unmask the rôle of foreign imperialisms — British, French and Russian — in the civil war, and in particular to expose the rôle of the PS and CGT — "agents of French imperialism" — and of the PCF — "agents of Russian imperialism."[54]

The revolutionary front as opposition to the reformist Front populaire and as "revolutionary front of solidarity with Spain" were, then, linked in that they were based, initially at least, on the same analysis. And the campaign of support for Spain was not intended to work only one way, simply as a means of providing material assistance. One of the anarchists' main aims was to provide a counter-information service to compensate for the failings of the French Popular Front press, which, the asnarchists insisted, was far from even-handed in its coverage of the various sectors of Spanish antifascism. The French working class, "duped" by its own politicians, would have before them the example of a large and successful revolutionary labour movement, independent of politicians, and might be inspired by the example.[55] Thus, there would be eight French-language anarchist newspapers given over entirely to events in Spain, not to mention the scores of public meetings organised by the French anarchists that were addressed by leading representatives of the CNT-FAI, the POUM and returning French combatants, and many of which attracted very large audiences. Second, the campaign for international solidarity included repeated exhortations to the workers in transport and armaments manufacturing to take the law into their own hands and supply the Spanish antifascists with all they needed — going as far as general strike and insurrection if need be. As Sébastien Faure put it, speaking of the CNT-FAI: "Admiring their example is fine. Preparing to follow it is better."[56]

CO-OPERATION WITH THE NON-ANARCHIST LEFT

So what were the results of this policy in practical terms? Although between July and October 1936 the UA was involved in a Comité anarcho-syndicaliste pour la libération et la défense du prolétariat espagnol (CASLDPE), along with the GTSR and FAF — a kind of anarchist front—the UA was also cooperating at the same time with the PS, the Gauche révolutionnaire, the Jeunesses Socialistes Révolution-naires, the Comité de Vigilance des Intellectuels Antifascistes (CVIA, Vigilance Committee of Antifascist Intellectuals), Trotskyists and even, in a few rare cases, Communists.[57] According to Joyeux, his local UA group already had more or less regular contacts with "related revolu-tionary groups" even before the revolutionary front policy was adopted: pacifists, the CGTSR, freethinkers, Trotskyists and the local PS section, once it had joined the GR.[58] In Wattrelos, there was a *Comité antifasciste* which united Socialists, Anarchists and Communists in one group.[59] Cooperation with Communists, however, was unusual. The Trotskyists were not the only ones to be slandered by the stalinists in this period. The anarchist press regularly printed reports of physical intimidation and violence being practised against activists. The PCF was accused regularly by anarchists and syndicalists of employing all sorts of under-hand methods to suppress any propaganda critical of the party.[60]

THE "REVOLUTIONARY FRONT"

In October, the policy of cooperation between Socialists and the UA was formalised at a joint public meeting, proposed by the Socialists, on the theme "For the creation of a Revolutionary Front." The event was held at the Mutualité on 3 October, and *le Libertaire* claimed an audience of 4,000.[61] It was chaired by Pierre Audubert of the PS and, significantly, Paul Rivet (one of the intellectuals who had been among the first to call for antifascist unity) was originally intended as the main Socialist speak-er: in the event, Lucien Weitz of the Jeunesses socialistes, and Pivert of the Gauche révolutionnaire spoke for the Socialists, with Ringeas and Faure from the UA.[62] The meeting passed a resolution calling for the creation of an armed *Garde Populaire* in order to counter physical attacks by the right in France, and defined its position on the Blum government thus: "A Popular Front which did not attune itself to the revolution-ary events which are now taking place in Spain and will soon spread to France, would be betraying the proletariat of both countries."[63]

THE "REVOLUTIONARY FRONT OF SOLIDARITY WITH SPAIN"

As for the campaign of solidarity with the Spanish revolutionaries, the UA had decided that cooperating only with small anarchist organisa-tions was not achieving good enough results, whereas working together with "related revolutionary tendencies" had already enabled them to reach much broader sectors of the working class.[64] Their policy was that "outside of its own specifically anarchist activities, the UA is ready, as in the past, to cooperate with all other revolutionary organisations on clearly defined tasks, and particularly for the effective support of Spain."[65] This was to lead to the creation of the Comité pour l'Espagne libre (Committee for Free Spain). And in fact, despite the pretensions of the CGTSR and FAF to be a French version of the CNT-FAI, the CNT fully supported the UA's policy: most of the Spanish anarchists were far more "popular frontist" than their French comrades.[66] On 16 October 1936, *le Libertaire* printed a telegramme from Horacio Prieto, secretary of the CNT National Committee, urging the UA to work together with anyone sympathetic to the cause of Spanish antifascism. Durruti's appeal to all French revolutionaries to unite in "a true people's antifascist front" was also advanced in justification.[67]

This was to widen the existing split in the anarchist movement between the UA on the one hand, and the FAF and CGTSR on the other, the latter rejecting any kind of formal or long-term cooperation with non-anarchists. When the CASLDPE held its congress in Paris, 24–25 October 1936, the UA's proposal for a "broadened front" was rejected overwhelmingly, since the CGTSR and FAF had a majority on the Paris Comité anarcho-syndicaliste.[68] The CGTSR's Confederal Committee declared at its meeting of 23 October that the UA's new committee "can in no way claim to represent either the CNT or the FAI in France."[69] A later statement of the residual Comité anarcho-syndicaliste went even further and insisted: "As far as we are concerned, those who practise such a liaison cease, *ipso facto*, to be anarchists."[70]

The main grounds for dissent from the revolutionary front policy on the part of the CGTSR and FAF were not so much the practice of alliances with non-anarchists as such, but rather the fact that such an alliance was perceived by the dissenters as an "organic" alliance, a long-term and even organisational link-up which would inevitably entail jettisoning anarchist principles. However, this was not how the UA saw the revolutionary front. It was made clear that such alliances were temporary: circumstantial cooperation on specific tasks.[71] Thus, contrary to what the CGTSR and FAF affirmed, the UA's understanding of the kind of revolutionary alliance into which it was entering was that (i) it would last only as long as proved necessary for the achievement of its specific aims; (ii) such an alliance entailed no abandonment by any constituent grouping of its own principles or methods of working, beyond those adjustments implied by the will to cooperate; and (iii) none of the groupings involved would exploit the alliance for partisan propaganda purposes.

However, this split became more complete as the UA went on to cooperate with an even wider range of political organisations. The most spectacular example was a meeting at the Vel d'Hiv organised by the UA in October 1936, at which the platform speakers included Léon Jouhaux and Marcel Cachin, the two bogeys of the anarchist movement, as well as speakers from the FAI (Magriñá), the Catalan CNT (Trabal), the Aragon Council (Mavilla), the UA (Huart), the POUM (Gorkin), the Esquerra and the Generalitat (Miravitlles), the PS (Zyromski), the JEUNES (Jeunes équipes unies pour une nouvelle économie sociale — Josse) and the Gauche révolutionnaire (Pivert). It is noticeable that Pivert was allowed to speak last and that it was his speech that received most coverage in *le Libertaire*'s report.[72] But from the autumn of 1936 the UA cooperated regularly with various groups and individuals on the left in organising public meetings, demonstrations and fund-raising: Jean Rous (Parti ouvrier internationaliste), Marcel Fourrier (Comité pour la révolution espagnole), André Ferrat (Que Faire?, Association communiste révolutionnaire), the Parti d'unité prolétarienne, the Parti frontiste, Robert Louzon and the Révolution prolétarienne group, *la Vague* and — not insignificantly — the "reformist" anarchists around the monthly *Plus loin*, who had been ostracised up until this point because of their support for the war effort in 1914.[73] There is some evidence of local manifestations of the *Front révolutionnaire*: in Aulnay-sous-Bois, the Trotskyists and the UA worked together, forming a group about 100 strong and — according to the UA — seriously worrying the local PCF.[74] In the ninth *arrondissement* the JAC and the youth section of the GR formally merged.[75] Joyeux gives a description of his delegation to joint talks with the local PS section in the 17th *arrondissement*.[76]

CONTRADICTIONS OF THE "REVOLUTIONARY FRONT" POLICY

It is difficult to separate the two aspects of the revolutionary front policy. On the one hand, it was intended as a reprise of the extra-parliamentary movement of 1934–35, able to unite the non-stalinist left in a revolutionary opposition to the Blum government. On the other, it was a means of drumming up as much support as possible for the Spanish republicans in general, and for the CNT-FAI and the POUM, in particular. In fact, as things developed, a clear contradiction emerged between the UA's position on the *Front populaire* and its solidarity work for Spain. At home, resolute opposition to the party hierarchies, to parliamentarism and to the myth of the antifascist crusade; in Spain, tacit acceptance of CNT ministers and of what was, in effect, a Popular Front government engaged in an antifascist war.

In certain ways, the anarchists were better placed than some to help make the revolutionary opposition to Blum and Jouhaux succeed: they were more resolute in their critique of Blum than the GR; they were more numerous, better established in the trade unions and less ideologically demanding of potential allies than the Trotskyists. Yet, on the evidence, the policy does not seem to have been a great success. Speaking at the UA's congress of October–November 1937, Charles Ridel (a member of the administrative commission) deplored the political incoherence and inconsistency of the UA, "which launched the campaign for the Revolutionary Front, only to abandon it later."[77] According to Joyeux, the UA's adoption of the revolutionary front policy had left each group quite free to contract alliances as and if it wished. Yet both the local membership and the national leadership were apprehensive about alliances—a hesitancy which Joyeux puts down to "fifteen years of struggle against marxist political parties and reformist syndicalists," and to alienation caused by anarchism's failure to prevent many of its supporters defecting to the various marxist groups since the war, an alienation which led many to shrink from further contact with such groups.[78] As for the 17th *arrondissement*, although Joyeux claims that the revolutionary front policy initially boosted his group, he and his fellow delegate Edrac felt alienated by the GR's middle-class intellectuals, and soon stopped attending what they felt was an ineffectual talking-shop. For Joyeux, the discourses of the different sectors of the revolutionary front were just too distinct.

Perhaps the principal function of the revolutionary front policy was to make possible the creation of the Comité pour l'Espagne libre in October 1936 and of SIA (Solidarité internationale antifasciste) in November 1937. Both were successful as campaigns of solidarity and support, but again showed up the inconsistency of the UA's policy. Both involved cooperation with supporters of the Popular Front government. The same policies that were accepted in Spain were opposed in France. There were various reasons for this: the acceptance of a *fait accompli* (the CNT's participation in government), the urgent need to defeat Franco, an unwillingness to criticise a CNT to which the UA was grateful for having put anarchism back on the agenda.

DIVISIONS WITHIN ANARCHISM

It is also possible to see the two different manifestations, as it were, of the united or revolutionary front policy as being the products of two different currents within the UA. Louis Anderson, editor of *le Libertaire* from 1936 to 1939, has (in interview) described this split within the UA as one between those who were above all humanitarian pacifists (typi-fied by Lecoin), and those who were above all socialist revolutionaries (such as Frémont). It was the latter tendency that produced the revolu-tionary front as opposition to the reformist *Front populaire*. It represented a move toward a more workerist and syndicalist view of the anarchists' rôle, and towards a less purist attitude to the thorny question of anar-chist organisation. The stereotypical "all or nothing" image was rejected in favour of a more constructive, pragmatic and "realistic" anarchism with heroes like Durruti and Makhno. Revolutionary frontists wanted the movement to leave the anarchist ghetto and become an integral part of the wider revolutionary labour movement.

The UA's other dominant tendency was that typified by Lecoin, a tendency perhaps more individualist than collectivist, more pacifist and "moralist" than revolutionary.[79] Lecoin's method—tried and tested in campaigns of a humanitarian nature in the 1920s—was to establish an unelected organising committee and to solicit the help of almost anyone whose name would be likely to draw attention and support. This meth-od of working mostly complemented the Spanish tendency to reduce the political conflict to two camps: fascism and antifascism. Lecoin himself tended to see the work of the Comité pour l'Espagne libre and of SIA as a humanitarian campaign.

Joyeux has argued that: "For decades anarchism has swung be-tween two extreme tendencies—isolation in its certainties, and the drift towards reformist or humanitarian organisations—without managing to find a point of equilibrium between doctrinal intransigence and com-promise."[80] If we accept this interpretation—and it is one that was al-ready being articulated by some revolutionary anarchists in 1938—then it could be argued that these two extremes were represented in the late 30s by the FAF on the one hand, and by Lecoin and others in the UA leadership on the other. In the middle were those who tried to put into practice their anarchist politics, maintaining a revolutionary class analysis and insisting on working-class autonomy and on the autonomy of the anarchist organisation, while at the same time cooperating with other groups whose position on specific points was close to theirs: as-serting the anarchist voice from *within* rather than *against* or *from outside of* the broader working-class movement. I would argue that this was the standpoint in the late 1920s of the platformists, and of activists such as Frémont, Ridel and Luc Daurat in the 1930s. Their critique of "tradi-tional" anarchism and of its performance in 1933–39 was taken up again forcefully by a group of young revolutionaries (which included Ridel and Daurat) who launched a new monthly discussion journal in Febru-ary 1938, aptly named *Révision*.

A RESURGENCE OF ANARCHISM?

In view of the rôle played by the UA in 1933–39, it would seem reasonable to reappraise Broué and Dorey's assertion that the anarchists were always "a minority swimming against the current."[81] Not only were the anarchists not as isolated as is often suggested, they also grew significantly in number in the Popular Front period, and this seems to have been, in part, a consequence of the UA's revised ideological positions. The JAC, reporting in January 1937 on the increase in sales of *le Libertaire*, argued that since the previous July the anarchist movement had come to be seen once more as belonging firmly within the labour movement, and that the revolutionary front policy was responsible for this. Others would argue much the same point in 1938, adding that the movement had thus regained a standing they had not enjoyed since the early 1920s.[82] Rabaut argues that, for the first time in forty years, the anarchists were again "the *avant-garde* of the *avant-garde*."[83]

Membership of the UA and the readership of *le Libertaire* had both expanded during 1935, and after July 1936 the increase accelerated.[84] *Le Libertaire* believed that the reasons for their new popularity were threefold: (i) the correctness of their stance on the Popular Front government; (ii) their consistent antimilitarism; and (iii) events in Spain. Between spring 1936 and spring 1937, UA membership more than quadrupled. There were some fourteen other anarchist papers besides *le Libertaire*, which, itself, on May Day 1937 — a few weeks after the violent clashes between the police and antifascists at Clichy — printed an exceptional run of 100,000 copies.[85] At the end of 1936 the UA opened an *Ecole propagandiste*.[86] Throughout 1936–38, new anarchist groups and regional federations were formed, and links between existing groups strengthened. Disabused ex-anarchists became active again, previously unaffiliated syndicalists discovered anarchism for the first time, and Socialists and Communists — including several in positions of responsibility — deserted their parties for the UA.[87] The non-anarchist press also began to talk about the anarchists much more. Even *le Temps* printed a feature based on police sources about "a dangerous resurgence of the anarchist movement": "It appears that the extremists, who thought that with the rise of the Communists they would see the triumph in France of revolution, insurrection and antimilitarism, are abandoning the Communist Party to go and swell the ranks of the anarchists."[88]

By the autumn of 1937, the leadership of the UA could confidently announce that it was "the only force having the authority and influence necessary to lead the revolutionary movement."[89] And there is no doubt that the anarchist movement achieved a great deal in 1936–39 — particularly as regards organising solidarity for their Spanish comrades. Yet, ultimately, the anarchists failed. For revolutionary anarchists, only the building of a revolutionary socialist antifascist movement in France (in opposition to the *Front populaire*), combined with the enlargement of the Spanish civil war into a revolutionary class war across Europe, could possibly have produced a revolutionary outcome.

However much of a resurgence of anarchism there may have been in 1936–37, new recruits were often not retained and the movement was still weak in comparison with the PS, the PCF and the "reformists" within the CGT. Internecine ideological disputes, the result of an almost impossible situation in Spain and of some extremely abstract and dogmatic analyses, divided the whole anarchist movement and alienated many (those who were already activists and doubtless many potential supporters too). Important strategic and tactical debates were never resolved satisfactorily; inconsistency both over time and between the national organisation and local groups was a major problem. The CGTSR failed to overcome its own isolationism and build a libertarian syndicalist movement capable of having any real influence (or even of being taken seriously) within the broader labour movement. And when it came to it, and despite the enormous sympathy felt in France for the CNT and the Spanish Republicans, the fear of the war spreading throughout Europe prevented the direct and massive intervention on the part of the French working-class movement which would have been needed. As Manfredonia has remarked, "The majority were simply not ready to die for Barcelona, any more than they were ready to die for the Sudetenland or Dantzig."[90]

Notes

1.   Daniel Guérin, *Front populaire, révolution manquée* (Arles: Actes Sud, 1997), pp.162–3. Quotation from *le Libertaire*, 31 July 1936.

2.   Quoted in Gaetano Manfredonia, "1936: Face au fascisme et à la Révolution" in *Les Oeillets rouges* no.1 (September 1986), pp.41–69, p.44.

3.   Frémont in *le Libertaire*, 7 July 1933.

4.   Manfredonia, "1936: Face au fascisme."

5.   *La Revue anarchiste*, August–September 1934.

6.   *Le Libertaire*, 1 June 1934.

7.   Jean Maitron, *Le Mouvement anarchiste en France* (Paris: Maspero, 1975) vol.II, p.27

8.   Georges Lefranc, *Histoire du Front Populaire (1934–1938)* (Paris: Payot, 1974), pp.23–4 and 441.

9. *Le Libertaire*, 5 July 1935.
10. Lefranc, *Histoire du Front Populaire*, pp.56–7.
11. *Le Libertaire*, 5 July 1935.
12. *Le Libertaire*, 12 July 1935.
13. Maitron vol.II, p.27.
14. *Le Libertaire*, 8 May 1936.
15. *Le Libertaire*, 15 May 1936; cf. *le Libertaire*, 3 January 1936.
16. Maitron vol.II, pp.87–8.
17. *Le Combat syndicaliste*, 5 June 1936.
18. *Le Combat syndicaliste*, 19 June 1936.
19. *Le Combat syndicaliste*, 5 June 1936. Such Italian-style factory occupations had in fact been proposed by anarchist syndicalists back in 1921, at a time when ordinary strikes were failing to get results because of surpluses of unsold stock (which meant that employers had little incentive to get their employees back to work). The tactic had been put forward, for instance, by the textile-worker Auguste Herclet in Vienne (Isère) and by the Loire metalworker Jean Seigne, and subsequently, there were a few brief occupations that year. Kathryn E. Amdur, *Syndicalist Legacy: Trade Unions and Politics in Two French Cities in the Era of World War I* (Urbana & Chicago: University of Illinois Press, 1986), p.182.
20. *Le Libertaire*, 12 June 1936.
21. *Révision*, May 1938.
22. *Le Libertaire*, 6 March 1936.
23. *Le Libertaire*, 18 December 1936. See the rubric "Dans les boîtes et sur les chantiers," which appeared in the paper from October 1936.
24. Jean-Pierre Rioux, *Révolutionnaires du Front populaire. Choix de documents 1935–1938* (Paris: Union Générale d'Editions, 1973), p.350; Jean Rabaut, *Tout est possible! Les 'gauchistes' français 1929–1944* (Paris: Denoël/Gonthier, 1974), p.252; *le Libertaire*, 4 and 11 November 1937. There were committees at the Trocadéro building site, Sauter-Harlé (Paris 15), Brandt, Renault, Citroën, Panhard-Levassor, SKF (Ivry), Somua (Saint-Ouen) and Gnôme et Rhône (Gennevilliers).
25. *Le Libertaire*, 11 November 1937.
26. Maurice Joyeux, *Souvenirs d'un anarchiste* (Paris: Editions du Monde libertaire, 1986), p.284.
27. In CIRA (Marseille), *Bulletin* no.26–27, "1886...1936 et quelques autres anniversaires," p.71.
28. Ibid, p.47.
29. Ibid, p.36.
30. Ibid, p.59; cf. Joyeux, *Souvenirs*, p.285.
31. CIRA, "1886...1936," pp.39–40; Pierre-Valentin Berthier in interview.
32. CIRA, "1886...1936," pp.56–8.
33. Ibid, p.36.
34. Jacques Kergoat, *La France du Front Populaire* (Paris: La Découverte, 1986), p.167.
35. The Stalin-Laval Pact included the famous statement that "Mr. Stalin understands and approves fully of the national defence policy adopted by France in order to maintain its armed forces at such a level as to ensure its security." It was at this time that the Communist Party, hitherto known as the "Communist Party—French Section of the Communist International" (PC-SFIC), changed its name to the "French Communist Party" (PCF) and began to have its supporters sing the Marseillaise on demonstrations rather

than the International. According to *le Libertaire*, anarchists who persisted in singing the International were sometimes attacked physically by PCF stewards—see, for example, *le Libertaire*, 21 February 1936.

36.   Nicolas Faucier, *Pacifisme et Antimilitarisme dans l'entre-deux-guerres (1919–1939)* (Paris: Spartacus, 1983), pp.112–4, 149–51; Rioux, *Révolutionnaires du Front populaire*, pp.26, 235, 247; Guérin, *Front populaire*, pp.132–3, 216, 242–3; Pierre Broué and Nicole Dorey, "Critiques de gauche et opposition révolutionnaire au Front populaire (1936–1938)" in *Mouvement social* no.54 (January–March 1966), pp.131–3.

37.   *Le Libertaire*, 5 July 1935.
38.   *Le Libertaire*, 10 May 1935.
39.   *Le Libertaire*, 20 March 1936.
40.   *Le Libertaire*, 1 May 1935.
41.   *Le Libertaire*, 7 April 1936. The "sic" is in the original.
42.   *Le Libertaire*, 3 January 1936.
43.   *Le Libertaire*, 22 May 1936.
44.   *Le Libertaire*, 5 July 1936.
45.   *Le Libertaire*, 21 February 1936.
46.   *Le Libertaire*, 10 April 1936.
47.   *Le Libertaire*, 21 August 1936.
48.   Ibid.
49.   *Le Libertaire*, 7 August 1936.
50.   *Le Libertaire*, 25 September 1936.
51.   *Le Libertaire*, 20 May 1937
52.   Ibid.
53.   *Le Libertaire*, 7 August 1936.
54.   *Le Libertaire*, 20 May 1937.
55.   *Le Libertaire*, 10 July 1936.
56.   *Le Libertaire*, 7 August 1936.
57.   See *le Libertaire* in August, September and October 1936.
58.   Joyeux, *Souvenirs*, p.275.
59.   *Le Libertaire*, 4 September 1936.
60.   See Hobsbawm's comments on the increase of anti-anarchist propaganda by the Communists in the mid-1930s: "Bolshevism and the Anarchists," *Revolutionaries* (London: Quartet, 1977), p.68.
61.   *Le Libertaire*, 9 October 1936.
62.   *Le Libertaire*, 25 September and 2 October 1936.
63.   *Le Libertaire*, 9 October 1936.
64.   *Le Libertaire*, 23 October and 6 November 1936.
65.   *Le Libertaire*, 6 November 1936.
66.   *Le Libertaire*, 7 August 1936 and F7/14721.
67.   *Le Libertaire*, 30 October 1936.
68.   *L'Espagne antifasciste (CNT-AIT-FAI)*, 28 October and 7 November 1936.
69.   *Le Combat syndicaliste*, 30 October 1936.
70.   *L'Espagne antifasciste (CNT-AIT-FAI)*, 7 November 1936.
71.   *Le Libertaire*, 20 November 1936.
72.   *Le Libertaire*, 30 October 1936.

73. *Le Libertaire*, 26 January, 25 February and 1 July 1937.

74. *Le Libertaire*, 1 January 1937.

75. *Le Libertaire*, 6 November 1936.

76. Joyeux, *Souvenirs*, pp.275–93.

77. *Le Libertaire*, 11 November 1937.

78. Joyeux, *Souvenirs*, pp.285–90.

79. Louis Lecoin, *Le cours d'une vie* (Paris: Edité par l'auteur en supplément du journal *Liberté*, 1965); Maurice Joyeux, "Louis Lecoin," in *la Rue (Revue culturelle et littéraire d'expression anarchiste)* no.11 (3rd quarter 1971), pp.4–17.

80. Maurice Joyeux, *Ce que je crois! Réflexions sur l'anarchie* (Saint-Denis: Cahiers du Vent du ch'min, 1984), p.43.

81. Broué and Dorey, "Critiques de gauche," p.92.

82. *Révision*, February 1938.

83. Rabaut, *Tout est possible!*, p.213.

84. Faucier in CIRA, "1886…1936," p.48.

85. *Le Libertaire*, 2 October 1936, 22 April and 13 May 1937.

86. *Le Libertaire*, 22 January 1937.

87. See for example *le Libertaire*, 4 December 1936, 8 January, 3 June and 8 July 1937; Louis Anderson in interview; Nicolas Faucier in correspondence.

88. *Le Temps*, 9 October 1936.

89. *Le Libertaire*, 11 November 1937.

90. Manfredonia, "Face au fascisme," p.69.

9

An Anarchist Front for Spain: the Anarcho-Syndicalist Committee

19 July 1936! ... All eyes are turned towards the flaming torch which has been lit beyond the Pyrenees, after a long night of tragic events, and which heralds fruitful battles.

Ernesto Bonomini[1]

After the series of defeats which the European proletariat has suffered, it is comforting for us that it is anarchists who have reopened a path which seemed to be closing implacably before us.

Luc Daurat[2]

Admiring their example is fine. Preparing to follow it is better.

Sébastien Faure[3]

Within a fortnight of the popular uprising that put a halt to the francoist coup of July 1936, the UA had held a meeting of its organizing committee in order to consider how best to support their Spanish comrades. On 22 August, a general assembly of the UA's Paris Federation on the theme "How to help our brothers in Spain" reached four decisions regarding future action. The Federation should (i) avoid, at all costs, the transformation of the Spanish civil war into an interstate war, "something which both fascists and stalinists want to see"; (ii) work within the trade unions to force the CGT into action; (iii) silence the French fascists, for instance by organizing intimidatory demonstrations outside the offices of pro-Franco newspapers; (iv) collect funds both for a publicity campaign in France, and also to help the families of those who had joined the Spanish militias.[4]

AN ANARCHIST FRONT

But the UA was not alone in its desire to help the Spanish anarchist movement. All French anarchists and anarcho-syndicalists, both inside and outside the UA, were under some pressure both from the CNT-FAI and from the many Spanish anarchists exiled in France, to work together closely in order to increase their effectiveness.[5] Hence the constitution, at the request of the CNT-FAI, of a national, Paris-based organization, the Comité Anarcho-syndicaliste pour la défense et la libération du prolétariat espagnol (CASDLPE, Anarcho-Syndicalist Committee for the Defence and Liberation of the Spanish Proletariat), under the auspices of the UA, the CGTSR and the FAF. The committee consisted of five delegates from each of the three constituent organizations; its secretary was Pierre Besnard and its treasurer was Albert Ganin.[6] The CASDLPE's manifesto, published in the CGTSR's organ *le Combat Syndicaliste* on 14 August, proposed two main tasks in its project to help "the Spanish people": first, it asked comrades in the provinces to set up local groups, or *Comités anarcho-syndicalistes* (CAS), and to establish contact with the Paris committee; and second, it announced its intention to publish a daily newspaper, whose main purpose would be to disseminate news received directly from Spain, to combat false stories put out by the press controlled by the Agence Havas (considered to be under the orders of fascism), to compensate for the failings of the "so-called left-wing press" and particularly to publicize the actions of the "heroic fighters of the CNT and of the FAI, systematically forgotten and often slandered by the extreme-left press."[7] This was to be *l'Espagne Antifasciste (CNT-FAI-AIT)*, whose fate will be discussed in more detail below. Indeed, the Spanish revolution and civil war were to provoke the creation of at least eight new anarchist newspapers or bulletins in France given over more or less entirely to the Spanish problem: *Boletin de Información. Edition en langue française*; *Bulletin d'information*; *l'Espagne Antifasciste*; *l'Espagne Antifasciste (CNT-FAI-AIT)*; *l'Espagne Nouvelle*; *Lu dans la presse libertaire syndicaliste espagnole*; *la Nouvelle Espagne Antifasciste*; and *SIA*. But how successful were the anarchists in achieving their other aims, preconditions of a propaganda or counter-information campaign: the establishment of a network of support committees and the raising of funds?

LOCAL SUPPORT GROUPS

As far as local groups are concerned, it is very difficult to tell: first, because we have no reason to believe that the newspapers — our primary source of information in this respect — reported all newly created groups; second, because in many cases the "new" groups seem to have been merely existing anarchist groups or CGTSR sections, which began to devote themselves to solidarity work; third, because many groups that do seem to have appeared spontaneously all over the country, though operating formally or informally with national organizations (the CAS-DLPE, or, later, the Comité pour l'Espagne libre and SIA), followed the Spanish revolutionary committees in adopting a wide variety of names — names that were sometimes modified over time. For example, in Toulon the FCL set up a Comité de Défense de la Révolution Espagnole to centralize the collection of funds in the area; in Marseille, the French, Spanish and Italian anarchist groups united with the Syndicat intercorporatif *(CGTSR)* to form a Comité révolutionnaire pour la défense de la révolution espagnole; in Wattrelos, there appeared a Comité antifasciste which united anarchists, socialists and even communists in one group; and St.-Etienne had a *CAS* according to the UA, a Comité d'Entr'aide according to the CGTSR.[8]

Even the situation in Perpignan is not easy to clarify, and Perpignan played a most important rôle throughout the civil war; money, material and militia volunteers were all sent through there from Paris, before crossing the border into Spain. But within the space of four weeks, there were references in *le Libertaire* to three differently named committees in Perpignan: the Comité régional de défense de la révolution espagnole, the Comité régional anarcho-syndicaliste and the Comité de défense de la révolution espagnole antifasciste.[9] The first remains a mystery; we only know that it had raised nearly 3,000 francs by the middle of August 1936. The second was the local CAS: all funds were forwarded to it from Paris and other collection points, and it then decided how best to use them.[10] The third committee shared the same chairman as the previous one — Louis Montgon, a leading Perpignan anarchist — and consisted at least partly, and perhaps entirely, of *émigré* Spaniards. By mid-September it had already raised over 13,000 francs (and 836 pesetas), and had spent some 6,000 francs on producing and distributing its own bulletin. In February 1937 it brought out a bi-lingual newspaper, the *Bulletin d'information du Comité de Défense de la Révolution Espagnole Antifasciste*, which, from June, was printed almost entirely in Spanish and was subtitled *"Porta-voz de la Federación de Comités Españoles de Accion Antifascista en Francia."* Both the CAS and this FCEAAF committee were housed in the disused military hospital in Perpignan.[11]

MATERIAL SUPPORT

Attempting to calculate the financial support provided by the anarchists in France is similarly problematic. There were three centralized funds established in Paris, although the accounts were not published regularly: an account established by the UA had reached around 21,000 francs by early September; by the middle of October, the CAS had collected over 26,000 francs, and the CGTSR's account—specifically for the CNT—raised nearly 46,000 francs in the same period. That money represented donations from organizations (e.g. the IWMA, the CGTSR, the St.-Etienne *Union locale*), or from particular groups of workers (the Personnel Emeris, the Sautter-Harlé workers, the Lavalette workers at Saint-Ouen), from collections at public meetings, from street collections by local committees, and from pledges by militants and other workers to donate one day's wages per week.[12]

But money raised was not always fed into the national account: often it was used immediately to help the families of local people who had gone to fight in Spain. Marseille's Comité révolutionnaire et groupe inter-corporatif syndicaliste (CGTSR) had raised over 5,000 francs by August and disposed of nearly half of it in this manner.[13] Nor was material assistance always given in an easily quantifiable financial form. According to a report from the Bayonne anarchist group, about ten of whose members had joined the militias, all the group's members still remaining in France took in a Spanish orphan to be looked after by them and their families.[14] Gerard Leretour (on behalf of the conscientious objectors' group) and Charles Marchal (for the FAF) gave the CASDLPE several large cases of medical supplies.[15] Such donations in kind became more common after the establishment by the UA of the *Centre de Ravitaillement* (Provisions Centre) in Paris in October; it was announced then that a convoy of supply lorries was to be sent to Aragon each week, and appeals went out for food, bandages, medicines and tobacco.[16] At the start of October, *le Libertaire* even announced that three ambulances had been acquired and were being sent to the three confederal militias on the Aragon front—one each for the International Groups of the Durruti and Ortiz-Ascaso Columns, and one for the Iron Column based in Valencia.[17]

PROPAGANDA

During August and September, scores of public meetings were held in towns large and small throughout France. These meetings were organized either by the CASDLPE, or the UA, or the CGTSR, or by local anarchist groups (many of which were still independent of any national organization). But this was a period of relative anarchist unity, with UA speakers like Faure, Frémont, Lashortes, Ringeas, Chazoff, Doutreau or Le Meillour sharing the platform with CGTSR speakers like Besnard, Couanault or the Lapeyre brothers and with militants known primarily as pacifists, like Roger Monclin and Aurèle Patorni of la Patrie Humaine.

The greatest single attraction at such meetings, however, was no doubt the presence of representatives of the CNT-FAI: David Antona (at that time temporary secretary of the CNT National Committee), for example, or Maria Ascaso (sister of Francisco Ascaso, who had died on 20 July) and Joaquin Ascaso (cousin of Francisco and Maria, and president of the Aragon Defence Council).[18] Although perhaps the best symbol of the special relationship between the French anarchists and Spain—"the Spain with which we have so much in common, the noble, courageous and proud Spain we love"[19]—was four-year-old Colette Durruti, daughter of the French anarchist Emilienne Morin and Buenaventura Durruti, who was introduced to a 5,000 strong audience in the Mutualité Hall at the beginning of August.[20]

It was also not long before a substantial number of French militants were returning from visits to Spain, where they had been either as combatants or on fact-finding missions. Although the impact of the Russian revolution of 1917 may have been greater in other respects, the Spanish revolution undoubtedly seemed much more immediate to those who came to listen to those of their compatriots, who, within weeks of the insurrection, could already give eye-witness accounts of the momentous events taking place just over the border. And the Spanish represented the single largest immigrant community in France, and many of them were of course political exiles.

It is hardly surprising, therefore, that public meetings were a great success, and continued to be so. The most impressive were those held in the "Mutualité" and "Wagram" meeting halls in August: described in *le Libertaire* as "magnificent" and "unforgettable," they attracted audiences of 5,000 and 8,000 respectively, and the CNT-FAI representatives— Rocca at the first, Antona at the second—were greeted with standing ovations.[21]

Yet such large, prestigious meetings in Paris can be concentrated on to the exclusion of a more modest but sustained effort in the smaller centres throughout the country. This would not do justice to the vigour and initiative of the scores of local groups and committees, whose public meetings attracted audiences ranging in size from a few hundred to a few thousand. Some of the provincial towns also attracted not insignificant crowds. The FCL's Var Federation got 2,000 to a meeting in Toulon, 3,000 went to listen to David Antona and others in Lyon, and the

CGTSR organized meetings in Perpignan and Toulouse which gratify-
ingly attracted 4,000 and 3,000 — for Toulouse it was the largest audience ever seen at a meeting organized by the anarchists.[22]

CO-OPERATION WITH NON-ANARCHISTS

It has already been noted that in Wattrelos the antifascist committee
united anarchists, socialists and communists. The cooperation with
communists was unusual, but it is certainly true that during this period, and especially from September onwards, there are indications of a
previously very unusual degree of cooperation between anarchists and
non-anarchists. For example, the FCL's meeting at Toulon, mentioned
above, was addressed by a member of the SFIO; the platform of a meeting at Aimargues in September included a member of the Socialist Youth
who had just returned from Spain, and who spoke about his opposition
to the non-intervention policy; Audubert, secretary of the SFIO in the
5th *arrondissement*, spoke at a meeting organized by the UA's Paris Federation at the Mutualité on 26 September; the Aulnay-sous-Bois anarchist group, reporting on its open meeting on French militarism, war
and Spain, went out of its way to stress the positive contribution to the
meeting made by the trotskyist Couzard; early in October, Saint-Henri
witnessed a joint meeting of the UA and of the Revolutionary Socialist
Youth in support of the CNT-FAI; and Fred Zeller foreshadowed what
was to become a much closer liaison between the UA and the GR, when
he spoke at two meetings organized by anarchist groups in the suburbs
of Paris — on one occasion sharing the platform with Couanault of the
CGTSR.[23]

But it was not until October that occasional contacts gave way
to a more concerted attempt at co-operation, and the UA clearly opted
for a "revolutionary front" policy. On 3 October, as we have seen, the
Paris Federation of the UA and the SFIO's Paris 5 section organized a
joint open meeting at the Mutualité: "For the Formation of the Revolutionary Front." The FAF and the CGTSR were not happy about this
rapprochement between the UA and the left wing of the SFIO, but they
were even less happy when the UA invited Léon Jouhaux to speak at
a mass meeting in the Vel d'Hiv on 23 October — Jouhaux who, for
twenty years, had been shunned by the anarchists because of his "reformist" syndicalism and because of his support for the state's war effort
in 14–18. But despite this disapproval by some anarchists, the Vel d'Hiv
meeting succeeded in attracting an estimated 15,000 people.[24] The meeting was chaired by Louis Lecoin, but Lucien Huart was the only French
anarchist to speak.[25] In fact, alongside three CNT-FAI representatives

on the platform, there was Julián Gorkin of the POUM, Jaume Miravitlles of the Catalan Esquerra (representing the *Generalidad*), Léon Jouhaux, Jean Zyromski of the SFIO, Josse of the JEUNES and Marceau Pivert, leader of the GR.[26] It was Pivert who stepped forward to address the audience last, and it was to his speech that *le Libertaire* in its account of the meeting devoted most space. It was Pivert who paid a tribute, symbolic of the new united front, to two militants who had both been killed in action at Farlete on 8 September: the anarchist Emile Cottin, and Merlin, a member of the GR. And it was Pivert who launched the climactic appeal for a united and revolutionary working-class front: "Are you ready, he asked the crowd in the hall, to form the revolutionary working-class movement that is becoming more and more necessary? And the hall, in one resonant, impassioned cry, answered: Yes!"[27]

THE INFLUENCE OF THE CNT-FAI

Why did the UA take the step of allying itself more or less formally with members of the SFIO and other non-anarchists? A widening of the CAS to bring in non-anarchists had in fact already been proposed at the Paris Federation's general assembly on 13 September,[28] but the Spanish influence was decisive. According to the UA, several Spanish comrades had already suggested the creation of a Comité pour l'Espagne libre, when Horacio Prieto, secretary of the CNT National Committee, sent a telegramme to the UA asking for the amount of aid sent to Spain to be increased as much as possible: "In our name, they have the right, in order to support us, to appeal to any personalities or organizations sympathetic to our cause."[29] The name of Durruti, especially, was drawn upon to defend the new policy. Having not been able to leave the front to attend the Vel d'Hiv meeting as planned, he sent the following message, which *le Libertaire* promptly published: "I appeal to the French revolutionaires, whatever their ideological or political allegiance, to unite strongly and sincerely to form a true people's antifascist front."[30] In the UA's eyes, the CAS had served a useful function, but it was now time to go beyond "the stage of little committees open only to certain organizations (and not the biggest) of the working-class movement."[31] And on 6 November the Administrative Committee of the UA, rejecting a suggestion from the FAI that the UA should organize a conference of all the different tendencies in French anarchism, offered this explanation: "The balance sheet of work in common with the other small fractions of the French anarchist movement was weak, whereas the wider activity of the UA, in association with other revolutionary tendencies with whom we have a certain amount in common, has resulted in the growth of our propaganda work which has as a consequence reached ever greater sections of the working class."[32] Anarchist unity was impossible at that particular juncture for two reasons: first, the unwillingness of the CAS to carry on working with the UA, if the UA continued to co-operate with non-anarchists; and second, "the tactical differences are such that the modest contribution of the anarchist groups not belonging to the Anarchist Union would only cause problems without producing any serious gains in compensation."[33]

DIVISION WITHIN THE ANARCHO-SYNDICALIST COMMITTEE

The CGTSR's opposition to the revolutionary front tactic, and thus to the Comité pour l'Espagne libre, was based on its refusal to co-operate in any "organic" way with non-anarchists.[34] The CGTSR's National Confederal Committee, at a meeting on 23 October, voted unanimously that Pierre Besnard should reject the UA's invitation to speak at the Vel d'Hiv the same day, either as a representative of the CGTSR or in a personal capacity.[35] The report of the meeting explained that past decisions of the CGTSR's congresses "make it impossible for any of our militants, *without exception*, to share a platform with politicians or with the man whose attitude during the last 20 years has been characterized by disavowal of the revolution and betrayal of the working class."[36] The conclusion was that "revolutionary unity" could exist only between anarchists and anarcho-syndicalists, and the committee declared—ironically, in view of the fact that it was the CNT-FAI that initially proposed the widening of the CAS—that the Comité pour l'Espagne libre "can, *in no sense*, represent the CNT or the FAI in France." Going even further, a joint protest against "the scandalous deviations of the UA and *le Libertaire*," by the CGTSR Local Union and the CAS in Saint-Etienne, asked Durruti, who they alleged had been invited to the Vel d'Hiv thanks to "the manœuvres of certain Parisian, so-called anarchist militants," not to share the platform with Jouhaux or Pivert; it regretted that Horacio Prieto had become "the plaything of the UA's harmful methods"; and it concluded: "The moment has come to remain closely united, but also to remain true to ourselves, on anarchist and anarcho-syndicalist ground, without compromises of any kind to politicians."[37]

The CASDLPE, then, claiming that it had had cause to complain about "certain insufficiencies, a certain negligence" on the part of the UA delegation right from the start, decided at its congress in Paris, 24–25 October, effectively to expel the UA. The proposal for a "widened front," was rejected by 8 votes to 2, with 1 abstention, and as a result the UA "was obliged to leave the Paris Anarcho-Syndicalist Committee and the Congress."[38] The CASDLPE, however, made it clear that it held the UA responsible: a motion proposed by the Saint-Etienne CAS and an individual UA member from Montpellier was passed by the same majority: "This split was provoked by the new tendency of the leaders of the UA delegated to the Congress, which is collaboration with political parties for antifascist purposes."[39] And as a later statement by the CASDLPE insisted: "those who conclude such alliances cease thereby, in our opinion, to be anarchists."[40]

Notes

1.   *Le Libertaire*, 23 October 1936. This was the paper's first non-ironic evocation of the *"Grand Soir"* or "new dawn" image since 1924. Coincidentally, it was in 1924 that the 21-year-old Bonomini had assassinated Bonservisi, a leading Italian fascist, in Paris. He served 8 years in prison, then lived illegally for a few years in Paris, before going to Spain in July 1936. He was to return to Paris in 1938, when he was arrested and sent to gaol for another year. He was a member of the Proofreaders' Union. *Le Libertaire*, 9 June and 28 July 1938.

2.   *Le Libertaire*, 4 September 1936.

3.   *Le Libertaire*, 7 August 1935.

4.   *Le Libertaire*, 28 August 1938.

5.   The "Federation of Spanish-language Anarchist Groups in France" appealed to "all revolutionaries" to forget their differences and unite behind the Spanish antifascist movement. *Le Libertaire*, 7 August 1936.

6.   *L'Espagne Antifasciste (CNT-AIT-FAI)*, 7 November 1936; *Le Combat Syndicaliste*, 7 and 28 August 1936. Ganin was also the treasurer of the CGTSR's "National Subscription for the CNT and the FAI" and of an International Committee for the Spanish Revolution, which had very close links with the CNT-FAI: *le Combat Syndicaliste*, 18 September 1936, published its manifesto.

7.   *Le Combat Syndicaliste*, 14 August 1936.

8.   *Le Libertaire*, 31 July, 4 September and 23 October 1936; *le Combat syndicaliste*, 14 August 1936.

9.   *Le Libertaire*, 21 August, 4 September and 18 September 1936.

10.   Its representative was Victor Giraud: *le Libertaire*, 4 September 1936.

11.   See F7/14721, dossier 3077.233: Sûreté Nationale report, "Renseignments sur les organisations rouges à Perpignan," dated 28 March 1937. The police refer to the FCEAAF as the *Fédération des émigrés antifascistes espagnols de France*. The communists' committee and the Secours Populaire de France also had offices in the same building. Maurice Jaquier, in his autobiography, refers to an anarchist committee in Perpignan which co-operated closely with Jaquier's own PS committee. The PS committee, which consisted entirely of GR supporters, met in the Continental Bar. *Simple Militant* (Paris: Denoël, 1974), pp.148 and 152.

12.   See various reports in *le Libertaire* and *le Combat syndicaliste* throughout the summer of 1936. See also René Lochu's autobiography, *Libertaires, mes compagnons de Brest et*

d'ailleurs (Quimperlé: La Digitale, 1983), pp. 142–143, for a description of how one particular group went about it, and of some of the problems involved.

13.   *Le Libertaire*, 11 September 1936.

14.   *Le Libertaire*, 25 September 1936.

15.   *Le Libertaire*, 11 September 1936.

16.   *Le Libertaire*, 2 October 1936. Notice that anarchist disapproval of tobacco did not interfere with solidarity.

17.   *Le Libertaire*, 2 October 1936.

18.   Chazoff acted as interpreter for Antona. *Le Libertaire*, 28 August 1936.

19.   Louis Lecoin, *Le cours d'une vie* (Paris: Edité par l'auteur en supplément du journal *Liberté*, 1965), p.152. The tremendous fascination which Spain held for libertarians of other countries was of course because of the extraordinary strength of anarcho-syndicalism there—Lecoin (p.153): "I know of no other country where Anarchism has put down such deep roots as in Spain. One could almost believe it was in the soil, the people seem so naturally impregnated with it."

20.   *Le Libertaire*, 7 August 1936.

21.   For accounts of the meetings, see *le Libertaire*, 7 and 28 August 1936, and *le Combat Syndicaliste*, 28 August 1936.

22.   *Le Libertaire*, 14 August, 4 September and 18 September 1936.

23.   *Le Libertaire*, 14 August, 11, 18 and 25 September, 16 October 1936. *Le Libertaire* described Couzard as belonging to the Fourth International (which had existed on paper—and only on paper—since March 1934); beyond this I have been unable to establish his identity. Zeller was a member of the GR from its foundation in October 1935, and was also one of the leaders of the Revolutionary Socialist Youth—see Daniel Guérin, *Front Populaire, Révolution Manquée* (Arles: Actes Sud, 1997), p.161; Jacques Roussel, *Les enfants du prophète* (Paris: Spartacus, 1972), pp.15–18; Fred Zeller, *Témoin du siècle* (Paris: Editions Grasset & Fasquelle, 2000).

24.   *Le Libertaire*, 30 October 1936.

25.   Sébastien Faure, who was intended to address the meeting, had not returned from Spain in time to attend; Lecoin read out a letter from him at the meeting.

26   Magrina for the FAI, José Trabal for the Catalan CNT, José Mavilla for the Aragon Council.

27   *Le Libertaire*, 30 October 1936.

28.   The proposal was made by Nicolas, the delegate for Aubervilliers—*le Libertaire*, 18 September 1936.

29.   *Le Libertaire*, 16 October 1936.

30.   *Le Libertaire*, 30 October 1936.

31.   *Le Libertaire*, 23 October 1936. This issue also saw the launch of a new rubric to which the entire back page was given over: "Le libertaire syndicaliste."

32.   *Le Libertaire*, 6 November 1936.

33.   Ibid.

34   *L'Espagne antifasciste (CNT-FAI-AIT)*, 7 November 1936.

35.   According to *le Libertaire*, 30 October 1936, Besnard himself had been "reasonable" about this affair—it was other members of the CGTSR who had insisted on the UA's "exclusion."

36.   *Le Combat Syndicaliste*, 30 October 1936.

37.   *Le Combat Syndicaliste*, 23 October 1936.

38.   *L'Espagne antifasciste (CNT-FAI-AIT)*, 28 October and 7 November 1936.

39.   Ibid.

40   *L'Espagne Antifasciste (CNT-FAI-AIT)*, 7 November 1936. This attitude was not unanimous within the CASDPLE, or the CGTSR, though. *Le Libertaire*, 30 October 1936, printed a statement by Huart, a founding member of the CGTSR who had chaired the CAS congress, in which he insisted that he wanted to work with all those who sincerely supported the Spanish antifascists, and claimed that the dispute between the UA and the CAS "was much more a question of personal feelings than of doctrine." Lecoin, Anderson, Faucier and Le Meillour, for the Comité pour l'Espagne libre, also asked why the decision to oppose the new committee had been taken so suddenly, since the previous week's *l'Espagne Antifasciste (CNT-FAI-AIT)* had actually carried an advertisement for the Vel d'Hiv meeting.

10

The Union Anarchiste and Antifascist Solidarity

> We can say with certainty that the defeat of our Spanish friends would be our own defeat, and that their victory · will be our own victory.
>
> *Sebastien Faure*[1]

So, in October 1936, the unity between the UA on the one hand and, on the other, the CGTSR supported by the newly created FAF was broken. Faced with a choice between a relatively narrow anarchist front and a broader antifascist front whose creation was encouraged by the CNT-FAI and which melded well with the revolutionary front policy, the UA did not hesitate. The CAS were to continue to campaign under the auspices of the CGTSR and FAF alone. These organizations will be looked at in more detail in the next chapter.[2]

THE COMITÉ POUR L'ESPAGNE LIBRE: MATERIAL SOLIDARITY

The initial response to the hundreds of thousands of leaflets printed and distributed by the CEL at its creation was that the *Centre de Ravitaillement* in the rue d'Alésia (Paris 14) was besieged.[3] In October, there were already local collection centres in the Paris suburbs and in several provincial towns.[4] By the following January, the *Centre de Ravitaillement* had been forced to move to bigger premises in the rue de Crussol (Paris 11), and 38 local collection centres had appeared in the suburbs and the provinces.[5] It is difficult to know exactly how much money was raised, or where it came from, because regular detailed accounts were not published. The same also applies to the nature and amount of donations in kind, and so the following details are unavoidably impressionistic.

Thus we know that the donations list in *le Libertaire* had raised 25,000 francs by September 1936, but we are only given two further figures for that list: 3,500 francs in the month of October, and 2,700 in November.[6] This would indicate a considerable dropping-off of the rate of donations after the first two months of the revolution and civil war. The opposite, though, is suggested by what we know of the Comite de Défense de la Révolution espagnole antifasciste in Perpignan. Having raised 13,000 francs by mid-September 1936, it had pushed that total up to 80,000 by November, and 87,000 by the following January.[7] In October 1937, the committee was able to give 25,000 francs to a Comité d'entr'aide aux familles des miliciens (Mutual Aid Committee for the Families of Militia Fighters).[8] Funds were also raised by holding "*Fêtes de Solidarité*" with song, dance, poetry and comedy[9]; and by charging an entrance fee at the many public meetings arranged by the anarchists. The speaking tour undertaken by Sébastien Faure and Achille Blicq, after the pair's visit to Catalonia in October 1936, produced a profit of 6,400 francs. This money was divided equally by Faure between the CEL and the CAS.[10] Money also came in from outside France. In January 1937, Faure announced the receipt of 76,000 francs from various groups and individuals in the USA, which he also divided between the two organizations.[11]

Donations of cash or of goods were often listed specifically if they came from groups of workers or from unions. The amounts concerned were sometimes small, sometimes quite considerable. The Glass-Blowers' Union, for example, gave 200 francs in October/November 1936, while the Printworkers' Union in the Seine collected 5,000 francs.[12] At the same time the Food Industry Workers' Union for the Paris region donated 100 kilos each of coffee and jam, and managed the same again a month later.[13] The Bespoke Clothing Industry Workers gave 10,000 packets of cigarettes, and, in their spare time, members of the Hatters' Union produced 1,000 balaclavas which they passed on to the CEL.[14] It is not clear whether they appeared spontaneously and purely for this task, but there appear to have been committees in some factories, which co-ordinated such collections for the CEL.[15] Several different workshops at the Renault factory in Boulogne-Billancourt, for example, organized collections of cash which a Purchasing Committee then used to buy goods.[16]

All these supplies were distributed through the CNT-FAI to Barcelona, Valencia and to the confederal militias. It was also possible to "adopt" a particular member of the militia fighting with the Centurie Sébastien Faure, to whom parcels (and letters) could then be sent personally. This was arranged by a Comité de liaison internationale des combattants antifascistes du front (part of the CEL) and was organized by Marguerite Bary at the French end, and by Berthe and Marie Ascaso (the wife and sister of Francisco) in Barcelona.[17] By December 1936 the CEL had four teams, each of three drivers, who ferried the supplies from the capital, via Perpignan, into Spain.[18] Some provincial centres arranged for their own lorries to go direct: Lyon, with 16 local committees and 3 collection centres, was an example.[19] At the UA's Paris congress, October–November 1937, Lecoin announced that an estimated 100 lorryloads—in other words 300–400 tonnes—had been sent to Spain in the 12 months of the CEL's existence.[20]

A large part of the CEL's effort was put into the financing and running of an orphanage at Llansá, on the Mediterranean coast road about 8 km south of the border crossing at Cerbère-Port Bou.[21] Pierre Odéon and Bonomini arranged for the Château Marly to be taken over, and the CEL re-named it the "Colonie Ascaso-Durruti." Initially the orphanage took in 50 or so children from Madrid, but very quickly the numbers had quadrupled and included children from Malaga and Aragon. It was run by Paula Felstein and six other women, and employed a teacher. Between March and September 1937, the CEL spent between 10,000 and 15,000 francs a month on Llansá, and a more or less independent support fund was established. This attracted, for example 1,250 francs from the Association of Precision Instrument Workers, 500 francs from a Comité des femmes libertaires pour l'aide au peuple espagnol (Anarchist Womens' Committee for the Spanish People) in Marseille, and at least 25,500 francs from British anarchists around the journal *Spain and the World*, who "adopted" 20 of the Llansá children. In April 1937, Lecoin went to visit the painter Maurice Vlaminck at his home in the Perche, and came away with a painting which was to be used in a tombola to raise money for Llansá.[22] Many other artists followed Vlamick's example, and very soon the CEL was able to mount a very successful exhibition in the large hall of the Union des Syndicats de la Seine.[23] By May, all 100,000 tombola tickets had been sold, and a further 100,000 had to be printed. Eventually 195,000 were sold.[24]

THE COMITÉ POUR L'ESPAGNE LIBRE: PROPAGANDA

The CEL was not only concerned with material solidarity: the collection of money and supplies. As had been the case with the CASDLPE, the CEL launched a propaganda campaign, which aimed not only to encourage the French people to help those fighting Franco, but which also aimed to spread news about the CNT-FAI's role in the war, and about the revolutionary changes being made in areas where the CNT-FAI were dominant. There was always a certain ambivalence about the extent to which the CEL and SIA were "pro-republican," "antifascist" solidarity organizations; and to what extent they used the CNT as a model for the French working class, a model of a large and independent, revolutionary syndicalist organization. The French anarchists were faced with something of a dilemma, given the lack of unity in the Spanish anti-Franco camp, and the imperious needs of the war. But despite criticisms from some quarters—notably the FAF—there was clearly a considerable propaganda drive on the part of the UA in which the focus was the Spanish revolution, rather than the Spanish civil war.

Such propaganda took the form firstly, of course, of articles in *le Libertaire* by anarchists who had visited Spain, usually Catalonia. Faure and Blicq, for instance, not only went on a speaking tour, they produced several articles about what they had seen, a *"Reportage Objectif"* covering everything from public health to political prisoners.[25] Lucien Haussard reproduced the text of an interview with Joaquin Ascaso, then chair of the Aragon Defence Council;[26] and a CGT delegate, Andre Mollot, wrote two articles for *le Libertaire* about a FAI-controlled factory and a CNT-controlled town.[27]

Speaking tours, especially those that involved the showing of films produced by the CNT-FAI, were very successful. In the winter of 1936–37, Charles Ridel and Lucien Huart covered the southern half of France on such a tour: they claimed a total audience of tens of thousands and a profit of around 10,000 francs (even though the hire of some halls cost 1,000 francs).[28] This was a considerable success and it was not the only such tour. But there is no doubt that the most spectacular successes, and the ones that attracted most attention at a national level, were the big meetings organized by the UA and CEL in Paris, at the Vel d'Hiv and the Mutualité. One of these, in May 1937, attracted 6,000 people—according to *le Libertaire*—to listen to representatives of the CNT, FAI and FIJL speak in detail about the Spanish situation. And the agenda made clear the organizers' political stance: "The workers of Paris ... affirm their contempt for the agents of the Spanish bourgeoisie and of English, French and Russian imperialism who have not hesitated to try to break up the antifascist bloc in order to ruin the revolutionary conquests won through the sacrifice of tens of thousands of workers in their gigantic struggle against Franco's hords."[29]

The significance of two other meetings is a little more problematic. No doubt they were both successful in terms of the attention they attracted. *Le Libertaire* claimed an audience of 12,000 for the meeting of 18 June 1937 in the Vel d'Hiv;[30] and the French authorities had been so concerned about an earlier one at the same venue, arranged for 6 December 1936, that they prevented Luis Companys, president of the Catalan Generalidad, from attending.[31] Both were revolutionist in tone. In December 1936, both Huart and Pivert encouraged the direct action of French labour to ensure support of the Spanish antifascists, "by taking control of the arsenals and armaments depots, and by boycotting anything being transported to the fascists."[32] The meeting held in June 1937 ended with the voting of a resolution reaffirming the audience's complete confidence in the CNT's ability to carry on the struggle against fascism, "and the struggle in favour of social reconstruction, which is equally necessary."[33] But both of these meetings caused something of a stir because of the people who were invited to speak. At the first, in December 1936, the list of invited speakers included not only Jouhaux and various other non-anarchists, but even Marcel Cachin. The meeting was intended to be a demonstration of the unity of the antifascist camp, putting the need to break the blockade of Spain "above partisan squabbles and self-interest."[34] And the front-page pre-publicity in *le Libertaire* was clearly designed with that aim in mind, giving most prominence to Companys, then to representatives of the CNT and UGT, and least of all to representatives of the PCF, SFIO, UA and CEL.[35] The account of the meeting in *le Libertaire* pointed out that the bourgeois press had made much of the event, choosing to interpret it in terms of the internal politics of the Popular Front. The intention of *l'Echo de Paris*, *le Jour* and *le Temps* was "above all political in that it was trying to create divisions within the Popular Front on the parliamentary level. Their hope was to aggravate conflicts between the left and extreme-left of the Popular Front in the government."[36] *Le Libertaire* declared its lack of interest in such partisan squabbles, the UA's only wish being to organize effective aid, and to "orient the French proletariat's desire for action towards an immediate and direct task."[37] Nevertheless, at the same time as calling on all those organizations "who could make a valuable contribution," the CEL emphasized "the libertarian character of this demonstration."[38]

The meeting of June 1937 also further increased the gulf between the CEL and the CGTSR and FAF, though not so much this time because of co-operation with representatives of the SFIO, PCF or CGT. This time it was because the two main speakers were Juan García Oliver and Federica Montseny, two of the four CNT delegates who had entered the socialist-dominated Largo Caballero government in November 1936 — Oliver as Minister of Justice, Montseny as Minister responsible for Health and Social Security.[39] Oliver directly and Montseny indirectly had also been instrumental in persuading CNT-FAI and POUM supporters to lay down their arms during the clashes of May 1937 in Barcelona.[40] An article by Faure that had appeared a week before the meeting, had hinted that beneath the surface of applause and admiration and solidarity, there were nevertheless some hesitations. Some comrades had been "greatly alarmed, even shocked" by the syndicalists' participation in the government; and these representatives of the CNT were coming to Paris to offer explanations to their supporters abroad.[41]

The potential problem here was whether there was a contradiction between the UA's revolutionary front policy, and the lengths to which the CEL was prepared to go in organizing effective aid for Spain. The revolutionary front proposed co-operation with non-anarchists in the struggle against both fascism and popular frontism. It was very clear in its opposition to the Popular Front, and it was clear in its rejection of the "myth" of fascism versus democracy/antifascism: the struggle to avert war in Europe was linked with the struggle against capitalism, and the Spanish war against francoism was linked with the defence and development of the revolution. But what position should the UA adopt with regard to CNT ministers—anarchists who had been involved in a Popular Front government which looked increasingly like it was engaged in an antifascist war?

SOLIDARITÉ INTERNATIONALE ANTIFASCISTE

These doubts came to the surface at the UA's congress of October–November 1937 in Paris.[42] The CEL had been approached some time before by the CNT-FAI about a further broadening of the organization, the intention being that the new group—Solidarité Internationale Antifasciste (SIA) would be "in the image of Spanish antifascism."[43] SIA was to be the French section of Solidaridad Internacional Antifascista, created by the CNT, FAI, FIJL, UGT and numerous political and literary figures.[44] Lecoin had been surprised by the opposition there had been to the idea of further enlargement, and a decision had therefore been postponed until the congress. Some of the criticism was directed against the giving of a platform to people like Jouhaux and, especially, Cachin. Guyard, Ridel, Martin and Rose all spoke out particularly against the presence of communist representatives at CEL public meetings. Others—Faucier, Lecoin, Huart, Servant—defended such a presence. Some were also unhappy about some of the names on the proposed Committee of Patrons of SIA, very few of whom were revolutionaries or anarchists.[45] The use of middle-class intellectuals and of reformists closely involved with the Popular Front was justified on the grounds that their task was not specifically anarchist, that their solidarity work was directed towards "a broad-based movement."[46] Lecoin himself defended such a tactic, attacking the objectors for their inconsistency. He had, on several occasions, been asked to intervene in various cases of arrest or expulsion and so forth, and had used similar methods: i.e. he had persuaded people with a certain influence to use that influence on his behalf.[47] "It was a humanitarian task," and nobody had complained. Now when Spain was in danger, militants were objecting because of principles to what Lecoin called "an enterprise of human solidarity." Lecoin was supported at the congress by the delegate of the Spanish anarchist groups in France, and the vote in favour of the creation of SIA was overwhelming: only 4 votes against, and 2 abstentions.[48]

SIA's manifesto, signed by the patrons, appeared in *le Libertaire* in December.[49] Interestingly, despite the discussion about whether or not to share platforms with communists, the SIA manifesto was clearly, if not explicitly, anti-stalinist: its aim was to help "more particularly the victims of the totalitarian States."[50] And Georges Pioch, speaking at SIA's first public meeting, on 17 December, in the Gymnase Japy, declared: "Neither Franco, nor Mussolini, nor Hitler must triumph in Spain, but we must also add: nor Stalin!"[51] And despite the use of personalities associated with the Popular Front, SIA also presented itself as being workerist and somewhat sceptical about the Popular Front. The aim, in Spain and elsewhere, was "the union of the forces of liberty," but SIA "wants … to see the unification of the two trade union organizations, the CNT and the UGT, so that they can assume the part in the struggle against Franco and in the social and economic administration of their country which is theirs as of right: the greater part."[52] A little later, Roger Hagnauer made a similar point in *le Libertaire*. SIA, he emphasized, was open to all tendencies within the labour movement; the one essential condition of membership was to put "the class spirit, fidelity to the international proletariat" above all other considerations.[53] And again at the Gymnase Japy, Jean Nocher spoke out about the lack of enthusiasm shown by the French Popular Front: "It would seem that some elements in the French *Front Populaire* feared the revolution in Spain."[54] So SIA was justified when in June 1938, it insisted that it was not only "a Red Cross, but also a revolutionary grouping."[55] But its stance on the Popular Front, on international communism and on the Spanish republican governments will become clearer as we look at the campaigns which developed naturally out of SIA's basic concerns, and when we look at the criticisms directed at the UA by other French anarchists.

As far as the job of material solidarity work was concerned, SIA basically took over from the CEL. With Lecoin as secretary, Faucier as treasurer, and Huart in charge of propaganda, it used the premises in the rue de Crussol, it carried on collecting money, clothes, bedding and medical supplies, and it assumed responsibility for the orphanage at Llansá.[56] From its issue dated 2 December 1937, two pages of the UA's organ was given over to SIA: one page in French, one in Spanish, the one not always a simple translation of the other. A series of illustrated posters was produced; printed in large numbers they, were distributed all over France.[57] And in November 1938 a separate paper, called simply *SIA*, was launched. It continued to appear, despite much official harassment, until August 1939.[58]

SIA was undoubtedly a success in terms of the support it attracted, and its constituency extended beyond the borders of the anarchist movement to include socialists, syndicalists, oppositional communists and others. A very early report in *le Libertaire* claimed that SIA had been generally well received by SFIO militants.[59] An antifascist group in Brest, about 80 strong and consisting of syndicalists, dissident communists and anarchists had, on the creation of SIA, immediately dissolved itself and formed a SIA "section."[60] In Perpignan, the group of more than 150 was composed mainly of anarchists and members of Pivert's Gauche Révolutionnaire.[61] And SIA seems in some cases at least to have overcome the differences between anarchist organizations at a national level: Hoche Meurant reported that SIA in Roubaix-Croix-Wattrelos had been joined by the local CGTSR.[62] There were even cases of support coming from grass-roots communists, despite opposition by the party leadership: Duperrier, a PCF activist from Poitiers joined SIA; in Froncles (Haute-Marne), a group secretary called Victor François and other communists were expelled from the party for joining SIA;[63] a militiaman called René Laurac left the PCF to join SIA, apparently tired of being told he was a trotskyist and anarchist; and several militants in Colombes left the PCF to join SIA despite attacks on it in the local party paper.[64] The following letter from a young communist militant called Piou, from Saint-Sébastien-sur-Loire (Loire Atlantique), gives an indication of how the creation of SIA must have helped the diffusion of anarchist ideas, if only because SIA supporters had initially to read *le Libertaire* for news of the organization:

> I have just read *le Libertaire* for the first time. I was a communist, but there are many of us here who will not pay our membership subscription to the PC for 1938. Since my comrades, all good militants, are young and as they want to take an active part in the emancipation of the proletariat, it seemed to us that we could make ourselves useful by working with SIA, which you have just created. We are not anarchists, we do not even know the theories behind your doctrine; we will try to study them in the future; but for the moment, if you accept us, you will have in us active campaigners for SIA. [65]

SIA had, then, a wide political base, and its fundraising efforts, like those of the CEL, were supported also by syndicalists from a broad range of trades and industries: print-workers, foundry workers, proof-readers, teachers, chemicals workers, Metro workers, quarry workers, car workers, etc. By April 1938, after only five months of existence, SIA claimed to have 40,000 card-carrying members and to have raised over 200,000 francs.[66] In November 1938 the organization brought out its own weekly newspaper, *SIA*: 130,000 copies of the first number were printed.[67] Out of its usual eight pages, *SIA* carried one page devoted to the Italian antifascist movement, and two pages to the Spanish.[68] In January 1939 *SIA* claimed to have 5,078 subscribers, and 7,000 by the following May.[69] By 1939 the organization reckoned to have 45,000 members in 350 "sections" and to have raised a total of 726,000 francs.[70]

THE NON-INTERVENTION PACT

Little has yet been said about the non-intervention pact of August 1936, "this truly scandalous and criminal decision, which lacks any basis in law and which objectively means supporting rebels against a legitimate government."[71] Maitron argues that because of their anarchist principles, and because of their desire to prevent the Spanish conflict from becoming an inter-state war, the French anarchists wanted solidarity to be exercised directly between the French working class and the Spanish working class, not *via* governments; and this to such an extent that they congratulated Blum on his policy.[72] Indeed, Maitron points out, Lashortes even titled an article in *le Libertaire* "Bravo Blum!"[73] This is, however, a misleading representation of the anarchists' stance.

As we have already seen, the anarchists were horrified that Blum did nothing to help the Spanish republicans: "This is treachery. Or worse—it is murder, deliberate and pre-meditated."[74] They were extremely critical also of the CGT for being so slow and so tepid in its response, and accused it of being tied to Blum's apron strings. In mid-August 1936, *le Libertaire* declared: "Now is not the time to shout 'Aeroplanes for Spain'. ... It was three weeks ago. Then, we were able to get a million people in the streets of Paris, and Hitler and Mussolini would probably have thought twice before trying to blackmail us."[75] *Le Libertaire* on 7 August 1936 carried the banner headline "Total Solidarity with the Fighters of Spain!," and titled its editorial "Treacherous Neutrality": "It is rare that we see a government demonstrate such incompetence in an affair of this kind, whereas, in fact it had the possibility, immediately, from the very first day, of adopting a clear stance in favour of its Spanish 'brother' government."[76] The editorial attacked the CGT for doing nothing but launching a financial appeal (whereas the UA was beginning a campaign to persuade the Popular Front to sell arms to Spain) and it attacked the PCF for seeing in the Spanish conflict only "a manoeuvre on the part of Hitler" and for wishing to use the situation to develop further "the neo-nationalism which it is inspiring in the French workers." For the UA, the events in Spain were the outcome of class conflict in Spain, and a banner headline in *le Libertaire* declared: "The Spanish proletariat is fighting ... FOR ITS OWN CAUSE."[77] Of course German nazism and Italian fascism were involved, the editorial continued: "But bending over backwards to present the defence of the antifascist struggle in Spain from the perspective of a possible crusade by the democracies against the fascist states is not doing our Spanish brothers (sic) any favours, and it certainly will not help them if we strengthen our own imperialism by associating the working class with it."[78]

So it would be quite wrong to suggest that the anarchists were somehow grateful to the Popular Front for adopting the non-intervention policy. At a public meeting on the theme *"Au secours du prolétariat espagnol,"* called by the UA's Paris Region Federation in the first week of August, it was made very clear that they opposed the pact. Pierre Besnard declared to the 5,000 strong audience: "The French government's policy of neutrality must stop; all non-intervention is in reality intervention against our Spanish comrades."[79] Frémont made it clear that the anarchists wanted the Blum government to sell arms to the Spanish republic, the legally elected government: "The most important thing right now is to put pressure on the government to deliver arms to the Spanish government." But the ending of the embargo was the only action the anarchists wanted to see: "We are not asking official France to run the risk of a war by becoming involved militarily in Spain. But the France of the Popular Front would be being unfaithful to its mission, it would be betraying the cause of the world proletariat, if it were to persist in maintaining an embargo which harms no one but the Spanish antifascists."[80] Two years on, Henri Jeanson, for SIA, stressed that they wanted Blum to be "neutral": "Staying neutral meant simply continuing to maintain normal diplomatic, commercial and political relations with the Spanish Government."[81] So they emphatically did not want positive intervention, and to the Spanish revolutionaries they issued this warning: "Do not allow your heroic struggle to be used as a pretext for the revolting schemes of rival imperialisms."[82] This is why, at the same time as demanding an end to the embargo—so that the republicans would be able to buy and sell in the normal way on the international market—the anarchists were also emphasizing the revolutionary nature of the Spanish civil war, and warning of the dangers for the revolution if Spain were to become entangled in the game of international power politics:

> We want our struggle to remain a revolutionary struggle, a *class struggle*. We believe that the defence of the revolution must be

a *class defence*. We refuse to fall into the trap of National Unity, and we will make sure, whatever happens, that we do not confuse the cause of the Spanish revolution with that of any capitalist power. However things turn out, we shall remember Lenin's teaching that our principle enemy is in our own country, that it is our own imperialism and that it is against our own imperialism that we must direct our blows.[83]

This emphasis on the class basis of solidarity with the Spanish revolutionaries was nevertheless a kind of second best. The anarchists' reaction was typified by Le Meillour's speech to the Wagram meeting in August 1936: firstly to attack Blum for not providing arms; and secondly to attack the communists for wanting to "transform the civil war into imperialist war."[84] Only after these comments did Le Meillour go on: "What do we care about the government's neutrality? It is the working class which in solidarity must takes matters into its own hands."[85] If the Popular Front was too cowardly to help its Spanish counterpart, then the anarchists must act and they must put pressure on the CGT to act in its stead.

Having said that, although the UA maintained this position for the duration of the civil war, it was not always made particularly clear, and their policy sometimes appeared contradictory. On the one hand, militants writing in *le Libertaire* and speaking at public meetings put the emphasis on the need to keep the Blum government out of the whole affair, and appealed for direct action on the part of the working class. This approach was typified by Faure's two articles "Blum, into action? No!" and "Workers, into action? Yes!"[86] A declaration by the Administrative Commission of the UA in December 1936 also insisted that it remained "in favour of a policy of autonomous working-class action as far as effective solidarity with the Spanish workers is concerned."[87] It was never entirely clear what this implied in practice, but an article that appeared in the same number of *le Libertaire* as this declaration contrasted the anarchist position with the communists': the latter wanted and expected Blum to lift the embargo; the anarchists believed Blum would not and could not do this and that the blockade must be broken "*just by the action and pressure of the working class and going as far as a general strike, as far as Revolution.*"[88]

On the other hand—and the difference is an important one—militants argued one of two things. Either the "more conscious elements of the government" were to be used to gain the tacit approval of the Blum government for certain forms of direct action, thus allowing the government to maintain "a façade of neutrality" whilst actually facilitating solidarity work.[89] Or direct action—if the expression can still legitimately be used in such a context—should be used simply to pressure the government into sending food and arms to Spain: "The French proletariat must *declare war on the embargo*. It must force its government to sell the Spanish government anything it needs to fight the war against fascism."[90]

This last position became the dominant one from early in 1937, and on 4 March the CEL co-organized a public meeting with the Comité d'action socialiste pour la levée de l'embargo.[91] This change in emphasis seems to have been linked to the realization that no amount of campaigning by the UA was going to produce the necessary direct action on a large enough scale to make any difference. This was stressed by Robert Louzon, for whom SIA's number one priority must be to get the blockade lifted: "But we have no illusions! What we are able to donate to the Spanish republicans will never amount to much compared to what they could buy with the profits from their sales ... if they were allowed to sell!"[92] By April 1938, SIA was campaigning unequivocally for the Blum government to supply the republicans: "What is needed now is not the occasional lorry-load. ... We must demand of our government, the Popular Front, sends to Barcelona, by the train-load, all the surplus wheat it possesses."[93]

Thus the UA and the organizations it created and more or less controlled—the CEL and SIA—were in favour of Blum's assisting the Spanish antifascists. But they were very wary about the risk of international war posed by the interference of foreign governments. This was the meaning of the article by Lashortes, "Bravo Blum!," of which the main thrust had been "opposition to the communists' war-mongering," as Faucier put it at the UA congress.[94] Lashortes had made a similar point at the public meeting at the Mutualité on 3 August 1936: "It is dangerous to allow the defence of Spain to be transformed into an anti-German crusade, as the communist press is doing."[95] The anarchists realized that if the war became a European war, the Spanish revolution would be destroyed: "We know that imperialist war, that is to say: any war which implies the national unity of the exploited with their exploiters—remember 1914!—spells the death of the revolution, the annihilation of the labour movement in nationalistic delirium and slaughter, the loss of workers' rights in a state of siege."[96] The anarchists believed that the German and Italian governments were not so sure of themselves, that Spain was a testing ground, and that the best way to stop international fascism and to avoid war was to support wholeheartedly the Spanish revolution:

The triumph of the revolution in Spain will have considerable repercussions in France as well as in Germany and Italy. The old capitalist world will not be able to resist such shocks, and even if it does not collapse completely, it will not dare launch itself into war with such a hotbed of revolution in its midst.

Our line of conduct is therefore clearly set out: ensure first of all the victory of the Spanish proletariat, for on it depends the maintenance of peace and our total liberation.[97]

PACIFISM

On the other hand, the anarchists were sometimes quite vicious in their attacks on the absolute pacifists, some of whom even opposed the lifting of the blockade on the grounds that it could signal the start of a European war. In response to a letter in *la Révolution prolétarienne* from the Primary School Teachers' Union in the Rhône, which had proposed mediation at diplomatic level, a militant wrote in *le Libertaire*: "What they call their pacifism, in reality their petit-bourgeois egoism, is so pure that it is shared today by Messieurs Bailby, Maurras, La Rocque, etc."[98] In 1939 la Patrie Humaine was to be condemned as "the dustbin of resignation," its supporters as "fascistic neo-pacifists."[99] On the pacifist wing of the movement a very few anarchists — "there are very few, but there are some," according to Faure, himself president of the *Ligue internationale des combattants de la paix*[100] — insisted that it was wrong for the CNT-FAI to take part in the war against Franco. But the vast majority were in no doubt as to the nature of the war: it was a Spanish-Spanish conflict, a war between the reactionary forces and the revolutionary forces in Spanish society.

Underlying the brutal and bloody conflict raging on the Peninsula is the conflict, which has now reached the point of explosion, between the Spain of yesterday which does not wish to die and the Spain of tomorrow which wants to live and to develop. ... It is ... the terrible and inevitable clash between the Spain of palaces and châteaux and the Spain of hovels and cottages; between the idle and parasitic Spain and the Spain which works and produces everything; between the Spain of the privileged and the Spain of the disinherited; between the miserable minority which lusts after power and domination and the vast masses who thirst for revolt and freedom. ... *This war is a holy war, it is a war for freedom.*[101]

Thus the CEL had no qualms about supporting the Spanish antifascists in the war against Franco, nor indeed about supplying them with arms and ammunititon.[102] When reacting to criticisms that it had turned its back on pacifism, the CEL responded: "We are and we remain complete pacifists. ... But we are not Tolstoyans, we are revolutionaries and as such we cannot stand idly by and watch what is happening in Spain."[103] Many anarchists whose militant activity was primarily in the pacifist movement had no hesitation in rallying round the Spanish antifascists.[104] Roger Monclin, for example, of la Patrie Humaine, who appears to have visited Spain during the war and who spoke at many public meetings, was very clear about the difference between imperialist war and revolutionary war. "Those who condemn any participation in imperialist war," he said in the Wagram Hall in August 1936, "will always be at the side of those who are defending their life and liberty."[105] The Seine Federation of the Union of Young Pacifists of France, in a "Resolution on Events in Spain," which it sent in to *le Libertaire*, remained "irreducibly opposed to all war," but refused to recognize that what was happening in Spain was a war.[106] The UA militant Chazoff resigned from the editorial board of *la Patrie Humaine* because of its insistence on a rigid pacifist stance. The letter of resignation, which the pacifist paper did not publish, appeared instead in *le Libertaire*. It referred to the "harmful consequences of non-violence raised to the level of an inviolable principle," and insisted that "those who only make a revolution in half measures are digging their own graves."[107] According to Chazoff, a revolutionary could not be an absolute pacifist since "capitalism has greater powers of passive resistance than the working class": "Now let us not mince words. However much we might dislike it, revolution and civil war can only be violent and bloody, and any general strike movement which is not able and willing to use violence in order to make and defend the revolution is doomed to complete failure."

STALINISM AT WORK

Relations with the stalinists were particularly hostile in this period. *Le Libertaire* and *SIA* are full of reports about intimidation of anarchists street-selling newspapers; about meetings being hastily arranged by communist cells in order to clash with those organized by local CEL or SIA groups; about SIA posters being covered by PCF posters; about how the communist press totally ignored successful public meetings; about returned militiamen being accused of being fascist agents. Around the spring and early summer of 1937, *le Libertaire* began to carry complaints about obstacles being placed in the way of French anarchists—

or of Spanish anarchists based in France—who were trying to cross into Spain with supplies. This caused real problems: "All antifascists should know that it is becoming more and more difficult to provide Spain with supplies of food and clothes. Those who have taken on the job of doing so are exposed to harassment of an increasingly serious nature, and are now risking their freedom and even their lives, for when you fall into the hands of the Spanish police—now under the orders of the stalinists—all guarantees have disappeared."[108]

It was not just a question of anarchist solidarity organizations being hindered by Spanish customs and passport control, though. In the first months of 1938, SIA in France also came under particular attack from the PCF.[109] SIA was accused of having used the names of certain people for its Committee of Patrons without permission. It was claimed that Jouhaux and Guiraud had resigned from the Committee. The source and destination of SIA's funds were questioned. Trotskyists—agents of fascism, according to the stalinists—were said to support SIA.[110] And it was claimed that internationally SIA had been created by only an unofficial minority within the CNT. The UA had at first refused to respond to such slanders: "We cannot descend to the stalinists' level; we cannot and do not want to waste our time refuting their inanities, their stupidly dishonest accusations. We want to do something more positive: organize effective solidarity."[111] But, faced with direct attacks on SIA, the anarchists published a detailed rebuttal of the accusations in *le Libertaire*. In a way, the UA was actually flattered, "since this suggests that our organization is doing well and is achieving its aims."[112] And the reason for this stepping-up of the anti-anarchist campaign was revealed in the communists' final point in their list of charges against SIA: the PCF denied that there were antifascists being held in Spanish republican prisons. It was in the spring of 1937 that the UA first began reluctantly to speak out about what the British communist historian Monty Johnstone has vaguely and euphemistically referred to as "measures of repression against honest revolutionaries."[113] In April 1937, in response to attacks on the CNT-FAI by communists, *le Libertaire* declared: "The Spanish revolution and the future of the Iberian proletariat are threatened not only by Franco's fascism, but also and above all by those false allies the socialists and communists who, harnessed to the policy of English, French and Russian imperialisms, are doing their best to crush the Spanish working class and its attempts to emancipate itself."[114]

This was the first time the UA had done anything other than emphasize the need to maintain antifascist unity; it was the first time, certainly, that socialists and communists were accused openly of being as

great a danger to the revolution as the francoists. It came, clearly, in response to the efforts of the Spanish communists to increase their control
over the Spanish republic, and to the repressive measures taken by the
Negrin government, beginning with the arrest of the POUM leaders in
June 1937. The May events in Barcelona were described in *le Libertaire*
as a "stalinist putsch."[115] With increasing numbers of non-communist
revolutionaries being imprisoned or murdered, the UA pointed out that
this helped nobody but Franco. This must also be seen in the context of
the argument over the Aragon front: the communists accused the confederal and POUM militias of being cowardly and disorganized, the
anarchists and POUMists accused the stalinists of deliberately starving
the confederal and POUM militias of arms. Given Stalin's strategy of
suppressing the revolution in order not to alienate Britain and France as
possible allies against Hitler, the French anarchists came to the conclusion that globally the communists were out to destroy not only trotskyism, but also anarchism:

> Where are they going? What do they want? Certainly not the
> revolution. But do they even want the defeat of fascism? One
> can be forgiven for doubting it, despite the arms from Russia.
> For the collapse of a front which has not been armed because
> of party political hate can lead to total defeat. … Above all,
> they want our extermination, the compete disappearance of our
> movement and of the revolutionary conquests of the people. …
> They prefer the victory of fascism to that of the revolutionary
> masses.[116]

To some, it even seemed that the destruction of the revolutionary
movement was Stalin's priority: "It is now much more important for
Stalin to eliminate the FAI and the CNT than it is to ensure the total
defeat of Franco."[117]

From the spring of 1937, then, there developed an outspoken campaign against the communists in France and Spain. This was launched
"officially," as it were, by a public meeting at the Mutualité on 3 October
1937, when the UA announced it was taking on itself the task that the
CNT-FAI could themselves not take on: "the task of denouncing the
stalinists."[118]

> It is *stalinism* which is doing most to ensure the victory of Fran-
> co. It is stalinism which provoked the troubles of 3 May. It is
> stalinism which, through its Cheka, has had some of the best
> revolutionary militants murdered and which is imposing the
> policy of repression against the CNT-FAI and the POUM. It
> is stalinism which has organised the remnants of the bourgeoi-

sie against the proletarian masses. It is stalinism which has just precipitated the division in the socialist ranks, and which did not hesitate, in the middle of the war, to create a criminal split within the UGT. History will be harsh on those who are responsible for this abominable policy, on those who, having led the proletariat of Central Europe into defeat after defeat, are now manoeuvring to compromise the victory of the working class in the only country up until now where, guided above all by the anarchists, it had actually succeeded in halting fascism.[119]

As has already been suggested, what caused the PCF most chagrin was the anarchist-initiated campaign against the repression of non-communist antifascists, and in particular against the trials of POUM members. It is also this campaign which honours most the anarchists and those associated with SIA; for as Pivert pointed out, few voices were raised against such procedures "on the pretext of not wanting to harm the Spanish Republic."[120] Some did support SIA's call for a general amnesty for antifascist prisoners: the Seine Federation of the SFIO, Hagnauer for the teachers, Chambelland for the proof-readers, Delsol for the gasworkers, Marcel Roy for the metalworkers.[121] Once SIA took the initiative, though, their argument seems to have gained much more support. When a public meeting was called for 18 February 1938 as part of this campaign, the Gymnase Japy was packed out, and the group which was delegated to meet Negrin considered itself directly mandated by about 12,000 people.[122] A similar meeting on 22 October 1938 demanding the acquittal of the POUM militants left the Mutualité with standing room only—and *le Libertaire* printed a photograph of the hall to prove it.[123] This second meeting not only brought together Gaston Bergery of *la Flèche* and the Parti frontiste, Hérard, secretary of the new Parti socialiste ouvrier et paysan, and the Socialist and founding member of the Rassemblement populaire Paul Rivet; the British Independent Labour Party was even present in the shape of Fenner Brockway.[124] The delegation that came out of the Japy meeting consisted of individuals connected closely with SIA: Lecoin, Pivert, Pioch, Nocher; the syndicalists René Belin, Largentier and Guiraud; and Henri Grandjouan representing the CVIA. They were received by the Spanish ambassador in Paris on 2 March 1938, but despite persistent attempts, circumstances in Spain prevented them from ever being able to meet with Negrin personally as had been arranged.[125] Letters to Negrin were written by all the members of the SIA delegation, by the lawyers Henri Torrès and Vincent de Moro-Giafferi, and by Léon Jouhaux acknowledging the release of some antifascists from gaol, but asking for a total amnesty.[126]

Further pressure on Negrin either to halt the POUM trials altogether, or if not then to allow Torrès to attend the trials and represent the defendants was to no avail.[127] The anarchists and their associates fought their campaign against the importation of stalinist methods into republican Spain on the basis of antifascist unity, on the basis of respect for the opinions of other sectors of the movement; on the basis that, as Pivert put it, and contrary to those who remained silent: "the greatest disservice one can do the antifascist cause is to allow people to believe that it requires attitudes and methods identical to those which characterize the fascist regimes."[128] Stalinist methods were justified by others in the name of realism and pragmatism, "and yet they have not led to the defeat of Franco, since ultimately they have played into his hands."[129]

DEMORALIZATION AND DEMOBILIZATION

There is no doubt that the suppression of the revolutionary forces in Spain by the stalinists or under stalinist pressure, and the further degeneration represented by the POUM trials contributed to an increasing demoralization in France: "We are a long, long way away from the early days of the Spanish revolution; two years have passed since then, two years which have brought with them many disappointments."[130] From the spring of 1938—"one of the greyest of years"[131]—*le Libertaire* had already started to complain of a slacking off of support, and of a widespread pessimism that was producing indifference. This was no doubt provoked by the nationalists' Aragon offensive of March–April, which was to cut republican Spain in two, and for perhaps the first time, in Spain, some began to believe the end of the war imminent. *Le Libertaire* tried, not very convincingly, to rally support: "To those who go around whining that it is too late, we say that we do not know for sure that it is too late, and that in any case there are hundreds of thousands of people who must be saved from an atrocious massacre."[132]

From a revolutionary's point of view, this was a significant date for another reason. The events of May 1937 had already represented a turning-point in terms of the decline of anarchist influence in Spain. April 1938 saw the eviction from the government, under communist pressure, of Indalecio Prieto, the Minister of Defence, who had struggled for a year to limit the growth of communist power. The period from April 1938 to March 1939 saw the political hegemony of the communists, and, in the last few months of the war, a series of crushing military defeats. The *"Anschluß"* of Austria in March 1938 also heightened fears of another world war, and SIA and the anarchists began to concentrate much more on this. In France, April saw the collapse of the last Popular

Front cabinet, and the installation of a government led by Daladier. This marked the beginning of a new repressiveness at home, with raids on premises, the prosecution of anarchist and SIA militants, the banning of public meetings and the seizing of newspapers.[133] The failure of the general strike of November 1938 also took its toll: "The failure of the strike of 30 November ... had, as far as we are concerned, one immediate consequence: it emptied the meeting-halls. The mystique of the Popular Front was finally crumbling. Force-fed for two and a half years with idiotic slogans, which were just so much hot air, the organized masses collapsed pathetically at the first serious hurdle."[134]

In the latter half of 1938, then, the UA and SIA were preoccupied with the anti-war campaign, and with a campaign launched to defend the right of asylum, under attack from a decree of the Daladier government—"accomplice of the fascist butchers," according to the UA.[135] From early in 1939, though, SIA was faced with a new problem: refugees from Spain crossing into France. Suffering from police harassment, increasing pessimism among its supporters in France and, consequently, from severe financial problems, SIA and the UA nevertheless did what they could to help evacuate non-combatants from Spain and guide the refugees as they crossed over into France. By February 1939, SIA alone claimed to have evacuated thousands of Spanish children.[136] The Llansá children were evacuated to the holiday home of some Parisian co-operatists on the Ile d'Oléron, Charente-Maritime; SIA tried to encouraged people to adopt the children, even if only temporarily, and undertook to complete all the administrative procedures involved.[137] SIA and the UA sent lorries with food, clothing and medical supplies to the border crossing points and to the camps to which the refugees were taken by the French authorities. They also helped refugees who were trying to locate friends and relatives—"Recherches" became a regular rubric in *SIA* and *le Libertaire* under which adverts could be placed by readers wanting news of missing friends or relatives.[138] Again, they were hindered by the French authorities: Haussard, delegated to oversee SIA operations in the border area, was arrested in February 1939 for aiding illegal immigrants even though he was co-operating with the local authorities.[139] A public meeting about the refugee problem took place at the Mutualité in Paris on 30 June 1939, but only 1,500 people attended.[140] This last effort, combined with the campaigns against the war and in defence of the right of asylum, combined with government repression, was the last straw. For the UA, Lucien Huart wrote despairingly in June 1939: "We have allowed the government to extend and reinforce its dictatorial powers; we have ruined our organizations. Today, we are at rock bottom. Funds: zero; action: zero; and, what is even worse, energy: zero."[141]

SIA, a month later, admitted it was finished: "For some time now, we have had the impression that we have been talking to ourselves. The situation appears to be the same in all left and extreme-left circles. The masses and even activists seem not to care about anything any longer."[142]

Notes

1. *Le Libertaire*, 25 September 1936.
2. The autobiographical accounts given by both Louis Lecoin and Nicolas Faucier, respectively secretary and treasurer of the Comité pour l'Espagne libre (CEL) and of its successor, Solidarité internationale antifasciste (SIA), make no mention of the CASDLPE. Lecoin's account dates the creation of the CEL as August 1936—*Le cours d'une vie* (Paris: Louis Lecoin, 1965), p.154. Maitron's account repeats that dating and judges the contribution made by the CASDLPE worthy of only a five line paragraph—Maitron, vol.II, p.30.
3. *Le Libertaire*, 30 October 1936.
4. Ibid.
5. *Le Libertaire*, 4 December 1936 and 18 February 1937. There were 3 collection centres in Paris, 16 in the suburbs and 22 in the provinces. The most successful centres outside of the Paris region were Brest, Croix, Carentan, Lille, Montreuil, Orléans and Lyon. For further details, see D. Berry, "The Response of the French Anarchist Movement to the Russian Revolution (1917–24) and to the Spanish Revolution and Civil War (1936–39)," (Unpublished DPhil thesis, University of Sussex, 1988).
6. *Le Libertaire*, 6 November and 4 December 1936. These are of course rounded figures.
7. *Le Libertaire*, 27 November 1936 and 15 January 1937.
8. *Le Libertaire*, 21 October 1937. It is not clear from the notice in *le Libertaire* whether this refers to families in Spain or in France, or both.
9. See, for example, the publicity for two such events at the Wagram meeting hall, in *le Libertaire*, 29 January and 19 March 1937.
10. *Le Libertaire*, 15 January 1937.
11. Ibid.
12. *Le Libertaire*, 6 November 1936. A CEL report in *le Libertaire*, 15 April 1937, picked out workers of the Syndicat du Livre-Papier as having given much support, and in particular workers at *Paris Soir* and *Paris Midi* newspapers, as well as the printers on the *Petit Parisien*.
13. *Le Libertaire*, 4 December 1936.
14. Ibid.
15. Ibid.
16. Ibid.
17. *Le Libertaire*, 27 November 1936. The *Centurie Sébastien Faure* will be discussed in chapter 12.
18. *Le Libertaire*, 18 December 1936. A report by Pierre Odéon, "Paris-Aragon et retour," in *le Libertaire*, 1 January 1937, talks of a convoy of five three-tonne lorries.

19. *Le Libertaire*, 25 December 1936.

20. *Le Libertaire*, 11 November 1937). This figure probably only applies to lorries sent by the central CEL in Paris. The paper had at first announced each week how many lorries had been filled, but soon gave up. Since initially the CEL was (according to *le Libertaire*) filling two to four three- or four-tonne lorries every week, a total for the year of 100 seems a reasonable estimate. *Le Libertaire*, 13 and 27 November 1936, 23 June and 28 July 1938 carried photographs of the CEL's and SIA's lorries in Paris, Perpignan, and at the front.

21. On Llansá see *le Libertaire*, 11, 18 and 25 February, 22 and 29 April, 27 May, 15 July, 30 September 1937. The 25 February and 15 July numbers contain photographs.

22. Later Vlaminck also agreed to contribute occasional articles to *SIA*: see for example "Le monde étouffe," about mechanization and militarism, in *SIA*, 5 January 1939.

23. Faucier, *Dans la mêlée sociale*, p.114. *Le Libertaire*, 20 May 1937, gave the following list of artists who had already donated paintings: Vlaminck, Luce, Kvapil, Cresson, Cermignani, Socrate, Frédéric, Pailloche, Darsac, Jouanno; and who had promised paintings: Antral, Germain Delatouche, Diener, Merio Ameglio, Aimé Milcent, Mercier de Latouche, Carlos Raymond, A. Weinbaum.

24. *Le Libertaire*, 20 May and 24 June 1937.

25. See for instance: Faure, "Un intéressant reportage;" Blicq, "Ce que nous avons vu en Espagne. Tribunaux, prisons, police"; Blicq, "La santé publique." 6 November, 4 and 11 December 1936 respectively. For the CGTSR's coverage of revolutionary Spain, see Jérémie Berthuin, *La CGT-SR et la révolution espagnole* (Paris: Editions CNT, 2000), pp.104–16 and 183–8

26. *Le Libertaire*, 18 March 1937.

27. *Le Libertaire*, 16 and 23 October 1936. Superior as such reportage undoubtedly was when compared to the flow of information coming out of revolutionary Russia 20 years earlier, one wonders whether more could have been made of such revolutionary experiments in the anarchist press and other publications. As S. J. Brademas pointed out in "Revolution and Social Revolution, Contribution to the History of the Anarcho-Syndicalist Movement in Spain: 1930–1937" (Unpublished DPhil thesis, Oxford University, 1953), the anarchists themselves, who of course had the greatest interest in publicizing examples of workers' control, only produced limited reports, and eye-witness accounts have only limited value in enabling a generalized analysis. See Frank Mintz, *L'autogestion dans l'Espagne révolutionnaire* (Paris: Maspero, 1976); Gaston Leval, *Collectives in the Spanish Revolution* (London: Freedom Press, 1975); Sam Dolgoff (ed.), *The Anarchist Collectives: Workers' Self-management in the Spanish Revolution 1936–1939* (New York: Free Life Editions, 1974).

28. 2,000 turned up for the meeting in Saint-Etienne and in Perpignan a whole crowd was said not to have been able to fit in the hall. Elsewhere audiences were 300–900. *Le Libertaire*, 25 December 1936, 15 January 1937, 18 February 1937.

29. *Le Libertaire*, 3 June 1937. The meeting took place on 28 May in the main hall of the Mutualité. The speakers were Haussard and Faure for the UA/CEL; Cortès for the CNT; Bernardo Pou for the FAI and Fidel Miro for the FIJL.

30. *Le Libertaire*, 24 June 1937.

31. He was stopped at the border and told he would be allowed to go only as far as Toulouse, until after the 6th. See Lecoin, *Le cours d'une vie*, pp.155–6; and Lecoin, "Blum à l'action ... contre l'Espagne libérale et ouvrière!," *le Libertaire*, 11 December 1936.

32. *Le Libertaire*, 11 December 1936.

33. *Le Libertaire*, 24 June 1937.

34. Lecoin, *Le cours d'une vie*, p.156.

35. *Le Libertaire*, 27 November 1936. The speakers, as they appeared in the publicity, were: Companys (Generalidad); Cortès (CNT) and Rafael Vidiella (UGT); Jouhaux (CGT), Victor Basch (Human Rights League) and Langevin (*Comité de Vigilance des Intellectuels Antifascistes*); Cachin (PCF), Zyromski (SFIO), Huart (UA) and Pivert (CEL). The writer André Chamson also spoke. (Lecoin claims, in *Le cours d'une vie*, p.156, that Faure was the speaker for the UA, but in fact it was Huart.)

36. *Le Libertaire*, 11 December 1936. This also contains a photograph of the platform at the Vel d'Hiv.

37. Ibid.

38. Ibid.

39. On "ministerialism," as it became known, see Burnett Bolloten, *The Spanish Civil War: Revolution and Counter-Revolution* (University of North Carolina Press, 1991); and for a critical, anarchist analysis, Vernon Richards, *Lessons of the Spanish Revolution* (London: Freedom Press, 1983).

40. On the political significance of May 1937, see Bolloten, *The Spanish Civil War*; Richards, *Lessons of the Spanish Revolution*; and Augustin Souchy, *et al*, *The May Days Barcelona 1937* (London: Freedom Press, 1987). Both *Lessons* and *The May Days* contain useful bibliographical articles by Richards.

41. Faure in *le Libertaire*, 10 June 1937.

42. Seventy-three groups were represented: 12 in Paris, 32 in the Paris region and 29 in the provinces. For further details, see Berry, "The French Anarchist Movement."

43. *Le Libertaire*, 11 November 1937. The phrase was Faucier's. The secretary of the Spanish SIA, based at first in Valencia and then in Barcelona, was Baruta Vila (*le Libertaire*, 2 and 9 December 1937). Montseny and the secretary of SIA's International Bureau, P. Herrera, were at the Paris congress as representatives of SIA. In May 1938 Herrera was replaced as International Secretary by Lucia Sanchez-Saornil, of the women's organization the Mujeres Libres — *le Libertaire*, 12 May 1938; see also L. Sanchez-Saornil, "La naissance de SIA," *SIA* no.1, 10 November 1938.

44. By 1939 there were also national sections of SIA in Algeria, Argentina, Australia, Belgium, Canada, Chili, China, Cuba, Great Britain, Holland, Japan, Mexico, Palestine, Poland, Portugal, Sweden, Uruguay and the USA.

45. The 25 patrons were: René Belin (reformist syndicalist; with Jouhaux, represented the CGT on the national committee of the Rassemblement Populaire); André Chamson (CVIA and Association des Ecrivains et Artistes Révolutionnaires, Association of Revolutionary Writers and Artists); Julien Cruzel (SFIO); Maurice Delépine (lawyer and SFIO politician); Georges Dumoulin (revolutionary syndicalist close to GR); Auguste Fauçonnet (taught sociology at the Sorbonne); Sébastien Faure; Gaston Guiraud (reformist syndicalist; secretary then treasurer of the CGT's Seine UD); Roger Hagnauer (primary school teacher and syndicalist, close to Monatte); Léon Jouhaux; Auguste Largentier (printworker and syndicalist); Robert Louzon (revolutionary syndicalist of the Monatte group; founder of *la Revolution Prolétarienne* in 1925); Victor Margueritte (novelist and pacifist); Jean Nocher (Jeunes Equipes Unies pour une Nouvelle Economie Sociale); Magdeleine Paz (feminist, GR militant and writer); Dr Marc Pierrot (anarchist associated with Grave); Georges Pioch (writer, journalist and socialist); Marceau Pivert (the founder of the GR in 1935, and of the PSOP in 1937); Gaston Prache (primary school teacher, syndicalist and cooperatist); Paul Reclus (anarchist associated with Grave); Maurice Rostand (writer and pacifist); Han Ryner (individualist anarchist, pacifist and writer); Marius Vivier-Merle (metalworker, secretary general of the CGT's Rhône UD and a so-

cialist); Georges Yvetot (veteran revolutionary syndicalist, anarchist and antimilitarist). *Le Libertaire*, 18 November 1937.

46. *Le Libertaire*, 11 November 1937.

47. The one example cited by Lecoin was the obtaining of permission for the exiled Italian anarchist Camillo Berneri—later to be murdered by the communists in Spain—to stay in France. Ibid.

48. Ibid. At the congress in Montpellier of the Fédération des comités antifascistes espagnols en France, 29–30 January 1938, at which over 300 groups were represented by 80 delegates, the French SIA was "adopted unanimously"—*le Libertaire*, 3 February 1938.

49. *Le Libertaire*, 2 December 1937.

50. Ibid.

51. *Le Libertaire*, 23 December 1937. Pioch was himself an ex-communist. Before the Great War he had been a contributor to *le Libertaire*, but had joined the SFIO in 1915. After Tours he joined the SFIC, but left in 1923. He moved closer to the anarchists again through his involvement with SIA. For the meeting in the Gymnase Japy in Paris, SIA claimed an audience in the region of 10,000.

52. *Le Libertaire*, 2 December 1937.

53. *Le Libertaire*, 3 March 1938.

54. *Le Libertaire*, 23 December 1937.

55. *Le Libertaire*, 23 June 1938.

56. On Llansá, see articles in *le Libertaire*, 6 January, 3 February and 14 April 1938. According to this last article, the orphanage was by then looking after 300 children. Some orphans were also brought to France. On 14 August 1938, 50 Spanish children arrived in Lyon, where the Antifascist Action Committee, affiliated to SIA, had rented a big house with a garden—*le Libertaire*, 25 August 1938. In December 1938 Odéon, acting for SIA, established an annexe to the Llansá orphanage—a house at Macanet de Cabrenys (about 30 km west of Llansá, 10 km southwest of Le Perthus), to be used as a convalescent home for 40 children. It was named after Louise Michel. *SIA*, 22 December 1938.

57. The first issue of *SIA*, 10 November 1938 carried miniature reproductions of seven posters. The print-run varied between 12,000 and 25,000.

58. *SIA* no.1 appeared 10 November 1938. According to Maitron, the last number to appear legally was no.33, 3 August 1939; he adds that, according to information supplied by Faucier, a further clandestine number appeared in September—Maitron vol.II, p.312. I have found 41 numbers of *SIA*, no.41 being dated 24 August 1939. Lecoin's autobiography is not very precise, but seems to confirm that after a police raid on the usual printers, a clandestine number of SIA was produced and indeed distributed in the first few days of September: "Thanks to the post office workers' turning a blind eye, we were able to send out the last number to our 6000 subscribers"—Lecoin, *Le cours d'une vie*, p.167.

59. *Le Libertaire*, 16 December 1937.

60. Ibid. and *le Libertaire*, 14 April 1938. On the CEL and SIA in Brest, see also René Lochu, *Libertaires, mes compagnons de Brest et d'ailleurs* (Quimperlé: La Digitale, 1983), pp.142–9.

61. *Le Libertaire*, 7 April 1938.

62. *Le Libertaire*, 20 January 1938.

63. *Le Libertaire*, 16 December 1937.

64. *Le Libertaire*, 17 March 1938.

65. *Le Libertaire*, 30 December 1937.

66. *Le Libertaire*, 7 and 21 April 1938.

67.   *Le Libertaire*, 3 and 10 November 1938; *SIA*, 10 November 1938. This print-run was exceptional, and *SIA* no.2 only appeared two weeks later.

68.   This format was established in no.2 (24 November 1938) and remained so until April 1939, when the paper was banned as a foreign paper because of these pages in Italian and Spanish. Of the two Spanish pages, one was devoted mostly to events in Spain, and one was given over to the FCEAAF.

69.   *SIA*, 5 January and 11 May 1939.

70.   *SIA*, 10 November 1938 and 24 August 1939. A list compiled from various notices in *SIA* and *le Libertaire* gives 142 sections: 14 in Paris, 63 in the suburbs, 65 in the provinces. For details, see Berry, "The French Anarchist Movement."

71.   Lashortes, "Les conséquences internationales de la révolution espagnole," *le Libertaire*, 31 July 1936. Lashortes was actually referring here, not to the formal non-intervention agreement as developed by the London committee, but to the immediate decision of the Blum government not to supply arms.

72.   Maitron vol.II, pp.31–2.

73.   *Le Libertaire*, 11 September 1936.

74.   *Le Libertaire*, 7 August 1936.

75.   *Le Libertaire*, 14 August 1936.

76.   *Le Libertaire*, 7 August 1936.

77.   *Le Libertaire*, 14 August 1936.

78.   Ibid.

79.   *Le Libertaire*, 7 August 1936.

80.   *Le Libertaire*, 16 October 1936.

81.   *SIA*, 15 December 1938.

82.   *Le Libertaire*, 14 August 1936.

83.   *Le Libertaire*, 1 August 1936.

84.   This phrase was an obvious jibe at the stalinists: in 1914–18, Lenin's position had of course been that the imperialist war should be turned into a civil war—the reverse of the Comintern's position in 1936–39, according to the anarchists. *Le Libertaire*, 28 August 1936.

85.   Ibid.

86.   *Le Libertaire*, 11 and 18 February 1937.

87.   *Le Libertaire*, 4 December 1936.

88.   Ibid. Emphasis in the original.

89.   Luc Daurat, "Utilisons le masque gouvernemental," *le Libertaire*, 25 September 1936.

90.   L. Militch, "A bas le blocus!," *le Libertaire*, 9 October 1936.

91.   The following took part in the meeting: Antona (CNT-FAI), Buisson (CGT), Gorkin (POUM), Zyromski (SFIO), Faure (UA), Weil-Curiel (GR), Josse (JEUNES), Fourrier (Comité pour la Révolution espagnole), Ridel (JAC), Rous (Parti ouvrier internationaliste), Huart (CEL), Weitz (Entente des jeunesses socialistes de la Seine), Zeller (Jeunesses socialistes revolutionnaires), Ferrat (Association communiste révolutionnaire), Brockway (Independent Labour Party)—*le Libertaire*, 25 February , 4 and 11 March 1937.

92.   "Deux tâches capitales de la SIA," *le Libertaire*, 10 February 1936. The other priority was to defend the revolution: "There is, in the present circumstances, no antifascism possible without Revolution."

93. *Le Libertaire*, 17 March 1938. According to the following week's *le Libertaire*, SIA spent 25,000 francs printing and distributing 10,000 copies of a poster entitled "Du Blé et des Armes!"

94. See "Bravo Blum!," *le Libertaire*, 11 September 1936. The article caused quite a stir, and Lashortes was criticized by Carpentier at the UA congress of October–November 1936. Anderson and Faucier defended Lashortes' intentions, but Anderson would admit to Maitron that the article only appeared in its original form because Anderson had been absent from editorial work. See *le Libertaire*, 11 November 1936; and Maitron vol.II, p.32. The communists' policy of "Uniting the French nation against the nazi threat" was seen by the anarchists as simply a new "Union sacrée," dictated by Stalin's foreign policy and having nothing to do with the Spanish revolution.

95. *Le Libertaire*, 7 August 1936.

96. Jean Bernier, *le Libertaire*, 10 June 1937. Bernier (1894–1975), a novelist who moved in avant-garde literary circles and who was in the 20s a journalist with *l'Humanité*, moved closer to the anarchists at the time of the Spanish revolution.

97. *Le Libertaire*, 11 December 1936.

98. Jacques Sanvigne "La paix exige-t-elle les cadavres des ouvriers d'Espagne?," *le Libertaire*, 14 April 1938.

99. *Le Libertaire*, 9 and 2 March 1939.

100. *Le Libertaire*, 14 August 1936.

101. Faure in *le Libertaire*, 31 July 1936.

102. Details as to the supply of arms are even more difficult to establish with any precision than is the case with other aspects of the solidarity campaign. *Le Libertaire* only ever hinted at the sending of arms. On the founding of SIA, for example, the paper referred to "the food, medicines, bedding, clothes ... and the REST the Spanish revolutionaries are asking for." —*le Libertaire*, 25 November 1937. And when the 43rd Division became surrounded in the Pyrenees, and could only be supplied from the French side, SIA launched a special appeal. Eventually, the Division collapsed through lack of ammunition, but SIA had by that time sent several lorryloads of supplies, "OF WHICH ONE TONNE OF A VERY SPECIAL NATURE"—*le Libertaire*, 23 June 1938. The principal rôle played by the CEL and SIA seems to have been that of go-between, putting CNT-FAI representatives in touch with French arms dealers—a rôle that they found most unpleasant because of some of the people it meant dealing with. Paul Lapeyre and Nicolas Faucier have mentioned in interview how their contacts with Marceau Pivert and the GR helped get lorries containing arms past Socialist customs officers at Port Bou—"Nous avons tant aimé la Révolution. Des militants parlent" [Interview of N. Faucier and P. Lapeyre by Thylde Rossel, Jean-Marc Raynaud and Gaetano Manfredonia], *Les Oeillets rouges*, no.2 (March 1987), pp.85–97.

103. Secrétariat du Comité pour l'Espagne libre, "Oui, des armes à l'Espagne ouvrière!," *le Libertaire*, 6 November 1936.

104. According to *le Libertaire*, 7 August 1936, Le Meillour, speaking at the Mutualité meeting, "jokingly declared himself pleased to see that so many genuine believers in nonviolence had been converted to the thesis of the armed defence of the Spanish revolution."

105. *Le Libertaire*, 28 August 1936. Some present-day pacifists seem to be less clear on this distinction, or still find the question a difficult one: any mention of the Spanish civil war was completely avoided both in a radio interview with Monclin and in an obituary— the text of the interview was reproduced in *Union pacifiste*, October 1982 and November 1982; the obituary, by Jean-René Vicet, appeared in *Union pacifiste*, October 1985. On the UA's attitude, see also M.D., "Pacifisme intégral et guerre civile," *le Libertaire*, 8 July 1937,

on the inevitability of war in a capitalist world and the necessity, therefore, of (violent) revolution as a precondition to true peace; and S. Faure, "Le pacifisme 'absolu,'" *le Libertaire*, 2 September 1937 and "La croyance au miracle," *le Libertaire*, 14 October 1937).

106.   *Le Libertaire*, 23 October 1936.

107.   *Le Libertaire*, 8 January 1937.

108.   "La répression stalinienne en Espagne," *le Libertaire*, 22 July 1937.

109.   See "La malfaisance bolcheviste. Réponse à des calomnies," *le Libertaire*, 31 March 1938.

110.   According to *le Libertaire*, 31 March 1938, some trotskyists were members of SIA, others opposed it, most were members of the SISL (Comité de Secours International Solidarité et Liberté). When *SIA* no.1 was seized by the police, the SISL supported SIA by protesting to the government—as did *le Populaire, le Peuple, l'Œuvre, la République, la Flèche, Juin 36* and *la Patrie Humaine. SIA*, 24 November 1938.

111.   *Le Libertaire*, 24 March 1938.

112.   *Le Libertaire*, 31 March 1938.

113.   "Trotsky and the People's Front," p.104, in Fyrth (ed.), *Britain, Fascism and the Popular Front*, pp. 89–114. The only "measure of repression" Johnstone can actually bring himself to mention is the murder of Andrés Nin of the POUM. Many other revolutionaries were of course imprisoned, tortured and murdered by the stalinists. My own research has revealed the names of nearly 40 French libertarians imprisoned by the stalinists in republican Spain. For details, see "Victims of political repression?," Appendix 6 to "Contribution to a Collective Biography of the French Anarchist Movement: French Anarchist Volunteers in Spain, 1936–39," paper presented to a conference on the International Brigades, University of Lausanne, 1997, available on the *Research on Anarchism* site at http://raforum. info/?lang=en; the conference proceedings in French translation, edited by Jean Batou, are forthcoming. For an account by the Swiss oppositional communists Pavel and Clara Thalmann of their imprisonment by the stalinists in Spain, see their *Combats pour la liberté: Moscou, Madrid, Paris* (Paris: Spartacus/La Digitale, 1983), pp.200–34.

114.   *Le Libertaire*, 8 April 1937.

115.   *Le Libertaire*, 13 May 1937.

116.   Gaston Leval, writing under his pseudonym Robert Lefranc, "La Politique Bolchevique en Espagne," *le Libertaire*, 26 August 1937.

117.   *Le Libertaire*, 13 May 1937.

118.   *Le Libertaire*, 14 October 1937. The UA claimed an audience of 4,000.

119.   Ibid.

120.   Pivert, "Tous debout contre le crime!," *le Libertaire*, 20 October 1938.

121.   *Le Libertaire*, 8 July 1937.

122.   *Le Libertaire*, 10 March 1938.

123.   See *le Libertaire*, 27 October 1938. The crowd was estimated to be 7,000 strong.

124.   Ibid. Brockway spoke in English, with Lucien Weitz acting as an interpreter. For Brockway's account of this period, see *Inside the Left* (London: George Allen & Unwin, 1942), pp.294–337.

125.   According to *le Libertaire* the Spanish Consulate refused visas, even though the ambassador had approved the delegation and Negrin had agreed to meet them. Louis Anderson then spent the first three weeks of March in Barcelona trying vainly to sort things out. See *le Libertaire*, 3, 10 and 24 March 1938.

126. *Le Libertaire*, 31 March 1938, printed the text of all these letters except the one sent by Jouhaux. From him there was just a note to Lecoin saying he would write to the Spanish trade union organizations and ask them to pass on his message "without publicity."

127. See *le Libertaire*, 21 July, 4 August, 1 September 1938. A second SIA delegation (led by Faucier) was also received at the Spanish embassy on 31 August—see *le Libertaire*, 8 September 1938.

128. *Le Libertaire*, 20 October 1938.

129. *Le Libertaire*, 17 February 1938.

130. *Le Libertaire*, 21 July 1938.

131. Pivert, "1938: Année des plus grises," *SIA*, 29 December 1938: "In the darkness of these decisive days, something gave in the collective consciousness of the masses."

132. "Criminelle indifférence," *le Libertaire*, 7 April 1938.

133. In April 1938, the authorities banned a public meeting organized by the UA on Spain and against the internationalization of the war—see the protest by Pivert, on behalf of the Seine Federation of the SFIO, published in *le Libertaire*, 7 April 1938. The same month, Roger Coudry was prosecuted for provoking soldiers to disobey orders "for the purposes of anarchist propaganda," for writing about the use of troops to break a transport workers strike—see *le Libertaire*, 28 April 1938. In June, Tixier of the JAC was arrested on the same charge—*le Libertaire*, 9 June 1938. The 23 June, 30 June and 14 July 1938 issues of *le Libertaire* were seized, but no charges were brought—see also *le Libertaire*, 7 July 1938. *Le Libertaire*, 21 July 1938, reported that more and more militants, even some who were no longer active, had been summoned by the Commissariat for questioning. This was interpreted as an updating of the "Carnet B," the list of militants considered a risk to the State in time of war or other emergency. The very first number of *SIA* (10 November 1938) was seized, and in April 1939 it was banned for a while as a foreign paper because of its foreign-language pages. The situation got gradually worse and worse, building up to the total repression following mobilization, and severely hindered both propaganda and solidarity work. See Nicolas Faucier, *Pacifisme et Antimilitarisme dans l'entre-deux-guerres (1919–1939)* (Paris: Spartacus, 1983), and Lecoin, *Le cours d'une vie*.

134. Lucien Huart in *SIA*, 2 March 1939.

135. *Le Libertaire*, 2 June 1938. The decree of 2 May 1938 also made it an offence to help an illegal immigrant directly or indirectly. SIA got together a *Conseil juridique*—a group of sympathetic lawyers to help in particular cases of refugees' being refused admission to France or in danger of being arrested and expelled—see *le Libertaire*, 26 May 1938. A public meeting was held on 10 June at the Mutualité with Chazoff, Pivert, Pioch and some of the lawyers; Jouhaux was unable to attend, but a telegram expressing his solidarity was read out at the meeting. According to *le Libertaire*, 16 June 1938, there was standing room only. SIA also organized a national petition against the decree—*le Libertaire*, 23 June 1938.

136. *Le Libertaire* and *SIA*, 9 February 1939.

137. *SIA*, 2, 9 and 16 February 1939.

138. On conditions in the camps, see, amongst other articles: "Dans les camps de misère et de mort," *le Libertaire*, 23 February 1939; "A notre honte—L'infamie des camps de concentration," *le Libertaire*, 1 June 1939; "Dans les camps de mort lente. Sinistre bilan," *le Libertaire*, 15 June 1939; "Une mise au point du groupe indépendant du camp de Gurs (îlot F)," *le Libertaire*, 20 July 1939; "Au camp de Rieucros: gardes-chiourme et staliniens contre les anarchistes," *le Libertaire*, 10 August 1939; "Dans les camps de la mort où la France officielle se montre l'auxiliaire de Franco," *SIA*, 16 February 1939; "De l'eau, de la boue, de la mort," *SIA*, 2 March 1939. See also Faucier, *Pacifisme et Antimilitarisme*, pp.163–7.

139.   See *le Libertaire*, 9 February 1939; and Chazoff and Haussard, "Visions d'horreur et d'épouvante," *SIA*, 9 February 1939. SIA co-operated with the French military authorities in ferrying refugees to centres in Perpignan and in supplying the various camps — see *SIA*, 23 February 1939.

140.   *Le Libertaire*, 22 June and 6 July 1939. The platform included Henri Jeanson, Pioch, Pivert, Nocher, Marcelle Capy and MacNair of the Independent Labour Party.

141.   *Le Libertaire*, 1 June 1939.

142.   *SIA*, 13 July 1939.

11

Schism in the Anarchist Movement: the CGTSR-FAF

> It is no longer a question of the overly abstract and more
> or less artificial quarrels of yesteryear between the vari-
> ous currents within anarchism, ... but of differences of
> opinion concerning the immense, infinitely varied and
> complicated problems which life and the present epoch
> confront us with urgently.
>
> *Voline*[1]

If one looks closely at the other anarchist organizations in the late
1930s—the CGTSR and especially the FAF—it is difficult not to come
away with an impression of marginal "groupuscules" concerned primarily with sectarian disputation and indulging in what Lenin would no
doubt have called "revolutionary phrase-mongering."

THE COLLAPSE OF THE ANARCHIST FRONT

After the expulsion of the UA from the Comité anarcho-syndicaliste
pour la défense et la libération du prolétariat espagnol in the autumn of
1936, it was the CNT-FAI that initiated the one and only attempt to re-
unite the French anarchist movement. The congress held at Lyon, 14–15
November 1936, was however to prove totally unsuccessful.[2] The congress brought together 55 militants representing various groups of the
UA and the FAF, independent groups and CGTSR unions. Practically
all were from the south of the country. José Elizalde of the CNT-FAI
delegation proposed a completely new organization that would bring
together all French anarchists. After a discussion, the idea of "organic
unity" was dropped in favour of "unity of action." A motion proposed
by Voline (of the FAF) and Huart (who had left the FAF for the UA
in November 1936) was adopted. This proposed the establishment of a
five-member commission that would deliberate on the unification of the
movement.[3] This was never to be. Very early on in the meeting it was
noted succinctly in the minutes that, "The discussions became venom-

ous." The whole congress simply rehearsed the arguments around what were to be the two central points of disagreement. These were summed up in a text written for the UA by Frémont, and read out at the congress by Louis Le Bot (Groupe intercommunal de Paris), explaining the split within the CASDLPE and why the UA as an organization had chosen not to attend the Lyon congress.[4] They were, briefly: the question of whether to co-operate with political parties; and the public criticisms of the CNT-FAI made by *l'Espagne Antifasciste (CNT-FAI-AIT)*, whose editors were André Prudhommeaux and Voline of the FAF.

THE UA AND THE CNT-FAI: SELF-CENSORSHIP

For its part, the UA had very early on committed itself to not passing judgement on some of the more questionable decisions of the CNT-FAI, beginning with the Spanish anarcho-syndicalists' rôle in the election of the *Frente popular* government in February 1936. As Pierre Mualdès put it at the time: "I have never been able to bear criticism and lesson-giving from comrades who are no doubt well-intentioned but who live thousands of kilometres from the scene of the action."[5] A few months later Louis Anderson, chief editor of *le Libertaire* in this period, spent three weeks in Barcelona, Saragossa and Madrid and on his return he wrote of the CNT-FAI:

> Even in our milieux we have not always been fair on them. The absence of liaison and the lack of precise information for a long time left us in ignorance of their reasons and sometimes led us to misunderstand why they acted the way they did. We have even sometimes allowed ourselves to criticize them unjustly when they have had to adopt some very delicate positions. And we have talked too often about developments in Spain as if they were happening just outside Paris.[6]

This kind of attitude was linked with affirmations of faith in the CNT-FAI to behave appropriately and responsibly. This unwillingness to criticize was characteristic of the UA and its organ for a long time. Some mild worries were expressed by certain militants about the process of militarization (the transformation of the revolutionary workers' militias into a "People's Army"), but *le Libertaire* on the whole was concerned to quell such fears. Ridel's article on "The militarization of the centuries" concluded: "There: the word is out. It sounds repellent. The reality of it is less so."[7] And Armand Aubrion wrote from the front: "We are at war and if we decide to take part in the war, we must do so with all our energy, with all our strength: we need organization; it is a vital necessity, indispensable for the struggle, indispensable for victory."[8]

The "Sébastien Faure Century," made up predominantly of French anarchists in the Durruti Column, also defended "the principle of technical
militarisation and that of centralized command," and dissociated themselves from "the campagne of denigration of the Spanish Revolution
undertaken in the name of 'pure anarchism' by some people who at one
time were our comrades"[9]

Similarly, the entry of CNT militants into the Generalidad—the
Catalan government—and into the national government at Madrid, was
greeted with some disquiet but certainly not with the uproar one might
have expected. In both cases, it was argued in the pages of *le Libertaire*
that these governments were not governments of the usual kind, they
were more like antifascist "juntas," and that such participation was indicative of the strength and influence of the CNT-FAI, and therefore to
be welcomed.[10]

DISQUIET INSIDE THE UA

The first real criticisms to be published in *le Libertaire* appeared in
March–April 1937, about the same time as did the first news of the
political manœuvres against the CNT-FAI in Spain, and this circumstance clearly discouraged much further criticism.[11] The public meeting at the Vel d'Hiv in June enabled Oliver and Montseny to present
at first hand their reasons for taking part in the regional and central
governments: the two main arguments advanced were the urgent need
to defeat Franco and maintain antifascist unity; and that to have done
otherwise would have been "dictatorial." Their speeches were reported
at length in *le Libertaire*.[12] It is true that shortly afterwards Sébastien
Faure wrote two articles entitled "The slippery slope," pointing out the
dangers of the CNT-FAI's policy, and insisting that it had damaged the
credibility of anarchism internationally.[13] But as was usually the case
with the inimitably courteous Faure, this was done in a most comradely
fashion, and he insisted: "Let us not exaggerate anything; let us talk
neither of renunciation, nor of betrayal; it can in this instance only be a
question of tactics."[14] So as far as the UA and its organ were concerned,
what little open criticism there was of the CNT-FAI was restrained and
usually qualified.

This does not mean that the entire membership of the UA agreed
with what the CNT-FAI had done and were continuing to do. The second day of the UA congress of October–November 1937 was dominated by the discussion of this question, and if the report in *le Libertaire*
is anything to go by, delegates were more or less evenly divided between
those who accepted the CNT-FAI's policy and those who were, on the

contrary, very concerned about it.[15] Faucier made it clear that, because of the difficulties the CNT-FAI found themselves in, the UA had deliberately kept quiet: "Whilst often making our concerns clear to our Spanish comrades, we toned down our criticisms and emphasized solidarity, as we did not wish our criticisms to be discussed in public and play in to the hands of our enemies or theirs."[16] This attitude predominated at the congress, and the delegates from Brest, Lyon-Vaise, Saint-Etienne, Orléans, Marseille (Germinal), Issy-les-Moulineaux and Paris 17 proposed the following motion: "Our brothers in Spain have a right to our total and unreserved solidarity. Considering the major contribution the Spanish anarchists have made to international anarchism by their participation in the antifascist struggle, Congress declares that any criticism which may weaken this solidarity is to be banished from our ranks."[17] It was passed by 54 votes to 18 (with 2 delegates absent).[18]

This act of self-censorship, this acceptance on a majority vote of some kind of notion of collective responsibility was a significant development for the UA. The "revolutionary individualists" of the FAF were certainly not prepared to accept such a surrender of the individual's freedom to the organization; and the anarcho-syndicalists of the CGTSR only came round to it somewhat belatedly, when arguably a great deal of damage had already been done both to the morale and support of the CGTSR, to relations between it and the CNT-FAI and, generally, to anarchist propaganda in France.

THE ANARCHO-SYNDICALIST COMMITTEE AFTER NOVEMBER 1936

It is true that the CASDLPE continued to do positive work after the split with the UA and the creation of the CEL. It is impossible to give precise figures for the amount of money raised for Spain, since the accounts published in *le Combat Syndicaliste* were so unclear and are contradicted by other accounts. Going by what seems to be a running total in that paper, one could estimate a total of around 100,000 francs raised by the spring of 1937. On the other hand, accounts to be found in the CNT's archives show a total of 437,000 francs raised between November 1936 and February 1937, of which 45,000 came from the IWMA.[19] The CGTSR's fund for the CNT—which seems in fact to have been an international one, centralizing fund-raising by the IWMA's member sections—had raised over 2 million francs by August 1937.[20]

However much was raised, the rivalry of the CASDLPE with the CEL very soon began to cause arguments, primarily because the CASDLPE considered itself the "sole committee in France recognized by the

Spanish CNT and the Iberian Anarchist Federation."[21] Pierre Besnard wrote to Horatio Prieto of the CNT on 12 October 1936, complaining that Lecoin had been authorized to represent the CNT in France, and accusing the CNT of preferring the UA and the CGT to the CAS and the CGTSR, "the natural representatives of the CNT in France."[22] When, at the Lyon congress, Couanault of the CGTSR asked why the CNT had given mandates to two different organizations, Torre of the CNT-FAI delegation had replied simply that the UA was the biggest anarchist organization in France and could not be ignored.[23]

Nevertheless, as we have seen, fund-raising did continue, and extensive speaking tours were arranged in the usual way. How successful were these? In November 1936, an announcement under the "CAS" rubric in *l'Espagne Antifasciste (CNT-FAI-AIT)* about a speaking and film tour by Aristide Lapeyre commented on the last series of public meetings arranged by the CAS "of a scale we have never before achieved." Signed by Julien Toublet, the announcement went on: "The results in terms of the mood and spirit of the proletariat are very good: many workers who until recently did not even know the name of our organization have now joined us; new unions have affiliated to us, others are in the process of being set up."[24] At their congress of 21–22 November 1936 the CAS formed a "Federative Union."[25] It is noticeable that there were very few CAS in the north of France, and the *Union Fédérative* began to co-operate with a similar organization that existed in Belgium: the Union des Comités Antifascistes Libertaires pour la Défense et la Libération du Prolétariat Espagnol.[26] This had member groups in Stembert-les-Vervies, Liège, Verviers and La Calamine.[27] At some stage, these two federations united to form the Union Fédérative des Comités Anarcho-Syndicalistes Franco-Belges (Franco-Belgian Federal Union of Anarcho-Syndicalist Committees). By the summer of 1937, this organization had 25 *"centres de ravitaillement"* in France.[28]

DIFFERENCES BETWEEN THE CGTSR-FAF AND THE CNT-FAI

In July 1937, in another step that was to widen the gap between the CGTSR and the CNT, the Union Fédérative transformed itself into a Comité d'Aide et de Secours aux Victimes de la Contre-Révolution Espagnole (Committee for the Assistance of Victims of the Spanish Counter-Revolution), whose aim was to help all those suffering political repression under the Negrin government.[29] Not surprisingly, the name of the committee was seen by the CNT as being damaging to them, and it put out a circular in France asking anarchists not to support the new committee.[30] After a meeting between the CGTSR and the CNT delegation in France, the name of the committee was changed to the Comité Anarcho-Syndicaliste d'Aide et de Secours.[31]

The conflict began when *l'Espagne Antifasciste (CNT-FAI-AIT)* — which was created under the auspices of the CNT-FAI specifically to support those two organizations — reacted very critically to the integration of the Catalan Economic Council into the Generalidad in September 1936, and to the suppression of the Central Committee of Antifascist Militias the following month.[32] Two editorials written by Pierre Besnard, which appeared in October, were very critical of the CNT leadership.[33] Besnard insisted that it was a serious mistake on the CNT's part to have accepted such moves, and that the revolution would be in danger if these mistakes were not immediately rectified. The integration of the Economic Council was seen as its transformation into "a cog in the machinery of State," and the suppression of the Central Committee of Antifascist Militias was opposed because the Committee represented "the supreme guarantee of the possession of armed force by the Proletariat":

> The Militia? It is the proletariat in arms, it is force put at the service of the workers, it is the formal guarantee that this force will never be used against the Revolution. It is the absolute certainty that no counter-revolutionary attempt to endanger the conquests of the revolution can ever succeed. The Army? It is force put back in the hands of the Government which — whatever its form, character or composition — will one day be able to use it against the revolution, to liquidate the revolution in the interests of a new clan, a new caste.[34]

Besnard also then went on to imply that the CNT leadership had failed and that there was a danger of "a profound divorce between the proletarian masses and the leadership charged with the defence of their ideal and of their interests."[35] As a result of such editorial comment, the editorial policy of *l'Espagne Antifasciste (CNT-FAI-AIT)* was debated, if somewhat inconclusively, at the CAS congress in Paris, 24–25 October 1936, and even the CNT-FAI delegates present at the congress were divided among themselves.[36] But the critical editorials continued to offer the CNT advice on how it should behave. In December, for example, the CNT was accused of having actually done harm to the anarchist cause internationally: "The new position adopted recently by the CNT-FAI in Spain: participation in the government, collaboration with the political parties, militarization of the masses, a tendency towards statism, etc, ... has represented a significant blow for the international anarchist movement."[37]

It was also in the pages of *l'Espagne Antifasciste (CNT-FAI-AIT)* that the question of tactical alliances with political parties was discussed, relevant as it was both to the split in the French movement and to the CNT's position within Spanish antifascism. The objections raised by the CGTSR and FAF to the UA's revolutionary front policy were based on a rejection of "organic" relations with political parties. In other words, alliances were acceptable if they were only short-term, and for a very specific purpose, after which there would be no more contact; they were unacceptable if they involved "close and long-term 'organic' relations, an established, prolonged, continuous collaboration":[38] "Any form of collaboration which obliges the anarchists to comply with the opinion, attitude or tactic of parties or political fractions, remaining silent about their own ideas and agreeing to reduce their activity, is an organic and harmful form of collaboration. It must be rejected, purely and simply, on principle, always and everywhere."[39]

For obvious reasons, the CNT found it intolerable that a newspaper produced with their money should then be allowed to attack them publicly, and financial support was stopped, thus bringing about the demise of the paper. The last number of *l'Espagne Antifasciste (CNT-FAI-AIT)* — no.31, 8 January 1937 — announced that the CNT-FAI had decided to close the paper down "because *l'Espagne Antifasciste* has achieved its aim," but nobody was fooled, and this "suppression" caused some disquiet.[40] According to Prudhommeaux, *l'Espagne Antifasciste (CNT-FAI-AIT)* was closed down, "suppressed arbitrarily,"[41] because "its success was worrying certain opportunists."[42] It was replaced by *la Nouvelle Espagne Antifasciste*, which was "confusionist and party political" according to Prudhommeaux.[43] According to the CNT's Manuel Mascarell, speaking at the congress of the FCEAAF in Nîmes, 21–22 August 1937, *la Nouvelle Espagne Antifasciste* was created because the Spanish proletariat did not have a newspaper "which faithfully represented its aspirations in France."[44] Mentioning *le Combat Syndicaliste*, Mascarell had continued: "It is clear to us that these papers which claim to be on our side, far from pursuing a campaign in defence of the positions adopted by their Spanish comrades, are actually engaged in a campaign to discredit them, a campaign which has often prevented the comrades of the Seine regional organization from maintaining good relations with them, because they have a very distinct conception of the Spanish revolution."

Such action by the CNT would not of course prevent criticisms of it. The first major critique of the CNT-FAI, the editorial "Attention" that appeared in *l'Espagne Antifasciste (CNT-FAI-AIT)* in late October 1936, also appeared as an editorial in the CGTSR's organ, *le Combat*

Syndicaliste, just two days later.[45] And if *l'Espagne Antifasciste (CNT-FAI-AIT)* was effectively suppressed by the withdrawal of financial support, the FAF—whose constitutive congress was held at Toulouse on 15–16 August 1936—was given access to the pages of *le Combat Syndicaliste*, as well as to those of *la Voix Libertaire*; and from February 1937 the new Federation had its own organs, *Terre Libre* and *l'Espagne Nouvelle*.[46]

THE POSITION OF THE CGTSR-FAF

The FAF had, in December 1936, only 15 paid-up member groups, but it attained more importance than its own size would perhaps merit through its association with the CGTSR.[47] For, ironically, the purpose behind the creation of the FAF was "the union of the CGTSR-FAF, in the image of the union of the CNT-FAI in Spain."[48] As Jean Dupoux put it in *le Combat Syndicaliste* in July 1936, the FAF wanted to create an organization with the same principles as the FAI: "complete federalism, absolute autonomy, the organization serving only as a link between our scattered forces and as a co-ordinator of initiatives."[49] The links between the FAF and the old Association des Fédéralistes Anarchistes, which had been created in opposition to the Plate-forme, are clear. For Dupoux, "the existing organizations" were too centralist, they were "organizations with a 'party line', which believe that theirs is the only truth, using authoritarian methods where possible to crush minorities and very often serving the ambitions or pride of a small number of irremovable committees."[50] The FAF aimed to unite "all anarcho-syndicalists who are truly anarchist, all libertarian communists who are truly libertarian, all individualists who are truly revolutionary." Each militant should be able to do whatever s/he wanted, "according to their means, their capacities, their temperament or their own chosen tactics." Significantly, the ultimate aim was not defined as socialism, however qualified, but as "the suppression of authority."[51] For Dupoux, it was preferable to work with an individualist who was not a member of a union, rather than with an anarchist-communist who was a member of the CGT.

For the CGTSR and the FAF the priority was very much the revolution, in France as well as in Spain. Hence criticism of the UA for being reformist, "not in its aims, but in its means," and of the CEL and SIA, "the gathering together of all the well-meaning."[52] According to *le Combat Syndicaliste* in November 1936, the UA "does not for a moment envisage the possibility of using the social revolution in Spain for the benefit of social revolution in the rest of Europe."[53] This was an unjust accusation, because the CEL and SIA always held up the CNT-FAI as a model, and their campaigns involved repeated calls for insurrectionary direct action. But the CEL/SIA campaigns were based on the need for a revolutionary working-class front. When the CNT-FAI urged the French workers to take over the arsenals and the railways, the CGTSR took up this call to revolution in a characteristically sectarian fashion — that is to say, by calling for a purge: "To be able to achieve this, it is necessary to move on immediately to the formation of a revolutionary minority which will eject from the proletarian ranks all those militants who are jaded, tired, corrupt, incapable and old."[54]

The CGTSR and FAF tended to interpret events in Spain in a revolutionist way, and they tended to idealize or exaggerate both the revolutionism of the Spanish people and the rôle of the CNT-FAI (as opposed to other antifascist organizations). The struggle going on in Spain was often reduced to one between "fascism on the one hand, the CNT and the FAI on the other."[55] There were frequent references to "the mass anarchist uprising of 19 July," as if only anarchists had taken part in stopping the francoist coup.[56] The basic conception underlying the FAF's analyses was that of a world-wide revolutionary situation: "The capitalist regime is not only rotten, it is already dead, it no longer exists."[57] Not only was capitalism believed to be in the throes of a terminal crisis, but the FAF was convinced that the ultimate outcome of the crisis would be a desirable one: "Step by step, humanity is approaching the realization of the anarchist idea."[58]

It is a difference of emphasis, but a significant difference. The UA tended rather to emphasize the need for antifascist unity, and spoke frequently and approvingly of co-operation between the CNT and the UGT. If the UA overstated the role of the CNT-FAI, it was made clear that this was simply in order to compensate for the more biased reporting of the French Popular Front press, which on the contrary tended either to ignore the CNT-FAI or even to denigrate them unjustly. This meant that the UA was more understanding of the CNT-FAI's difficulties in asserting itself within the broader antifascist movement. The CGTSR and FAF, on the other hand, tended to be somewhat uncomprehending when confronted with assertions of the CNT-FAI's helplessness with regard to certain problems, and tended to credit them with more power than did the UA.

The CGTSR was very insistent that what was referred to as the second stage of the revolution was absolutely decisive — that is, the stage after the initial chaotic explosion, when for the revolutionary forces it was a question of taking stock, reorganizing and consolidating.[59] The revolution would fail, according to the CGTSR, if the revolutionary forces were not decisive enough in their destruction of reaction and the consolidation of the revolution — if they had a tendency, in other words, "to call for help to the forces of the past, to compromise with them, to make concessions to them, to listen to their advice, to agree to the co-habitation of these forces of the past with those of the present."[60] Any such compromise, any concession to non-revolutionaries or even to non-anarchists was therefore to be avoided: "Any deviation, however insig-nificant it may seem, ... risks compromising the entire edifice by making it weak and unstable."[61]

The CGTSR was also convinced that it was right and proper for it to voice its concerns in public: "We believe that the greatest assistance we can give the CNT-FAI is to open their eyes to what we are obliged to call their mistakes: to draw their attention to the consequences these mistakes may have."[62] Indeed, the argument as it developed in France was not so much one over the correctness or otherwise of the CNT-FAI's tactical decisions, but rather about whether it was right or not to discuss such criticisms publicly. For the CGTSR, criticism was not only a duty, but a right: "We will never, whatever the circumstances, abdicate our right to criticize; we will never ask anyone not to exercise the same right with respect to ourselves."[63]

So the criticisms continued, and despite the agreement that came out of the Lyon congress that the two sides would not interfere with each other's campaigning, the dispute even led to fisticuffs. At the CEL's Vel d'Hiv meeting of June 1937, Oliver's speech was interrupted by CGTSR militants, and there was a fight between them and UA stewards. The CGTSR had several complaints: (i) that the CNT had not bothered to inform them of the meeting or invite them, never mind ask them to help organize it; (ii) the CNT speakers—Oliver and Montseny—avoid-ed all the important questions; (iii) the UA stewards were very young militants "who only yesterday were in the ranks of the communists, the trotskyists and even of La Roque"; (iv) that it was a deliberate provoca-tion to have Lucien Huart, late of the FAF and of the CGTSR, chair the meeting; (v) that the selling of *le Combat Syndicaliste* was forbidden.[64] The UA insisted that the selling of all newspapers—including *le Liber-taire*—had been forbidden at the meeting in order to prevent any pos-sible appearance of sectarianism or disunity; and it complained of the CGTSR's "incomprehension" and "narrow-mindedness."[65]

CRISIS IN THE IWMA

It was around this time that the cracks in the IWMA started becoming obvious to everybody, and that the CNT began to lose patience with the CGTSR and FAF. On 11–13 June 1937—just a few weeks after the fateful events of May in Barcelona—the IWMA held an extraordinary plenary congress in Paris. In *le Combat Syndicaliste*, on the first day of the plenum, there appeared an article asserting that the CNT's "collaborationist" policy had led to "the greatest failure in history," and making public the fact that the previous IWMA congress (15–17 November 1936) had seen "a *complete and general* disagreement" between the CNT and all the other IWMA sections: "Nevertheless, in order to maintain the unity of the world anarcho-syndicalist movement and after having received assurances that the CNT would effect the indispensable rectification of its policy as soon as circumatsnces allowed it, Congress declared that it 'understood' the CNT's position, without being able to approve of it."[66]

On this note, the extraordinary congress opened in Paris, and according to the CGTSR's organ, "the IWMA is strengthened by this congress, its morale and unity reinforced."[67] And this despite the fact that the CNT's interventions at the congress were interpreted as an attempt to abolish "the freedom of the anarchist and anarcho-syndicalist press with regard to events in Spain."[68] The congress also saw an unsuccessful attempt by the CNT to have the secretariat transferred from France to Spain.[69] The CNT-FAI had begun to counter-attack. Mariano Vazquez, secretary of the CNT National Committee, attacked "the stupidity" and "the fanaticism" of the CNT's critics, especially in France: "Stop your criticisms and your foolishness, for in reality you are the only ones who are betraying the cause of the world proletariat, through your incomprehension and your sectarianism."[70] Simultaneously, the FAI's Peninsular Committee attacked both the CGTSR and the FAF: "By the attitude they have adopted, these groupuscules ... have deliberately turned away from fraternal relations with the CNT and the FAI and, consequently, our organizations can no longer regard them as belonging to the same movement."[71]

In August 1937, having failed to get the IWMA secretariat moved to Spain, the CNT's National Committee wrote to the IWMA complaining about the secretariat's "generally obstructive attitude," demanding a reconsideration of its structure and rôle, and demanding the replacement of its then general secretary Pierre Besnard.[72] In the extremely long "Rapport Moral" that Besnard then produced in time for the extremely long extraordinary congress of the IWMA, 6–17 December 1937, Besnard gave in to pressure and resigned as general secretary, becoming instead one of the assistant secretaries. But he was unrepentant: "Without false modesty, I am not afraid to declare that if these doctrines and methods had been applied *fully and everywhere*, the revolution would have triumphed completely and rapidly."[73] The congress was presented in *le Combat Syndicaliste* as having been a success: there was much more

consensus than at previous congresses; unconditional support was declared for the CNT; the publication of a new review was decided on.[74] It
was in fact decided that criticisms of the CNT-FAI would not in future
be discussed in public, but only in the new review, *Internationale*, which
was to be for members only.[75] This was another step towards the total
isolation of the FAF. Prudhommeaux—for whom *Internationale* was a
"bureaucratic organ filled with the hollow fanfares of self-glorification
of Mascarell and his friends"[76]—was later to write:

> From December 1937, by a tacit agreement, all our organs had
> stopped the polemics over the 'errors', the 'failings', the 'faults'
> of the Spanish anarcho-syndicalist movement, to content them-
> selves with fighting the declared enemies of the movement. As
> for the rest, in all the papers, we limited ourselves to reproduc-
> ing the more or less 'conformist' opinions more or less 'dictated'
> by the government and the GPU, which the CNT-FAI them-
> selves published in their press.[77]

The CNT had tended, not unjustly, to conflate CGTSR and FAF,
but Besnard, in his report, had distanced himself from the extreme critical stance of the FAF.[78] After the Barcelona events of May 1937, which
the FAF believed to be proof of the correctness of their position, *Terre
Libre* published a declaration in which it viciously attacked the CNT-
FAI leadership:

> The ministerialist leaders of the CNT-FAI no longer have the
> right to speak. No! Those who aborted the Spanish workers'
> new 19 July no longer have the right to speak; we should listen
> instead to those who *still fight for the Revolution despite everything*:
> the Libertarian Youth and the grass-roots militants in the FAI;
> the Friends of Durruti and the militia-fighters at the front; the
> mass of workers and peasants in the CNT. It is the turn of the
> *true* antifascist fighters to speak, those who do not want to sac-
> rifice the only thing which to them was worth fighting for. The
> true freedom of the people. It is the turn of the *real CNT-FAI*,
> not the phrase-mongers, not the comedians, not the indeci-
> sive or cowardly, not the impostors, renegades or traitors![79]

This was one of the most violent attacks on the CNT-FAI leadership to date, and was all the more offensive to many in France as well as
in Spain because it implied a total divorce between a treacherous leadership and a revolutionary grass-roots membership. And an editorial in
l'Espagne Nouvelle at the same time declared that there was no longer a
revolutionary war in Spain: "There is the war between the government

in Valencia (France-England-Russia) and the government in Burgos (Germany-Italy). And there is above all the war made by the Spanish bourgeoisie—whatever its political ideology—on the working people of Spain, whatever their trade union or ideology. The other war is just a pretext. The hour of mediation is at hand ...".[80]

A SPLIT IN THE ANARCHIST "MOVEMENT"

In July, as we have seen, the FAI had declared that it no longer considered itself part of the same movement as the FAF. In France also, the FAF was going too far for most comrades. *Le Libertaire* returned no.5 of *l'Espagne Nouvelle* and broke off its exchange agreement with the paper.[81] The Italian Pro-Spagna committee in Nice returned no.6 of *l'Espagne Nouvelle* and asked for no more copies of the paper to be sent to them.[82] By July 1937, the FAF's own supporters were beginning to be alienated. Dupoux had an article published in *Terre Libre* opposing the paper's editorial line, on the grounds that it did no good and that it could only damage the anarchist movement in Spain and internationally. The editors' reply insisted that it would be unjust and unanarchist to hide things from "the masses," "unless, like the political parties, one regards the masses as a herd above which the solemn pundits engage in their deceitful manœuvres behind the political scenes, carefully hidden from the imbeciles below."[83] The brothers Aristide and Paul Lapeyre of Bordeaux also criticized the paper's editorial line, arguing that it was wrong to accuse the CNT-FAI leadership of outright treachery even if they had made mistakes. They added that the editors of *Terre Libre* were behaving undemocratically in that they were expressing only their own opinions, not those of the whole FAF. The brothers ended by insisting that if the editors really believed what they wrote about the CNT-FAI, then logically they should break off all contact and not support the Spanish organizations at all.[84] The editors' response was: "We believe a schism in the ranks of the CNT and of the FAI themselves and indeed in the international anarchist movement to be inevitable."[85] At the FAF congress of 14–15 August in Clermont-Ferrand this uncompromising stance was maintained, despite increasing noises of discontent from the Bordeaux group "Culture et Action," which tried unsuccessfully to get a motion passed curbing criticisms of the CNT-FAI in the press. This was interpreted as censorship, so it was re-phrased to exclude from the newspaper any articles "which might harm the general propaganda of the FAF."[86] It was generally agreed, however, that this motion was too vague to make any difference.

Not only did the attacks on the CNT-FAI leadership continue, but *l'Espagne Nouvelle* identified more and more with a radical oppositional minority within the CNT-FAI, especially the Friends of Durruti Group.[87] "Read in the (clandestine) revolutionary press of the Spanish proletariat" became a regular rubric in *l'Espagne Nouvelle*.[88] In January 1938, André Prudhommeaux was joined on the editorial committee by Aristide and Paul Lapeyre—whose own Bordeaux-based paper *l'Espagne Antifasciste* was read by only a few hundred people—and by Alphonse Barbé—whose pacifist, individualist *le Semeur* disappeared in November 1936.[89] By the following September, though, the editorial committee was hardly functioning any longer. Dautry—who had joined the group at the same time—had disappeared. Barbé and the Lapeyre brothers had agreed to leave the editing to Prudhommeaux, who also seems to have been burdened with all the administrative work.[90] Despite the doctrinal judgements being handed down regularly by Prudhommeaux and Voline, in May/June 1938 the FAF's Clermont-Ferrand group circulated a proposal that the FAF should unite with the UA and with the independent groups: the proposal received a favourable reply from "most" groups.[91]

A lengthy exchange began in January 1939 between Prudhommeaux—writing in *l'Espagne Nouvelle*—and Paul Lapeyre—writing in *le Combat Syndicaliste*.[92] Lapeyre argued basically that in the circumstances the CNT-FAI had had no choice; that antifascist unity was necessary to win the war; and that the government would have been even more counter-revolutionary without anarchist input. As for the policy of open criticism, Lapeyre became convinced that it had done no good. The CNT had not changed its tactics. Propaganda had, if anything, been harmed. The FAF had not gained respect for being honest: its criticisms had been seen as sectarian bickering, and had been used against the CGTSR, the circulation of whose organ had suffered as a result. It was not even the case always that the cause of truth had been served, since many of the criticisms were ill-founded. There was now a split between, on the one hand, the CGTSR and the FAF, and on the other, the CNT-FAI leadership and membership, practically all the Spanish militants living in France and the UA. The IWMA had been severely damaged. "The consequence has been widespread feelings of mistrust, disputes in all anarchist milieux and in every town in France."[93] Many militants were now convinced there was nothing to choose between Negrin and Franco, and there was widespread cynicism in the movement.

Irrespective of whether the analyses produced by the FAF and CGTSR were right or wrong, there is no doubt that the only results of their campaign of criticism was the demoralization of militants and

the splintering of the movement both nationally and internationally —
including their own organizations.

THE STATE OF THE CGTSR, 1936–39

It is true that, after the summer of 1936, support for the CGTSR increased significantly. Was this increase due to events in France, or in
Spain, or both? Certainly as late as April 1936, *le Combat Syndicaliste* was
not very healthy, and this would suggest the CGTSR had not benefitted
greatly from the increased militancy of 1934–35. According to the paper's administrators, writing in April 1936, "our *Combat* is not in a won-
derful state"; and a "Phalanx of Support" established by the congress
of November 1934, and whose members undertook to give 5 francs per
month, was at that time producing only 100 francs monthly.[94] As we
have seen, Paul Lapeyre claimed that the membership of the CGTSR
increased from 3,000 to 5,000 in the summer of 1936.[95] According to
Besnard, in his report to the IWMA, membership doubled after May
1936 to 6,000.[96] Nevertheless, until September 1936, both the editorial
and administrative work involved at *le Combat Syndicaliste* was done by
one person, Adrien Perrissaguet. After that date, a second militant took
on the editorship.[97] After November, the paper, although still only four
pages long, was produced in a larger format.[98] The congress of 9–11
January 1937, at which 39 unions were represented, registered an (un-
specified) growth in the number of member unions as well as of individual members, and was described in the paper as "the congress of renewal."[99] The congress also decided to move the paper from Limoges to
Paris in order to improve communications and access to news, etc.[100] In
December 1937, Dimanche reported from the latest meeting of the CCN
that the CGTSR was growing, but this contradicted remarks made by
other militants.[101] Lapeyre, we have seen, reckoned *le Combat Syndicaliste*
to be suffering by the end of 1938. A police report of November 1938
put the paper's print-run at 4,000.[102] Helmut Rüdiger of the IWMA,
writing in its internal review *Internationale* in the summer of 1938, spoke
of "the organic, political and moral failure, in a word the total failure, of
the IWMA at a decisive moment of contemporary history."[103] He went
on, in a rather negative assessment of the IWMA's conduct, to claim that
no national section of the IWMA had grown since 1936. The relative
lack of influence of the IWMA and its French section were also brought
out by an article on the IWMA's December 1937 congress in *l'Espagne
Antifasciste* — a paper produced by supporters of the CGTSR and FAF,
and which yet admitted both the "weakness" of the CGTSR, and the

fact that the vast majority of French militants probably did not realize the IWMA even existed.[104]

THE ISOLATION OF THE FAF

What of the FAF, which was, after all, only created in 1936? It certainly failed in its primary aim, which was to win over groups affiliated to the UA, and create with the CGTSR a twin organization modelled on the Spanish CNT-FAI. According to a report produced in June 1938, the FAF consisted almost entirely of groups which had been independent before the FAF's creation.[105] In February 1937, the Federation claimed to have 57 member groups.[106] If one compiles a list of groups mentioned in the pages of *Terre Libre*, it adds up to 59: 5 in Paris, 15 in the suburbs, 39 in the provinces.[107] However, only 30 groups were represented at the Clermont-Ferrand congress of August 1937, and several groups which were suggested as possible candidates to take over the secretariat from Paris had to refuse on the grounds that they would not be able to cope with the work-load.[108] *Terre Libre* claimed initially to have sold 6,500 copies out of 8,000 printed, and just after the newspaper's appearance the FAF's funds amounted to only 300 or 400 francs.[109] The public of *l'Espagne Nouvelle*—whose readership did not complement that of *Terre Libre*, but overlapped with it—was even more restrained. It started off with 3,000 francs and a print-run of 5,000.[110] By the end of the year, it claimed a readership of 4,000, though only about 100 subscribers, which the paper itself described as "derisory."[111] In December 1937, Prudhommeaux pointed out that the newspaper and its editors were totally isolated, and that 98% of the international movement were against them.[112] Very soon after that the paper was losing money, and in September it became a monthly. By April 1939 less than 2,000 people were buying *l'Espagne Nouvelle*.[113] Reports in the FAF's *Bulletin intérieur*, six issues of which appeared between September 1938 and July 1939, attest repeatedly and unequivocally to the Federation's complete failure in every respect: organizationally, politically and financially.

If the CGTSR managed to maintain some kind of existence, with around 5,000 or 6,000 supporters concentrated predominantly in the south, the FAF, on the other hand, was destroyed by its own intransigence, as its ideologues argued it into total isolation. Even the CGTSR was eventually condemned by Voline as having "washed its hands" of any interest in the Spanish revolution.[114] For Prudhommeaux and Voline UA militants were "revisionists," "deviationists," who like the CNT-FAI leadership had taken "the military, political and ministerial path."[115] Their approach had a precedent, according to Voline, in (i) those who had signed the "Manifesto of the Sixteen," who had thought a French victory in the Great War preferable to a German victory; (ii) the "plat-formists" of the mid/late 1920s (who, to Voline, were almost as bad as the bolsheviks); and (iii) the "treintistas," the Pestaña-Peiro tendency within the CNT who had adopted a more conciliatory and reformist and less insurrectionary attitude towards the republic of 1931.[116]

On the other hand, the FAF distinguished itself from what it called "sceptical" or "cynical" individualism, which "in general consists in denying the possibility of any revolution which merits the name; in contempt for the proletariat and for humanity in general; in artfulness, machiavellian cynicism, *arrivisme* and the exploitation of others."[117] The FAF had already made its attitude towards absolute pacifism clear—as, indeed, had the CGTSR and the UA—but being more closely linked to the individualists, it seems to have had more pacifists within its own ranks, especially younger militants, "and especially those from intellectual milieux."[118] Such pacifists believed with the individualist Madeleine Vernet that, "We cannot accept the idea of a war having revolution as its aim. For a revolution to be worthy of man, it must be achieved through peaceful means."[119]

Prudhommeaux, though, directed his criticisms rather towards *l'en dehors*, the paper of Vernet's colleague Armand. The paper was eclectic in the extreme. Some articles expressed sympathy with the CNT-FAI, or with the antifascists in general; many expressed the opinion that there was no difference between a Popular Front government and a fascist government; others were pacifists whose main concern was that the war should not be allowed to spread to France. And all these points of view were discussed with that curious kind of disinterested and intellectual cynicism characteristic of Armand and *l'en dehors*.

Who then was not to be excommunicated? For Voline, only the FAF and *Terre Libre* were, in the end, anarchist; those who disagreed were "false anarchists," or ignorant and naïve.[120] He was even convinced that those who attacked the FAF for being "sectarian" were "the sworn enemies of anarchism."[121] The true anarchist—the supporter of the FAF—was defined by Prudhommeaux thus:

> An anarchist individualist may consider the revolution an opportunity for personal liberation for himself and for other men, as a source of exaltation and human energy which he defends as such against all attempts to smother or monopolize it or to divert it towards any kind of regime which absorbs the capacities and denies the rights of the individual. This kind of revolutionary individualism (which has produced the most upright con-

sciences, the most intransigent attitudes in the struggle towards the ideal, the most magnificent and most enlightened devotion to the cause of freedom) constitutes, in our opinion, the irreplaceable treasure of all social movements.[122]

Given the high priority accorded by the FAF to ideological purity and its consequent readiness to criticize others, it is just as well that certain leading members of the FAF believed "quality" and "quantity" to be mutually exclusive.[123]

Notes

1. "V." (most probably Voline), "Discussion et Action," *Terre Libre*, 25 September 1937.
2. The congress is mentioned briefly in *l'Espagne Antifasciste (CNT-FAI-AIT)*, 18 November 1936. The typed minutes (in French) are to be found in the CNT Archive at the IISG — Paquete 60/C/2: "Comités Antifascistas del Extranjero."
3. The militants elected to the commission were: Torre (FAI), Darcola (Comité Italien Pro-Spagna, Italian Committee for Spain), Louis Laurent (CASDLPE), Felix Garrec (Toulon, UA), Victor Nan (Toulouse, FAF).
4. At Gabriel Diné's suggestion, those UA members present sent a telegram to the UA in Paris regretting the absence of any official delegation. These were delegates from UA groups in Toulon, Clichy, Montpellier, and from the UA's Bouches du Rhône Federation.
5. *Le Libertaire*, 28 February 1936.
6. *Le Libertaire*, 10 July 1936.
7. *Le Libertaire*, 16 October 1936.
8. Armand Aubrion, "Du front de Sastago. La militarisation des milices et les miliciens," *le Libertaire*, 27 November 1936.
9. "A propos de la militarisation des milices," *le Libertaire*, 22 July 1937. On the dilemmas of the CNT and of the IWMA and its other affiliates in this period, see Wayne Thorpe, "Syndicalist Internationalism Before World War II" in Marcel van der Linden and Wayne Thorpe, *Revolutionary Syndicalism. An International Perspective* (Aldershot: Scolar Press, 1990), pp.237–60, esp. 252–7.
10. See, for example, "Le nouveau conseil de la Généralité," *le Libertaire*, 2 October 1936; and Charles Robert, "Le Gouvernement de Madrid et la CNT," *le Libertaire*, 13 November 1936.
11. See Bonomini's article "La révolution espagnole est menacée. Anarchistes, plus que jamais serrons nos rangs," *le Libertaire*, 22 April 1937. The first sign of disquiet was provoked by Garcia Oliver who, as Minister of Justice, made comments at the military college in Barcelona about the need for "iron discipline," etc. See "D'étranges déclarations attribuées à Garcia Oliver," *le Libertaire*, 8 April 1937: "We remained silent, for we always had in mind, whatever the ideological sacrifices, the ultimate aim towards which the Spanish revolution was directed: libertarian communism."
12. *Le Libertaire*, 1 July 1937.

13. *Le Libertaire*, 8 and 22 July 1937.

14. *Le Libertaire*, 22 July 1937.

15. *Le Libertaire*, 11 November 1937. Ridel made the point that "we have to produce a critique of the Spanish movement because it highlights the failings of all anarchist movements: no economic plan, no programme." The platformists at the congress seem to have been among those most disturbed by the CNT-FAI's actions.

16. Ibid. Contrary to what the CGTSR and FAF seemed sometimes to believe, the UA did actually make its views clear to the CNT-FAI—but privately. See, for example, a letter dated 15 May 1937 from the UA's Commission Administrative to the FAI's Comité Peninsular expressing serious concern about developments in Spain, and urging that the international anarchist congress planned for July should be brought forward. This conference would not only be a show of solidarity at a difficult time for the CNT-FAI, the UA said, but would also allow the international anarchist movement "to tackle together the necessary decisions." IISG, FAI Archive, Paquete 57/Carpeta 3.

17. *Le Libertaire*, 4 November 1937.

18. A letter from the secretary of the Paris 19 UA group to *Terre Libre* accused Frémont, Faucier and Anderson of rigging the conference in order to silence opposition. *Terre Libre*, 14 January 1938. A resolution proposing a complete break from the UA, "a political and demagogic organization," at the FAF's Clermont-Ferrand congress 14–15 August 1937, also insisted that there was much opposition within the UA to its official policy—*Terre Libre*, 10 September 1937.

19. Paquete 61/A/2: "CGTSR," CNT Archive, IISG.

20. Various reports in *le Combat Syndicaliste*.

21. This claim—which the CASDLPE knew full well was untrue—was repeated in *le Combat Syndicaliste* and *Terre Libre* and on the Comittee's letterhead, of which there are examples in Paquete 60/B/1: "CASDLPE/CGTSR"—CNT Archive, IISG.

22. Paquete 61/A/1: "AIT, Paris"—CNT Archive, IISG. See also a letter to the CNT from the CASDLPE dated 3 November 1936, asking for clarification of the situation—Paquete 60/B/1, "CASDLPE/CGTSR," CNT Archive, IISG.

23. Minutes of the congress, Paquete 60/C/2: "Comités Antifascistas del Extranjero"—CNT Archive, IISG.

24. *L'Espagne Antifasciste (CNT-FAI-AIT)*, 11 November 1936.

25. See *le Combat Syndicaliste*, 27 November 1936, according to which Besnard was secretary, Toublet assistant secretary and Giraud treasurer. According to *l'Espagne Antifasciste (CNT-FAI-AIT)*, 2 December 1936 Toublet was the treasurer and Ganin was in charge of money being collected for the CNT.

26. According to *l'Espagne Antifasciste (CNT-FAI-AIT)*, 28 November 1936.

27. *L'Espagne Antifasciste (CNT-FAI-AIT)*, 11 December 1936.

28. One in Paris (33 rue de la Grange-aux-Belles), 24 in the provinces.

29. *Le Combat Syndicaliste*, 23 July and 6 August 1937. Toublet was secretary, and René Doussot treasurer.

30. Along with a publicity leaflet of the Comité d'Aide et de Secours, a copy of the circular, dated 19 October 1937, can be found in the CNT Archive, IISG: Paquete 61/A/1, "AIT, Paris."

31. Letter from the AIT Secretariat (Besnard, Galve, Rüdiger) to the CNT National Committee, 12 January 1938, Paquete 61/A/1: "AIT, Paris"—CNT Archive, IISG.

32. According to Marchal of the FAF, *L'Espagne Antifasciste (CNT-AIT-FAI)* had a print-run of 22,000 once it had been moved to France from Barcelona—see minutes of the Lyon

congress, Paquete 60/C/2: "Comités Antifascistas del Extranjero"—CNT Archive, IISG. Marchal also claimed that after no.7 (i.e. after the move to Paris) the paper was funded no longer by the CNT but by the CGTSR. This seems difficult to believe: (i) because the CGTSR's coffers were not overflowing, and *l'Espagne Antifasciste* appeared twice weekly at a time when *le Combat Syndicaliste* was appearing as per normal; (ii) because it then becomes difficult to understand how the CNT could prevent the paper from appearing, as it was later to do.

33. It is according to Voline that they were written by Besnard—see minutes of the Lyon congress, Paquete 60/C/2: "Comités Antifascistas del Extranjero"—CNT Archive, IISG. The anonymous editorials, which caused so much anger, were "Attention" and "Redressement necessaire" in the issues of 21 and 24 October 1936.

34. *L'Espagne Antifasciste (CNT-FAI-AIT)*, 21 October 1936.

35. *L'Espagne Antifasciste (CNT-FAI-AIT)*, 24 October 1936.

36. See the second part of the account of the congress in *l'Espagne Antifasciste (CNT-FAI-AIT)*, no.17 (4 November 1936). It has proved impossible to unearth a copy of no.16, containing the first part of the account.

37. Editorial, "Confusion et maladresse," *l'Espagne Antifasciste (CNT-FAI-AIT)*, 18 December 1936.

38. Part I of the anonymous three-part article "Discutons un peu," *l'Espagne Antifasciste (CNT-FAI-AIT)*, 7, 11 and 28 November 1936.

39. *L'Espagne Antifasciste (CNT-FAI-AIT)*, 28 November 1936.

40. See for example the undated letter from the Fédération Communiste Libertaire des Alpes-Maritimes, signed by Michaud, asking why the paper was "suppressed by order." Paquete 60/C/2: "Comités Antifascistas del Extranjero"—CNT Archive IISG.

41. *L'Espagne Nouvelle*, 1 May 1937.

42. *Terre Libre*, 8 October 1937.

43. Ibid.

44. Quoted in *la Nouvelle Espagne Antifasciste*, 6 October 1938. The first number of the paper appeared 20 September 1937. Produced in Paris, it was edited by Albert Soulillou, a former editor of Barbusse's *Monde*, and was very much a propaganda instrument for "antifascist unity."

45. *L'Espagne Antifasciste (CNT-FAI-AIT)*, 21 October and *le Combat Syndicaliste*, 23 October 1936.

46. Report of the first meeting of the FAF's Administrative Commission, *le Combat Syndicaliste*, 25 December 1936. The CA members were: Andrès, Baudon, Babaud, Bono, Hermann, Henri, Moisson, Planche, Perron, Ricros, Sanzy, Laurent, Prospéro. The CA was at that time already negotiating to take over *Terre Libre* as the FAF's official organ, which would eventually happen the following February. The editorial committee of *Terre Libre* was to be Voline, Hermann, Sanzy, Ricros, Moisson, Laurent. *Terre Libre* and *l'Espagne Nouvelle*, both fortnightly, appeared alternate weeks.

47. Ibid.

48. Paul Lapeyre (a leading member of the CGTSR and the FAF), letter to the author, 3 February 1986. This "union" was never to be achieved, but 3 December 1936 did see the "Unification Meeting" in Paris of the Jeunesses Syndicalistes Revolutionnaires and the Jeunesses Anarchistes FAF—*Le Combat Syndicaliste*, 27 November 1936. I have found no information regarding the size or influence of these two youth organizations.

49.   "Pour une FAI française," *le Combat Syndicaliste*, 17 July 1936. See also the "Charte de la Fédération anarchiste de langue française (FAF)" in the first issue of the *Bulletin intérieur de la FAF*, 15 September 1938.

50.   *Le Combat Syndicaliste*, 17 July 1936. For Dupoux to speak of "other organizations" in the plural is of course nonsense, as it was clearly the UA which was the object of these strictures: the FAF and CGTSR were very close ideologically and organizationally, and both constantly attacked the UA.

51.   *Le Combat Syndicaliste*, 17 July 1936.

52.   *Le Combat Syndicaliste*, 6 November 1936. It is noticeable that although the UA was under almost constant attack from the CGTSR and FAF, it very rarely responded in the pages of *le Libertaire*: see "Le combat contre la vérité," *le Libertaire*, 1 July 1937, which insisted the UA would not bother to reply "the untruths, inanities and slanders of the CGTSR."

53.   *Le Combat Syndicaliste*, 6 November 1936.

54.   *Le Combat Syndicaliste*, 4 December 1936.

55.   *Le Combat Syndicaliste*, 7 August 1936.

56.   For example, *Terre Libre*, February 1937.

57.   Ibid.

58.   *Terre Libre*, 10 September 1937.

59.   See the editorials "Le problème reconstructif de la Révolution Espagnole" and "Les stades de la révolution," *le Combat Syndicaliste*, 21 August and 13 November 1936.

60.   *Le Combat Syndicaliste*, 13 November 1936.

61.   *Le Combat Syndicaliste*, 21 August 1936.

62.   *Le Combat Syndicaliste*, 23 October 1936.

63.   Editorial, "Considérations sur la critique," *le Combat Syndicaliste*, 6 November 1936. See also Paul Lapeyre, "Le droit à la critique," *le Combat Syndicaliste*, 16 July 1937, which argues the same point.

64.   *Le Combat Syndicaliste*, 25 June 1937; *Terre Libre*, July 1937.

65.   For the UA's version of events, see *le Libertaire*, 24 June 1937.

66.   "LE MOMENT DECISIF. Où ses dirigeants entraînent-ils la CNT? Les travailleurs du Monde veulent le savoir!," *le Combat Syndicaliste*, 11 June 1937. The text of this article was voted on at a meeting of the CGTSR's Commission Administrative Confédérale on 4 June, and passed unanimously.

67.   The account of the congress appeared in *le Combat Syndicaliste*, 18 June 1937. For a brief summary, see Thorpe, "Syndicalist Internationalism," pp.255–6.

68.   Alexander Schapiro in *le Combat Syndicaliste*, 23 July 1937. Schapiro was one of the most persistent and outspoken critics of the CNT-FAI.

69.   Ibid. On the grounds that such a move would be detrimental to international communications, the move was supported only by Spain; Sweden, Holland, Italy, Poland and France voted against; Belgium and Chile abstained. The secretariat remained therefore in Paris, with a sub-secretariat in Barcelona.

70.   "L'anarchisme espagnol ne peut être discrédité par ceux-là même qui ne recueillirent que des échecs," *le Combat Syndicaliste*, 23 July 1937. The article first appeared in the CNT's organ, *Solidaridad Obrera*, 6 July 1937. A letter from the CNT to the IWMA dated 16 August 1937 also pointed out that the last National Plenum of the CNT's regional organizations had considered the press of the different IWMA sections, and had demanded an end to attacks on the CNT by the CGTSR — Paquete 61/A/1, CNT Archive, IISG.

71. Ibid. The article originally appeared in the Committee's *Bulletin d'Informations et Orientation Organique*, 4 July 1937.

72. "Considering that the present Secretary of the IWMA, comrade Pierre Besnard, is not equal to the task in the present circumstances and does not have the mental capacity necessary to be able to interpret events and to work not only for solidarity with the CNT but for the reinforcement of the IWMA, we believe it indispensable that he be replaced"— Paquete 61/A/1, CNT Archive, IISG. David Antona also thought Besnard was dogmatic and lacking in common sense: "Comrade Besnard is a man who is exhausted physically and even intellectually"—quoted by Besnard himself, "Rapport Moral" (n.d.[late 1937]), 97pp. TS, p.58—Paquete 61/D/5, CNT Archive, IISG. Besnard, who had been IWMA secretary since 1936, was replaced in 1938 by the Spaniard Manuel Mascarell. From 1938 until after the Second World War, the secretary was the Swede John Anderson. Thorpe, "Syndicalist Internationalism," p.249.

73. "Rapport Moral" (n.d.[late 1937]), 97pp. TS, p.96—Paquete 61/D/5, CNT Archive, IISG. Postal elections after the congress elected Prieto (CNT) as general secretary, with Besnard, Rocca (CNT), Rüdiger (German FAUD) and Das Neves (Portuguese CGT) as assistant secretaries—see circular dated 31 January 1938, Paquete 61/A/1, CNT Archive, IISG.

74. *Le Combat Syndicaliste*, 24 December 1937. The congress also resolved to approach the IFTU with a view to co-organizing a boycott of "fascist" countries and "fascist" goods, but repeated advances were rejected by the IFTU.

75. See *l'Espagne Nouvelle*, 15 February 1939. *Internationale* does not appear to have lasted very long. I have found only five numbers: no.2, June 1938 to no.6, October 1938.

76. *L'Espagne Nouvelle*, July–August–September 1939.

77. *L'Espagne Nouvelle*, 15 February 1939.

78. "Rapport Moral," p.51.

79. *Terre Libre*, June 1937.

80. "La fin des illusions," *l'Espagne Nouvelle*, 29 May 1937.

81. *L'Espagne Nouvelle*, 12 June 1937.

82. *L'Espagne Nouvelle*, 5 June 1937.

83. *Terre Libre*, July 1937.

84. *Terre Libre*, August 1937.

85. Ibid.

86. The report of the congress is in *Terre Libre*, 10 September 1937.

87. On the Friends of Durruti, see Georges Fontenis (ed.), *Le message révolutionnaire des "Amis de Durruti" (Espagne 1937)* (Paris: Editions 'L' [Union des Travailleurs Communistes Libertaires], 1983); The Friends of Durruti Group (Barcelona 1938), *Towards a fresh revolution* (Orkney: Cienfuegos Press, 1978 [first published 1938]); Agustín Guillamón, *The Friends of Durruti Group: 1937–1939* (Edinburgh/San Francisco: AK Press, 1996).

88. *L'Espagne Nouvelle*, 17 September 1937, referred to "a flourishing of new organs, breaking the conformist silence and unanimity of previous months. In these organs: *Anarquia, Esfuerzo, Ideas, Ruta, Libertad* and, above all, *El Amigo del Pueblo* (organ of the Friends of Durruti), we can read of the theoretical and practical renaissance of the proletarian movement in the semi-legal situation imposed on it by the temporary victory of the stalinist-bourgeois counter-revolution."

89. See *l'Espagne Nouvelle*, 21 January 1938.

90. *L'Espagne Nouvelle*, September 1938.

91. *Terre Libre*, 3 June 1938.

92. P. Lapeyre in *le Combat Syndicaliste*, 13 January, 20 January and 3 February 1939; A. Prudhommeaux, in *l'Espagne Nouvelle*, 15 January, 15 February and 15 March 1939.

93. *L'Espagne Nouvelle*, 3 February 1939.

94. *Le Combat Syndicaliste*, 10 April 1936.

95. Letter to the author.

96. "Rapport Moral," p.37. Besnard, one of whose characteristics was surely a tendency to overestimate the importance and influence of the CGTSR, also added: "The authority and prestige which it enjoys in the country surpass by far what one might expect from the organization's limited numerical strength."

97. *Le Combat Syndicaliste*, 11 September 1936.

98. Starting with the 20 November 1936 issue.

99. *Le Combat Syndicaliste*, 15 January 1937. The only unions represented at the congress which were specified in the report were: the Saint-Etienne Inter-union Group, the Old Building-workers' Federation (represented by J.-S. Boudoux), the Lyon and Bordeaux Metal-workers (the latter represented by P. Lapeyre) and Paris Leather-workers — *le Combat Syndicaliste*, 22 January 1937.

100. *Le Combat Syndicaliste*, 22 January 1937.

101. *Le Combat Syndicaliste*, 17 December 1937.

102. BA/1713.

103. *Internationale*, July–August 1938.

104. "Le congres de l'AIT," *l'Espagne Antifasciste*, 31 December 1937.

105. *Terre Libre*, 17 June 1938.

106. *Le Combat Syndicaliste*, 26 February 1937.

107. For details see Berry, "The French Anarchist Movement."

108. These groups were: Bordeaux, Toulouse, Lyon, Clermont-Ferrand and Thiers. *Terre Libre*, 10 September 1937.

109. *Terre Libre*, 12 March 1937.

110. *L'Espagne Nouvelle*, 19 April 1937.

111. Various reports in *l'Espagne Nouvelle*.

112. *L'Espagne Nouvelle*, 24 December 1937.

113. *L'Espagne Nouvelle*, 15 April 1939.

114. Voline in *Terre Libre*, 20 May 1938.

115. Voline in *Terre Libre*, 17 December 1937.

116. Ibid.

117. *L'Espagne Nouvelle*, 24 December 1937.

118. Editorial, "Pacifisme et Révolution," *Terre Libre*, May 1937. Cf. Lagrange in *le Combat Syndicaliste*, 26 November 1937: "Madeleine Vernet, like many complete pacifists: Han Ryner, Félicien Challaye, etc., moves in circles where there are only cultured people, to whom violence is inexplicable; because for all these educated people society ought to be in their image, that is everybody ought to be good, just and humane."

119. "Guerre et Révolution," *la Voix libertaire*, 24 October 1936. See also various articles by pacifists such as Pierre Ramus in the same newspaper and in *Rectitude*, "Organe des Pacifistes d'action et de la Ligue des Objecteurs de Conscience" (French section of the War Resisters' International).

120. See *Terre Libre*, 17 December 1937 and 20 May 1938.

121. *Terre Libre*, 17 December 1937.

122. *L'Espagne Nouvelle*, 24 December 1937.

123.   Jean Dupoux, in *le Combat Syndicaliste*, 17 July 1936, criticized a speaker at the UA congress of April 1936 who—according to Dupoux—had said that "you never find quality where you do not also have quantity." Dupoux's response?—"I think that quality is most often in a minority."

12

Volunteers in Spain, 1936–39

> The obscure, the nameless! They are the true heroes of
> history. We know no books they have written. Not au-
> thors, nor orators they. Yet how lifelike they tower before
> our mental eye in all the glory of their self-sacrifice, their
> noble passion and immortality. We see them, these brave
> unknown, in the thick of combat, their eyes aflame, their
> fists clenched. We hear their songs of battle, witness their
> inspiring devotion. We behold them dying, serenely joy-
> ous, the devoted martyrs of a noble cause.[1]

Jean Maitron and others have already pointed out the difficulties involved in establishing a clear picture of the contingent of French militants who went to fight alongside their Spanish comrades during the
civil war: "How many were there? How many killed? How many
wounded?"[2] Since much of the documentation relating to foreign volunteers in Spain is of communist origin, establishing the extent of anarchist intervention is particularly difficult. For anarchists there was
no nationwide recruitment organization (like the communist-organized
International Brigades) to keep records of volunteers — for in the words
of René Lochu, "those who took themselves off to Spain went off their
own bat, individually."[3] Indeed, many of those of whom some record
has survived were already on the Aragon front before any kind of support or solidarity organization — of any political persuasion — had been
established in France. Inevitably therefore, estimates of numbers have
varied — even amongst veteran militants of the anarchist movement.
Maurice Joyeux — whose own desire to volunteer was frustrated by a
prison sentence provoked by his political activities — put the number at
only about a hundred.[4] Nicolas Faucier, who was perhaps in a better
position to judge in view of his leading rôle in the UA, the Comité pour
l'Espagne Libre and SIA, suggests several hundred.[5] This estimate is
supported by a short piece by the Orléans UA group in *le Libertaire* in
May 1937, which claimed that the UA had "several hundred members"
fighting in Spain, of whom "a great number, alas," had already fallen.[6]

Some of this chapter originally appeared as "French Anarchists in Spain, 1936–1939" in
French History vol. 4, no. 4 (December 1989) pp. 427–65.

Attempting to penetrate the anonymity of the anarchist volunteers is, then, a difficult task, and beyond sparse newspaper reports or even sparser police files, and the memories of those who survived, one is reduced to estimation based on a little archival evidence and a number of tantalizing glimpses. Pierre Odéon, for instance, reported on New Year's Day 1937 that "a good and still young militia fighter" had just died fighting in the Sébastien Faure Century; but we learn nothing more about him.[7] Militants speaking at public meetings back in France were very often described as having just "returned from Spain"—but why had they been in Spain? Did they go to collect information, or to fight, or for some other purpose? It is impossible to know if no other information is forthcoming. Very often, it seems, a whole group of comrades would set off to Spain together, and yet, if we are lucky, we hear about just one of them—perhaps the group delegate, or simply the most articulate militant with most experience of public speaking or of writing articles. Thus, we know for example that Armand Aubrion left Paris on 22 July 1936 with a whole group of Parisian comrades; yet he is the only one we can name, because it was Aubrion who was asked by *le Libertaire* to send regular reports.[8] Similarly, we know that Pierre Albert, of the Narbonne group, went to Spain with "a certain number of mates," but we know neither their identities nor how large their group was.[9] Ridel wrote in October 1936 that a militant called Boudoux had been killed, along with several anonymous comrades from the same UA group in St-Denis.[10] Such examples abound.[11]

Ordinary working-class women—as opposed to well-known, bourgeois intellectuals like Simone Weil[12]—suffered a similar fate, often being reduced to the status of *compagne* of a better-known man. Georgette, for instance, who was the companion of Fernand Fortin, died serving as a nurse with the Durruti Column, but the announcement of her death does not give her surname.[13] Léa was the first name of the companion of Hoche Meurant—another leading figure in the anarchist movement—and with Meurant she was a delegate of the Union Fédérative des Comités Anarcho-Syndicalistes Franco-Belges to the French anarchist group in Puigcerdá; yet, again, we are not given her full name.[14] And even less helpfully, *le Combat Syndicaliste* tells us about the imprisonment of René Prince whilst in Spain, but neglects to tell us anything about his companion other than that she was in gaol with him.[15]

Is it therefore reasonable to assume that for every militant we can actually name, there were five or ten or twenty others who have remained anonymous? Perhaps not, but the 330 or so whom I have been able to name probably do not represent the total number.[16] By all accounts, the number of *émigré* anarchists living in France in 1936 who immediately left for the front — Spaniards, Italians, Bulgarians, Poles and others — was greater than the number of French anarchists who volunteered (although this is another area that needs more research).[17]

Of those 330 or so, about 250 were at the front (whether combatant or non-combatant — we can not normally tell); over 50 fulfilled some kind of support rôle in Spain (these are for the most part members of the French Sections in Barcelona and Puigcerdá); 10 were present in Spain as members of visiting delegations (on fact-finding or speaking tours, for instance) or as resident official representatives of French organizations (such as the FAF or CGTSR); over 20 fulfilled some kind of propaganda rôle (either through speaking tours in France after visiting Spain or, as representatives of the CNT-FAI, speaking to French members of the International Brigades); 4 were involved with security; 3 worked; and in 22 cases, we have no information as to their rôle in Spain.

There are a number of important reasons for the relatively small number of French anarchist volunteers, quite apart from the fact that the anarchist movement, despite its recent rapid growth, was of course still much smaller than either the SFIO or the PCF. Firstly, the French anarchists were locked in struggle with both the employers and the Popular Front government; and as well as being fervent supporters of the strike movement of 1936, anarchists became increasingly involved — along with their revolutionary front allies — in anti-colonial and anti-militarist campaigns in the period 1936–9.[18]

Secondly, the UA refused to become "recruiting officers" for the Spanish war, as Frémont put it, because "we felt the appropriate place for French anarchist militants to be active was in this country, ensuring solidarity."[19] In fact, as early as September 1936, the Anti-Fascist Militias Committee in Barcelona let it be known through the pages of *le Libertaire* that no additional personnel — combatant or non-combatant — was required in Spain: "Comrades should cease sending anyone to the Perpignan Committee, as they will turned away."[20] By October, the Perpignan committee was actually turning away several aspiring volunteers every day.[21] When, on 27 November (only seven days after his death), *le Libertaire* printed "Durruti's Last Letter," which contained a complaint about those foreign volunteers who came to the front, yet objected to the "self-discipline" of the Spanish militias and expected preferential treatment. Durruti asked French comrades to limit their "tourist visits," unless on a special mission; and he insisted on the value to the Spanish revolution of solidarity work in France: "There is an enormous amount of propaganda work to be done abroad and comrades who sympathize with our antifascist struggle can help us greatly; they will be just as useful as at the front, perhaps more so."[22]

THE EFFECTS OF NON-INTERVENTION

A further consideration is that after 20 February 1937, a ban on the sending of volunteers to Spain was implemented by the French government as part of the non-intervention pact, and the Prefect of the Pyrénées Orientales—previously considered relatively liberal by the local militants—responded by flooding the border area of his department with police: according to one local anarchist, the whole region resembled an occupied territory and Perpignan itself—the main transit centre for all anarchist solidarity organizations—seemed like a "town under occupation."[23] Broué and Témime have suggested that "stopping the flow of volunteers into Spain in March or April 1937, when the war had already been going on for nine months, was relatively easy as the great majority of foreigners coming to fight in Spain had already crossed the border."[24] This is true to some extent, but the implementation of such measures did make life very difficult for support organizations in France, for Spanish anti-fascists living in France (who were automatically suspect in the eyes of the authorities and subject to much harassment), and for French volunteers wishing to go home on leave and return to Spain afterwards. Spot-checks and searches of individuals and vehicles became frequent. On 3 December 1936, for instance, three anarchists were arrested trying to take a train from Toulouse to Bourg-Madame, and by April 1937 the Comité de Défense de la Révolution Espagnole in Perpignan warned that it was almost impossible to cross into Spain without a passport and visa.[25]

STALINIST COUNTER-REVOLUTIONARY REPRESSION

Anarchists of all nationalities in Spain—even foreign volunteers with the militias—increasingly suffered harassment at the hands of the communists. In August 1937, the Association des anciens miliciens libertaires (Association of libertarian militia veterans)—soon to be rebaptized the Association révolutionnaire des miliciens d'Espagne (ARME, Revolutionary association of militia fighters in Spain)—claimed that many French militia volunteers had had to leave Spain altogether, against their will, because of the ever more repressive and dictatorial activities of "the communist bourgeois."[26] Several French anarchists suffered in this way: Félix Danon, for instance, spent a year in the Carcel Modelo as a result of the Barcelona events of May 1937 (he had helped guard the Casa CNT-FAI);[27] and in another case, Thourault and Tissier, two volunteer militia fighters returning home on leave, had all their belongings confiscated at the border by a political commissar with the International Brigades—money, papers and anarchist pamphlets were taken, the latter on the grounds that they were "fascist literature." Tissier was eventually arrested.[28] My research has produced nearly 40 *prima facie* cases of French anarchists imprisoned in Spain on purely political grounds, but this remains a very under-researched area.[29]

AT THE FRONT

Within days of the armed popular uprising of 19 July, many anarchists had already crossed the border, either in the Pyrenees at Bourg-Madame/ Puigcerdá, or on the coast road at Cerbère/Port Bou; they would pass through Barcelona and, in the vast majority of cases, Lérida, and go on from there to join the CNT-FAI militias on the Aragon front. Of the 247 militia volunteers it has been possible to name, we know that 149 belonged to the Durruti Column. Of these 149, Lacroisille (also known as Marseille) also fought with the 124th *Brigada Mixta*; and Georges Longuet with the 14th International Brigade (though we do not know in which order). Apart from the Durruti Column, there were only two other significant groups of French libertarians (or French volunteers with the CNT-FAI militias): 21 with the Italian Column under Ascaso (a further two being described as belonging to the Ascaso Column) and 17 with the Ortiz Column. Apart from 7 with the Los Aguiluchos Column and 5 with the Libertad Column on the Madrid front, the rest were scattered around different units. A very small number—possibly only a handful—seem to have served with two different units, but we have no information as to why or when.

Table 4

French Volunteers with CNT-FAI Militias

Hilario Zamora Column	1
G. Oliver Column	1
Del Rosal Column (Madrid)	1
"Col. Españole"	1
Ascaso Column	2
Iron Column	2
Aviators' Column	2
Libertad Column (13th Century, 11th Group, Madrid)	5
International Brigades (11th, 13th, 14th, 15th, 35th)	5
Los Aguiluchos Column	7
Ortiz Column	17
Italian Column (Ascaso Column)	21
Durruti Column	149

Sources: Berry, "French Anarchists in Spain"; "Liste des miliciens français" (n.d.—September/October 1936?), TS., 4pp. and Sección Francesa de Propaganda CNT-FAI, "Lista de Franceses Llegados a España Despues Del 19 de Julio 1936 (Entregada el 18 de Octubre de 1938)," TS., 9pp., FAI "Propaganda Exterior"—Archive, IISG.

So it was to the Durruti Column, and therefore to the sector of the front facing Saragossa, that the majority of French anarchists gravitated: Durruti was well known and much loved in France, and indeed, as we have seen, owed his freedom to the efforts of his French comrades. The column had its headquarters at Bujaraloz, to the north of the Ebro, and its International Group—or Brigade—operated on the sector of the front from the Ebro north to Tardienta—though they were also involved in the attack on Teruel in January 1938.[30] The International Group—"known for its activity and for its true heroism," according to *le Libertaire*[31]—consisted of French, Swiss, Italian, German, Bulgarian and, strangely enough, even some Spanish militants (perhaps those who had lived in exile in France for so long they were more familiar with their French comrades?[32]). A photograph of the French section taken in August 1936 shows a group of twenty-five men, two women and two small boys.[33] Carpentier and Ridel confirm this number in one of their many letters to *le Libertaire* from the front.[34] In the next two months, though, the number of French volunteers doubled to about fifty; among them was a group of about a dozen members of the CGTSR, who made their own banner in black and red, bearing the names of their organizations: "CGTSR-FAF-AIT."[35]

By September 1936, and on the initiative of *le Libertaire*, a Sébastien Faure Century had been founded, which seems to have united French and Italian volunteers within the International Group; the Century had its own independent internal organization, and even a mascot, a dog.[36] According to Georges Sossenko, who as a teenage student in Paris had run away from home and joined the militia under an assumed name (Georges Jorat), the Century was about 100 strong when it left Caspe for the front at Azaile in October 1936.[37] The French appear to have played a leading rôle: Georges Monnard and Jean Martin were both delegates of the Sébastien Faure Century at different times, and Louis Berthoumier was the "general delegate" of the International Group as a whole. He was succeeded after his death in combat by Saïl Mohamed of the Aulnay-sous-Bois UA group.[38]

But as has already been made clear, those fulfilling a support rôle in the effort to defeat Franco were considered no less important than those engaged directly in the fighting. As the ARME put it: "They departed to become combattants in Spain, carried along by their enthusiasm, their temperament and their idealism ... Other militants have accomplished revolutionary tasks in staying at their posts here in France."[39]

IN THE REAR: PUIGCERDÁ

There were two groups of anarchists who were involved in various non-military tasks within Spain, and all the French libertarians coming and going would have been in contact with them at one time or another.

The Section Française, or French-language anarchist group, in Puigcerdá—just over the border from Bourg-Madame, and one of the main crossing points—was constituted in November 1936 with the FAI's agreement, in order to strengthen the liaison between Barcelona and French libertarian organizations. The group's delegate was Albert Perrier (or Périer?), a 39-year-old labourer from Périgueux and secretary of the local CGT Building-workers' Union, and included the veteran Toulouse militant Alphonse Tricheux.[40] Initially the group seems to have fulfilled a propaganda rôle only, selling French translations of CNT-FAI booklets, postcard-sized photographs of Francisco Ascaso and red-and-black scarves of the type worn by the confederal militias.[41] But in February 1937 the group was reorganized and integrated into the border-control structure of the CNT-FAI, with special responsibility for keeping a check on all French libertarians crossing the border at that point—as well as giving them information and guidance.[42]

Alphonse Tricheux had not gone to Puigcerdá alone: his wife, Pauline, or Paule, had also joined the French Section, though her primary involvement was with a Groupe d'action culturelle et d'éducation des femmes libertaires à Puigcerdá, a group consisting mainly of Spanish women, which existed early in 1937.[43] As well as being in charge of propaganda for this women's group, she also played a leading rôle in the Comité Pro-Refugiados de Puigcerdá, and all three of these Puigcerdá groups were last reported as sharing the job of looking after 300 refugee women and children from Malaga, who arrived in the area just after the nationalist offensive of February 1937.[44] It is to be presumed that most of the anarchists in the area, French and Spanish, either fled, or were killed or arrested, at the time of the government offensive against anarchist control of the border around April 1937.[45]

IN THE REAR: BARCELONA

There was another, more important group, which had been established several months earlier, but that collapsed at about the same time as the Puigcerdá group. This was the Section Française (CNT-FAI) de Barcelona, which was set up in July 1936, and was at first housed in the Casa CNT-FAI.[46] There also existed three other groups, all of which seem to have overlapped considerably with each other and with the Section Française: a group of French-speaking CNT members, one of French-speaking FAI members, and one of members of the CGTSR resident in Barcelona.[47] The Section Française was also represented by three of its members on an International Anarchist Committee.[48] We are now able to identify 24 members of the Barcelona French Section, of whom 9 seem to have formed a core group which effectively ran the Section, and to whom can be added René, the Section's driver.[49] The number of people attending the weekly meetings of the French Section varied, as anyone passing through was welcome—militia members convalescing or on leave from the front, visiting delegations, and so on. Significantly, the group was also often visited by "foreign militia fighters, ex-communists and ex-socialists who had become anarchists."[50]

However, although the Section Française had been set up by the CNT Regional Committee and was used by it as a propaganda department, the subsidy of 12 pesetas per day at first provided by the CNT was discontinued in November 1936. What the French Section at first believed to be an administrative oversight clearly was not; the result was that the French complained continually of the lack of interest and support from the CNT, and for the rest of its existence the group did not enjoy good financial health, being dependent on the sale of newspapers and membership cards, and on donations from comrades.[51]

The function of the French Section was twofold: firstly, to organize French-language propaganda for the CNT-FAI, and, in the process, to strengthen links with French anarchist and syndicalist organizations; secondly, to act as a centre in Barcelona for French-speaking libertarians of all tendencies. The French edition of the CNT-FAI's *Boletín de Información*, published by the French Section, was used in France as a primary source of propaganda for the CNT-FAI.[52] The bulletin—typewritten and mimeographed—appeared at intervals of between three days and a fortnight from November 1936 to July 1937, and consisted predominantly of excerpts from the official CNT-FAI press, excerpts that were then reused by the French libertarian press. Not surprisingly in view of the genesis of the group and the bulletin, both were uncritical of the CNT-FAI leadership.

In its rôle as a propagandist and link between France and Spain, the French Section was also involved in other ventures. In November 1936 it established a Commission of Inquiry made up of three suitably qualified French comrades, to investigate two questions of paramount importance to French anarchists. Firstly, there was the armaments position of the Aragonese militias, because this was where most French volunteers fought and, even at this early stage, it was being claimed that arms and ammunition were being deliberately withheld by central government—under communist influence—for political reasons. Secondly, there was concern to establish the truth about the collectivized factories of Barcelona: clearly of interest to the international anarchist movement as the first significant experiment in libertarian industrial organization.[53] Public meetings were also organized with guest speakers from France. In December 1936, for instance, one such was organized on behalf of the Catalan CNT, with Aristide Lapeyre and Pierre Besnard, Gaston Leval (a Frenchman resident in Spain and involved with the CNT) and the CNT representative Bernardo Pou.[54]

At a more routine level, it was the French Section that welcomed and looked after French volunteers on their way to the front, but also Spanish anarchists who now returned home to fight after many years' exile in France. These Spanish comrades would be directed to their respective union headquarters. The French were given information and advice and money for food and transport if required; there was always a delegate on duty at the Bakunin and later the Spartacus Barracks, where French volunteers were sent to register and be armed. The group established its own library with books sent by the Comité pour l'Espagne Libre, and arranged the delivery of mail to and from French anarchists in Spain. Morale-boosting tours of the front and of the hospitals in the rear were undertaken by several members, and the group also liaised between French militants — whatever their political affiliation — in Spanish prisons and the CNT's legal commission.[55]

And yet, despite continual reaffirmation by the French Section of its desire to unite all the different tendencies within the libertarian movement, the same political tensions that destroyed anarchist unity in France by the autumn of 1936 had the same effect in Barcelona. The source of the tensions was a series of confrontations between the group and Jean Dupoux, an official delegate of the FAF in Barcelona.[56] A first clash at a meeting on 2 January 1937 resulted in an almost unanimous vote criticizing the CGTSR's "tendency to provoke disunity," and reaffirming the group's confidence in Fernand Fortin.[57] Very soon afterwards, a dispute arose over access to the CNT's radio transmitter in Barcelona. Augustin Souchy — co-ordinator of external propaganda for the CNT — had to be called in to mediate, and it was decided that French-language broadcasts should be divided equally between the representatives of what the French Section called, on the one hand, "anarcho-syndicalism" and, on the other, "anarchism."[58] At a meeting on 6 February, there was a further serious argument, this time between Styr-Nhair and Dupoux. The trigger was a letter from Besnard, on behalf of the CASDLPE, claiming certain rights over the French Section and in particular over its bulletin. After Dupoux had left the meeting, a motion condemning the CGTSR's attempts at "appropriation" was passed unanimously.[59] Eventually, a final accusation was made against Dupoux — namely, that having been delegated to the International Anarchist Committee, he had usurped the rights of the French Section "in order to intervene in favour of his friends" — and a vote was taken removing him from all positions of responsibility.[60]

Thus, solidarity work in Spain was hampered by the same political dissensions that had produced similar counter-productive results in France. The conflict seems to have been one between, on the one hand, the French Section and the Regional Committee of the CNT, and, on the other, the FAF and CGTSR who were critical of the CNT's "ministerialism." It is certainly true that Fortin was attacked by some French anarchists as a "traitor" and a "sell-out," because of his unquestioning work as propagandist for official CNT policies.[61] But two months after Fortin had abstained in the vote to remove Dupoux from all official positions, he was himself expelled because of an article he had written for the bulletin.[62] The article was said to be "anti-anarchist," "anti-revolutionary" and full of "insinuations" about other French comrades in Spain: Fortin "was always anti-syndicalist and an enemy of the revolutionary anarchist movement in France," according to Schlauder and Lobel.[63] Very soon afterwards, though it remains unclear why, how or by whom, the French Section was dissolved. Pierre Besnard, writing in *le Combat Syndicaliste*, regretted the disappearance of the group, "whose mission has not been accomplished and whose existence is more necessary than ever"[64] —a reference, no doubt, to the events of May 1937 and the stalinists' increasingly bold and violent attempts to counter anarchist influence in Spain. While Besnard, perhaps surprisingly, demanded a review of Fortin's expulsion, those involved with the FAF sided with the other members of the French Section against Fortin and against the CNT-FAI leadership. *L'Espagne Nouvelle* pointed out that Fortin—along with Juan Garciá Oliver, Federica Montseny, Mariano Vazquez Ramon and Jaqinto Toryho—had been instrumental in persuading CNT-FAI and POUM supporters in Barcelona to lay down their arms in May 1937.[65] *Terre Libre* further accused Fortin and Souchy of censoring correspondence between individual anarchists and their organizations.[66] Ultimately, André Prudhommeaux concluded that the dissolution of the French Section was a dictatorial act of censorship on the part of the Catalan CNT against the ordinary members of the group, "for having acted in a non-conformist way against the iron rule of its secretary: F. Fortin."[67]

Notes

1. *Mother Earth*, March 1908.

2. *DBMOF*, vol.16, p.448.

3. Letter to the author.

4. In conversation with the author. Joyeux also claimed that the majority of French anarchists who fought in Spain were either anarcho-syndicalists, or those who had come to anarchism *via* communism.

5. Letter to the author.

6. *Le Libertaire*, 27 May 1937. The article was a reply to attacks on the UA in the local communist newspaper *Le Travailleur*.

7. *Le Libertaire*, 1 January 1937.

8. Aubrion and his comrades joined the Hilario Esteban Column (part of the Ortiz Column), and were based at Sastago in the old Guardia Civil barracks—the outside of the building apparently bore the legend *"Vive l'Union Anarchiste Française!"* Having agreed to send back reports to *le Libertaire*, he wrote several articles on life at the front and on the debate over "militarization" of the popular militias ("Discipline? We have none. Our enthusiasm is quite enough to replace it," he wrote in September 1936). He took part in the battles of Zaïda and Belchite, and his last letter from the front appeared in November

1936. The following August, back in Paris, he became a member of the provisional committee of the newly formed Comité des anciens miliciens d'Espagne and, at the constitutive assembly of ARME in April 1939, he was elected to the secretariat. *Le Libertaire*, 25 September, 2 October, 16 October, 27 November 1936, 5 August 1937; *la Nouvelle Espagne Antifasciste*, 5 May 1938.

9.   *Le Libertaire*, 31 July 1936.

10.   *Le Libertaire*, 23 October 1936.

11.   For further details regarding some of the volunteers, see the appendices to D. Berry, "French Anarchists in Spain, 1936–1939" in *French History* vol.3, no.4 (December 1989), pp.427–65, and to my "Contribution to a Collective Biography of the French Anarchist Movement: French Anarchist Volunteers in Spain, 1936–39," paper presented to a conference on the International Brigades, University of Lausanne, 1997, on the *Research on Anarchism* web site (http://raforum.info/?lang=en).

12.   Simone Weil (1900–43) contributed to *la Révolution prolétarienne* and to a lesser extent to *le Libertaire* during the 1930s. She joined the Durruti Column in August 1936, and wore the usual boiler-suit, forage cap, espadrilles and red and black neckerchief. Despite her poor eyesight and her inexperience with weapons, she took part in one reconnaissance operation behind nationalist lines, but thereafter was put on kitchen duty. After her return to Paris, she appeared at public meetings, always wearing her forage cap. She was appalled by the violence she witnessed on both sides in the Spanish war, and the experience contributed to her conversion to catholicism. Jean Rabaut, *Tout est possible! Les "gauchistes" français 1929–1944* (Paris: Denoël/Gonthier, 1974), p.609, note 2; Nicolas Faucier, letter to the author; Simone Weil, *Journal d'Espagne* in *Ecrits historiques et politiques* (Paris: Gallimard, 1960), pp.209–16; Phil Casoar, "Louis Mercier, Simone Weil: Retour sur une controverse," in David Berry, Amedeo Bertolo, Sylvain Boulouque, Phil Casoar, Marianne Enckell and Charles Jacquier, *Présence de Louis Mercier* (Lyon: Atelier de création libertaire, 1999), pp.21–36; for a photo of Weil with the Durruti Column, see Abel Paz, *Durruti: The People Armed* (New York: Free Life Editions/Black Rose Books, 1977), p.252.

13.   Her full name was, in fact, Georgette Kokoczinski and she was a nurse with the International Group of the Durruti Column: she is described by Paz as having been a "sort of mascot of the Column." Having taken part in many surprise attacks on the enemy rear-guard with the "Sons of the Night" (Hijos de la Noche), she was finally shot and killed during an attack on Perdiguerra, 17 October 1936. An anarchist since the age of 15, she had previously been the partner of Fernand Fortin, and was well known in the circles around *le Libertaire*, *l'Insurgé*, *l'en dehors* and especially *la Revue anarchiste*, of which she had been a regular seller. She had performed at anarchist galas under the name Mimosa. *L'Espagne Antifasciste (CNT-FAI-AIT)*, 18 November 1936; *le Combat syndicaliste*, 20 November 1936; Paz, *Durruti*, p.277.

14.   Léa was from Wattrelos in the north. *Le Combat syndicaliste*, 5, 12 and 19 February 1937.

15.   Prince was the pseudonym of Georges Marcel Desbois, born in Montluçon in 1902, living in Marseille in July 1936. A member of both the FAF and the CGTSR, he was delegated to represent the FAF in Barcelona, and was a member of the French Section there. He was suspected by the French police of having been involved in the theft of machine guns and small arms from the Saumur Cavalry School in February 1937. *Boletín de información*, 6 and 13 January 1937; *le Combat syndicaliste*, 25 December 1936 and 23 July 1937; F7/14677.

16.   It should be noted that my "Contribution to a Collective Biography of the French Anarchist Movement" lists French men and women who were either clearly a part of the

libertarian movement, or of whom we know only that they chose to join CNT-FAI militias. In the latter case, those concerned may well have been united only by their anti-stalin-ism — see Clara and Pavel Thalmann, *Combats pour la liberté* (Paris: Spartacus/la Digitale, 1983), p.175.

17.   For example, the accounts of the "Comité anarchico-italiano pro-Ispagna," repro-duced in *le Libertaire*, 6 November 1936, state that 152 Italian volunteers had departed — of whom 12 had been killed and 13 wounded — and that 53 volunteers' families in the Paris area, and 14 in the provinces, were receiving assistance from the committee. In July 1936 *le Libertaire* reported that many Spanish anarchists on their way home to fight were still leaving their families in France, and asking their French comrades in the UA to help their dependents. A special appeal for 10,000 francs in two weeks was launched: *le Libertaire*, 31 July 1936. According to Skirda, there were even two ex-Makhnovites who fought and died in Spain: Alexandre Skirda, *Nestor Makhno, le cosaque de l'anarchie: la lutte pour les Soviets libres en Ukraine, 1917–1921* (Paris: A. Skirda, 1982), p. 335. I have found evidence of only one: Alexandre Staradolz, who was killed near Saragossa in 1936: *le Libertaire*, 23 October 1936 and 15 July 1937.

18.   From 1937 onwards, when *le Libertaire* and *SIA* were banned or confiscated and their collaborators prosecuted, it was because of their campaign against the coming war and, to a lesser extent, their anti-colonialism.

19.   *Le Libertaire*, 26 January 1939.

20.   *Le Libertaire*, 18 September 1936; a similar notice had already appeared on the 4th.

21.   *Le Combat Syndicaliste*, 2 October 1936.

22.   *Le Libertaire*, 27 November 1936.

23.   *Le Libertaire*, 25 March 1937.

24.   Pierre Broué and Emile Témime, *La révolution et la guerre d'Espagne* (Paris: Minuit 1961), p.314.

25.   *Le Libertaire*, 8 and 22 April 1937.

26.   *Le Libertaire*, 19 August 1937.

27.   Danon was the librarian-archivist of the French Section and an active member of the CNT and of the FAI. He seems to have been arrested by the NKVD and held in the Carcel Modelo without any form of trial until June 1938. Whilst there, he was the rep-resentative of other French prisoners. His correspondence and "Rapport confidentiel sur tous les étrangers de langue française détenus à la première galerie de la Carcel Modelo" (6 August 1937), MS., 2pp., preserved in the FAI "Propaganda exterior" archive, IISG, are a good source of information on the political repression of non-stalinist revolutionaries in Spain.

28.   *Le Libertaire*, 24 June 1937.

29.   See "Victims of political repression?," Appendix 6 to my "Contribution to a Collec-tive Biography of the French Anarchist Movement."

30.   See Paz, *Durruti*, for the most detailed study of the Durruti Column; also Phil Ca-soar, "Avec la colonne Durruti: Ridel dans la révoltion espagnole," in *Présence de Louis Mercier*, pp.13–20. The words "group," "century," "column," "brigade," etc., varied in their precise meaning even in official usage, and some were used almost interchangeably by ordinary militants. Attempting to establish the exact composition of the confederal militias is therefore not always easy.

31.   *Le Libertaire*, 25 September 1936. Saïl Mohammed also referred to the International Group as "the elite of the Durruti Column," in *le Combat Syndicaliste*, 23 October 1936.

32.   Juan Mayol, who signed Jean Mayol in letters to *le Libertaire*, would be a case in point. A Catalan anarchist responsible for the assassination of Barcelona's chief of police in 1931, he fled to France where he remained until July 1936, then, accompanied by Frenchman Georges Sossenko, he joined the Durruti Column's International Group and ultimately the Sébastien Faure Century. Information supplied by G. Sossenko, correspondence with the author; see also *le Libertaire*, 22 July and 18 November 1937.

33.   Reproduced in Paz, *Durruti*, p.236. Only the men in the picture are armed. Paz also reproduces a photograph taken in Bujaraloz in September 1936 showing Durruti, Sébastien Faure, Sol and Mora Ferrer (daughter and granddaughter of Francisco, both active in the French movement), and members of the International Group. This same photograph appears in Nicolas Faucier, *Pacifisme et Antimilitarisme dans l'entre-deux-guerres (1919–1959)* (Paris: Spartacus, 1983), p.139. See also a photograph of the Centurie Sébastien Faure on its arrival at Caspe, posing by a lorry of the French SIA, in *le Libertaire*, 13 November 1936. The lorry bears the slogan *"Vive la FAI—Paris—Aragon!"* Unfortunately, it has as yet proved impossible to identify any other individuals in these photographs.

34.   *Le Libertaire*, 18 September 1936. Charles Carpentier and Charles Ridel joined the Durruti Column as soon as possible after the insurrection, and sent back regular reports to *le Libertaire*. On their return to France, they toured the country giving talks on the Spanish situation and showing propaganda films produced by the CNT-FAI. On Ridel (aka Louis Mercier-Vega), see Casoar, "Avec la colonne Durruti."

35.   *Le Libertaire*, 25 September 1936 and *le Combat Syndicaliste*, 23 October 1936.

36.   Ridel and Carpentier reported in a letter in *le Libertaire*, 21 August 1936, that the French and Italians had united to form a group, although the column also contained several other nationalities; and we know that R.-A. Neveu and G. Monnard belonged to what was called "the first century of the International Group." See also *l'Espagne Nouvelle*, 24 December 1937 and *le Libertaire*, 25 September 1936. After militarization in 1937, the century became the 3rd Battallion, 121st Brigade, 26th Division, but the French anarchists continued to refer to it as "the old Sébastien Faure Century."

37.   Correspondence with the author.

38.   Monnard would be killed at Quinto. *Boletín de información*, 18 December 1937. On Martin, see *le Libertaire*, 1 January, 22 July and 18 November 1937. Berthoumier was a captain of artillery in the Great War, and had been living in Spain for several years when the revolution broke out. He was among those killed when they were surrounded by nationalists at Perdiguerra on 17 October 1936 (only 70 out of 240 escaped). S. Weil gives the impression that he struggled constantly to instil some military sense into many members of the group, and he was also responsible on more than one occasion for preventing the summary execution of prisoners and of suspected nationalist sympathizers. As for politics, Ridel wrote: "He would have nothing to do with questions of tendencies, claiming that he did not understand any of it." *Le Libertaire*, 23 October 1936; *le Combat syndicaliste*, 20 November 1936; *Terre libre*, 25 February 1938; Letter to the author from Charles Carpentier; Weil, *Journal d'Espagne*; Jacques Delperrie de Bayac, *Les Brigades Internationales* (Paris: Fayard, 1968), pp.63–4. Mohamed was one of the first to join the Durruti Column, and was one of a dozen CGTSR members there. Wounded and hospitalized in November 1936, he had returned to Aulnay by January 1937. He was later involved in a bitter dispute with some FAF members who allegedly passed on a rumour started by non-anarchists that he had wounded himself deliberately. *Le Combat syndicaliste*, 23 October and 4 December 1936; *le Libertaire*, 27 November 1937; *SIA*, 22 December 1938; *L'Espagne antifasciste (CNT-FAI-AIT)*, 4 November 1936, contains a photo of Mohamed at Farlete.

See also Sylvain Boulouque, "Saïl Mohamed, un anarchiste en France," in *Migrances* no. 3 (1er semestre 1994), pp. 14–18.

39. *SIA*, 1 December 1938.

40. *Le Combat Syndicaliste*, 4 December 1936. Périer went to Puigcerdá and seems not to have left until 1939. For more information about the remarkable Tricheux family—five of whose members, from two generations, were anarchist militants—see the no less remarkable dossier on the Toulouse anarchist group compiled by the police between 1926 and 1932, in F7/13059. Alphonse, Pauline and two of their children (Marius and Noëla) would all be among those arrested during the clampdown on revolutionaries after May 1937.

41. *Le Libertaire*, 26 February 1937.

42. *Le Combat Syndicaliste*, 26 February 1937.

43. *Le Libertaire*, 4 March 1937.

44. See *le Libertaire*, 22 April 1937 and *le Combat Syndicaliste*, 12 and 19 March 1937.

45. It was at this time that Antonio Martin, anarchist president of the revolutionary committee of Puigcerdá, was killed in a clash with Assault Guards. See Burnett Bolloten, *La Révolution espagnole. La gauche et la lutte pour le pouvoir* (Paris: Ruedo ibérico, 1977); Broué and Témime, *La Révolution et la guerre d'Espagne* and J.-L. Blanchon, "1936–1937: Une expérience libertaire en Cerdagne" (Mémoire de Maîtrise, Toulouse, 1986), for a fuller account of these incidents.

46. *L'Espagne Antifasciste (CNT-FAI-AIT)*, 14 November 1936. The Casa CNT-FAI was in the Via Layetana, later renamed Avenida B. Durruti. In late November 1936, the Section Française had to find its own premises and moved to the Calle Consejo de Ciento.

47. Fernand Fortin in *Boletín de Información. Edition en langue française*, 9 January 1937. Many French militants who stayed in Spain for any length of time became CNT and/or FAI members.

48. *Boletín de Información. Edition en langue française*, 13 March 1937. This may have been the committee that was established under the Belgian, Hem Day (Marcel Dieu), to organize an international anarchist conference in Spain. That committee, which had a first preparatory meeting on 19 October 1936, was made up of anarchist "celebrities": Sébastien Faure, Louis Bertoni, Diego Abad de Santillan and Emma Goldman (who was involved with the British section of SLA). *L'Espagne Antifasciste (CNT-FAI-AIT)*, 24 October 1936. Roger Pantais was one of the delegates to meetings of this committee—letter to the author.

49. The committee consisted of Marcel Schlauder (secretary), Fernand Fortin (propaganda delegate), Roger Pantais and Chatris (joint treasurers) and Roger François (barracks duty delegate). In March 1937, Alfred Lobel was elected assistant secretary, Styr-Nhair treasurer, Félix Danon archivist-librarian and Chauvet barracks duty delegate. *Le Libertaire*, 18 December 1936, and *Boletín de Información*, 13 March 1937. Schlauder was, according to G. Sossenko who knew him well, a pseudonym adopted in order to avoid military service; later imprisoned in France, he would be released and mobilized in September 1939, then taken prisoner by the German army—correspondence with the author. For a list of other members, see Appendix 5 to my "Contribution to a Collective Biography of the French Anarchist Movement."

50. *Le Libertaire*, 29 April 1937.

51. Membership cards cost 1 franc. Despite the loss of the subsidy, however, the group had a turnover of nearly 2,000 francs between October 1936 and February 1937. See *l'Espagne Antifasciste (CNT-FAI-AIT)*, 14 November 1936; *le Libertaire*, 18 February 1937; and *Boletín de Información*, 13 March 1937.

52. The paper's full title was *Boletín de Información. (Informes y noticias facilitadas por la Confederación Nacional del Trabajo y la Federación Anarquista Iberica)*. The paper was normally referred to by the French as the *Bulletin d'information*, and should not be confused with the bilingual *Bulletin d'information du Comité de Défense de la Révolution Espagnol Antifasciste* published by the anarchists in Perpignan.

53. *Boletín de Información*, 30 November 1936.

54. *Boletín de Información*, 18 December 1936.

55. On the day-to-day activities of the French Section, see *Boletín de Información*, 18 and 25 December 1936, 6 January, 13 February, 3 July 1937; *le Libertaire*, 18 December 1936, 12 May 1937; *l'Espagne Antifasciste (CNT-FAI-AIT)*, 14 November 1936.

56. *Le Combat Syndicaliste*, 29 January 1937. According to an account of the first meeting of the Commission Administrative of the FAF, published in *le Combat Syndicaliste*, 25 December 1936, René Prince was also delegated to represent the FAF in Barcelona. Dupoux was often erroneously referred to as the representative of the CGTSR. In fact, the official CGTSR and AIT delegate was Alexandre Mirande: *le Combat Syndicaliste*, 30 October and 4 December 1936.

57. *Boletín de Información*, 6 January 1937. It is not made clear how or why Fortin specifically was involved, though it may have been because of the control he had over the contents of the bulletin in his capacity as "propaganda delegate": the FAF would have wanted the bulletin to be more critical of CNT policy.

58. *Boletín de Información*, 9 January 1937. Augustin Souchy, the prominent German anarchist and syndicalist, had arrived in Barcelona on 10 July 1936, and remained in Spain until the fall of Catalonia. See his autobiography, *"Vorsicht: Anarchist!" Ein Leben für die Freiheit (Politische Erinnerungen)* (Reutlingen: Trotzdem Verlag, 1982), pp. 103–23.

59. *Boletín de Información*, 13 February 1937.

60. *Boletín de Información*, 27 February 1937. The accuser this time was Schlauder. There were three abstentions: Félix Danon, Fernand Fortin, Henry.

61. See Fortin's letter to *le Libertaire*, 7 April 1938.

62. He was expelled at a meeting on 17 April 1937, the same day the article in question appeared in the bulletin. Unfortunately, it has not been possible to trace a copy of that issue, so the causes of the split remain somewhat obscure.

63. *Le Combat Syndicaliste*, 7 May 1937.

64. *Le Combat Syndicaliste*, 4 June 1937.

65. *L'Espagne Nouvelle*, 17 July 1937.

66. *Terre Libre*, August 1937.

67. *L'Espagne Nouvelle*, 12 June 1937. If this is true, it seems odd that on previous occasions the FAF representative was so heavily censured by the French Section as a whole. On the other hand, as "propaganda delegate," Fortin probably had control over the bulletin, and so the published accounts of the dispute may well not be entirely reliable.

13

Antimilitarism, Resistance
and Collaboration

> How could we *not* be disoriented? And who could we
> trust?
>
> *Fred Zeller*[1]

In the prologue to his "novel," *La Mémoire des vaincus* (The Memory of the
Vanquished), Michel Ragon introduces the person whose life-story the
book is to recount. In fact, the character in question is not an individual; he
stands for Anarchism: "He was not very old, but seemed much older than
his years. I mean, he had lived through so much, he had experienced so
many adventures, he had known so many famous, even legendary people,
he had himself played such a rôle in History, that he seemed untouched
by time."[2] And yet, Ragon goes on, in those grey post-war years, nobody
was interested: "Time—the new times of the post-war era—rejected him.
Imprisoned from 1939 to 1945, and having therefore played no rôle in the
Resistance or in the Collaboration, or indeed in the scramble for vacant
posts at the Liberation, he now appeared utterly anachronistic."
    It is striking that in a quasi-historical account of over 400 pages,
which is clearly intended to reaffirm the memory of a revolutionary movement and reassert its timeless relevance, a veil of silence is pulled over a
period as important as 1939–45, and over that period only. It is a conve-
niently unambiguous veil: the hero was locked away in the Gurs concentration camp in south-western France because of his antimilitarism and
lived there among "the just, the innocent, the pure."[3] This fits with the
most common representation of the French anarchists' reaction to the Occupation and Vichy: a fragmented, disoriented and despairing majority reduced to *"attentisme"* (wait-and-see passivity) and playing no active rôle of
any kind; a small minority imprisoned more or less for the duration of the
war because of their attempts to prevent it or their wish to bear witness
against it; a minority of *"résistants"*; and an even smaller minority of collaborators. Maurice Joyeux—a Parisian locksmith and determined war-

A version of this chapter was originally published as "The French Anarchist Movement,
1939–1945: Resistance and Collaboration" in Andreas Graf (ed.), *Anarchisten gegen Hitler*
(Berlin: Lukas Verlag, 2001, pp. 29–55).

resister who was to play a leading rôle in the anarchist movement after the Liberation—summarised the situation in typically virile fashion, insisting that *"on n'était pas beaucoup à bander!"* which, loosely translated, means that not many of the French anarchists responded vigorously enough.[4] In fact, however, there seems to be little available research on which to base such an assertion, and a published version of this interpretation in which Joyeux makes similar claims has been seriously questioned on factual grounds by other anarchists who had been involved in Resistance activities.[5] The neglect of this period of the history of the French anarchist movement is quite astonishing: while work has been done on the interwar years and on the postwar years (beginning with the reconstruction of the movement from 1944), historians of anarchism—and, oddly, anarchists themselves, despite their typically French passion for their own historical roots—have paid little attention to the war years themselves.[6]

THE COMING WAR AND THE DISINTEGRATION OF THE ANARCHIST MOVEMENT, 1938–39

We have already noted that after the hopeful days of 1936–37, it was in the spring of 1938 that the UA began to complain of growing apathy and widespread pessimism: for Marceau Pivert, 1938 was "the greyest of years." As well as the defeat of the revolutionary forces in Spain, the *"Anschluß"* of Austria in March 1938 also heightened fears of another world war, and SIA and the UA began to concentrate more on this than on events in Spain.

The French anarchists' reaction to the *Anschluß* was that "in the present unleashing of expansionist appetites—some of which have been satisfied, others not—German imperialism is doing no more nor less than playing its rôle. …. In which case, it is hardly of importance whether the imperialism concerned is adorned with the swastika or not."[7] Hitler was seen by the anarchists as "the child of Versailles" and Austria as an absurd statelet born of the chaos of the first imperialist world war. The *Anschluß* did not concern the French working class, and the danger for the anarchists was that it would be used to "push people towards total acceptance of the idea of antifascist war."[8] The problem of Czechoslovakia was similarly regarded as "an imperialist conflict for which the international working class will pay the cost."[9]

Munich does not seem to have elicited an entirely unequivocal response from anarchists. For Lashortes, a member of the editorial committee of *le Libertaire*, "the Munich compromise is better than war. No one is happier than we are that war has been avoided." On the other hand, it was to be seen as "a respite to be utilized."[10] Others refused outright "to

applaud the work of Chamberlain and Daladier," and Doutreau, a leading member of the UA, organized a public meeting tour on the theme:
"Their war is not our war. Their peace is not our peace."[11] For the UA,
"The only just war the workers can make is the social war, class war";[12]
and the only alternative to fascism and war was revolution.[13]

April 1938 saw the collapse in France of the last Popular Front
government and the installation of a government led by Daladier. This
marked the beginning of a new repressiveness at home, with raids on
premises, the prosecution of anarchist and SIA activists, the banning of
public meetings and the seizing of newspapers. When the police started
summoning activists for questioning—even some who were no longer
active—from the summer of 1938, it was interpreted as an updating of
the infamous "Carnet B," the list of militants considered a danger to
the state in time of war or other emergency. This repression became
gradually worse and seriously hampered the anarchists' activities. In
the latter half of 1938, the UA and SIA were preoccupied with the anti-
war campaign and with the defence of the right to political asylum, under attack from a decree of the Daladier government—"accomplice of
the fascist executioners," according to the UA.[14] From early in 1939,
SIA was faced with a new problem: refugees crossing into France from
Spain. Suffering from police harassment, increasing pessimism among
its own supporters in France, and consequently from severe financial
problems, SIA and the UA nevertheless did what they could to help
evacuate non-combatants from Spain and guide the refugees as they
crossed over into France.

A public meeting about the refugee problem, which took place in
Paris on 30 June 1939, however, attracted only around 1,500 people.[15]
This last effort combined with the campaigns against the war and in
defence of the right to asylum, accompanied by government repression,
was the last straw. SIA, a month later, admitted it was finished: "For
some time now, we have had the impression that we have been talking to
ourselves. The situation appears to be the same in all left and extreme-
left circles. The masses and even activists seem not to care about anything any longer."[16] In the months leading up to the declaration of war
on 3 September 1939, anarchists and their organizations were under
continuous attack from the state, and morale had plummeted. A survey
conducted by *le Libertaire* in April showed that the majority of UA members still refused to support the war effort, but neither did they see any
revolutionary potential in the imminent outbreak of war: "This is what
generally distances our comrades from the theory of the transformation
of the imperialist war into civil war."[17] As André Prudhommeaux of the
FAF put it:

Armed revolutionary struggle on a world scale is out of the question in the present situation and given the parlous state of our forces. The retreat has been too generalized since July 1936 for us to have any chance of fighting effectively for our cause, and while we still have so many wounds to heal and are still suffering from so many losses. As for getting ourselves killed for capitalism, too many of our comrades have already fallen in Spain and elsewhere.[18]

At the UA's Paris Region Federation congress in March 1939, the position put forward by René Frémont was adopted: "In the event of war, comrades should first of all save their lives in order to be able to create a clandestine organization which will allow them to remain in contact, even if all propaganda is impossible; in this way, when the moment comes, they will be able to act cohesively and rationally."[19]

A last desperate attempt to avert war—or at least to bear witness against it—was the distribution by Louis Lecoin and Nicolas Faucier of the famous tract, "Paix immédiate!," ten days after mobilization.[20] But as Faucier himself concedes, this was in practical terms completely ineffective.[21] For Daniel Guérin and Georges Fontenis, it was a naïve appeal to the goodwill of governments, which ignored such questions as class struggle, fascism or imperialism; it was a final spectacular example of the "pacifist phraseology and illusions" which caused so much confusion and ambiguity in these years, and that would even lead some to convince themselves that Vichy and Hitler's Germany could be forces for peace in Europe.[22] The seeming resignation of some anarchists-turned-pacifists (such as Lecoin or Pierre Le Meillour) when faced with the armistice, nazi occupation and Vichy has also seemed questionable to some anarchists in the post-war years.[23] Both Lecoin and Faucier had already been condemned to two years imprisonment and a fine of 1,000 francs for having published antimilitarist articles in *SIA*. Lecoin would eventually be released from gaol only in 1941; Faucier—having been sentenced to a further three years for refusal to join his unit—had to go underground for the remainder of the war after escaping from the prison camp at Neuville (Vienne) in 1943.

THE "*DÉBÂCLE*": CHAOS AND REPRESSION

The picture painted by Maitron is of a movement in utter disarray, which, even as late as 1941–42, managed to organize only walks in the country.[24] It certainly seems to be the case that the anarchist organizations, which, as we have seen, had been seriously weakened by 1939, had no concrete strategy and were not practically prepared for dealing with war or occupation and simply disappeared, as did their newspapers.[25] The clandestine organization proposed by the UA's Paris Federation in 1939 seems to have been built only during 1943–44 — albeit after three years' difficult and dangerous preparatory work. Up until that point, networks of small groups of anarchists involved in resistance activities of one sort or another were established in towns across the south and in the Paris region, but only very gradually. The majority of supporters were thus left more or less isolated, with no organized solidarity, no structures within which the social and political situation could be debated and thus no framework for collective action. Hence the large numbers of activists who by all accounts fell into "*attentisme*," that is, they became inactive, waiting on developments. As one post-war anarchist newspaper put it: "a very few were Germanophiles or Gaullists, the majority just relied on their own devices to stay alive."[26] Others simply left (or tried to leave) the country — André and Dori Prudhommeaux, accompanied by another anarchist, Alexandre Croix, sought refuge in Switzerland, Dori's country of origin; Charles Ridel (soon to be become Louis Mercier-Vega) and others fled to South America; some crossed the border into Belgium; others chose Sweden.[27]

Henri Bouyé (treasurer of the FAF in 1939) has talked of "the whole country's descent into anarchy — in the negative sense of the word!"[28] Day-to-day survival became a major preoccupation. From the viewpoint of the revolutionary, in particular, transport and communications of all kinds were disrupted, there were arrests, surveillance increased, sentences were severe.[29] Many anarchists were picked up by the police immediately after mobilization was announced, on the basis of the "Liste S," the list of subversives to be arrested in the event of any trouble — Huart and Haussard, for instance, both well-known members of the UA.[30] Many others were harassed more or less for the duration of the war simply because they were known to the authorities for their pre-war activities. It is worth quoting at length Charles Ridel's description of the situation in Marseille in September 1939:

> The organizations could do nothing, deprived of their members by mobilization, paralysed by police surveillance. The few offices still open were known to the police and avoided by activists as traps. Only a few old men, past the age of military service, came to sweep the floors of empty rooms, gather up the few letters that were still being delivered and pile up the foreign publications that continued to arrive but which nobody came to read.

Even the old *Bourse du Travail* had become suspect for all those who were in danger either because of the files they knew were kept on them, or because of their youth, or simply because of their accent or their demeanour. Women, the very young or the very old could still act as messengers.

... It was no longer a question of the hunt for an individual. Whole streets were being raided now, whole quarters. Anybody at all who did not blend perfectly into the background was systematically stopped and questioned. It was still possible to move around during the day so long as your clothes and your language were utterly ordinary, and so long as you had some presentable ID, a military service record book for a cohort that had not yet been called up ... But once night fell, the black out transformed the rules of the game and every shadow became dangerous for the hunters as for the hunted.

Collective action, movements, neighbourhood groups or factory groups, publications, all that had just disappeared. The parameters of the struggle had been suddenly reduced. Every militant was betting their freedom, some were gambling with their lives. A handful of die-hards in Paris, defiant and refusing to despair, were still publishing a *Courrier des Camps* which maintained a minimum of solidarity amongst the Spaniards and the cosmopolitan survivors of many defeats. There were now only individuals, backs against the wall, hunted, reduced to their meagre capital of personal connections, to the handful of change in their pocket and to their last, most acceptable suit.

France was a trap inside a bigger European trap, and the trap was closing.[31]

René Lochu, who was not even involved in the resistance, remarks how, after the German occupation, "any militant who had been involved with the *Maison du Peuple* had everything to fear. From time to time we would learn of the arrest of another comrade, or a group of comrades. If ever, early in the morning, I heard steps on the stairs, I would think: Gestapo!"[32] Hardly surprising, in these circumstances, that many did as Clotaire Henez: "I got through the war years by offering all the various authorities the lowest possible profile, and was thus able to avoid youth labour camps, STO and raids by the 'Milice.'"[33]

CONSCIENTIOUS OBJECTION

With the declaration of war, some chose to declare themselves as conscientious objectors. Conscientious objection had for many years been rejected by the anarchist movement for a variety of reasons: it was an individualistic response to a social problem; it implied that some duty was owed to the state; it meant the loss of an activist for the period that they were imprisoned. There was however a change in the anarchists' attitude to war-resistance after 1914. This was caused by the realisation that the anti-war movement was simply too weak to bring about effective *collective* resistance to war. Hence, whilst continuing to campaign within the labour movement and participate in specifically pacifist organisations, as well as in unitary campaigns (with the communists and others) against the occupation of the Ruhr (1923–25) and so forth, there was a certain tendency in the inter-war years towards increased acceptance of *individual* responses, and notably conscientious objection. As late as 1929, the secretary of the Anarchist Union, René Frémont, was still condemning the "individualism" of conscientious objection and reaffirming the value of the slogan: "Transform the capitalist war into a revolutionary war!"[34] Nevertheless, at the April 1930 congress of the Anarchist Union, conscientious objection was accepted as a valid form of anarchist "propaganda by the deed."

We have already seen what happened to Lecoin and Faucier. The former would remain inactive for the rest of the war after his release from gaol in 1941, the latter was underground from 1943 until the Liberation.[35] For a brief period from December 1943, he worked for the Todt Organization (which provided labour for the Germans' military infrastructure building projects), near Neuville.[36]

There were others who refused to answer the call-up. Maitron mentions two other anarchists who refused on grounds of conscience, one a member of the Versailles anarchist group, the other from Rennes, but he adds: "If there were others, they were very few."[37] According to Arru, there were a good dozen activists in the Bordeaux anarchist group who planned to refuse to answer the call-up, but in the end only he and one other comrade went through with it.[38] Faucier speaks of "a few dozen" conscientious objectors who declared themselves in 1939, but can provide the names of only a handful of anarchists: Joseph Briand,[39] Pierre Martin,[40] Gilles Dubois,[41] André Le Marc[42] and Boncoeur.

In fact, it depends what exactly one means by "conscientious objection." The idea was originally opposed by the UA between the wars partly because it involved allowing oneself to be arrested and making a statement to the authorities explaining one's refusal to serve in the military (which meant a good militant was lost to the cause while they served their sentence). According to this definition, it is true that very few anarchists were conscientious objectors. If, on the other hand, one includes comrades like Dubois who simply refused to answer the call-up and went underground, then CIRA's research has brought to light many such cases. Indeed many spent the war years underground, often involved more or less directly with the Resistance, only to be imprisoned after the so-called Liberation for having refused to answer the call-up in 1939 — Georges Burgat, shoemaker, anarchist and pacifist, would be a typical example.[43]

Probably a majority of those who were called up, however, did respond. René Frémont of the UA, for instance, joined up and was killed during the French army's retreat in June 1940. Other activists even joined the Free French. Charles Ridel (from this point on known as Louis Mercier-Vega) refused the call-up in 1939 and fled to Chile, before joining up with the Free French in June 1942.

RESISTANCE

Many (most?) anarchists seem to have engaged more or less actively in a wide range of forms of resistance — although of course it depends what we mean by "resistance." Some — Spanish comrades in particular, but not only — joined the armed Resistance. Sonia Picqueray, daughter of May, worked for the *"maquis"* in the Dordogne as an *"agent de liaison."*[44] André Respaut, a farrier in Coursan (Aude), answered the call-up in 1939, but as soon as he was demobilized he joined the *"Combat"* movement, as well as remaining active amongst other anarchists, both French and Spanish, in Ales and Perpignan. He was arrested by the Germans in October 1943 and deported to Buchenwald, which he survived to write about.[45] René Cavanhié was also active in the resistance. Having gone underground in 1942, he created an independent resistance group in the Lot. He and his group then worked for a while with the "Mouvements Unis de la Résistance" before joining the FTP in the winter of 1942–43.[46] There are many other examples of such commitment.

Many more activists "resisted" in other ways, without bearing arms. They took part in networks that sheltered comrades being sought by the authorities — for example, providing false papers and/or organizing escape routes out of the country.[47] Constant Planas, a hair-dresser in Aix-en-Provence, acted as a "letter-box" for a local Resistance group after having been approached by some Socialist militants with whom he was personally friendly. The actor Léo Campion, working in theatres in Paris and in Brussels, was a messenger for the "Nord-Normandie-Bretagne" network.

Some of those who contributed in this way gave their lives in the process. Georges Gourdin, an active member of the UA, of the Anarchist Youth and of the Technicians' Federation of the CGT, contributed a great deal to the reestablishment of links between anarchists, and helped many comrades and other refugees escape the Gestapo. Arrested in May 1944, he was tortured by the Gestapo but gave nothing away, and eventually died in the camp at Elbrück, near Nordhausen. He was 29.

Learning about the different ways in which comrades behaved during the war years also makes one aware of the many levels of resistance that existed. Pierre-Valentin Berthier, a journalist in Issoudun at the time, "did not belong to the Resistance" as he puts it.[48] And yet, he knew members of the Resistance, and had them supply him with false papers in order to help a cousin escape STO; he hid his cousin in his home for a fortnight before finding him a more permanent hiding place in the country; he warned the local "*maquisards*" that a letter denouncing them had been sent to the newspaper for which he worked; and he refused the Vichy authorities permission to use his office window for putting up propaganda posters. "Low-level" resistance maybe, but resistance nevertheless.

Perhaps the best known anarchist "*résistant*" was Jean René Saulière, "a militant pacifist and anarchist" and a travelling salesman by trade, who had adopted a false identity—André Arru—in order to avoid the call-up in September 1939. Having lived in hiding in Bordeaux for five months, he moved to Marseille and set himself up with a bicycle repair shop. He established contact with exiled Italian and Spanish anarchists. With an old comrade from Bordeaux, Armand, he began to print stickers and leaflets which they slipped into mail-boxes and posted up around the town. Gradually, an anarchist group about 10–12 strong was created, which included, amongst others, the exiled Russian anarchist Voline, as well as French, Spanish and Italian comrades. Contacts began to be established with comrades outside of Marseille: in the Var to begin with, then in Nîmes, Lyon, Montpellier, Perpignan, Toulouse, Agen, Villeneuve-sur-Lot, Foix and even Paris. The Lion brothers of Toulouse, Raoul and Henri, who also printed material for the "*Combat*" Resistance network and who would ultimately both die in a German concentration camp, produced posters and leaflets for the Marseille group. In 1943, they printed 1,000 copies of a pamphlet entitled "Les Coupables" (The Guilty) and, in June the same year, about 2,000 copies of the first number of a review called *La Raison* (The Reason).[49] The posters were for use principally in Marseille, but the leaflets, the pamphlet and the review were distributed to all Saulière's contacts. This network would become the basis for the reconstruction of the movement from 1943 onwards. Simultaneously with these activities, Saulière had also acquired false stamps and other materials from the Lion brothers, and with these

he supplied Jews and political refugees—many of whom stayed temporarily in the rooms next to his workshop—with false papers.

In August 1943, whilst working on the second issue of *La Raison*, Saulière was arrested along with his partner, Julia Vinas, a Spanish political refugee, and Etienne Chauvet, a comrade from Lyon who
was on the run to avoid STO. They were all imprisoned, Chauvet and
Saulière at Chave. After having been left behind for political reasons
when the communist and Gaullist prisoners organized a mass escape
in March 1944, they were transferred to the prison at Aix, from which
they escaped with other "*résistants*" a few weeks later. After an unevent-
ful three or four weeks in the "*maquis*" with the FTP, they decided to go
their own ways. Saulière, having been reunited with Vinas, eventually
arrived back in Toulouse at the end of June 1944. The network established by Saulière, Albert and others had become inactive because of the
risks involved after the arrests, but it was quickly reactivated. When the
town was liberated in August 1944, a *Manifesto of the Anarcho-Syndicalist
Libertarian Groups* in leaflet form was distributed throughout the town
the same day the German army withdrew.[50] Saulière—described by another veteran, Maurice Laisant, as "the heart and soul of the Resistance
in those troubled times"[51]—concludes: "Our movement was of very little
importance, but it was nevertheless quite coherent. Contrary to what
some historians have written, I think we were ready and adapted to
clandestine activity."[52]

COLLABORATION

A small number of anarchists compromised themselves with Vichy and/
or the German occupying forces, although it is important (if frequently
difficult) to distinguish between the differing motivations of "collabora-
tionists," "collaborators" and others who deliberately used certain organizations created by Vichy in order to help comrades in difficulty and/or
aid antifascist Resistance.[53]

May Picqueray, for instance, concerned with the plight of ordinary
refugees, worked initially with the Quakers and with the humanitarian, politically-neutral Commission d'aide aux enfants espagnols. This
enabled her not only to contact and aid comrades in the French concentration camps, but also to help nine *émigré* German antinazis escape
from the camp at Le Vernet (with the help of a French army officer);[54]
and later—in a move which she compares in her memoirs to her visit
to Trotsky, some 20 years earlier, in order to have Russian anarchists
released from bolshevik gaols — she would even visit Vichy's Minister of the Interior, Pucheu, and successfully negotiate the release of the

revolutionary syndicalist Nicolas Lazarevitch from Le Vernet, as well as that of his wife and children from another camp.[55]

Lecoin, Guyard and Carpentier worked with Vichy's "Restaurants communautaires." Other anarchists activists worked within the COSI (Comité ouvrier de secours immédiat, Committee for Workers in Urgent Need).

A case perhaps of a different kind is that of Charles Dhooge, an anarchist from Reims and the director of a clinic before the war, who actively supported Vichy's "Labour Charter" and was president of the "Trade Union Propaganda Centre."[56] He also wrote for the pro-Vichy paper, *l'Atelier* (The Workshop). This collaboration, however, seems to have enabled him to save some comrades, and his clinic was apparently used to hide arms and refugees, and at the Liberation, his services to the Resistance were acknowledged.[57]

Perhaps one of the best-known and one of the most intriguing cases is that of Pierre Besnard. Besnard joined Pétain's Légion des Combattants, for reasons which he is said to have explained.[58] He also published a book during the Occupation entitled *Pour assurer la Paix, comment organiser le monde* ("In order to ensure peace, how to organize the world"), which apparently caused some disquiet among comrades.[59] At the Agen congress of October 1944—effectively the founding congress of the post-war anarchist movement—Besnard claimed that he had been delegated by "a syndicalist organization" to join the Légion des Combattants "to carry out a particular task," and promised to make available documentary proof. The conference delegates declared their personal trust in Besnard, but decided that the movement would collectively judge Besnard's conduct when it had seen the promised documentary evidence. The documents appear never to have been produced.[60]

Although much more rare, there were some cases of outright collaboration, even collaborationism.[61] According to Picqueray, "Maurice W." (Wullens?), whom she describes as the editor of a left-wing paper, who "became something of a Germanophile" after 1940, was accused in another anarchist's memoirs of having collaborated with the police.[62] Picqueray could not believe that he had gone that far, and the accusation was denied by all of "W.'s" friends: "All of his friends, including myself, maintained their respect for him."

Others who were known as libertarians between the wars went even further in their links with fascism. Louis Loréal, for instance, after first supporting the notion of a war between "Democracy" and "Fascism" during the "*drôle de guerre*," ended up writing for the pro-nazi papers *Germinal* and *La Gerbe*.[63] The following article, entitled "Choisir!" (Choose!) appeared in *Germinal* on 7 July 1944:

I would like to appeal, in these pages, to my old comrades in the
syndicalist and pacifist movements. ... those who understand
that the old world is dying and who wish with all their hearts
for a better future, but who are concerned that the Social Revolution which is under way is not following the way planned for
it by the theoreticians of socialism and syndicalism. ...

We want to abolish class struggle by destroying its causes. We
want to create a regime based on community and socialism.

Those who still resist have not yet understood that this war is
not like any war which has gone before. It is the final war between, on the one hand, all the evil forces of the past, a world
rotten with privilege, theft, slavery and crime and, on the other,
the virile, healthy forces of the people which at last is trying to
free itself. ...

It used to be thought that the Social Revolution would be made
through conflict and violence. We thought the people would
"triumph" by installing some system of workers' and peasants'
councils, within which different factions would tear each other
apart in order to gain as much power as possible for themselves.
There was supposed to be some sort of dictatorship of a party or
a trade union in the name of the poor proletariat which would
in fact end up paying with its misery, its money and its blood for
the more or less disastrous experiments of the revolutionaries
for whom socialism meant simply their own sect.

That would have produced a lovely mess in which the different
factions of the working class would have excommunicated and
exterminated each other in the name of liberty. We saw what
that led to in Spain between 1936 and 1938. ...

You have spent all your lives combatting capitalism, and yet
here today capitalism is about to be destroyed forever, and you
are beginning to miss it!

By your presence, you would infuse the revolution with an au-
thentic socialist spirit. As Marcel Déat has proclaimed: "The
Social Revolution will only be made with the people." Join
us!"

Loréal was not alone in being seduced by the twisted logic of the
extreme-right's appeal to syndicalists and socialists. Gérard de Lacaze-
Duthiers, a writer previously known for his libertarian sympathies, also
wrote for *La Gerbe*. René Gerin, a conscientious objector and one-time
editor of the pacifist newspaper *Le Barrage humaine*, who had earlier rejected the "Légion d'Honneur," nevertheless worked as literary critic for

the pro-Vichy paper *l'Œuvre* between 1940 and 1944.[64] René de Sanzy donned the uniform of the RNP (Rassemblement national populaire, the "People's National Rally") created by the socialist-turned-national-socialist, Marcel Déat. A certain Léger even wore that of Vichy's *Milice*.[65]

THE RECONSTRUCTION OF THE ANARCHIST MOVEMENT, 1943–45

One thing that clearly emerges from the first-hand accounts gathered by the Marseille CIRA is that the accounts of the reconstruction of the French anarchist movement provided by Maitron, Biard and Joyeux are incomplete and, in some respects, misleading and even factually incorrect.[66] What follows is an attempt to reproduce an accurate account of the series of meetings that had as their aim the reconstitution of a national anarchist movement or organization. It was a parallel process, centred largely on the efforts of two people: Henri Bouyé in Paris and Jean René Saulière in the south.

The very first meetings held with a view to reconstruction seem to have been organized by Charles Carpentier in Paris in September 1940, but little came of it.[67] Further meetings in Paris were held at the *Bourse du travail* in the offices of the CGT's Florists' Union (which had been created by Henri Bouyé in 1936) and elsewhere. In 1943, around 30–35 comrades from the Paris region met in Montmorency forest, under the pretext of a ramble organized by a fictitious naturist group (an arrangement which may account for the conclusion drawn by Maitron that the movement managed to organize only social walks in the country).[68] On 15 January 1944, Bouyé and Louis Laurent organized a meeting in Paris, which brought together Emile Babouot, Georges Vincey and a dozen or so others — mostly activists from the pre-war years. At this meeting, the declaration of principles and the statutes of a new federation were produced.[69] During February–March 1944, Bouyé travelled around France under a false identity, in order to establish links between the different groups, and leaflets and manifestos produced under the auspices of a Federalist Movement were distributed. A Unified Libertarian Federation emerged in the spring of 1944, along with an internal discussion bulletin, *Le Lien* (The Link), and a two-page manifesto was produced that called for revolutionary action in the spirit of internationalism. A pamphlet entitled "Libertarians and the Social Problem" was also prepared, and was printed. Immediately the Germans began to withdraw from Paris. There would be three reprints. In July 1944, a leaflet entitled "Return to Freedom" was produced under the auspices of an Anarchist Federation and fly-posted in large numbers around the capital.

In the south, the first important meeting was in 1943 at Bon En-contre, the home of Pierre Besnard near Agen, held nominally to discuss the production of the pamphlet Les Coupables, and at which five or six other militants were present.[70] On 19 July the same year, a "mini-congress" was held over two days at the home, near Toulouse, of veteran militants Alphonse and Paule Tricheux under the auspices of an Inter-national Revolutionary Syndicalist Federation. Saulière, Voline and a Spanish comrade called San Clemente represented the Marseille group; there were also delegates from Toulouse, Agen, Villeneuve-sur-Lot and Paris; a few individuals; and a CNT-FAI observer, Joseph Ester, from the clandestine Spanish libertarian movement in the departments of Ariège and Haute-Garonne.[71] The discussions were both theoretical and practical. The question of whether the movement should remain in-dependent or cooperate with other resistance groups was a particularly thorny one, according to Saulière.

After Saulière's return to Toulouse in June 1944, the network was reactivated, contacts were re-established with Agen and Villeneuve-sur-Lot, and a pre-congress was held in Agen on 29–30 October 1944.[72] It had always been the hope of Saulière and his associates to reunite all the French anarchists, and the Agen meeting succeeded in this—at least for a time. Saulière also saw an opportunity to bring together the French movement and the Spanish movement in exile when he was asked in August 1944 by the National Committee of the CNT to become na-tional secretary of SIA. In order to give SIA a higher profile, Saulière organized a congress in Paris in April or May 1945. Unfortunately, the anarchists in Paris were already divided, and they attended the con-gress as two separate delegations: Simone Larcher and Louis Louvet (who produced the review *Ce qu'il faut dire*[73]) on the one hand, and on the other, Henri Bouyé and others who were preparing to relaunch *le Libertaire*. The congress was a heated one, the CNT National Committee disapproved of Saulière's approach, and so he resigned as SIA national secretary in July.[74]

The founding congress of the Anarchist Federation in Paris, 6–7 October and 2 December 1945, finally saw the coming together of the two networks. The first post-war issue of *le Libertaire* having appeared on 21 December 1944 (printed in Toulouse), issue no.2 came out on 15 February 1945.

PROVISIONAL CONCLUSIONS

What conclusions, if any, can we draw regarding the history of French anarchism in this period? Firstly, it seems clear that "Resistance" had a different meaning for anarchists than that which is/was usually attributed to the word. This was not an interruption, a temporary state of affairs prompted by the invasion of France by Germans: "It was *anarchist* Resistance," in the words of Maurice Laisant.[75] It was a *continuation* of the struggle against war and militarism, against capitalist and imperialist exploitation, against authoritarianism of all kinds. Saulière, for instance, writes that the "specifically libertarian clandestine group," which he managed to create gradually in Marseille, was "doubly clandestine," since "our propaganda attacked not only fascism, but *all* those responsible for the war, including capitalism and the stalinist dictatorship."[76] This was made clear in the text of the poster "Mort aux Vaches," produced by Saulière's group in 1943, and which encouraged proletarian conscripts of all countries to turn their bayonets not on each other but on their own leaders, "whether they wear the swastika, the red star, the Order of the Garter, the Cross of Lorraine or the Frankish axe."[77] A 1943 leaflet, A tous les travailleurs de la pensée et du bras (To all workers of the brain and of the hand), composed by Saulière, Voline and other members of the Marseille group, is also quite explicit in separating the anarchists' position from that of most other sectors of the Resistance:

> If it is true that it was Hitler and Mussolini who, in the immediate term, precipitated the war, others also bear responsibility: international finance and the industrial and financial trusts which, from 1919 to 1930, financed the Italian fascist movement and German national-socialism and, from 1930 to 1939, paid the press of the different democratic and fascist countries to conduct the bellicose campaigns which provoked a massive rearmament of all nations, a rearmament which would lead to the present war and which at the same time prevented any movement for the liberation of the working masses.
>
> Today, the imperialists of yesterday pose as liberators. Those who produced and pushed the Treaty of Versailles, the inventors and the saboteurs of the League of Nations, the accomplices of Hindenburg and Dollfuss, those who strangled the Spanish revolution, the fomentors of counter-revolution in Mexico, the suppliers of Hitler's Germany and Mussolini's Italy claim— oh, what irony!—to be bringing order to the world, those who have never lived other than by disorder and by conflict between the nations of both hemispheres.[78]

Secondly, one is struck by the variety of responses on the part of anarchists. To some extent, as Roger Pantais has pointed out, this was due to force of circumstance: taking part in armed resistance, for instance, was only conceivable in certain parts of the country.[79] Bianco's individualistic gloss on this variety of forms of engagement is that it was "doubtless due to the fact that there is no 'anarchist truth', every individual being obliged to forge for themselves, day after day, their own 'credo' and adopt, when faced with such and such an event, whichever attitude they judge to be the most in accord with their own conscience."[80] This is reflected in May Picqueray's comments on her own involvement: "I entered into relations with various comrades belonging to different Resistance networks. We helped each other out, but I never wanted to join any organization. I wanted to be free, I wanted to make decisions and define my responsibilities myself. I think it is that which saved me, whilst so many other men and women were arrested and deported."[81]

Others have been less happy with what they see as symptoms of one of the anarchist movement's major weaknesses and one of the reasons why so many "activists" seem to have been inactive during the war, and why some even allowed themselves to be taken in by the supposed "pacifism" of the extreme-right. Henri Bouyé:

> When, in the summer of 1940, Hitler ... made a 'pacifist' speech, how many of our friends rejoiced, explaining to us that the enlightened dictator was going to build peace! ... How many did we see of these ex-'war resisters' who chose to believe in such sweet talk in order to justify their own acceptance of a *fait accompli*, apparently unmoved by the criminal acts of violence and barbarism committed by the nazis under our very eyes .... Such activists' earlier antimilitarism seems to have evaporated when it came to the 'revitalization' of the race in the name of values advocated by national-socialism. And very often, we would leave these ex-companions, after debating the situation with them, with pained hearts and clenched fists. Among these forgetful comrades, there were some who went so far in their indulgence towards or their compromises with Hitler's and Pétain's forces of repression, that when the Germans were leaving Paris, they came to ask us to intervene on their behalf, so afraid were they of being violently denounced and punished. The best thing for them to do was to disappear as quickly as possible .... That is what we managed to help them to do, with the necessary discretion.[82]

What seems to me interesting about this is the indulgence shown towards such collaborators. This can also be seen in the case of May Picqueray, who speaks of "the sad and shameful spectacle of revenge" at the Liberation.[83] She helped "F.B.," the editor of a right-wing newspaper who had "collaborated" (Picqueray's inverted commas) by providing him with forged identity papers. He was nevertheless finally arrested, and was imprisoned alongside Robert Brasillach (the right-wing intellectual and collaborator) at Fresnes: "Although his ideas were the opposite of my own and horrified me, as an anarchist I felt I had to help him. Once he was freed, we had no further contact."[84] This seems to have been a common attitude among libertarians at the Liberation (nor was it limited to libertarians, of course).

Finally, to answer the question posed at the beginning of this book, it would seem that earlier published assessments have not given the anarchists' sufficient credit either for their contribution to the Resistance or for the efforts made from 1940 onwards to rebuild their own movement nationally. Bouyé:

> It must be said that in our circles, those who took risks did so essentially because of their ideals, and for them this went without saying. ... Our comrades had no ulterior careerist motives, and glory-seeking was the last thing on their minds. ... That said, let us be modest: we would be exaggerating if we claimed they had had a determining impact on events. But they were present in the struggle, with the means (and numbers) at their disposal, and they did what they could. That's all they want to say.[85]

Notes

1. Fred Zeller, *Témoin du siècle* (Paris: Editions Grasset et Fasquelle, 2000), p.116.

2. Michel Ragon, *La Mémoire des vaincus* (Paris: Albin Michel, 1990), p.11.

3. Ibid, p.418.

4. Interview with the author. Joyeux may, in fact, have been a partial model for Ragon's central protagonist, since he spent the duration of the war in prison at Montluc, near Lyon.

5. See Maurice Joyeux, "L'affaire Fontenis," in *La Rue* no.28 (1980); R. Saulière in CIRA (Marseille), *Bulletin* no.21/22 (1984): "Les Anarchistes et la Résistance," p.34; M. Laisant in CIRA (Marseille), *Bulletin* no.23/25 (1985): "Les Anarchistes et la Résistance," vol.II: "Témoignages 1939–1945," p.4.

6. By far the most important sources are two volumes of the Marseille CIRA's *Bulletin* (nos.21/22, 1984 and 23/25, 1985), which contain first-hand accounts and a certain amount of primary material (leaflets, letters, pamphlets, newsletters), which compensates to some extent for the absence of archival material—most activists at the time not having kept anything which might have been incriminating—and in certain respects enables us to correct errors in earlier published accounts. It is interesting to note that apart from the

fact that some of those involved in the Resistance did not wish to reawaken unpleasant memories, others refused to contribute for different reasons. One, for instance, wrote: "I really do not want to be mentioned in the planned issue of the *CIRA Bulletin*, because, you see, I absolutely detest being put in the spotlight. It was always a case of *anonymous team-work*, and I insist on it staying that way." Quoted in Bianco's preface, *Bulletin* no.21/22, p.3.

7.   *Le Libertaire*, 18 February 1937.

8.   *Le Libertaire*, 24 March 1938.

9.   *Le Libertaire*, 8 September 1938.

10.   *Le Libertaire*, 6 October 1938.

11.   *Le Libertaire*, 6 October 1938.

12.   *Le Libertaire*, 4 August 1938.

13.   *Le Libertaire*, 15 September 1938.

14.   *Le Libertaire*, 2 June 1938.

15.   *Le Libertaire*, 22 June and 6 July 1939.

16.   *SIA*, 13 July 1939.

17.   *Le Libertaire*, 27 April 1939.

18.   *L'Espagne nouvelle*, 15 April 1939.

19.   Report of 20 March 1939, Box 50, Dossier UACR, Paris Police Archives.

20.   Louis Lecoin, *Le Cours d'une vie* (Paris: Lecoin/Liberté, 1965), pp.169–87; Nicolas Faucier, *Pacifisme et Antimilitarisme dans l'entre-deux-guerres (1919–1939)* (Paris: Spartacus, 1983), pp.191–94.

21.   Faucier, *Pacifisme*, p.194.

22.   Quotation from Georges Fontenis, *L'autre communisme. Histoire subversive du mouvement libertaire* (Mauléon: Acratie, 1990), p.73. For an analysis of the debates around pacifism and revolutionary defeatism on the left in the late 30s, see Daniel Guérin, *Front populaire révolution manquée* (Arles: Actes Sud, 1997).

23.   Fontenis, *L'autre communisme*, p.36.

24.   Maitron vol.II, p.37.

25.   This latter point is important, as newspapers played a somewhat different rôle in the anarchist movement than they did in other sectors of the labour movement: given anarchism's traditionally loose structures, papers and bulletins of various kinds were far more important as an organizational link between individuals and groups and between local groups and national organizations.

26.   *Le Trait d'union*, the internal bulletin of the Anarchist Federation's Paris region, 16 October 1949.

27.   CIRA, *Bulletin* no.23/25 (1985); Fontenis, *L'autre communisme*, p.74.

28.   Interview with the author.

29.   The Vichy State even introduced a law directed specifically at "communist or anarchist activity" (Law no.3515, 14 August 1941).

30.   May Picqueray, *May la réfractaire. Pour mes 81 ans d'anarchie* (Paris: Atelier Marcel Jullian, 1979), p.174.

31.   Louis Mercier-Vega, *La Chevauchée anonyme* (Geneva: Editions Noir, 1978), pp.13–14.

32.   Lochu names three comrades from Brest who were arrested and deported and who died in Germany: Jules Le Gall, Charles Berthelot and a "Louis B."

33. Clotaire Henez, "Passé simple: Itinéraire idéologique," in *Bulletin du CIRA* no.33 (1992), pp.1–15, p.12. STO, the *"Service du travail obligatoire"* (Obligatory Labour Service) was the system whereby young French men were forcibly sent to work in Germany. It was a common reason for people deciding to go underground and join the Resistance. The *"Milice"* was a political police on the nazi model, formed by Joseph Darnand from the more active political elements of the *"Légion des anciens combattants."* Basically an association of the various ex-soldiers' organizations that existed before the war, the *"Légion"* was a vanguard for the values of Pétain's "National Revolution."

34. *Le Libertaire*, 12 October 1929.

35. Faucier, *Pacifisme*, pp.199–200; Maitron vol.II, p.36.

36. See Nicolas Faucier, *Dans la mêlée sociale. Itinéraire d'un militant anarcho-syndicaliste* (Quimperlé: La Digitale, 1988), pp.172–75. For Fontenis—concerned with an analysis of the political inconsistencies, which he argues were exhibited by the movement during the war—this is a contradiction: "We cannot be satisfied with Faucier's failure to explain how it was that he was a draft-dodger in 1939 and yet was drafted into the *Todt Organization* in 1943" (*L'autre communisme*, p.67). According to Faucier's own account (*Pacifisme*, pp.196–200), which includes the text of declarations made before various courts, Faucier was underground from 3 September to 25 September 1939 (producing "Paix immédiate!"), was taken to the Santé prison on 8 October, then to the Cherche-Midi prison and then to the military camp at Avord (Cher). Having refused again to serve, he was imprisoned in Orléans, then Poissy and, after the German invasion, a forced labour camp at Fontevrault. His sentence completed in February 1943, Faucier was nevertheless held for some months longer on the order of the German authorities, before being sent to another labour camp at Neuville (Vienne), from which he escaped in December 1943, "to avoid the fate of so many of my comrades who disappeared in Hitler's camps." It is in Faucier's 1988 autobiography that he mentions the couple of old friends and comrades who sheltered him in a small village south of Orléans, and with whom he shared his "wages from the Todt factory" (pp.171–73).

37. Maitron vol.II, p.36, note 113.

38. CIRA, *Bulletin* no.21/22 (1984), p.1.

39. Joseph Briand, of Rennes, was arrested on 18 September 1939 and, although sentenced to five years, was released at the end of September 1940 "thanks to fortuitous circumstances." He managed not to draw attention to himself for the rest of the war, and was thus able to help other comrades in difficulty. He was rearrested in January 1946 and sentenced to serve the rest of his five years, but was definitively freed after the amnesty of 14 July that year. Faucier, *Pacifisme*, pp.200–2.

40. Pierre Martin, a teacher, had been sentenced to 18 months imprisonment in 1937 for refusal to carry out his military service, and was sentenced to a further 2 years in April 1939 for persisting. Having begun a hunger strike in protest at the particularly severe conditions imposed on conscientious objectors in prison, Martin was transferred to Clairvaux prison in the winter of 1939–40. Having been granted certain responsibilities and privileges, he used these to establish a network of solidarity among all the objectors at Clairvaux. When the prison was bombed in June 1940, the prisoners were evacuated and Martin ended up being released in April 1941. Shortly afterwards he was once more arrested and sent to do STO work in Germany, from which he escaped some months later. Faucier, *Pacifisme*, pp.202–3; Pierre Martin, *L'Armée? Non merci! Candide face au Moloch. Récit d'une aventure de la non-violence* (Arudy: Editions d'Utovie, 1983).

41. Gilles Dubois, an anarchist from Brest, attempted to escape as a stowaway on a boat to Montevideo when war was declared. The boat was, however, turned back to Rotterdam, Dubois arrested and deported. He was imprisoned first at Loos-lès-Lille, then at the Santé, Fresnes and Clairvaux, where he knew Martin. He was wounded in the bombing, but eventually sent back to Clairvaux. He was released in April 1942. Faucier, *Pacifisme*, pp.204–5.

42. André Le Marc of Rennes was sentenced to five years and was sent to Clairvaux and then Riom; Boncoeur was sentenced to five years by a Versailles tribunal, and eventually posted as missing. (Faucier, *Pacifisme*, p.205).

43. CIRA, *Bulletin* no.23/25, pp.47–8.

44. Picqueray, *May la réfractaire*, p.179.

45. CIRA, *Bulletin* no.23/25, pp.51–54.

46. Ibid., pp.57.

47. Picqueray, *May la réfractaire*, p.174–78.

48. CIRA, *Bulletin* no.23/25, p.15.

49. The pamphlet bore the title of an organization: the "International Revolutionary Syndicalist Federation," and carried articles on the Katyn forest, the Spanish revolution and syndicalism. Saulière had discussed the contents with Pierre Besnard, who at the time was living near Agen.

50. Reproduced in CIRA, *Bulletin* no.21/22, p.27.

51. CIRA, *Bulletin* no.23/25, p.4.

52. CIRA, *Bulletin* no.21/22, p.33.

53. For a brief discussion of the historiography of Vichy, the meaning of "Resistance" and "Collaboration" and the evolution of the debate (including the concept of the "vichys-to-résistant") see Daniel Lindenberg, "Vichy, la mémoire, la République," in *L'Etat de la France 95–96* (Paris: La Découverte, 1995), pp.30–33.

54. Picqueray, *May la réfractaire*, pp.168–69.

55. Ibid, pp.171.

56. All national trade union organizations and employers' associations were dissolved by the Vichy régime in August 1940, and the "Charte du travail" (Labour Charter) was introduced in October 1941. Its supposed aim was to create an organic unity at the workplace: "It made claims to inaugurate a new era in industrial relations, but since the organic structures were heavily weighted towards the owners, management and white-collar staff, it did no more than dress up a long-standing system of economic inequality in the tinsel of corporatism" H. Roderick Kedward, *Occupied France: Collaboration and Resistance, 1940–1944* (Oxford: Blackwell, 1985), p.30.

57. CIRA, *Bulletin* no.23/25, p.46.

58. Ibid, p.17.

59. I have been unable to trace a copy of the book.

60. Fontenis, *L'autre communisme*, pp.64 and 277. Annexe II (p.277) contains quotations from the minutes of the conference which were supplied to Fontenis by Henri Bouyé.

61. According to Fontenis, "Certain others are said to have gone even further in their collaboration, but the absence of detailed documentation or testimony prevents us from naming names." Ibid, p.64.

62. Picqueray, *May la réfractaire*, p179. I have as yet been unable to establish whose memoirs she was referring to here.

63. Louis Loréal was the pseudonym of Louis Raffin (1894–1956). According to Paul Jamot and Louis Dorlet, Loréal was not a serious militant: he was a drunkard, he was emotionally immature and had been thrown out of the *Le Libertaire* group in 1931 for having spent the group's money on himself. He ended up, however, being more pitied than anything else, and Jamot concludes that his comrades were right to intervene and save him at the Liberation. CIRA, *Bulletin* no.23/25, p.6.

64. CIRA, *Bulletin* no.23/25, p.14. Bianco points out that there is absolutely no evidence to support Pascal Ory's bald assertion in his study of collaboration (*Les collaborateurs, 1940–1945* (Paris 1976), p.128) that Sébastien Faure also contributed to *l'Œuvre*.

65. Fontenis, *L'autre communisme*, p.64. This was not Robert Léger.

66. Maitron vol.II; Roland Biard, *Histoire du mouvement anarchiste en France, 1945–1975* (Paris: Galilée, 1976); Joyeux, "L'affaire Fontenis."

67. Fontenis, *L'autre communisme*, p.75.

68. According to Bouyé, those present included Georges Vincey, Rachel Lantier and Emile Babouot. CIRA, *Bulletin* no.23/25, p.105.

69. Maitron vol.II, p.37; Bianco and Bouyé in CIRA, *Bulletin* no.23/25, p.6 and p.105. There were still disagreements between the different tendencies at this stage over the name of the reconstituted organization. It was only at the constitutive congress in October 1945 that "Anarchist Federation" was definitively chosen. For an explanation, see Bouyé in CIRA, *Bulletin* no.23/25, pp.105–6.

70. CIRA, *Bulletin* no.21/22, p.33.

71. According to M. Laisant (CIRA, *Bulletin* no.21/22, p.64), those present were Alphonse and Paule Tricheux, Saulière, Voline, two women comrades from Paris, Joseph Ester and another Spanish comrade, some comrades from Agen and Villeneuve-sur-Lot and Laisant himself.

72. Laurent and Lapeyre attended the Agen congress delegated by the Bordeaux group (Saulière in CIRA, *Bulletin* no.21/22, p.35).

73. Larcher and Louvet represented the more individualist and pacifist wing of the movement. A manifesto was published in November 1944, and *Ce qu'il faut dire* appeared from December 1944 as an internal discussion review, becoming public in 1946.

74. It was at this congress, according to Saulière, that he met Maurice Joyeux for the first time. CIRA, *Bulletin* no.21/22, pp.34–5.

75. CIRA, *Bulletin* no.23/25, p.4.

76. CIRA, *Bulletin* no.21/22, p.1

77. In other words, the symbols of nazism, bolshevism, the British aristocracy, Gaullism and Vichy. The poster is reproduced in CIRA, *Bulletin* no.21/22, p.16, as is correspondence between Saulière and Rabaut over the latter's accusation that it included reference to the star of David and was therefore antisemitic. Saulière, "Réflexions sur des histoires" in CIRA, *Bulletin* no.21/22, pp.29–38; Jean Rabaut, *Tout est possible! Les 'gauchistes' français (1929–1944)* (Paris: Denoël/Gonthier 1974).

78. Printed in Toulouse, between 3,000 and 5,000 copies of this leaflet were distributed. It is reproduced in its entirety in CIRA, *Bulletin* no.21/22, pp.11–14.

79. CIRA, *Bulletin* no.23/25, p.145.

80. Ibid, p.3.

81. Picqueray, *May la réfractaire*, p.176.

82. CIRA, *Bulletin* no.23/25, p.114. For Fontenis, who is similarly critical of certain currents within the anarchist movement in those years, such about-turns were a symptom of the movement's theoretical paucity.

83. Picqueray, *May la réfractaire*, p.178–79.

84. Ibid, p.179.

85. CIRA, *Bulletin* no.23/25, p.103.

Conclusion

Mobilization, Constituency and Ideology

> Must we ... conclude that Anarchy is irrelevant to real life and that, in the coming Revolution, it will be impossible to put it into practice?
>
> *Léon Chantesais*[1]

> The anarchists are and always will be few in number, but they are everywhere. They are what I will call the yeast that makes the dough rise.
>
> *Sébastien Faure*[2]

> Indeed *anarchy* is, above all else, synonymous with *socialism*.
>
> *Daniel Guérin*[3]

By way of conclusion, let us try to summarize what we know about the changing nature of the anarchist movement in the inter-war years. There are three aspects to this: (i) its numerical strength and the extent of its influence; (ii) which social categories (in terms of social class, geography and gender) provided the most fertile ground for anarchist ideas; and (iii) what I would argue were significant developments in the ideological and political positions adopted by anarchists.

MOBILIZATION

How can we assess the size or influence of the anarchist movement between the wars? This is by no means unproblematic. Maitron has already outlined some of the problems: the irrelevance of election results, the looseness of the anarchist organizations, the absence of well-kept membership or subscription lists and so on.[4]

The anarchist press

Because of these various difficulties, Maitron chose to concentrate on the number of anarchist newspapers appearing each year as an index of the movement's vitality. [5] Having worked out the total number of newspapers to have appeared each year, he then worked out the average for certain periods, as follows:

Table 5

The number of newspapers produced per annum in five
periods, 1891–1972

1891–95	204
1911–13	333
1921–23	237
1936–38	254
1971–72	107

If we accept that such statistics do in fact give an indication of the movement's vitality, then we can conclude, firstly, that the zenith of French anarchism was just before the Great War; secondly, that between the wars anarchism was nevertheless stronger than at the turn of the century (a period when anarchism hit the headlines more and which has attracted the attention of historians much more than the inter-war years); and thirdly, that the movement was stronger in the 1930s than in the 1920s.

There are however problems with this. Maitron justified this concentration on the press partly on the grounds that in the anarchist movement greater importance was attached to the need for education and self-improvement, and that the press therefore had a privileged rôle to play. Was this still true after the Great War? Jean Grave, Maitron pointed out, was emphatic about the need "to stuff ideas into individuals' heads."[6] However, it was also Grave who was criticized by other anarchists for being dry, doctrinaire and intellectual, and who remained reserved towards syndicalism, which, as I have argued, was seen by many anarchists in the inter-war years as the primary site for revolutionary activity (indeed, for some, syndicalism became virtually synonymous with anarchism). The inter-war period, it seems to me, saw far less of an emphasis by anarchist communists on the need for education, and greater stress on organization and practical action. It is true that the anarchist press was different from that of more structured movements in that it acted as a link between supporters of a weakly structured organization. But as far as its supposed educational rôle is concerned, it seems to me debatable whether the anarchist communist press played a significantly different rôle than the syndicalist, socialist or communist press.

The one exception to this would be the individualist press. Here, the difficulty of using the production of newspapers as an index of the movement's vitality is of a different kind. For if one were to apply Maitron's approach to the individualist press, one could easily overestimate the strength and influence of that tendency, for the publication of newspapers, reviews and booklets seems to have been practically the sole activity of relatively small groups of individuals. This was natural enough, given their emphasis on self-improvement and their lack of interest in organization, social action or revolution.

Maitron's use of subscriber numbers as an index of the diffusion of anarchist ideas also seems questionable, firstly because statistics relating to subscriptions are particularly difficult to come by (and it is therefore difficult to get together a significant corpus), and secondly because one thing we do know about subscribers is that they were a minority of readers of the major anarchist papers.[7] Given the working-class nature of the readership of the anarchist communist and anarcho-syndicalist press, it is not surprising that the vast majority of readers preferred simply to buy their paper every week as it appeared. Indeed, the weekly street-selling of *le Libertaire* and other anarchist newspapers was a major regular activity of local anarchist groups and, at least in Paris, especially of the JAC. And even when we know how many papers were sold (as opposed to how many were printed, which is much easier to find out), we do not know how many people actually read the paper. Workers would often share the cost of a newspaper and pass it round their friends or workmates. So if we work on the assumption that of the 20,000 copies of *le Libertaire* printed, perhaps 10,000–15,000 were sold, the total readership could have been anything between 10,000 and 40,000 or even more (during a strike wave, for instance: there are plenty of photographs of striking workers in June 1936 posing for the camera in their occupied factory and holding up their preferred paper, including *le Libertaire*).

A final problem is the question of which newspapers one should take into account when assessing the vitality of the movement (or ideological change). Whereas I have considered as part of the revolutionary anarchist communist current such periodicals as *l'Avenir international, l'Internationale* and *le Communiste*, Maitron was more selective and discussed only the FCS organ, *le Soviet*; yet at the same time *SIA* was considered by him to be anarchist on the grounds that the initiative for its creation came from anarchists, even though its readership was by no means limited to anarchists or even to closely-related tendencies. Decisions as to where to draw the line inevitably involve a degree of arbitrary judgement. One's interpretation of the meaning of anarchism has an effect on the parameters adopted.

The implantation of Anarchist Union groups

Estimating the number of anarchist groups is also far from straightforward. Contact lists under rubrics like "The Life of the UA" in *le Libertaire*—our main source of information—were not complete directories, far from it. Sometimes they included groups that were not technically affiliated to the UA—they could also be, for example, *la Patrie Humaine* readers' groups, which happened to contain a number of anarchists. Many groups were not mentioned in these lists, but they turned up in accounts of public meetings, either in the press or in police reports. On the other hand, successful public meetings in the provinces could often be organized by just one or two militants with support from Paris, and cannot therefore always be seen as evidence of strong local implantation of the movement. If a UA group is listed in *le Libertaire*, is it because it is a well-established group, or because it has just been set up and is looking for new members? How big is it? What do we think of groups with names like *"groupe d'études sociales"* or *"groupe d'action sociale,"* since these seem sometimes to have been anarchist groups and sometimes mixed groups of anarchists, syndicalists and revolutionary socialists?[8] There is no way of answering these questions without complementary information from different sources, and such information is rarely forthcoming. Police archives for instance have not proven very useful in this respect.

With all these caveats in mind, though, if we compile lists of groups from *le Libertaire*, one relating to the 1919–24 period, one to 1936–39, the results do seem to confirm the conclusion that the movement was stronger in the later period than just after the Great War. Such lists suggest that the UA had a total of 86 groups over the period 1919–24: 11 in Paris, 27 in the Paris suburbs, 48 in the provinces.[9] By 1936–39, that total appears to have risen to 107: 12 in Paris, 44 in the suburbs, 51 in the provinces.[10] As well as this, by the late 1930s the UA's youth organization, the JAC, had established its own national federation and had a total of 29 groups: 24 in Paris and the suburbs, 5 in the provinces. All but two of these seem to have functioned independently of their local UA group.[11]

Table 6

Estimated numbers of Anarchist Union groups in 1919–24
and 1936–39

	1919–24	1936–39
Paris	11	12
Paris suburbs	27	44
Provinces	48	51
Total	86	107

The growth of support for anarchism in the 1930s

Sébastien Faure—who had been active on the extreme left since the
1880s—was convinced that there were more anarchists in France in
January 1936 than ever before, and that was before the events of that
summer.[12]

    Although the UA may have been smaller as a membership orga-
nization than the CGTSR—at least in the provinces—it was no doubt
less isolated than the CGTSR and more influential in the wider labour
and socialist movements. Support for the UA increased significantly in
the 1930s, and as well as creating the CEL and SIA, it played an important rôle in the antifascist movement in France, in the revolutionary
minority within the CGT and in the anti-war movement. Although the
UA's actual membership has been estimated at 2,500–3,000 in 1938, the
readership of the UA's organ would suggest a much wider audience.[13] In
October 1936, the UA, conceding that in the previous decade "there had
been a regrettable disaffection towards the propaganda of which our old
lib is the best instrument," pointed out that the reasons for the increasing
popularity of the paper over the preceding year had been threefold: (i)
the anarchists' position on the *Front Populaire*; (ii) their firm and continuing opposition to war which had gained them "the sympathy of many
workers"; (iii) most importantly, events in Spain "which brought our
doctrines to the attention of the more lucid of those who had hitherto
been totally disoriented by the political confusionism and the incredible
recantations of a certain, supposedly extreme-left party."[14]

    Le Libertaire certainly experienced an impressive increase in its
print-run between 1934 and 1937. It rose from a nadir of around 6,000–
7,000 in 1934 to a minimum of 17,000 by October 1936.[15] By the end of
that year *le Libertaire* claimed to have 2,000 subscribers and a print-run
of 20,000.[16] It increased to 25,000 after the shooting of demonstrators
at Metlaoui in Tunisia and the events at Clichy in March 1937—when

an attempt to prevent a meeting of the extreme right Parti social français turned into a riot and caused seven deaths.[17] The special number
produced for May Day 1937 — whose slogans were the defence of republican Spain and the lifting of the blockade — represents something
of a record for the anarchist movement, with a print-run of 100,000.[18]
The paper increased in size from four pages to six in August 1936; in
March 1937, it increased to eight pages and also began to carry a regular "proletarian literature" page, edited by Henri Poulaille. According
to the police the print-run of *le Libertaire* was still 18,000 as late as the
autumn of 1938.[19]

This was associated with a generally higher public profile. The anarchist movement was commented on increasingly in the non-anarchist
press of both left and right,[20] and massive increases in sales of books and
pamphlets, as well as of newspapers, were registered.[21] The UA responded and demonstrated a more energetic approach to campaigning. At the
end of 1936 or early in January 1937, the UA created an "Ecole propagandiste" with courses at the offices of *le Libertaire*, which had a good
response.[22] In May 1937, the UA reorganized the running of *le Libertaire*
and of its book shop in order to cope with the increased work-load.[23]

Given this higher profile, then, *le Libertaire* was no doubt right to
talk early in 1937 of "the growing influence we are gaining within the
revolutionary movement."[24] But who were the new anarchists? *Le Libertaire* attributed the growth of anarchist influence to a combination of
two factors: (i) winning people over to anarchism for the first time; and
(ii) greater input through the creation of closer links between anarchist
groups and individuals.[25] The creation of tighter links involved the reconstitution of groups and of regional federations (as in the Languedoc,
for example). Already well-established groups also grew. In September 1936, the Aulnay-sous-Bois UA group claimed to have grown to be
about 100 strong and that this was causing concern among local PCF
militants, "who had thought they had the monopoly of propaganda in
Aulnay-sous-Bois."[26]

Frémont, who had himself been a member of the Communist
Youth, introduced a third factor: he said in his report to the October–
November 1937 congress of the UA, that 1936–37, had been characterized by "the regrouping of anarchist forces on the one hand, and a
significant recruitment of new elements or of militants from the political
parties."[27] There do indeed seem to have been many disabused militants
of political parties who had become sympathetic to anarchism. The La
Ciotat group, for example, having re-formed, announced in December
1936 that local sales of *le Libertaire* had doubled and were increasing
every week, and also that its membership had doubled: "A lot of com-

rades are coming to join us because they are disgusted with politics."[28] After Clichy and Metlaoui, six members of the Socialist Youth in Paris 15 left to join the JAC.[29] A group of young soldiers — "young radicals, socialists and communists sick of the baseness of their leaders" — wrote from their barracks at Reims to express support for the UA's policy on Spain.[30] The great majority of cases cited by the anarchist press, though, concerned the PCF. The potential was recognized by the UA, and Escabos of the Paris 15 group urged UA groups to re-organize if necessary and to ensure sustained and cohesive activities in order to attract and keep such militants: "We know a lot of militants these days who are disappointed by the bourgeois and ultra-nationalist policies of their party. Such people are now wavering, and joining the UA would be the logical next step for them."[31]

Thus we read a report from the UA group in Nice — which claimed to have between 200 and 300 members by the summer of 1937 — that many local communists bought and read *le Libertaire*: "The policies adopted by the French stalinists are making our movement, the Anarchist Union, bigger every day."[32] In January 1937, the Groupe intercommunal de la Banlieue Sud also emphasized the presence in the group of several "grass-roots communist comrades."[33] After a talk by Faure in Aulnay in January 1936, three "undisciplined communists" were reported to have joined the UA group there.[34] The UA also found an eager audience among PCF members in Gentilly.[35] The Popular Front policy was seen by many militants as a turn to the right. Within a very short period the communists went from being workerist, antimilitarist and revolutionist, to being proponents of a *"Front français"* which involved accepting national defence, an alliance with the bourgeoisie and moderate, legalist reforms.[36] Successful as the move clearly was in terms of mass support for the PCF, there were also many in the party unhappy with such changes.[37] Félix Guyard (of the FCL tendency within the UA) wrote: "There are many communist militants who are so disgusted with the harmful, nationalistic policy followed by their party that they are joining the ranks of the UA."[38] When the secretary and 15 or so other young militants of the Communist Youth in Valenciennes left to join the JAC, the reason they gave in their letter to *le Libertaire* was that "*we* have remained revolutionaries and anti-militarists."[39] The same number also carried an article entitled "The Popular Front has deceived us," written by militants who had left the Socialist or Communist Youth to join the JAC. A Georges Viujard, who claimed to have been expelled from his PCF cell in Saint-Priest (on the outskirts of Lyon) in December 1936, and who had joined the UA, wrote in a letter to *le Libertaire* that he was tired of all the party's changes of tactic, its "self-contradictions" and its "sectarianism."[40] A letter from another militant who had left the PCF for the UA, this time in Nantes, made similar accusations of "changes of position," and also spoke of the party's policy of *"Union Sacrée."* In this last case, an introductory note from the Nantes UA group said it was "typical of the rebellion of an ever growing number of honest workers who have been abused by the communist leadership and who are now turning to libertarian communism."[41]

But of course all the evidence presented here is drawn from an anarchist newspaper, and we must ask ourselves just how significant was this apparent haemorrhage from the left of the PCF, and to what extent a few, statistically insignificant cases may have been concentrated on by the UA for propaganda purposes. The evidence produced by a reading of *le Libertaire* consists to a large extent, not of editorial comment but of activity reports from local groups, and might therefore perhaps be considered worthy of credence. But on the other hand, the suggestion of a significant influx into the UA from the PCF has been questioned by Anderson and Faucier, both of whom were in a position to have a reasonable overview. Anderson has emphasized that there was a constant filtering of communists leaving their party to join the UA right through the interwar period; but that most of the individuals who joined in 1936–37 were militants who were already sympathetic to anarchism or who had actually been involved with the anarchist movement at an earlier point—"the weary, the disillusioned."[42] And Faucier: "There were, it is true, a certain number of disillusioned communist party militants who joined us in the inter-war years, but not very many. It was above all the trotskyist groups who benefitted. It was particularly our campaign of action in favour of the Spanish revolution which won us the sympathies of many outside the revolutionary syndicalist movement which was our main source of support, both morally and materially."[43]

Of course, the UA was not the only anarchist organization, although there seems little doubt that it was the biggest and most influential. As well as the growth experienced by the UA, the CGTSR had 5,000–6,000 members in 1936–37, and *le Combat syndicaliste* may have been read by many more than that. The FAF—which brought together many (but not all) of those provincial anarchist groups had, for some years, been independent of any national organization—claimed to sell 6,500 copies of its organ, *Terre libre*. There was, of course, a certain overlap between the CGTSR and the FAF, and even between the CGTSR and the UA, so it would be nonsense simply to add up the membership figures of the three organizations.

A final point worth making in any attempt to assess the influence of anarchism is that these three national organizations were not the whole of anarchism, indeed Maitron's approach was criticized for regarding as anarchist only those who called themselves anarchist: "It is perhaps this that leads him to produce some rather questionable estimates of the respective strength of organizations and to neglect non-organized currents, such as readers of newspapers or reviews, discussion groups, camps and the influence of anarchist ideas in domains outside of the movement proper."[44] In trying to assess the broad support the anarchists had at the turn of the century, Maitron drew a distinction between activists, supporters (such as readers of anarchist newspapers) and sympathizers.[45] Noting that the ratio of Socialist Party members to Socialist Party voters was 1:20, Maitron calculated that if there were 5,500 more or less active anarchists, there would have been around 105,000 sympathizers—people who would have "voted for" anarchism, as it were. If we were to apply that methodology to the inter-war years, the total would clearly be much higher since the activists and supporters numbered in their tens of thousands.

CONSTITUENCY

As Kathryn Amdur has commented: "Only by reintegrating the study of politics and ideology with the analysis of economic and sociological conditions can one hope to achieve a full understanding of labor history or of the historical reality of any social class."[46] We too often review political debates in the labour movement as if they were conducted in abstraction from social and economic realities. We only need to read Amdur's or Colson's accounts of the syndicalist and socialist movements in Limoges and Saint-Etienne to remind ourselves of the importance for developing modes of struggle of the conditions in which different groups of workers lived and worked, but also of the enormous local and regional disparities caused by different historical conditions.[47] Given the political, ideological and organizational focus of the present study, and the fact that this is an area where very little research has been carried out, what follows is an unavoidably brief overview of the state of our knowledge of the social constituency of the anarchist movement.

Class

Shoemakers are usually produced in discussions of the sociology of anarchism. With regard to the nineteenth century, this would be largely justified; whether the same could be said of the inter-war years is doubtful. Still less convincing would be the simplistic presentation of the anarchists as having support only among a bohemian fringe, intellectuals, the petty bourgeoisie or the *Lumpenproletariat*.[48] Yet this is how anarchism has often been represented, especially by marxists. The classic marxist interpretation of the historical significance of anarchism is that it was an essentially backward-looking reaction against the development of industrial capitalism with its concomitant economic concentration and urbanization; that it was the fearful response of a relatively privileged artisanal working class gradually being displaced by a factory proletariat. Given the fact that French working-class consciousness had its roots in the mid-nineteenth century in precisely those social categories (and not in a factory proletariat),[49] it is not surprising that a significant proportion of anarchism's constituency in the latter half of the nineteenth century was to be found among workers in traditional, highly-skilled jobs that required a long apprenticeship and that were usually carried out in small workshops. The irate anarchist shoemaker, the eponymous hero of Émile Pouget's newspaper *le Père Peinard*, who every week berated the bourgeois in the robust *argot* of the working-class quarters of Paris, is emblematic of this constituency.

Some qualifications are however necessary. Firstly, the sociological nature of anarchism's support varied enormously from region to region. Although research has shown that whereas in the Bouches du Rhône and the Alpes Maritimes, for instance, the *artisanat* represented well over half of known anarchists in the 1890s, the same was not true of the Var, and in the Isère and the Nord a clear majority worked in more modern, concentrated industries.[50] Secondly, from the early 1890s onwards, the proportion of anarchists in the artisanal trades was declining in relation to the proportion employed in concentrated, rationalizing industries. Similarly, the proportion of self-employed artisans was declining in relation to wage-earners. This is borne out by research on the Bouches du Rhône before the Great War,[51] and by research relating to the whole of France before 1914 and during the inter-war period.[52] My own study of French volunteers with the CNT-FAI militias showed that of the 48 individuals for whom we have information, a clear majority (28) were blue-collar workers, 7 were private sector white-collar employees, 5 were school teachers and 3 were shopkeepers or market traders. The branches most represented were the metalworking industries (12), construction (6), education (6) and paper and printing (5).[53] A final point which needs to be made concerns categories such as small shopkeepers, café proprietors, market-stall holders, hawkers and proofreaders, who often seem overrepresented among anarchists and indeed among other revolutionaries. This is because such forms of work were very often a last resort for troublesome workers sacked and blacklisted by employers because of their activities on the shop-floor. A typical example would be Nicolas Faucier, a car worker with Renault in Paris, who was fired and blacklisted in 1925 for having led a strike. He was reduced to working as a street hawker for a while before eventually finding work as a proofreader.[54]

Few studies of the sociology of anarchism have been published, and those that have are all limited in scope. Taken together, however, the available evidence seems to be that, by the 1920s, there was no significant sociological difference between the membership of the French Communist Party and that of the Anarchist Union, and that by the time of the Popular Front the anarchist movement was significantly more "proletarian" than the Socialist Party.

Gender

How well represented were women in the anarchist movement? Very little research has been done on the question.[55] Research on the anarchist movement generally is problematic for the reasons we have already mentioned. Doing research on anarchist women is doubly so. With regard to police reports, for example, René Bianco has found accounts of public meetings and galas organized by anarchists and syndicalists in Marseille in the 1890s at which anything between 20% and 60% of the audience were claimed to be women or "women and children" counted together. And yet comparing estimates of attendance produced by different police officers present at the same meetings, disparities of 100% or more were found to be not uncommon.[56] A further problem is that the police seem not to have believed women could possibly represent a danger to the State, and simply did not include women activists in their surveillance of the movement, even at the height of the terrorist phase of the 1890s.[57] Another problem is the frequent use of surnames alone, both in the press and in police reports, which gives us no indication as to an activist's sex. Alternatively, women are referred to by their first name only, or sign their articles just with their first name.[58] Whether this was conscious imitation of the Saint-Simonian women who refused to use their surname on the grounds that it was the name of their father or husband; or for the same reason women involved in the 1970s MLF (Mouvement de libération des femmes, Women's Liberation Movement) preferred not to use surnames, namely to prevent attention from being focussed on individuals, we do not know. But it makes it difficult to find out anything more about them. As for oral testimony, its usefulness in this domain is sometimes limited by the sexism of male activists or the unwillingness of women activists to speak frankly in front of their male partners.[59] Despite all these problems, what is it possible to establish about the participation of women in the French anarchist movement?

We know that women were forming separate groups within the movement as early as the 1880s—groups with names like les Humanitaires, les Insoumises and les Révoltées—but the names are all we have.[60] We also know that there was an anarchist Groupe féminin in Paris, which had regular weekly meetings during 1914. In the 1920s and 30s, more women began to attend local anarchist group meetings, often accompanying their male partners, whereas in some towns they had been almost totally absent before the Great War.[61] And there are more references in the anarchist press, however brief, to women's groups and sections. A feminist group within the Anarchist Union was created in 1925—though apparently not without some of the men objecting—based on the recognition of the specificity of women's oppression.[62] Toulouse had a Comité Anarcho-Syndicaliste Féminin in 1936–37.[63] In Marseille in 1937 women anarchists set up a Comité des femmes libertaires pour l'aide au peuple espagnol.[64] By 1937 there appears to have been a women's section attached to the CGTSR, the Section Féminine des Amis du Monde Nouveau, led by Lucie Job, partner of Pierre Besnard.[65] And 31 March 1939 saw the somewhat belated constitutive meeting of the Groupe Féminin de l'Union Anarchiste.[66]

Some French anarchist women—though very few in comparison with the number of men—went to Spain during the civil war: only 16 out of the 254 whose gender we know. Only seven of those were with the militias: Thérèse Bardy, Juliette Baudard, Suzanne Girbe, Suzanne Hans, the nurse Georgette Kokoczinski, Emilienne Morin and a 34-year-old textile worker, Hélène Patou, who were all members of the Durruti Column. Emilienne Morin was the French partner of Buenaventura Durruti and a member of the Durruti Column, in which she was responsible for coordinating technical services at the front. Baudard and Kokoczinski died at Perdiguera in October 1936. Hans, a 22-year-old from Paris, was killed during an attack at Farlete the previous month. Of the others, Paula Felstein and Renée Lamberet ran the Llansá orphanage; Pauline and Noëla Tricheux were in Puigcerdá; Eugénie Casteu, as far as we are aware, was not a volunteer of any kind, but was killed in a bombardment whilst visiting her wounded brother at the front; Léa Meurant, a 53-year-old garments industry worker from the Nord, was as we have seen, delegated with her husband by the Union Fédérative des Comités Anarcho-Syndicalistes Franco-Belges to visit Puigcerdá; Montégud visited Spain between October and December 1936 as the delegate of the Fédération anarchiste provençale. We have already mentioned the total anonymity of the wife of René Prince, beyond the fact that she accompanied him to Barcelona and was also imprisoned with him. Dori Prudhommeaux, 29 at the time, accompanied her husband André to

Barcelona in September–October 1936 when he was launching *l'Espagne Antifasciste*, but she does not seem to have taken a public rôle herself.

In his monumental study of the French anarchist press over a hundred-year period, René Bianco has calculated that of all the contributors whose sex we can be sure of, 10% were women.[67] Around the turn of the century, many anarchist papers were concerned at the small numbers of women writing for them and appealed to women to join the cause and be more active in their support. According to police reports, there were at least two or three attempts to found "anarchist-feminist" newspapers.[68] Some newspapers were very self-critical about the attitudes of the anarchist movement in the past, and if there was undeniably a certain patronizing tone in some male anarchists' calls for "their womenfolk" to be given a "social education" and "encouraged" to become politically active themselves, women anarchists were by no means passive, vigorously criticizing their male comrades in the pages of the movement's press. Some papers established more or less regular rubrics reserved for women activists. *La Revue Anarchiste*, for instance, which appeared in the mid-1920s, had a regular rubric "Écoutons nos compagnes" (literally: "Listen to our women comrades") signed by "Une Révoltée." *Le Libertaire* carried a somewhat irregular "Tribune Féminine,"[69] and even when it did not have a "Tribune," it normally carried at least one article per number about women and/or feminism, usually by a woman. Indeed one of the most prolific contributors from 1919 through to the mid-1920s was the libertarian socialist feminist Madeleine Pelletier—who, incidentally, also wrote one of the two entries on feminism in the four-volume *Encyclopédie Anarchiste* published in 1934.[70]

One particular topic, which was given some prominence in the anarchist press, was the question of female suffrage. Of course, this presented the anarchists with something of a dilemma given, on the one hand, their public declarations in favour of women's "complete emancipation" and, on the other, their antiparliamentarism. The result was some lively discussion of the arguments for and against female suffrage. The argument against supporting the campaign for the vote for women was basically the same as anarchists always used with regard to elections. The Paris Groupe Féminin saw suffragism as being of interest only to the ladies of the bourgeoisie; for them, "proletarian" women should organize on an economic basis—i.e. in trade unions—and should not cooperate with individuals whose interests were the opposite of their own.[71] Other anarchist women argued that rather than deceiving working-class women by encouraging them to believe in the myth of parliamentary democracy, anarchists should be working towards their "moral and intellectual emancipation."[72] Madeleine Pelletier, on the other hand, whilst expressing little faith in electoral politics, nevertheless argued that if the act of voting was not important to women, having the right to vote was; the fact that no man would be able to say to a woman that he was any more of a citizen than she, would make a difference to the way women would be seen and to the way they would see themselves.[73] Pierre Martin—one of the very few men to intervene in the debate—insisted that women Deputies would not legislate in the interests of all women, but only in the interests of their class.[74] Julia Bertrand, on the other hand, believed that the presence of women in the Chamber would have a positive influence on the type of laws passed and on the nature of government—a remarkably familiar debate.[75] And so the discussion continued at more or less regular intervals, with a majority of contributors upholding the anarchist rejection of electoralism, whilst otherwise supporting feminist positions. These contributors could, however, be seen as self-selecting. As we have already noted, very few men took part in the debate in the press, and we do not know why. It is possible that the debate was tolerated in the pages of the anarchist press and simultaneously marginalized by the male majority, to whom it may simply not have appeared important. For women anarchists, the suffrage question was of such importance that quite a few of them became unsure about their previously absolute opposition to parliamentary politics.

On the basis of the available evidence, it would probably be wrong to exaggerate the anarchist movement's commitment to women and feminism, even if it is worth noting positive elements such as the importance attached to discussion of the "woman question" in the anarchist press and other publications, the existence of women's groups (probably more than in the SFIO), the importance attached to the notion that "the personal is political," the rejection of traditional family structures and the active involvement in campaigns for the right to contraception and abortion. Thanks largely to the increasing proportion of women working outside the home and the concomitant change in attitudes (particularly after the experiences of 1914–18), there was a significant shift from the proudhonist misogyny (or what has been called the "left-wing patriarchalism")[76] of the First International years, to a more pro-feminist stance in the period following the 1880s. But it was obviously a slow and gradual process and practice clearly often failed to live up to theory. If, in later years, women were encouraged to participate more actively and more visibly in the movement, it was sometimes by fulfilling what were traditionally "feminine" rôles—knitting scarves for the Durruti column, for instance.[77] And there was certainly a disparity between the public, political sphere on the one hand, and the private, on the other. As one woman activist told Claire Auzias: "I've often told my partner that the anarchists rail in public against other peoples' authority, only to come home and impose their own authority there."[78] The world of the anarchist activist was still overwhelmingly a world of men and still very sexist. In introducing the autobiography of René Michaud (who started his political life among the anarchists), Thierry Paquot felt it necessary to apologize for the author's sexism: "a sexism widely shared at the time — and still today — by the great majority of men, whether working-class or middle-class, anarchist or non-anarchist."[79]

Geography

What of the geographical implantation of the anarchist movement? If we look first at the distribution of UA groups, the first and most obvious point is the strength of the anarchist presence in Paris and especially in the working-class suburbs. In both the earlier period and the later, the Paris area represents a significant proportion of groups nationally. In 1919–24, 38 groups out of a total of 86; in 1936–39, 56 out of 107. It is noticeable that in the earlier period, a majority of groups—48 out of 86—were in the provinces, while in the later period the majority were on the contrary in the Paris area. This is confirmed if we look at the distribution of the 29 JAC groups in the late 1930s. Of these, 24 were in Paris and the suburbs, and only 5 in the provinces.

This has also been confirmed by a study of the geographical origin of those who became involved in Spain in 1936.[80] This is a small corpus, as we only have information in 74 cases out of 327 as to where individuals were living at the time they left for Spain. That notwithstanding, one thing, immediately obvious from the data, is the predominance of Paris and the Paris region: 29 of the 74 had been living in Paris, and a further 12 in the Paris region with notable concentrations in the northern and western *banlieue*. The only other noticeable concentration is in the Gard and Haute-Garonne, doubtless a result of the rôle of Spanish anarchist immigration and of geographical proximity. If we limit our investigation to those at the front, we have data for 35 out of 247, but the concentration in Paris and the northern and western *banlieue* remains true, as does the showing of the south-western departments.

Two further points can be made about the movement's presence in Paris and the suburbs. First, the number of groups in Paris itself remained stable between the two periods: 11 to 12; and their distribution also remained more or less the same: a very weak presence in the central *arrondissements* of the right bank (1st, 2nd, 3rd and 4th arr.) and no presence at all in the bourgeois west end (7th and 8th), but with fairly even representation in all other parts of the city.

Second, this period saw an increase in the number of groups in the *"banlieue rouge,"* the industrializing working-class suburbs where the Communist Party was also strong. In the 1930s there was an effort on the part of the UA to strengthen the organization of groups in the Paris region and to increase co-ordination of their work. This began with the creation of "inter-communal" groups: the *"Banlieue Nord,"* which covered Clichy, Gennevilliers, Asnières and Levallois; and the *"Banlieue Sud,"* which covered Montrouge, Malakoff, Vanves and Châtillon. Later on, there was mention in the "Vie de l'UA" rubric of *le Libertaire* of a *"Secteur Sud-Ouest,"* covering the 14th and 15th arr., Issy-les-Moulineaux, Clamart, Vanves, Malakoff, Antony and Boulogne-Billancourt; and of a *"Secteur Nord-Ouest,"* covering the 16th, 17th and 18th arr., Clichy, Levallois, Gennevilliers, Saint-Ouen, Colombes, Puteaux and Courbevoie. Nothing further is known about this apparent attempt at re-organization, but the very existence of such an effort is in itself significant.

So the first conclusion that can be drawn is the importance for anarchist communism of the Paris area, and the increasingly dominant rôle of the suburbs. This conforms to impressionistic evidence suggesting that the UA was dominant in the Paris area, whereas the AFA, the FAF and the CGTSR were at their strongest in the provinces, and in particular in the south: Limoges, Clermont-Ferrand, Nîmes, Saint-Etienne, Lyon and Bordeaux.

As for UA implantation in the provinces, we can point to three major centres of activity between the wars: the Nord and the Pas-de-Calais (and to a lesser extent the Somme and the Oise and the Seine valley between Paris and Le Havre); the Rhône and the Loire; the Var, the Bouches-du-Rhône, the Gard, the Hérault, the Aude and the Pyrénées-Orientales. Again, given the lack of detailed research, one can only ask more questions about why anarchists seem to have been present and active in greater numbers than usual in these areas. Lyon, of course, had an anarchist tradition going back to Bakunin's attempted insurrection of 1870 and beyond that to the mutualists. Both Lyon and the industrial area that centres on Lille were major manufacturing centres. Lyon and Saint-Etienne were also among the areas where the CGTSR was strongest.[81] The Rhône and the Loire were the two departments which gave the largest number of votes to Besnard's CDS and to the anti-communist Groupes Syndicalistes Révolutionnaires at the CGTU's Bourges congress of 1923.[82] The economy of the departments on the Mediterranean coast was very diverse, from wine growing throughout the region, to the docks at Marseille or the arsenal at Toulon. The number of anarchist groups in this region appears to have increased significantly by the

1930s, and it is likely that Spanish and Italian immigration played a not insignificant role.[83]

We have already come to the tentative conclusion that between the wars there was little difference in the sociologies of communism and of mainstream anarchist communism. This conclusion would seem to be supported by our look at the UA's geographical distribution, since the Paris *banlieue* and the mining area of the Nord/Pas-de-Calais were also strongholds of the PCF. This would suggest a change in the constituency of anarchism—or at least of mainstream anarchist communism. Although the economic changes undergone in France between the wars are sometimes exaggerated, this was a period of technical and financial concentration in industry, of taylorization, of increasing numbers of semi-skilled workers (*"manœuvres spécialisés"* or *"ouvriers spécialisés"* as they became known later); it was a period that saw the development of new industries (e.g. cars and chemicals); it was a period that saw increased state intervention, and the organization of the employers—first in the Confédération générale de la Production française, founded in 1919, then from 1936 in the Confédération générale du Patronat français. Such changes are often advanced to explain the development of a communist movement finding support in an expanding factory proletariat, and the disappearance of an anarchist movement whose allegedly artisanal constituency was disappearing and whose strategies for social change were becoming increasingly irrelevant. It is however by no means easy to explain or define the relation between such changes and their effect on political or ideological choices. Amdur has stressed the extent of ideological continuity within the labour movement from the pre-war period through to the 1920s and 30s: "It would of course be a little simplistic to link syndicalist strategies to economic conditions, especially in the short term. One can say that working-class attitudes either maintained a considerable degree of autonomy from economic changes, or that they were characterized by a certain inertia which meant that they responded to economic developments with a greater or lesser time-lag."[84]

Further, the anarchist movement seems not to have been so tightly anchored in the declining sectors of the economy as has often been suggested. It also seems to have experienced something of a renewal in this period, both in generational terms and ideologically. André Lorulot wrote of the anarchist movement in 1922 that "the personalities, apart from a few exceptions, are no longer the same."[85] There was a second influx of fresh militants in the mid-1930s. Was there a connection between the recruitment of a younger generation and the ideological revisionism of 1917–20 and 1936–39? Certainly the periods of rapid growth coincided with periods of severe criticism of "traditional" anarchism and of increased emphasis on anarchism as socialism. Faucier has pointed out that those who supported most strongly the "platformist" tendency were — apart from the Languedoc groups heavily influenced by exiled CNT-FAI militants — militants from the industrial north (Nord, Pas-de-Calais, Somme, Oise) and the many young militants in the Paris area.[86] At the 1937 UA congress, René Frémont, whilst emphasizing the rôle of the Spanish revolution in proving to many French workers that anarchism was relevant to the labour movement and was not about "philosophical and romantic speculation," also felt the need to point out that many recent young recruits to the UA were "still too impregnated with bolshevist ideas."[87] Servant, of the JAC group in Paris 12, denied the accusation of bolshevism, but it is clear from the exchanges as reported in *le Libertaire* that there was a certain ignorance amongst the younger militants of anarchist "traditions" and "principles." This would obviously imply more openness to revision — indeed the debate in question was about the need for re-organization of the UA.

IDEOLOGY

This study may be one principally of ideology and organizations, but it has tried to emphasize the ideas and actions of grass-roots militants rather than those of theorists; it has tried to get beyond the generalizations of political philosophers' accounts of anarchist ideology (in the singular) and has tried to analyse anarchism as the ideology of a social movement, with its internal contradictions, its equivocal responses to new challenges, its continuous development in changing circumstances; it has also challenged the very idea of an anarchist *movement* of the type posited by Faure's "Synthèse," and has implied a reconsideration of the usual, simplistic border-line between "authoritarian" and "anti-authoritarian" socialisms.

The whole of the inter-war period was, I would argue, one of revisionism. The individualist Lorulot, in the 1922 article quoted above, had already pointed out the increased homogeneity of the movement, now dominated by the anarchist communism of the UA and *le Libertaire*, and less preoccupied with individualist concerns: "There is greater cohesion and harmony; there is therefore more intense action. Some view this with satisfaction, others find it regrettable on the grounds that the present-day revolutionary anarchist tendency tends to neglect education and reflection, preferring instead to launch itself into action and violence."[88]

The challenge of the Russian and Spanish revolutions

The Russian and Spanish revolutions represented moments of crisis for
the anarchist movement. It was confronted for the first time with actual
revolutions in which anarchists played a significant rôle. On both occasions, the anarchists were provoked into questioning their own theories and their own visions of the Revolution. Significant sections of the
movement found anarchism as a revolutionary doctrine and practice
severely lacking. Important aspects of anarchist doctrine and practice
were questioned and rejected, or so modified that it was difficult to per-
ceive any clear and significant distinction between anarchism and other
sectors of the revolutionary socialist movement. The much-vaunted
"specificity" of anarchism became somewhat problematic: what exactly
was it that distinguished the socialist varieties of anarchism from non-
anarchist socialisms?[89] This doctrinal crisis was a problem of which the
militants themselves were very well aware at the time:

> Each time that the problem becomes concrete and serious, each
> time that life demands a true, real, exact solution, each time that
> the revolutionaries in general and the anarchists in particular
> are obliged to give their opinion, to declare their position and to
> act on it, we are forced to consign our ideas to the museum and
> to contribute to the application of ideas which we believed are
> wrong. But, incontestably, an idea is wrong if at the precise mo-
> ment when it needs to be put into practice it is seen every time
> to be invalid, sterile, inoperable. Such an idea must be rejected
> definitively. Because an idea which is impracticable at the very
> moment when it needs to be put into practice is not worth the
> paper it is written on.[90]

The organization of the anarchist movement

There were various interlinked questions thrown up by the two revolutions and debated at length in the anarchist press. The major one was organization. It is of course something of a cliché to raise this point when
considering the reasons for what has no doubt been the historic failure
of anarchism as a movement, and the movement's inability to shake off
what was for Trotsky the "traditional French disease," the inability to
organize.[91] Looking back from a position of isolation, Jean Grave was
bitter and harsh on his erstwhile comrades, but there was much truth in
what he wrote:

> The anarchists, who pride themselves on being lucid and ra-
> tional, contented themselves rather too often with verbiage:
> "Let us make the revolution, we will see afterwards what needs

to be done to organize the future society"! — "Let us produce *conscious* rebels"! — "There is no need for organization, free initiative suffices"! — "Free Association is the best form of organization"! — All that would have been fine if there had been anything behind it. Unfortunately, in most cases, they were just phrases devoid of meaning ... [92]

Sébastien Faure, though, took a different view. In a speech given more than once on speaking tours around 1920–21, he did more than highlight one of the problems involved in trying to define and quantify the anarchist "movement." Faure himself made clear what must be the major historical failure of the anarchist movement: the incapacity to provide an organization or framework capable of co-ordinating effectively the activities of thousands of supporters. Why did so many militants *need* to join the SFIO? Why did so many come to devote themselves exclusively to the syndicalist movement? Why were their activities in the rationalist or co-operatist movements not clearly integrated, both theoretically and practically, within a broader anarchist framework?

> They can be seen infiltrating everywhere. Alongside the several thousand declared anarchists who are organized in groups, one can see thousands and thousands who are in other kinds of group: some with the Freethinkers; others in the Socialist Party; yet more in the CGT. I even know many, in such and such a small town in the countryside, who, feeling the need to do something, to become involved in local struggles and in campaigns going on around them, join the socialist movement; they do not for all that abandon their anarchist ideas; there are also many such people in the syndicalist movement, in the co-operative movement, they are everywhere ... There are even many who do not know they are anarchists! For as soon as one explains to them what anarchism is, they reply: "But if that is what anarchism is, then I'm an anarchist! I am with you!" Yes, anarchism is everywhere. [93]

This kind of cheerful and complacent acceptance of the atomized nature of the "movement" was (and still is) characteristic of a certain type of anarchism. It seems to be formed of a mixture of principle — a belief in the "*synthèse*" and in the "*minorité agissante*" (the "active minority") that comes and goes spontaneously with fluctuations in the level of social conflict — and of resignation to the numerical weakness of anarchism as compared to other doctrines of social change. [94]

But whereas most commentators content themselves with registering a failure, the evidence presented here surely forces us to emphasize the constant efforts in the inter-war years of a significant and frequently very influential minority to provide anarchism with a more consistent and cohesive organizational and ideological framework.[95] From the critique developed by those associated with *Ce qu'il faut dire* and *l'Avenir international*, through the efforts of the sovietists to reconcile ideological and organizational unity with anti-authoritarianism, to the different Libertarian Communist Federations, the *Plate-forme* and the organizationalist UA of the 1930s, the trend throughout this period was towards tighter organization and towards co-operation with other sectors of the labour movement. The editors of *le Libertaire*, introducing an article by Gaston Leval on this very question, wrote in 1937 that "the repugnance felt by anarchists with regard to organization is nowadays definitely on the decrease in France and ... we are glad of it."[96] Leval emphasized that all the major anarchist theorists and militants had favoured organization: "If anarchy were the negation of organization ... it would have to be rejected, as many who interpreted it that way have done. It would have to be rejected because the dilemma of life is organization or death. The isolated individual does not exist. What differentiates us from other tendencies in the labour and socialist movement is not the rejection but the conception of organization. ... Repudiating organization as such is not anarchism, it is nihilism."[97]

Anarchism's place in the wider socialist movement

The emphasis on organization was always linked in the 1920s and 30s to a desired *rapprochement* with other sectors of the wider socialist and labour movements. This was a major and recurrent theme from 1917 onwards, as we have seen. The Versailles UA group, putting forward new organizational proposals in 1937, insisted that anarchism could not be separated from socialism, that anarchism was socialism "taken to its logical conclusion."[98] Ridel — a member of the FCL tendency and of the UA's Administrative Commission — made an interesting intervention at the 1937 congress, deploring the political inconsistency of the UA: "We are overburdened with the weight of outdated ideas. Anarchism is not a philosophical system. It is situated both in space and time. It is a socialism, a sector of the labour movement."[99] This desire on the part of the UA to see itself as part of the wider socialist movement was linked with a workerism that stressed the "essential rôle which the producers have to play in the social struggle" and that was reminiscent of the sovietists and the platformists and, of course, of the French revolutionary syndicalist tradition.[100]

This was not all just wishful thinking. With the phenomenal growth of the UA in 1936–37, and the success of SIA, the anarchists had some reason to congratulate themselves on their "return to the so-cial scene."[101] The achievements of the CNT-FAI and the prestige that brushed off on anarchism worldwide had a lot to do with this, as René Frémont made clear: "The Spanish revolution, for many workers, has meant the birth of a new socialist doctrine. As a consequence, anar-chism has left the domain of theory and become a practice. For the first time, our doctrine became the subject of a practical experiment."[102] Since 1914 the anarchists had been extremely sensitive to accusations of the impracticability of anarchism: "Despite the concrete proof which the anarchists have provided in France and elsewhere of their practi-cal sense in the unions and in the co-operatives, many still felt able to say that although the anarchists knew how to struggle and die, they did not know what for."[103] The anarchists were very keen, especially when faced with communist critics who had behind them the concrete achievement of a soviet state, to refute allegations that they were mere dreamers capable only of negative criticism. After 1936, revolutionary Spain provided the anarchist movement with their own concrete model. Sébastien Faure in 1938: "Unless from ignorance or in bad faith, no one will in future be able to claim that the Anarchists are mere dreamers, utopians and destroyers and that although their ideal is superb, it is in practice unachievable."[104] Leading UA militants began in the 1930s to talk positively of "revolutionary realism" and "revolutionary opportun-ism,"[105] but not just in the context of the Spanish revolution. Makhno and Durruti were both elevated, in the 1930s, to the status of heroes, acclaimed as "realistic anarchists of action," recuperated for the organi-zationalist tendency, their names linked to the quest for a working-class, sovietist anarchism.[106]

Confusion or revisionism? The "transitional period"

This was not an uncommon attitude between the wars. Anarchism was increasingly regarded as a historically determined ideology whose prin-ciples should in no sense be regarded as immutable. Analyzing the ste-reotypical representations of anarchism produced by its political enemies and how these images had been contradicted by events in Spain, the French-speaking Belgian anarchist Ernestan wrote: "This is where we see the paucity of words and how erroneous it is to consider anarchism as a pure philosophy and an idealist dialectic, rather than as an eminent-ly realistic doctrine and a social technique. We have too often been the slaves of words, of absolute and abstract formulae, without concerning ourselves with their concrete content and their transposition into real-ity."[107] Ernestan went on to examine three anarchist "principles" which had been much discussed both in connection with Spain and, over a decade earlier, in connection with Russia: anti-statism, anti-militarism and opposition to leaders. He argued that anarchism must oppose leaders but must accept mandated delegates, "and have confidence in them within the limits of their remits. The main thing is that they must never escape being monitored and criticized." Militarism he defined as "that authoritarian mystique and that submission complex which create an inhuman discipline"; and he argued that the popular antifascist militias were in no way "militaristic." These two points would probably have caused offence to only a minority of anarchists on the individualist wing of the movement. His third point concerned the meaning of anarchist anti-statism in a revolutionary situation, and can be read as a defence of the CNT's participation in the Caballero government. This was also not an uncommon position, though hotly contested by some, but his general reinterpretation of the anarchist position, which he based on the Spanish experience, was much more revisionist. Ernestan accepted that anarchists must oppose "statism," which he defined as "the tendency to maintain a political privilege for the benefit of a particular fraction," or as the maintenance of "a central power from which all initiatives emanate and which controls all social activity." But he went on: "That does not mean denying that certain aspects of the State cannot be replaced in a day, and that residual structures persist for a certain length of time. The essential thing is that from the first day of the revolution, State structures must be replaced as quickly as possible by Proletarian Federalism. This is the opposite of Statist marxism, which wants to actually strengthen the State in order to create a dictatorship."

So Ernestan, writing in the organ of the UA, argued that in certain circumstances anarchists may not be able to destroy the state entirely, and would have to accept the survival for a while of some kind of state. Albert Jensen, the Swedish anarcho-syndicalist, argued in the French edition of *Internationale*, the review of the IWMA, that events in Spain demonstrated the weakness of anarcho-syndicalist ideology and that the situation there required the creation of a national assembly, "a new expression of power, convening representatives of the workers', peasants' and soldiers' councils."[108] But what does such an attitude mean, if not an acceptance of a "transitional period" of some kind? And if the anarchists accept some kind of a transitional period, with some kind of representative structure still in place, what exactly is it that constitutes the distinctiveness or specificity of anarchism? Has it not just been reduced to a matter of degree: a question of the degree of authority which is acceptable?

This was of course nothing new. The response to the Russian revolution had already highlighted the lack of clarity of many anarchists' thinking and provoked a serious questioning of anarchist ideas of what the revolution would be like. That this ambivalence towards "the State" and towards notions of a "transitional period" existed among the sovietists is clear. But such an ambivalence was also demonstrated to a remarkable degree by militants of all tendencies. Since this question is always cited as being the major point that distinguishes anarchist revolutionary strategy from other revolutionary strategies, this is surely an important point. *La Mêlée*, for instance, published one militant who wrote: "I am one of those who have doubts as to whether our ideal could be realized without preparation and without a transitional period, especially in the larger towns and cities and during a period when basic necessities will be scarce."[109] Marie Isidine, a leading member of the *Temps nouveaux* group, expressed similar doubts: "We do not expect, of course, that after the first day of the revolution everything will be sorted out without conflicts and without the persistence of some elements of the bourgeois past. We know it is extremely unlikely that complete, pure communism can be achieved all at once."[110] In 1921 Sébastien Faure, even as he finally pronounced his disapproval of bolshevik policies, also brought into question the rejection of a transitional period: "It was not, one must agree, the immediate and complete realization of the anarchist ideal; but was it possible to clear with one bound the abyss separating bourgeois society and the libertarian communist society ...? Nevertheless, a door had been opened on new prospects for the future."[111] The fudge was even more blatant with Lecoin's judgement on the practice of bolshevism. He rejected "authoritarianism" and "dictatorship," but admitted that a "transitional period" would probably be necessary. But if "authority" had been totally abolished, what did Lecoin understand by a transitional period?

> The anarchists do not deny that between the first days of a revolution with anarchistic tendencies and the ultimate aim of anarchism, the anarchic commune, there must be a certain period of time during which the remains of the old servitude gradually disappear, and the new forms of free association develop. This period, full of mistakes, of errors and of constant improvements can be called the period of accumulation of antiauthoritarian experience, or the period of consolidation of the social revolution, or the setting in motion of the anarchist commune.[112]

Fifteen years later, Faure and his comrade Blicq would be justifying the existence of prisons and political prisoners in revolutionary Spain, emphasizing how good the prison library was, how the prisoners wore no uniform and did no forced labour.[113] And the supposedly purist and dogmatic Besnard was to do exactly the same, presenting a rosy view of contented, well-fed and repentant prisoners—even antifascists being punished for disciplinary offences: "I also saw the prisons. For the situation, the defence of the revolution, demands, unfortunately, that the prisons be maintained still."[114]

The long-term decline of anarchism

A major contributory factor in the long-term decline of the anarchist movement was surely its failure to clarify its own ideology and to put itself on a sound organizational footing after the humiliating collapse of 1914. It found it impossible to campaign effectively against the implantation of bolshevism in France. This has no doubt been linked, over the longer term, to economic concentration and to what, in 1919, *la Mêlée* called the "general tendency towards statism": growing corporatism and the increasing marginalization of antiparliamentary strategies as the other sectors of the labour and socialist movements took on board parliamentary and statist strategies in response to the relative success of the previous decades of reformism.[115] It was also due to a factor sometimes concentrated on, to the exclusion of all else, by anarchists but ignored completely by others: persistent vilification (and worse) at the hands of the communists. But of course the very existence of the USSR also played an immensely important rôle. As Annie Kriegel put it:

> In social and political struggle, the success of a formula makes the quest for any other formula temporarily superfluous, even though other formulae might be better suited to objective conditions. As the Bolsheviks were the first to succeed in establishing a régime claiming to be socialist, their achievement, by virtue of its anteriority, was a "precedent" which was transformed naturally into a "model." A "model": this term in itself implies no value judgement. It simply means that the bolshevik-style revolution was sheared of its real attributes, of its environment, of the individuality of its protagonists, of the contingent nature of its unfolding. It was frozen in its abstraction: it now became the incarnation of the universal proletariat's dream of subversion.[116]

Curiously, the repeated attempts throughout this period to build a more coherent, stable and effective anarchist organization were at once provoked by the appearance of bolshevism and also later hindered by it. Initially a model, later a rival and enemy, bolshevism became demonized, and accusations of "bolshevization" became an easy way of foreclosing on discussion of any organizational innovation or attempt at theoretical clarification.[117] Lenin wrote that "anarchism was not infrequently a kind of penalty for the opportunist sins of the working-class movement. The two monstrosities complemented each other."[118] If we were to substitute "communist movement" for "working-class movement," this might help us understand the ironic mechanism whereby, while communists would criticize the organizational and doctrinal confusion of anarchism, it was to a large extent the authoritarianism and perceived opportunism of the communists that prevented the anarchist movement from correcting such confusion.

Having said that, if we look at the inter-war period and compare it to earlier phases of the history of anarchism in France, what stands out is the dominance of communist anarchism, the increasing identification of anarchism with organized labour, and repeated attempts to tighten both organization and ideology. Those militants whom Chazoff called "the absolutists, those in favour of all or nothing" were increasingly isolated.[119] Indeed I would argue that it is misleading to refer to the "anarchist movement" in this period: a study of the anarchists' reactions to the Russian and Spanish revolutions and of the ideological revisionism of the 1920s and 30s surely indicates the increasing distance between the individualists on the one hand, and the anarchist communists and syndicalists on the other. At the same time, the majority of anarchists seem to have been constantly co-operating with non-anarchist socialists of various types throughout this period. The emphasis was continually put on anarchism as a part of the wider labour and socialist movement. To suggest, therefore, as do Broué and Dorey in their study of the revolutionary opposition to the Popular Front, that the anarchists were always a minority "swimming against the current" seems to me misleading.[120]

It depends on one's own political standpoint whether one interprets the ideological revisionism of those years as symptomatic of a failure—a tacit admission that anarchist doctrine should be jettisoned—or as a commendable attempt to adapt to new historical circumstances, taking on board what were felt to be the lessons of the Great War, October 1917 and June–July 1936: the need for a more cohesive organization, the need to take account of the existence within the revolutionary camp of different ideological movements, the problems of civil war and foreign intervention, the changing nature of war, the problem of post-revolutionary structures and so on.

The *Révision* group: for a revolutionary libertarian socialism

One group of militants stood out in the late 1930s by virtue of their attempt to conduct a thoroughgoing, reasoned critique of both anarchism and the wider revolutionary movement from the standpoint of a consistently revolutionary, antiauthoritarian socialism. The group had diverse origins: most of them were from an anarchist background, but several had previously belonged to other political or syndicalist organizations: the PCF, the PS, the PSOP, the JEUNES, the Révolution prolétarienne group.[121] The group had two things in common: their youth and their conviction—after the experience of the preceding twenty years and particularly after their own direct experience of popular frontism in France and in Spain—that the entire working-class movement was in dire need of a radical ideological and strategic rethink. The *raison d'être* of the group was to help produce the new ideas which they believed the existing organizations of the left lacked. They did this by launching a new "review of revolutionary studies," the monthly *Révision*:

> Within or on the margins of the official tendencies, a group of sincere and honest revolutionaries reject the outdated credos and catechisms and are searching for an interpretation and a method of action which can take account of the new factors which the events of this century have thrown up and by which we are all influenced. ... Reformism, bolshevism, syndicalism and anarchism are all doctrines whose dogmas are no longer adequate for any militant. It is time to *revise* the entirety of our socialist and revolutionary conceptions through a fresh study of the reality of yesterday and of today.[122]

The *Révision* group saw itself as a rallying point for all those, whatever their political "labels," who wished to work for "a free and human socialism, a libertarian socialism", which "refuses to neglect the human side of socialism and which conceives of the social struggle and of the future society only in terms of a true democracy." They undertook to be independent of all existing tendencies and to criticize the Second International, the Third International, the "hypercritical and sterile doctrinalism of the various oppositional communist groups" and the "opportunism and purism which are to be found closely associated in certain anarchist tendencies." Charles Ridel, in particular, used *Révision* as a platform from which to denounce what he saw as the negative aspects of the "anarchist milieu"—a term which itself underlined "the vagueness and incoherence of anarchism":

> The lack of solid organizations, the absence of a written programme and statutes, the elasticity of the doctrine, its impreciseness, the generalities and contradictions it contains all make it peculiarly difficult to formulate global interpretations and clear analyses. ... The movement is divided, tendencies co-exist,

the links between groups in the provinces and those in the capital are weak and ill defined. Mentalities and campaigns vary from one region to the next. The doctrine, which is entirely theoretical and is drawn from an inexhaustible stock of out-of-date pamphlets, brings together different categories of socialist to the extent that it is only thanks to the particular character of the 'study group', the usual form taken by anarchist groups, that it is possible to unite them at all.[123]

For Ridel, "organic" involvement in labour struggles was essential, and the anarchist movement had ended up in its present state because of 15 years' absence from such struggle. Even though the PCF's tactical change after 1933 had brought new recruits to anarchism, the movement had not been able to transform itself in order to retain them. Many militants had left to work with more effective organizations that shared some of anarchism's anti-authoritarianism and revolutionism, and the movement was now dominated, he argued, by militants who had abandoned revolutionary action in favour of essentially humanitarian, liberal democratic campaigns in the framework of the bourgeois republic. This, for Ridel, fostered corrupting relations with "progressive" bourgeois elements and even with government officials. Any serious discussion about anarchist doctrine was rendered impossible by recourse to the absolute principles of "Authority" and "Liberty" — "A logic as irrefutable as it is unreal."[124]

What made this possible, ironically, was the lack of organization, Ridel insisted. What would, 40 years later, be called the "tyranny of structurelessness" meant that "on the pretext of defending freedom, a *de facto* hierarchy is installed with a few men [sic] at its summit":

> Democracy presupposes organization, it depends on it. Without organization, we get confusion and incoherence, and the natural result is the dictatorship of a clique or of mandarins. Anarchism ends up having no public existence other than in the shape of these few individuals who write, speak and act in the name of and in place of a movement which could determine itself, through the co-operation and the contribution of each one of its members, united around a doctrine, trying to influence social struggles as a vigorous and self-confident force, able to carry with it the whole of the proletariat towards its emancipation.[125]

The target of such remarks was clearly the UA. Ridel was biting in his criticisms of supposedly anarchist campaigns void of any revolutionary content and headed by committees full of "independents," "hams and posers with a tear always at the ready." For Ridel, any campaign, any movement, any action that was not anchored in the class struggle lost all validity for a revolutionary anarchist and resulted in the anarchist organization becoming "a mere annexe of the political 'left.'"[126]

After the absence of organization and of internal democracy, after the failure to adopt a consistent class analysis, another major cause of the weakness of the anarchist movement was to be found in what Ridel called its "lack of character":

> A lack of character, of independence, of autonomy means a lack of confidence and of faith in the principles and theories being advocated. The inevitable result is compromise and the abandonment of what is essential to anarchism every time social conditions make revolutionary action and the application of the revolutionary programme possible.
>
> Spain has suffered this cruel experience. Anarchism, or rather those who acted in its name, far from trying to crush en bloc what anarchism calls the forces of authority, instead attempted, from the very beginning, to gain admittance to the great liberal, republican, federalist family. Suddenly ashamed of the arguments they had been putting forward just days before, they outdid in their talk of 'realism' the bourgeois republicans, who were stunned to see this explosion of new forces happily donning the suit and tie of a minister or of a councillor.[127]

Despite what seems to me to be a remarkably perceptive critique of the anarchist movement in the 1920s and 30s, Ridel nevertheless remained optimistic and reasserted the essential correctness — in the face of the futile reformism of the Socialist Party and the stalinists' increasingly cynical and violent counter-revolutionary manœuvres — of the anarchist critique and he sang the praises of a working-class, revolutionist anarchism symbolized for him as for many others by Makhno and Durruti:

> Distinguishing itself clearly from other movements by its refusal to have anything to do with the putrescence which is bourgeois democracy, anarchism represents, in the eyes of thousands of revolutionary workers, the Barbarian who will raze to the ground the old society collapsing in blood and chaos and guarded by its mercenaries and its corrupt morality, in order to replace it with a higher form of civilization.[128]

Notes

1. *Le Libertaire*, 27 July 1919.

2. Sébastien Faure, "Les Forces de Révolution," in *Propos Subversifs* (Paris: Les Amis de Sébastien Faure, n.d. [1950?]), p.291.

3. Daniel Guérin, *L'anarchisme. De la doctrine à la pratique* (Paris: Gallimard, 1981), p.21.

4. Maitron vol.II, pp.123–35.

5. Maitron vol. II, pp.124–28.

6. *Les Temps Nouveaux*, 12–18 December 1896.

7. Maitron vol.II, pp.128–29. Because of this problem, Maitron looks at only three moments in the movement's history, none of which is much use to an examination of the inter-war period: 1893, 1913, 1975; and only very few papers are taken into account. The periodicals themselves—no doubt simply because it was easier than calculating weekly sales—tended only to publish figures relating to print-runs. The same is therefore usually true of militants' accounts, and also of police reports.

8. Such mixed groups existed for example in Bordeaux and Villeurbanne in 1919.

9. For details of these groups, see David Berry, "The Response of the French Anarchist Movement to the Russian Revolution (1917–24) and to the Spanish Revolution and Civil War (1936–39)" (DPhil thesis, University of Sussex, 1988).

10. Ibid.

11. Ibid.

12. *Le Libertaire*, 3 January 1936. See also Frémont's comments on the movement's progress in *le Libertaire*, 27 March 1936.

13. The figure 2,500–3,000 is based on estimates by both Nicolas Faucier and the police, the latter in a report of 1941. Maitron vol.II, pp. 131–32.

14. *Le Libertaire*, 2 October 1936.

15.. Ibid.

16. *Le Libertaire*, 18 December 1936.

17. *Le Libertaire*, 1 April 1937.

18. *Le Libertaire*, 13 May 1937. Maurice Joyeux claimed that no anarchist newspaper had ever had a print-run of 100,000 until the number of *le Libertaire* devoted to the Renault strikes of 1947. *L'anarchie dans la société contemporaine* (Paris: Casterman, 1977), p.57.

19. Report of November 1938, BA1713. For comparison, the PSOP's weekly *Juin 36* had a print-run of 20,000 at that time and the PCF's daily *l'Humanité* 346,000.

20. *Le Libertaire*, 29 April 1937. Articles on anarchism and anarchist syndicalism had appeared in *Vendémiaire, Esprit, Liberté* and *la République*.

21. *Le Libertaire*, 22 April 1937. The same article noted a continuing influx into the UA of ex-members of the SFIO and PCF.

22. *Le Libertaire*, 22 January 1937 and 13 October 1938. The school was to tour the provinces.

23. *Le Libertaire*, 27 May 1937.

24. *Le Libertaire*, 5 February 1937.

25. Ibid.

26. *Le Libertaire*, 4 September 1936. See also "La progression anarchiste inquiète le Parti Communiste," *le Libertaire*, 8 January 1937, which claimed that street-sellers of *le Libertaire* were being attacked by communist militants.

27. *Le Libertaire*, 11 November 1937.

28. *Le Libertaire*, 4 December 1936.

29. *Le Libertaire*, 25 March 1937.

30. *Le Libertaire*, 4 March 1937.

31. *Le Libertaire*, 5 February 1937.

32. *Le Libertaire*, 11 June 1937.

33. *Le Libertaire*, 15 January 1937.

34. *Le Libertaire*, 5 February 1937.

35. Ibid.

36. For a libertarian revolutionary interpretation of the period, see Daniel Guérin, *Front populaire, révolution manquée* (Arles: Actes Sud, 1997).

37. From its nadir of around 28,000 in 1932–33, PCF membership increased to about 330,000 in 1937. The SFIO, whose lowest point had been the three years after Tours — when it had a membership of around 50,000 — gradually re-built to a membership of 280,000 in 1937. Figures from Georges Lefranc, *Le mouvement socialiste sous la troisième république* (Paris: Payot, 1977), vol.II, p.461; and Henri Dubief, *Le déclin de la IIIe République (1929–1938)* (Paris: Seuil, 1976), p.195.

38. *Le Libertaire*, 4 September 1936.

39. *Le Libertaire*, 8 July 1937.

40. *Le Libertaire* ,8 January 1937.

41. *Le Libertaire*, 29 January 1937.

42. Louis Anderson in interview with the author.

43. Nicolas Faucier, letter to the author. On French trotskyism, see Jacques Roussel, *Les enfants du prophète* (Paris: Spartacus, 1972).

44. Marianne Enckell, review of Maitron, *Le Mouvement anarchiste*, in *Bulletin du CIRA* (Lausanne), no.29 (Spring 1975), pp.20–1.

45. Maitron vol.I, p.130.

46. Kathryn E. Amdur, *Syndicalist Legacy: Trade Unions and Politics in Two French Cities in the Era of World War I* (Urbana & Chicago: University of Illinois Press, 1986), p.13.

47. On the other hand, as Amdur and Colson convincingly argue, this does not mean that we should accept the simplistic, economistic analysis of those for whom anarchism, "anarcho-syndicalism" and communism represented successive stages of development of the labour development, more or less directly determined by technological and economic developments. Daniel Colson, *Anarcho-syndicalisme et communisme. Saint-Etienne 1920–1925* (Saint-Etienne: Université de Saint-Etienne/Centre d'Etudes Foréziennes/Atelier de Création Libertaire, 1986).

48. See Eric Hobsbawm's consideration of "a long lost era of bohemians, rebels and avantgarde" in "Reflections on Anarchism" in *The Debate on Anarchism* (Nottingham: The Bertrand Russell Peace Foundation for *The Spokesman*, 1973); Jean Baechler's somewhat inaccurate summary of anarchist doctrine and history in *Revolution* (Oxford: Basil Blackwell, 1975) and his claim that anarchist movements "must inevitably draw their recruits from a very narrow field. The only sizeable groups they could possibly attract make up the rabble, the social category that, by its very nature, plays no part in society and is conspicuous for its utter fragmentation" (p. 115); and John Hutton's assertion that anarchism had its support among "the small shopkeepers, independent workers and artisans, labourers, barbers, cooks and the unemployed" and especially among "artists and intellectuals" — "Camille Pissarro's *Turpitudes Sociales* and Late Nineteenth-Century French Anarchist Anti-Feminism," *History Workshop Journal* vol.24 (Autumn 1987), pp.36 and 40.

49. Roger Magraw, *France 1815–1914: The Bourgeois Century* (London: Fontana, 1983), pp.96–7.

50. See René Bianco, *Le mouvement anarchiste à Marseille et dans les Bouches du Rhône (1880–1914)* (Unpublished Doctorat de 3ème Cycle, Université de Provence, 1977), pp.297–99.

51. Ibid, pp.310–19.

52. Jean Maitron, "Un 'anar', qu'est-ce que c'est?," in *Mouvement social* no.83 (April–June 1973), pp.23–45; Nicolas Faucier, "Souvenirs d'un permanent anarchiste (1927–1929)," in *Mouvement social* no.83 (April–June 1973), pp.47–56; Nicolas Faucier, "Rapport sur le mouvement anarchiste en France, sa composition, son comportement durant la période 1930–1940" (Unpublished TS, 13pp.). Nor are Jean-Louis Robert's attempts in *La Scission Syndicale de 1921* (Paris: Publications de la Sorbonne, 1980), pp.174–75, to draw significant conclusions regarding the relation between ideology and sociology in the context of voting patterns in CGT congresses very convincing. Daniel Colson: "Whether they are 'anarcho-syndicalist' or 'pro-communist', the trade unions which rallied behind different motions at Saint-Etienne and Bourges were all characterized by the great heterogeneity of their industrial and geographic bases as of the representations and discourses which they developed. Only the arbitrary presupposition of 'currents', with the historic mission of marking the progress of technological developments and of class consciousness, makes it possible to read into them hidden 'correspondences'." *Anarcho-syndicalisme et communisme. Saint-Etienne 1920–1925* (Saint-Etienne: Université de Saint-Etienne/Centre d'Etudes Foréziennes/Atelier de Création Libertaire, 1986), p.66.

53. David Berry, "Contribution to a Collective Biography of the French Anarchist Movement: French Anarchist Volunteers in Spain, 1936–39," conference paper, University of Lausanne, 1997.

54. "Souvenirs," p.48. This was one reason for the number of anarchists and revolutionary syndicalists in the Fédération du Livre and in particular the Proofreaders' Union. As a proofreader, the pay was relatively good, the hours were short, and the work was often done at night, which meant that militants could devote the daytime hours to their trade union or political activities. See Guérin, *Front populaire*, pp.41–3; Yves Blondeau, *Le Syndicat des Correcteurs de Paris et de la région parisienne 1881–1973* (Paris: Syndicat des Correcteurs, 1973).

55. See Marie-Jo Dhavernas, "Anarchisme et féminisme à la Belle Epoque. Quelques réflexions sur les contradictions du patriarcat en milieu libertaire à la fin du XIXe siècle et au début du XXe" in *la Revue d'en-face* no.12 (Autumn 1982), pp.49–61, and no.13 (Winter 1982), pp.61–80; John Hutton, "Camille Pissarro's *Turpitudes Sociales* and Late Nineteenth-Century French Anarchist Anti-Feminism," in *History Workshop Journal* no.24 (Autumn 1987), pp.32–61; Hubert van den Berg, "Pissarro and Anarchism," in *History Workshop Journal* no.32 (Autumn 1991), pp.226–28. See also Dominique Loiseau, "Les militantes de l'ombre: femmes de ..." in Michel Dreyfus, Claude Pennetier and Nathalie Viet-Depaule (eds.), *La Part des Militants* (Paris: Editions de l'Atelier, 1996), pp.257–68.

56. Bianco, *Le mouvement anarchiste à Marseille et dans les Bouches du Rhône*, pp.264 and 282.

57. Ibid., p.293, note 13.

58. Five of the women who contributed to the "Tribune Féminine" which appeared in *le Libertaire* after the Great War signed only with their forenames: Mariette, Sonia, Milly, Maxiole and Estelle. Who were they?

59. See Claire Auzias, *Mémoires libertaires: Lyon 1919–1939* (Doctorat de 3ème Cycle, Université de Lyon-II, 1980), pp.345–48.

60. *Les Humanitaires* published a protest against war and the death penalty in *le Révolté* no.45 (26 March 1887); a further notice from the group in the same paper mentioned *les Insoumises* and *les Révoltées*.

61. Faucier, "Rapport," p.6; Maitron, "Un 'anar,'" p.44.

62. See the group's manifesto in *le Libertaire*, 26 March 1925.

63. *L'Espagne Antifasciste (CNT-FAI-AIT)*, 11 December 1936.

64. *Le Libertaire*, 11 March and 27 May 1937.

65. *Le Combat Syndicaliste*, 29 January, 12 February and 21 May 1937.

66. *Le Libertaire*, 31 March 1939.

67. René Bianco, *Un siècle de presse anarchiste d'expression française dans le monde, 1880–1983* (Unpublished Doctorat d'État, Université de Provence, 1988), p.253.

68. BA1497 and 1498, cited in Dhavernas, Anarchisme," pp.76–77.

69. The "Tribune Féminine" in *le Libertaire* in the years after the Great War was written by Eugénie Casteu and the five other women, mentioned above, who signed only with their forenames.

70. Sébastien Faure (ed.), *Encyclopédie anarchiste* (Paris: Œuvre internationale des éditions anarchistes, 1934–35), 4 vols.

71. *Le Libertaire*, 28 March 1918.

72. *Le Libertaire*, 8 June 1919.

73. *Le Libertaire*, 4 April 1914. A similar point is made in the *Encyclopédie anarchiste* — see "L.," "Liberté de la femme," pp.1248–50: "However intelligent she may be, a woman does not even have the right to vote, granted to even the most ignorant and brutish of men."

74. *Le Libertaire*, 11 April 1914. See also the *Encyclopédie anarchiste* — "Emancipation de la femme," pp.672–73, by the syndicalist Georges Bastien.

75. *Le Libertaire*, 18 April 1914. See Gill Allwood and Khursheed Wadia, *Women and Politics in France* (London & New York: Routledge, 2000).

76. Claire Moses, *French Feminism in the Nineteenth Century* (New York: SUNY, 1984).

77. See the appeal in *le Libertaire*, 16 October 1936.

78. Auzias, "Anarchisme," p.345.

79. Preface to René Michaud, *J'avais vingt ans* (Paris: Syros, 1983), p.13.

80. Berry, "Contribution to a Collective Biography of the French Anarchist Movement."

81. See Maitron vol.II, p.72. The other areas were Clermont-Ferrand and Bordeaux, the Seine, Seine-et-Oise and Seine-et-Marne.

82. K. E. Amdur, "La tradition révolutionnaire entre syndicalisme et communisme dans la France de l'entre-deux-guerres," *Mouvement social* no.139 (April–June 1987), p.37, note 58.

83. Girault has pointed out the difficulties faced by the PCF in the Var, firstly because of the strength of the SFIO in the department, and secondly because "the workers, often not originally from the departement, are also strangers to it ideologically since most of them are of anarchist extraction" — "Pour une problématique de l'implantation du Parti communiste français dans l'entre-deux-guerres," p.56, in Girault (ed.), *Sur l'implantation du Parti communiste français*, pp.17–59. Unusually, the Var had its own departmental Fédération Communiste Libertaire, which in September 1936 called for groups to be set up in every village and town quarter — *le Libertaire*, 4 September 1936. There was also a Fédération des Bouches-du-Rhône. Many workers in the Var and the Bouches-du-Rhône were of Italian origin. Further west in the Aude, on the other hand, immigrant workers

were more likely to be Spanish: the anarchist group in Coursan (Aude) attracted many CNT-FAI militants—see Maitron, "Un 'anar', qu'est-ce que c'est?"

84. Amdur, "La tradition révolutionnaire," p.48.

85. *Le Réveil de l'Esclave*, 1 January 1922.

86. Faucier, "Rappport," pp.3–5.

87. *Le Libertaire*, 18 November 1937.

88. *Le Réveil de l'Esclave*, 1 January 1922.

89. Cf. this editorial comment from the launch issue of a new journal belonging to the present-day Anarchist Federation: "It is precisely the specificity of anarchism in relation to the authoritarian socialist tendencies, whether reformist or revolutionary, which is to-day its greatest strength." *Les Oeillets Rouges (Cahiers de réflexion anarchiste)* no.1 (September 1986), p.2.

90. *L'Espagne Antifasciste (CNT-FAI-AIT)*, 11 November 1936.

91. Trotsky, quoted in Roussel, *Les enfants du prophète*, p.25.

92. *Publications de "la Révolte" et "Temps Nouveaux"*, May 1922.

93. Sébastien Faure, "Les Forces de Révolution," in *Propos Subversifs* (Paris: Les Amis de Sébastien Faure, n.d. [1950?]), p.291–92.

94. It may also be seen as recognition of the fact that in the case of many individual militants, formal membership of particular organizations did not necessarily always imply that much doctrinally or in terms of who they worked with politically or who they supported in trade union elections and so on. Borders between movements were often very fluid. This is one reason why reductionist analyses of the socio-economic origins of movements in this period are so problematic. See for example Colson's comments on the supposed affiliations of two prominent Saint-Etienne militants in the early 1920s, *Anarcho-syndicalisme*, pp.124–25.

95. Maitron's assertion in his doctoral thesis that the anarchists were "hostile to any discipline, to any brigading, to any organization" (a point repeated in Maitron vol.II, p.188), and Maitron's general lack of emphasis on the organizationalist current in anarchism was rightly criticized by Georges Fontenis when it was published as *Histoire du mouvement anarchiste en France* in 1951—see the review in *le Libertaire*, 2 October 1952.

96. *Le Libertaire*, 6 May 1937.

97. Ibid.

98. *Le Libertaire*, 22 April 1937.

99. *Le Libertaire*, 11 November 1937. The inconsistencies Ridel was referring to in particular were the printing of Lashorte's "Bravo Blum!" article and the failure to pursue more energetically the revolutionary front policy.

100. Epsilon, welcoming the UA's taking part in the antifascist movement, defended "workerism" against its individualist critics: "To be workerist does not mean that in order to have correct ideas it is necessary and sufficient to have calloused hands. It means that we are conscious of the essential rôle to be played by the producers in the struggle for social revolution, a rôle from which they must not allow themselves to be diverted." *Le Libertaire*, 3 January 1936.

101. See the JAC report on sales of *le Libertaire* in the 8 January 1937 issue: "Since July, the workers of France have begun to see the anarchist movement as playing an important part in the social struggle, a part which the anarchists have claimed for themselves and which they must never again abandon. The Revolutionary Front initiative has in practical terms and officially put the seal on anarchism's return to prominence in the working-class movement."

102. *Le Libertaire*, 15 July 1937.

103. Luc Daurat in *le Libertaire*, 4 September 1936.

104. *Le Libertaire*, 21 July 1938.

105. Daurat in *le Libertaire*, 4 September 1936; and Chazoff, "Opportunisme révolution-naire," *le Libertaire*, 17 March 1938.

106. See Charles Robert and Ridel in *le Libertaire*, 27 November 1936; and Robert, in *le Libertaire*, 22 July 1937.

107. "Les principes anarchistes à l'épreuve de la Révolution," *le Libertaire*, 15 January 1937. A five page MS of the same article, which is only very slightly different in its wording and which is accompanied by a typed Spanish translation, can also be found in the CNT Archive at the IISG—Paquete 60/C/2, "Comités Antifascistas del Extranjero." This suggests the article may have been submitted as a paper for the planned international anarchist conference.

108. Jensen, "La CNT-FAI, l'Etat et le Gouvernement," *Internationale* no.2 (June 1938): "It is reality which determines theory, and not theory which is superior to reality."

109. *La Mêlée*, 1 March 1919.

110. *Les Temps nouveaux*, 15 April 1920.

111. *Le Libertaire*, 15 April 1921.

112. *Le Libertaire*, 23 May 1920.

113. *Le Libertaire*, 4 December 1936.

114. *Le Combat Syndicaliste*, 8 January 1937.

115. "We cannot deny that there is a general tendency towards statism. Not only did the bourgeoisie accept, during the war, a certain restriction of commercial freedom … but even some big labour organizations (the railway-workers and miners, notably) have declared themselves to be in favour of the nationalization of their respective industries. The anarchists are not numerous enough, nor do they have enough influence over the masses … for them to hope to be able to impose their point of view." *La Mêlée*, 1 March 1919. For an intelligent anarchist appraisal of the implications of these developments in the longer term, see Louis Mercier-Vega, *Le syndicalisme révolutionnaire: Une pratique qui cherche une doctrine*, in L. Mercier-Vega and V. Griffuelhes, *Anarcho-syndicalisme et syndicalisme révolutionnaire* (Paris: Cahiers Spartacus, Série B, no.97, September–October 1978), pp.5–86. For an academic analysis, see Richard F. Kuisel, *Capitalism and the state in modern France* (Cambridge: The university Press, 1981) and M. Fine "Toward Corporatism: The Movement for Capital-Labour Collaboration in France, 1914–1936" (Ph.D. Thesis, University of Wisconsin, 1971).

116. Annie Kriegel, *Aux origines du communisme français* (Paris: Flammarion, 1969), p.80. The difficulty remained, even during the darkest periods of Stalin's rule: "The belief that Soviet Russia, even if one admitted that it had certain unattractive traits, was nevertheless the only fundamentally progressive country and the great social experiment of our time is a particularly elastic and consoling opinion. It makes it possible to dispose of reality with a sweep of the hand through a general reference to provisional expedients and emergency measures." Arthur Koestler, quoted in Pierre Daix, *Les Hérétiques du PCF* (Paris: Robert Laffont, 1980), p.130.

117. It was an accusation commonly levelled at the platformists, for example. The French delegate to the extraordinary congress of the AIT in Limoges, December 1937, referred to notions of a transitional period and to the idea that participation in a revolutionary government might be progressive as "the bolshevization of anarchism." *L'Espagne Nouvelle*, 15 March 1939.

118.   V.I. Lenin, *"Left-Wing" Communism, an Infantile Disorder* (Moscow: Progress Publishers, 1968), p.18.

119.   *Le Libertaire*, 17 March 1938.

120.   Pierre Broué and Nicole Dorey, "Critiques de gauche et opposition révolutionnaire au front populaire (1936–1938)" in *Mouvement social* no.54 (January–March 1966), p.92, note 3.

121.   Marie-Louise Berneri and Suzanne Broido of the Libertarian Students; Luc Daurat, Marester and Charles Ridel of the JAC and the UA; René Dumont of the UA; Greta Jumin, ex-member of the Communist Youth; Jean Meier of the Autonomous Federation of Socialist Youth and the Gauche révolutionnaire, who would the following June participate in the creation of the PSOP; Jean Rabaud, another ex-communist and now a member of the Socialist Students close to Pivert; and Sejourne, who had been expelled from the JEUNES. The administrator, Lucien Feuillade, was also an anarchist. Ridel was simultaneously a member of the "Cercle syndicaliste Lutte de classes" (Class Struggle Syndicalist Group), and contributed to its organ *le Réveil syndicaliste*, which appeared in January 1938.

122.   "Manifeste," *Révision*, February 1938.

123.   "Anarchistes de gouvernement," *Révision*, February 1938.

124.   Ibid.

125.   Ibid.

126.   Ibid.

127.   Ibid.

128.   Ibid.

Selected Bibliography:
Anarchist movement
publications and
other primary sources

1. ANARCHIST NEWSPAPERS AND REVIEWS

I have listed here only those periodicals consulted for this study. For a more comprehensive catalogue, see René Bianco, "Un siècle de presse anarchiste d'expression française dans le monde, 1880–1983" (Doctorat d'Etat, University of Provence, 1988), 7 vols.

L'Action d'art. Organe de l'individualisme héroïque. Paris. No.1 (15 October 1919) to no.8 (22 May 1920).

L'Anarchie. Paris. No.1 (21 April 1926), no.52 (April 1929).

L'Avenir International, Revue Mensuelle d'Action Sociale, Littéraire, Artistique, Scientifique Paris. No. 1 (January 1918) to no.32 (August–October 1920).

La Bataille Syndicaliste, Hebdomadaire prolétarien. Paris. No. 1 (1 May 1922) to no.9 (29 June 1922); no.10 (8 September 1923).

Boletín de Información (Informes y noticias facilitadas por la Confederación Nacional del Trabajo y la Federación Anarquista Ibérica) Edition en langue française, publiée par la 'Section Française' de Barcelone. Barcelona. New Series: no.2 (30 November 1936) to no.30 (3 July 1937). Irregular.

Bulletin d'information du Comité de Défense de la Révolution Espagnole Antifasciste. Perpignan. No.1 (6 February 1937) to no.11 (23 September 1937). From no.5 (10 June 1937) became *Boletín de Información del Comité de Defensa de la Revolución Española Antifascista y porta-voz de la Federación de Comités Españoles de Accion Antifascista en Francia*, with very little material in French.

Bulletin intérieur de la Fédération anarchiste de langue française. Paris. No.1 (15 September 1938) to no.6 (July 1939). Irregular.

Ce qu'il faut dire. Paris. No. 1 (2 April 1916) to no.83 (22 December 1917).

La Clameur, Organe mensuel d'action libertaire. Paris. 1932–36 (?).

Le Combat, Organe anarchiste du Nord et du Pas-de-Calais. Lille, then Wasquehal. No.1 (May 1923), no.12 (April 1924).

Le Combat Syndicaliste, Organe officiel de la Confédération Générale du Travail Syndicaliste Révolutionnaire, A.I.T. Paris. No. 1 (December 1926) to no.62 (25 April 1933); no.1 (12 May 1933) to no.310 (16 June 1939). Monthly, then weekly from May 1933.

Le Communiste, Hebdomadaire, Organe Officiel du Parti Communiste et des SO-VIETS adhérents à la Section Française de la 3ᵉ Internationale de Moscou, des Conseils d'Ouvriers, Paysans et Soldats. Rédigé et contrôlé par le peuple lui-même. Paris. No.1 (25 October 1919) to no.5 (14 December 1919).

Le Communiste, Hebdomadaire, Organe officiel du Parti Communiste, Section Française de l'Internationale Communiste. Paris. No.1 (11 July 1920?) to no.5 (8 August 1920).

L'en dehors, bi-mensuel. Paris & Orléans. No.1 (31 May 1922) to no.335 (October 1939). From no.64 (8 August 1925), sub-titled: *Organe de pratique, de réalisation, de camaraderie individualiste.*

L'Espagne Antifasciste, Organe trimensuel au service de la Révolution espagnole. Bordeaux. No.1 (1 September 1937) to no.7 (30 November 1937). Merged with *l'Espagne Nouvelle.*

L'Espagne Antifasciste (CNT-FAI-AIT), Edition française de Solidaridad Obrera. Barcelona then Paris. No.3 (28 August 1936) to no.31 (8 January 1937).

L'Espagne Nouvelle. Nîmes. First series: *Bulletin hebdomadaire d'information, Edité par le Secrétariat de Documentation Ouvrière.* No.1 (1 February 1937) to no.10 (5 April 1937). New series: no.1 (19 April 1937) to no.67–69 (July–August–September 1939). From no.34–35 to no.56–57 includes *le Semeur* and *l'Espagne Antifasciste*, and sub-titled *Organes réunis pour la défense des militants, des conquêtes et des principes de la Révolution sociale ibérique.*

La Feuille, Organe d'éducation sociale (Organe d'éducation libertaire from no.6, December 1934). Saint-Genis-Laval (Rhône). 1917 (?) to August 1939.

Le Flambeau. Brest. No.1 (June 1927) to no.80 (5 June 1934).

Franchise, Organe de combat. Paris. No.1 (31 March 1918) to no.3 (14 April 1918).

Germinal, Journal du peuple. Organe communiste libertaire de la Somme et de l'Oise (from October 1920; 2 editions). *Organe libertaire de la Somme et de l'Oise* (from July 1924; 2 editions). *Organe libertaire de la Somme, de l'Oise, du Nord et du Pas-de-Calais* (from July 1925; 3 editions).

Journal du Peuple, Libertaire (from February 1926; 3 editions). *Journal du Peuple, Syndicaliste-Révolutionnaire Socialiste-Libertaire* (1933; 1 edition). Amiens/Crillon. Second series (weekly): no.1 (29 August 1919) to no.725 (15 July 1933). Third series (fortnightly): no.1 (20 May 1938) to no.7 (2 September 1938).

Les Glaneurs, Recueil éclectique mensuel. Lyon. No.1 (March 1917) to no.19 (September 1918).

L'Idée anarchiste. Paris. No.1 (13 March 1924) to no.13 (15 November 1924).

L'Idée libre, Sciences, Philosophie, Sociologie. From no.2, sub-titled: *Culture individuelle. Rénovation sociale.* Saint-Etienne, then Conflans-Sainte-Honorine (Seine et Oise). No.1 [2nd series] (July 1917) to no.12 [15th series] (December 1933) [?].

L'Insurgé. Journal d'action révolutionnaire et de culture individualiste. Paris. No.2 (14 May 1925), no.32 (15 December 1925).

Internationale, Organe mensuel de l'Association Internationale des Travailleurs (A.I.T.). Destinée exclusivement aux militants de l'organisation. Editée par le secrétariat de l'A.I.T. Paris. No.2 (June 1938) to no.6 (October 1938).

L'Internationale, Journal hebdomadaire. Paris. No.1 (15 February 1919) to no.36 (16 December 1919). *L'Internationale Communiste* from no.30 (15 September 1919).

La Jeunesse Anarchiste, Organe de la Fédération des Jeunesses Anarchistes. "Ni Dieu Ni Maître." No.4 (15 July 1921).

Libération. Saint-Genis-Laval (Rhône). No.1 (July 1927), no.2 (March 1928) (?).

Le Libertaire. "Les anarchistes veulent instaurer un milieu social qui assure à chaque individu un maximum de bien-être et de liberté adéquat à chaque époque". Paris. No.1 (26 January 1919) to no.668 (31 August 1939).

Libereso. Organe des anarchistes idistes. Auxerre. No.15 (August 1924); no.23 (June 1927). Irregular.

Lucifer. Organe de pensée libre et de culture individuelle. Bordeaux. 17 nos. (1929–31 and 1934). Succeeded by *la Révolte.*

La Lumière. Saint-Etienne. No.1 (May 1923), no.3 (July 1923).

La Lueur. Organe de la Fédération anarchiste du Centre. Tours. No.1 (19 February 1924), no.5 (1 June 1924).

Lueurs, Cahiers individualistes d'études et de documentation. Lyon. No.1 (15 December 1924) to no.5 (15 April 1925). Succeeded *les Vagabonds.*

Le Malthusien, Mensuel, Revue néo-malthusienne, économique et eugéniste. "Bonne naissance. Bonne éducation. Bonne organisation sociale." Paris. No.69 (January–February 1920).

La Mêlée, Libertaire, Individualiste, Eclectique. Paris. No. 1 (15 March 1918) to no.38–39 (February 1920). Succeeded *Par delà la mêlée,* followed by *L'Un.*

Le Néo-Naturien, Revue des Idées Philosophiques et Naturiennes. "Beauté. Liberté. Art et Nature." Parthenay (Deux-Sevres). No.3 (February–March 1922) to no.21 (October–November 1925); no.22 (August–October 1927). Irregular.

La Nouvelle Espagne Antifasciste/Nueva España Antifascista (Organo de los Españoles Residentes en Francia y Portavoz del Antifascismo Internacional). Paris. No.1 (20 September 1937) to no.60 (17 November 1938).

L'Ordre Naturel, Organe du Mouvement Individualiste. Paris. No.1 (9 December 1920) to 1927 (?).

Par delà la mêlée, Acrate, individualiste, éclectique, inactuel. Paris/Orléans. No. 1 (26 January 1916) to no.41 (31 January 1918). Followed by *la Mêlée.*

La Plèbe. Paris. No.1 (13 April 1918) to no.4 (4 May 1918), plus a special issue (1 May 1918).

Plus Loin, Mensuel. Paris. No.1 (15 March 1925) to no.169 (July–August–September 1939).

Publications du "Groupe de Propagande par l'Ecrit" (Publications de "La Révolte" et "Temps Nouveaux" from no.9). Robinson (Seine). No.1 (n.d.[August 1920]) to no.99 (September 1936).

La Raison, Journal du Peuple. Rouen. 1933–36 (?). Monthly (?).

Le Réfractaire. Organe de la Ligue internationale des réfractaires à toutes guerres. Paris. No.4 (April 1929).

Le Réveil de l'Esclave, Organe Mensuel de Propagande, d'Education, de Combat. From no.16 (November 1921), sub-titled: *Organe mensuel d'Education individualiste libertaire.* Pierrefitte (Seine). No.1 (May 1920) to no.42 (1 April 1925).

Le Réveil libertaire. Organe de la Fédération Anarchiste du Sud-Est. Lyon. No.1 (June 1923) to no.11 (April 1924).

Révision, Revue d'Etudes Révolutionnaires (Editée par un groupe de jeunes révolutionnaires). Paris. No.1 (February 1938) to no.6 (August 1939). No.6 entitled *Courrier des camps*.

La Révolte, Organe Anarchiste du Sud-Ouest. Bordeaux. No.1 (28 April 1922) to no.10 (15 September 1922).

La Revue Anarchiste. Paris. No.1 (January 1922) to no.35 (August 1925).

La Revue Anarchiste, Cahiers Mensuels d'Etudes et d'Action. "*Libre de toute hérédité... elle ne possède encore ni dogme ni directive, ce ne sera donc l'organe ni d'une individualité ni d'un groupe*". Paris. No.1 (December 1929) to 1936 (?) (no.13–15, January–March 1931).

La Revue Internationale Anarchiste. Paris. No.1 (15 November 1924), no.8 (15 June 1925). Merged with *la Revue Anarchiste*.

Le Semeur, Bi-mensuelle de Culture Individuelle. Falaise (Calvados). No.1 (15 October 1923) to no.281 (28 November 1936).

S.I.A., Hebdomadaire, Organe de la Solidarité Internationale Antifasciste. Paris. No.1 (10 November 1938) to no.41 (24 August 1939).

Le Silence du peuple. Organe bimensuel des travailleurs libertaires. Saint-Etienne. 13 January to 1 August 1929.

Le Soviet, Organe de la Fédération Communiste des Soviets (Section de Langue Française de l'Internationale Communiste de Moscou). Bimensuel. Paris. No.1 (21 March 1920) to no.13 (1 May 1921).

Le Sphinx, Journal Naturien-Néo-Stoïcien. Allias "Contre le Chaos" du "Foyer Naturien" de Brest. Naturisme et Subjectivisme. Individualisme-Rynériste. Trimestriel/Bimensuel. Brest. 3 nos. in 1922 (one in March) (?). New series entitled *Le Sphinx de Brest, Poétique, Philosophe et Satirique. Rynérien et Naturiste. Littérature. Science*. No.1 (May–June 1936). Irregular.

Le Syndicaliste Révolutionnaire, Sous le contrôle du Comité Central des Comités Syndicalistes Révolutionnaires. Paris. No.1 (22 December 1921) to no.15 (6 April 1922).

Les Temps nouveaux. Paris. *Bulletins* (Irregular): No.1 (May 1916) to no.16 (Jure 1919). *Revue internationale des idées communistes (Revue internationale des idées communistes libertaires* from no.13) (Monthly): No.1 (15 July 1919) to no.23–24 (June–July 1921).

Terre Libre, Organe Bi-Mensuel de la Fédération Anarchiste du Sud. "*De Chacun selon ses forces. A Chacun selon ses besoins.*" Marseille. No.1 (20 June) to no.10 (5 November 1922).

A History of the French Anarchist Movement, 1917 to 1945

Terre Libre. Nîmes/Paris. No.1 (May 1934) to 65 (June–July 1939). *Organe de la Fédération Anarchiste de langue Française (F.A.F.)* from no.29 (February 1937).

Le Tocsin. Contre tous les fascismes! Pour la liberté! Antony. No.1 (2 March 1934) to no.4 (11 May 1934).

Le Trait d'Union libertaire, Bulletin de l'Association des fédéralistes anarchistes (A.F.A.). Paris. No.1 (January 1928), no.4 (April 1928). Succeeded by *la Voix libertaire.*

L'Un, Libertaire, Individualiste, Eclectique. No.1 (March 1920). Became: *Un, Individualiste, Libertaire, Bi-Mensuel Eclectique.* No.1 (June 1920) to no.7 (December 1920). Succeeded *la Mêlée.*

Les Vagabonds. "Vagabonds de la Pensée, rien ne nous est sacré. Nous alimentons notre Esprit des fruits les plus savoureux du domaine immense des Idées". Lyon. No.1 (January 1921) to no.10 (October 1921). Became: *Les Vagabonds Individualistes-Libertaires.* No. 1 (June 1922) to no.31(?) (August 1924). Followed by *Lueurs.*

Le Végétalien. Vence-Ermont. No.1 (November 1924) to no.7/8/9 (November 1928–January 1929).

La Voix Libertaire. Organe de l'Association des Fédéralistes Anarchistes, then *Organe anarchiste hebdomadaire* from June 1934, then *Organe anarchiste mensuel* from October 1937. Paris then Limoges. No.1 (May 1928) to no.394 (July 1939).

La Voix du Travail. Bulletin mensuel de l'A.I.T. Paris. No.1 (August 1926), no.15 (October 1927). *Bulletin mensuel de la C.G.T.S.R.* from April 1927.

2. ANARCHIST BOOKS AND PAMPHLETS

Archinoff, P. *L'Histoire du Mouvement Makhnoviste (1918–1921).* Paris: Editions Anarchistes, 1928. Preface by Voline. (Main text written in Russia, January–June 1921; Preface written May 1923.)

Armand, Eugène. *Les Ouvriers, les Syndicats et les Anarchistes.* Orléans: 'l'en dehors', n.d. (1925/27?).

Armand, Eugène. *L'illégaliste anarchiste est-il notre camarade?* Paris & Orléans: 'l'en dehors', 1927 .

Armand, Eugène. *Subversismes sexuels.* Orléans: 'l'en dehors', 1927.

Armand, Eugène. *Les précurseurs de l'anarchisme.* Orléans: 'l'en dehors', 1933.

Armand, Eugène. *Petit manuel anarchiste individualiste.* 1934.

Armand, Eugène; Despres, Marguerite. *Est-ce cela que vous appelez "vivre"? L'en-dehors. Pensées pour la vie quotidienne. La ruse. L'Amour libre.* With ido translation by C. Papillon. Paris & Orléans: 'l'en dehors', 1927.

Bastien, Georges. *Pour la Rénovation du Syndicalisme.* Amiens: Syndicat autonome des Tisseurs d'Amiens, n.d. (1922–25).

Bergeron, Paul (ed.). *Idées et Conceptions de Pierre Chardon.* Lyon: 'Aux Vagabonds', 1924. Foreword by Albin.

Berneri, Camillo. *Guerre de Classes en Espagne. Les Cahiers de 'Terre Libre',* April–May 1938.

Bernier, Jean. *La revolution espagnole et l'impérialisme.* Paris: J.A.C., 1936.

Besnard, Pierre. *Les syndicats ouvriers et la révolution social.* Paris: Le Monde nouveau, 1930.

Besnard, Pierre. *Le Monde nouveau.* Paris: CGTSR, 1936.

Besnard, Pierre. *L'Anarcho-Syndicalisme et l'Anarchisme, Rapport de Pierre Besnard, Secretaire de l'A.I.T. au Congrès Anarchiste International de 1937.* Preface by A. Schapiro (dated 30 May 1937); iipp. + 6pp. Republished as supplement to *le Monde Libertaire,* 1963.

Besnard, Pierre. *L'Ethique du syndicalisme.* Paris: CGTSR, 1938.

Byington, Stephen T.; Carpenter, Edward; Mackay, John Henry; Owen, Wm. C.; and Seymour, Henry. *Les Différents Visages de l'Anarchisme.* Paris & Orléans: 'l'en dehors', 1927. Foreword and trans. E. Armand.

CGTSR. *La révolution sociale par la baisse des prix.* Nîmes: Cahiers du Travailleur Libre, January 1939.

Comité International de Défense Anarchiste. *Comme au temps des Tzars: L'exil et la Prison, parfois la mort, contre les meilleurs révolutionnaires.* Paris: CIDA, 1927.

D., Edmond. *La République Fédérative, Fondée sur les bases du Syndicalisme Révolutionnaire: Schéma constitutif du milieu social de demain (Réponse aux partis politiques).* Bordeaux: l'Union Syndicale Autonome de la Gironde, 1924.

Darrow, Clarence S. *Qui juge le criminel? Inconséquences des lois pénales.* Paris & Orléans: 'l'en dehors', 1927. Trans. E. Armand.

Devaldes, Manuel. *Han Ryner et le Problème de la Violence (Suivi d'une lettre de Han Ryner).* Conflans-Honorine: L'Idee Libre, 1927.

Emile Cottin: son geste, sa condamnation, son supplice. Paris: L'Union anarchiste, n.d.

Fabbri, Luigi. *Qu'est-ce que l'Anarchie?* Paris: Librairie Internationale, 1926.

Faure, Sébastien. *Les Anarchistes. Qui nous sommes. Ce que nous voulons. Notre révolution.* Paris: Editions Anarchistes, Librairie Internationale, n.d. (1928?).

Faure, Sébastien (ed.). *Encyclopédie anarchiste.* Paris: Œuvre internationale des éditions anarchistes, 1934–35. 4 vols.

Fédération communiste libertaire, *Le Communisme libertaire. Précis d'économie libertaire.* Marseille: Editions du 'Travailleur libertaire' no.3, January 1935. 39pp.

Gaudeaux, Jean. *Six mois en Russie bolcheviste: documents inédits.* Paris: Romans Nouveaux, 1924.

Grave, Jean. *Le mouvement libertaire sous la troisième République.* Paris, 1930.

Groupe d'anarchistes russes à l'étranger. *Plate-forme d'organisation de l'Union Générale des Anarchistes (Projet); Supplément à la Plate-forme d'organisation de l'Union Générale des Anarchistes (Questions et Réponses).* Paris: Librairie Internationale, 1926.

Groupe d'anarchistes russes à l'étranger. *La Réponse aux confusionnistes de l'anarchisme.* Paris: Librairie Internationale, 1927.

Groupe d'études anarchistes-communistes; Groupe de secours à la presse anarchiste, *et al. Déclaration et Protestation —A propos du Manifeste des Seize.* Paris: May 1916.

Un Groupe de Syndicalistes. *Centralisme et Fédéralisme.* Paris: Union des Syndicats des Chemins de Fer de l'Etat, Secteur de Paris, New edition, 1919. 23pp.

Hanot, Marius. *Soviet ou Parlement.* Paris: La Productrice, 1919.

La Jeunesse Anarchiste-Communiste. *Programme d'Action.* Editions de la JAC, no.1, September 1936. 14pp.

Imbard, Maurice. *Ordre et Anarchie.* Paris: Bibliothèque de l'Artistocracie, 1984.

Lapeyre, Aristide. *Le problème espagnol.* Bordeaux: Tierra y Libertad, 1946. 36pp.

Lapeyre, Paul. *Révolution et contre-révolution en Espagne. Lueurs sur l'Espagne républicaine.* Paris: Cahiers Spartacus, 1938.

Libertad, Albert. *La Liberté. Nous allons ... Ultime bonté.* Paris & Orléans: 'l'en dehors', 1927.

Makhno, Nestor. *La Révolution Russe en Ukraine (Mars 1917–Avril 1918).* Paris: l'Union Anarchiste Communiste de Paris, 1927).

Malatesta, Errico. *Anarchistes de Gouvernement—Réponse de Malatesta au Manifeste des Seize*. n.d.

Mauricius. *L'Affaire Malvy. Ce que j'aurais dit en Haute Cour*. Paris: Mauricius, n.d.

Mauricius. *Au Pays des Soviets. Neuf Mois d'Aventures*. Paris: Eugène Figuière, n.d. [1922].

Mélet, Pierre Guillaume. *Mesure d'homme. Itinéraire d'un militant*. Levallois-Perret: la Mère Educatrice, 1937. Preface by Han Ryner.

Pelletier, Madeleine. *L'Emancipation Sexuelle de la Femme*. Paris: La Brochure Mensuelle, 1926.

Prudhommeaux, André; and Prudhommeaux, Dori. *Spartacus et la Commune de Berlin*. Paris, 1934. Republished in *Cahiers Spartacus*, August 1972.

Ryner, Han and Lorulot, André. *La Morale peut-elle se passer de la Science?* Paris: 'l'Idée Libre', 1925.

Roulot, André [Lorulot]. *Le Soviet*. 1919.

Roux, Maxime. *Essai de conduite intérieure (Diogène dans son taxi)*. Paris: Bibliothèque de l'Artistocratie, 1934.

Serge, Victor; Croix, Alexandre; and Bernier, Jean. *L'Anarchie*. Special number of *Le Crapouillot*, January 1938.

Sobol; Fléchine; et al. *Réponse de quelques anarchistes russes à la Plateforme*. Paris: Librairie Internationale, 1927.

Solidarité Internationale Antifasciste. *S.I.A.: son but, sa ligne de conduite, ses moyens d'action, ses réalisations*. Paris: SIA, n.d. [January 1938].

Vilar, Albert. *Les lois de 1893–1894 dites "lois scélérates"—Etude Historique*. Paris: l'Unité Ouvrière, 1930.

Voline, *La Révolution en Marche*. Nîmes: 'Vie et Pensée', 1938.

La Brochure Mensuelle

The pamphlet series "La Brochure Mensuelle" (Editions du Groupe de Propagande par la Brochure) was primarily the work of the anarchist bookseller, Bidault (1869–1938), working from his shop at 33 rue de Bretagne, in the 3rd *arrondissement* of Paris. The following is the nearest to a comprehensive list of the pamphlets I have been able to establish.

No.1, January 1923: Kropotkine, Pierre. *Aux jeunes gens* and *L'ordre*.

No.2, February 1923: Kropotkine, Pierre. *La loi et l'autorité* and *La Révolution sera-t-elle Collectiviste?*

No.3, March 1923: Ryner, Han. *Une conscience pendant la guerre, L'affaire Gaston Rolland*.

No.5, May 1923: Rhillon. *Les Capitalismes en guerre, 1903–1923: De Briey à la Ruhr.*

No.11B, November 1923; new edn. August 1927: Tolstoi, Léon. *Tu ne tueras point.*

No.12B, December 1923 (2nd edn.): Hugo, Victor. *Déshonorons la guerre!* and Ermenonville. *La Morale de la Guerre déduite par ses Professionnels.*

No.15, March 1924: Rhillon. *La Propriété-Vol.*

No.24A, December 1924: Pelletier, Doctoresse M. *L'âme existe-t-elle?*

No.24B, December 1924: Chaughi, René. *Les Trois Complices: Les Tueurs, Les Faiseurs de Pluie, L'Homme qui Juge.*

No.25, January 1925: Lux. *Parasitisme social, Les Morts Glorieux.*

No.27, March 1925: Thonar, G. *Ce que veulent les Anarchistes.*

No.29, May 1925: Odin, Raoul. *Propos Subversifs.*

No.30, June 1925: Vernet, Madeleine. *L'Amour Libre.*

No.38, February 1926: Hébert, E. *Le Crépuscule des Partis.*

No.39, March 1926: Ghislain, René. *Contre le Fascisme.*

No.41, May 1926: Lux. *L'instinct de conservation, Vive la vie!*

No.42B, June 1926: Gohier, Urbain. *Aux Femmes.*

No.44, August 1926: Ritz, F.-O. *Les Origines de la Vie.*

No.52, April 1927: Barbedette, L. *Pour l'ère du coeur. Essai de Psychologie Morale.*

No. 54, June 1927: Reclus, Elisée. *Evolution et Révolution.*

No.57, May 1927: Kropotkine, Pierre. *La Morale Anarchiste.*

No.58, October 1927: Faure, Sébastien. *La Question Sociale.*

No.59, November 1927: Barbedette, L. *A la Recherche du Bonheur. Essai de thérapeutique Morale.*

No.61, January 1928: Ryner, Han. *Elisée Reclus (1830–1905).*

No.63, March 1928: Kropotkine, Pierre. *Le Gouvernement Représentatif.*

No.72, December 1928: Barbedette, L. *Le Règne de l'Envie.*

No.73, January 1929: Beaure, Armand. *Arguments Anarchistes.*

No.74, February 1929: Bastien, Georges. *Anarchisme et Coopération.*

No.75, March 1929: Lux. *Travail et Capital* and Levieux. *Homme Libre — Policiers — Magistrats.*

No.76, April 1929: Trencoserp. *La Stagnation de l'Anarchie.*

No.77, May 1929: Relgis, Eugen. *Un livre de paix.*

No.79–80, July-August 1929: Malatesta, Errico. *L'Anarchie.*

No.81–2, September–October 1929: Rothen, Edouard. *La Liberté Individuelle.*

No.83, November 1929: Barbedette, L. *Par delà l'intérêt. Essai de Psychologie Morale.*

No.85, January 1930: Pelletier, Madeleine. *Le Travail: Ce qu'il est, Ce qu'il doit être.*

No.90, June 1930: Elosu, Dr. F. *Le poison maudit.*

No.96, December 1930: Rothen, Edouard. *Politiciens (Pièce en Un Acte).*

No.97, January 1931: de la Boëtie, Etienne (1530–1563). *De la Servitude volontaire.*

No.98, February 1931: Griffuelhes, Victor. *Le Syndicalisme Révolutionnaire.*

No.99, March 1931: Withoutname, Georges. *De l'Origine et de l'Influence Sociale des Religions.*

No.103–4, July-August 1931: Yvetot, Georges. *A.B.C. Syndicaliste.*

No.109 (?), January 1932: Roule, Jean. *Ce que Veulent les Révolutionnaires*; and Dr. M. N. *Quelques idées fausses sur l'Anarchisme.*

No.113–4, May–June 1932: Barbedette, L. *Vers l'Inaccessible. Essai Philosophique.*

No.116, August 1932: Meslier, Curé. *Non! Dieu n'est pas!* and Elmassian, Dikran. *Dieu n'existe pas.*

No.117, September 1932: Retté, A. *Réflexions sur l'Anarchie.*

No.118, October 1932: Fuszka, Maurice. *Communisme et Naturisme.*

No.123, March 1933: Freedom Press. *Qu'est-ce que l'anarchisme?* Labadie, Joseph. *L'Anarchisme, ce qu'il est et ce qu'il n'est pas.* Meulen, Henry. *L'anarchisme individualiste.* Mackay, John-Henry. *O Anarchie!* de Cleyre, Voltairine. *L'Idée dominante.*

No.126, June 1933: Withoutname, G. *Spiritisme.*

No.132, December 1933: Trafelli, Prof. Luigi. *Lettre à 'L'Avocat du Diable' dans le procès de béatification d'un 'Pape de Guerre'.*

No.137, May 1934: *Pour qui? Pourquoi? ou 'La Guerre par les Citations' (Résumé).*

No.138, June 1934: Rothen, Edouard. *La Propriété et la Liberté.*

No.142, October 1934: *Francisco Ferrer Anarchiste.*

No.143, November 1934: Ramus, Pierre. *Le Communisme-anarchiste comme réalisation pour les temps actuels.*

No.145, January 1935: *Les Calendriers du Passé: le romain, le républicain.*

No.147, February–March 1935: Barbedette, L. *En marge de l'action. Recherches sociologiques.*

No.148, April 1935: Faure, Sébastien. *La Liberté: Son aspect historique et social.*

No.150–1, June–July 1935: F. A., *La Peste Noire: le Fascisme.*

No.154, October 1935: Ramus, Pierre. *La préparation à la Guerre sans la résistance du peuple — Pourquoi?*

No.160, April 1936: d'Axa, Zo. *Le candidat de 'La Feuille'* and *Aux Electeurs.*

No.162, June 1936: Boron, Ali. *L'initiation sexuelle par les parents pour leurs enfants.*

No. 163–164, July–August 1936: Vergine, S. *Le sabre et la soutane.* Supplement to no.163–164, August 1936: Rhillon, *Léon Blum, Lavallien de Genève. L'Hégémonie des Fascismes sur le Continent. Paix Féodale ou Guerre.*

No. 168, December 1936: *Un homme, une œuvre — Han Ryner.*

No.172, April 1937: Devaldes, Manuel. *La Guerre dans l'Acte Sexuel.*

No.177, September 1937: Kropotkine, Pierre. *La Guerre, Les Minorités Révolutionnaires, L'Ordre.*

No.177–8, October-November 1937: Riéchelber, W.-A. *Dossier de la Révélation Humaine.* and *Le Végétarisme par principe.*

3. FIRST-HAND ACCOUNTS

The following were kind enough to share their memories of the period with me and/or to discuss my ideas and interpretations, either in interview or in correspondence.

Interviews:

Anderson, Louis (Paris, 6 April 1985).

Berthier, Pierre-Valentin (Paris, 21 April 1984).

Bouyé, Henri (Tours, 10 June 1993).

Joyeux, Maurice (Paris, 3 May 1984).

Maitron, Jean (Paris, 28 May 1984).

Senez, André (Tours, 10 June 1993).

Correspondence:

Anderson, Louis (15 February 1985, 2 February 1986).

Berthier, Pierre-Valentin (28 April and 21 June 1984, 20 February 1986).

Carpentier, Charles-François (31 January 1986).
Faucier, Nicolas (13 June 1984, 27 May 1985, 12 March and 19 May 1986).
Fontenis, Georges (29 September 1986).
Guérin, Daniel (12 and 26 February 1986).
Lapeyre, Paul (3 February 1986).
Lochu, René (4 December 1984).
Pantais, Roger (6 March, 15 May and 20 June 1986).
Sossenko, Georges (4 December 1998 and 3 May 1999).

4. ARCHIVES

Archives Nationales, Paris.

The richest source is the F7 series ("Police Générale"). The archives of the Ministry of Justice (BB18) are also useful. The following "cartons" were used: F7/12891, 12907, 13053, 13054, 13055, 13056, 13057, 13059, 13060, 13061, 13062, 13068, 13090, 13091, 13956, 13957, 13964; BB18/2543, 2587, 2600, 2609/2, 2613, 2627, 6465, 6466, 6467, 6468, 6469, 6472, 6476. The "Section Contemporaine" of the Archives Nationales is essential for the 1930s, though access can still be restricted. I found useful material in F7/14676, 14677 and 14721, but was unable to consult many other valuable looking archives, including some relating to the Spanish civil war.

Bibliothèque Nationale, Paris.

The Salle des Imprimés has a bound collection of leaflets: *Tracts politiques de groupements anarchistes et libertaires 1919–1939*.

Centre de recherches d'histoire des mouvements sociaux et du syndicalisme, Paris.

The CRHMSS contains the archives of Jean Maitron and Nicolas Faucier.

Institut Français d'Histoire Sociale, Paris.

The IFHS contains the archives of Renée Lamberet, Mauricius, Raymond Péricat and Jean Grave.

Internationaal Instituut voor Sociale Geschiedenis, Amsterdam.

The IISG holds the archives of many militants of international standing, some of which have been useful—Ugo Treni, Jean Grave—but by far the most useful for this study were the archives of the CNT and of the FAI.

The Kate Sharpley Library, Peterborough, UK.

The KSL Libertarian Archive and Documentation Centre contains a range of useful material, notably the IWMA *Bulletin of Information* (English and French versions) and the bulletin of the IWMA Press Service (edited by J. Dupoux). Web site: http://flag.blackened.net/ksl/Sharpley.htm

Préfecture de Police, Paris.

The relevant archives are those in the sub-series BA, but access was often refused. Dossiers used: BA/1494, 1513, 1545, 1562, 1713.

Index

SUPPORT AK PRESS!

AK Press is a worker-run collective that publishes and distributes radical books, visual/audio media, and other material. We're small: a dozen people who work long hours for short money, because we believe in what we do. We're anarchists, which is reflected both in the books we publish and the way we organize our business: without bosses.

Currently, we publish about 20 new titles per year. We'd like to publish even more. Whenever our collective meets to discuss future publishing plans, we find ourselves wrestling with a list of hundreds of projects. Unfortunately, money is tight, while the need for our books is greater than ever.

The Friends of AK Press is a direct way you can help. Friends pay a minimum of $25 per month (of course we have no objections to larger sums), for a minimum three month period. The money goes directly into our publishing funds. In return, Friends automatically receive (for the duration of their memberships) one free copy of every new AK Press title as they appear. Friends also get a 20% discount on everything featured in the AK Press Distribution catalog and on our web site—thousands of titles from the hundreds of publishers we work with. We also have a program where groups or individuals can sponsor a whole book. Please contact us for details.

To become a Friend, go to www.akpress.org.